全問正解する
新TOEIC® TEST
990点対策

CD2枚付き

加藤 優
エッセンス イングリッシュ スクール
主任講師

SCORE

990

難問
攻略

語研

はじめに

　最近の TOEIC では，Part 1 から上級者を迷わせる難問が登場し，Part 7 でも読むべき文章量が多くなっています。900 点をすでに持っている方でさえ，最後まで解き終わらないこともあるほどです。本書は，最高点の「990 点」を目指す上級者の方のために，毎回のテストで数問出題される「難問」だけを集めたものです。TOEIC は回やテストフォームにより，難易度にかなりの差がありますが，いつ受験しても全問正解できる真の英語力を身につけられるよう，「TOEIC の範疇を越えないギリギリの難問」を，一問一問究極に追求しています。もちろん，TOEIC の最新傾向も随所にちりばめています。本書の問題は，「クオリティ」と「難度」の両方の点で，TOEIC 最高レベルです。

　「990 点満点」を取ること自体には，TOEIC 講師を志望されている方を除き，それほど大きな意味はないのかもしれません。それでも，最高点にたどり着く道のりの中で，数多くの意味ある体験をされることと思います。学習のプロセスを楽しみながら，ぜひ問題に臨んでください。

　本書を，「TOEIC を通じて真の英語力を高めたい！」と切望するすべての方にささげます。

　本書の執筆にあたり，私のスケジュールに臨機応変に対応してくださった語研の田尻さん，エッセンスの教材の使用を許可してくれた中村紳一郎学校長と Susan Anderton 副学校長，私の完璧主義的な要望にも常に応じてくれたネイティブ講師の Paul，そして，執筆で休みなく働き続けた私を常に支えてくれた家族に，心から感謝します。

2012 年 7 月

加藤　優

目次

【装丁】山田英春

【CD 吹き込み】Bianca Allen, Iain Gibb, Nadia McKechnie, Jack Merluzzi, Jason Takada

＊ 本書の音声 CD には，書名やトラック名などの文字情報は含まれておりません。本 CD をパソコンに読み込んだ際に表示される書名やトラック名などの文字情報は，弊社の管理下にない外部のデータベースを参照したものです。あらかじめご了承ください。

本書の構成と使い方

　本書は，TOEIC で 800 点以上の学習者が 990 点満点を達成するだけでなく，その一歩先の「全問正解での満点」を目指して，難問の攻略法を身につけ，英語力を鍛える対策書です。TOEIC には高得点者をねらった難しい問題パターンやひっかけがあります。「全問正解での満点」を達成するには，これらの問題パターンやひっかけを理解し，的確な攻略法と豊富な練習問題をとおして，確実に正解できるようトレーニングを積んでおく必要があります。

　本書では，TOEIC 指導の「全国最優秀校」エッセンス イングリッシュ スクールの講師であり，TOEIC を毎回受験して分析と研究を行っている著者が厳選した「満点ポイント」を 27 紹介しています。この「満点ポイント」は，990 点を目指すうえで必ずクリアしなければならない項目であり，また最新のテスト傾向を反映したものです。

リスニング・セクション

リスニング全体	満点ポイント 1	
Part 1	満点ポイント 2-5	練習問題 12 問
Part 2	満点ポイント 6-9	練習問題 35 問
Part 3 & Part 4	満点ポイント 10-14	練習問題 56 問

リーディング・セクション

リーディング全体	満点ポイント 15-16	
Part 5	満点ポイント 17-20	練習問題 40 問
Part 6	満点ポイント 21-22	練習問題 18 問
Part 7	満点ポイント 23-27	練習問題 64 問

　「満点ポイント」は高得点者が苦手とするパターンや見落としがちな点をパートごとに明確にし，その対策を解説しています。「満点ポイント」を習得するために，豊富な練習問題（リスニング 103 問＋リーディング 122 問）を用意しています。練習問題には，類書に見られるような「複数正答」を含むものは一切ありません。なぜなら，TOEIC は「ベストな答え」を選ばせるテストだからです。ネイティブでさえ，消去法でしか答えの出ない問題が実際に登場すること

があります。この点を踏まえ，正答はすべてひとつにしています。本書のハイレベル問題に慣れておけば，実際のテストで難問に出くわしても動じることなく，落ち着いて解けるようになります。間違えた問題は繰り返し解き直し，「満点ポイント」や重要表現を確実に定着させていってください。リスニングは，シャドーイング（音声を聞きながら，聞こえたとおりに声に出していくトレーニング）を繰り返し，聞き取れない部分がなくなるまで練習しましょう。

　また，Part 7 の文書は，速読トレーニング用に音声を用意しています（ディスク 1：Questions 1-35　計 7 題，無料ダウンロード：Questions 46-64，計 4 題）。音声を利用して黙読・音読のトレーニングを繰り返し，Part 7 の文書を時間内にすべて読めるリーディングスピードを身につけましょう。

実戦模試 200 問

リスニング (47分)	リーディング (75分)
Part 1 (10 問)	Part 5 (40 問)
Part 2 (30 問)	Part 6 (12 問)
Part 3 (30 問)	Part 7 シングル (28 問)
Part 4 (30 問)	ダブル (20 問)

　模試は通常の TOEIC より難しめになっています。リーディングは 75 分間をタイマーで計り，一気に解いてください。解答・解説には問題を再掲載していますので，問題文でわからなかった点，見逃していた点を確認しながら答え合わせをしてください。それでは，全問正解への道を，ともに歩んでいきましょう！

【CD 収録項目】
DISC1：　リスニング・セクション「満点ポイント」の練習問題
　　　　　Part 7「満点ポイント」Questions1 ～ 35 の文書（計 7 題）
DISC2：　模試のリスニング・セクション

【無料ダウンロード】
下記の項目は弊社ホームページから無料ダウンロードできます。
http://www.goken-net.co.jp/catalog/toeic-7.htm#9784876152575 にアクセスしてください。
▶ Part 7 まとめの練習（Questions 46-64，計 4 題）の音声
▶「満点ポイント」練習問題用マークシート
▶ 模試用マークシート

990

900

800

700

600

500

400

300

1
....

リスニング・セクション
満点ポイント

97 問以上正解する *Listening Test*

　リスニング・セクションでは，3問まで間違えても満点（495点）が出る場合がほとんどです。満点を取るためには当然すべてを聞き取れるリスニング力が求められますが，つい聞き逃してしまったり，知らない単語が出てきてミスをすることは，誰にでもあります。それでも，「まだあと2問間違えられる」と考え，常に気持ちに余裕を持つようにしましょう。リスニング・セクションでもっとも必要なのは「集中力」です。各 Directions の間や，問題の間の数秒をうまく利用し，集中する時と気持ちを緩める時のメリハリをつけることで，最後まで集中力を保つことができ，聞き逃しもなくなります。

Part 1
写真描写問題

Directionsの間はPart 1に集中する

テスト開始の合図があったら，封のついたテスト用紙の間に片手を入れ，手の横側を使って一気にシールを破ります。その後，まず10枚の写真をめくりながら，「今からこの10問を解くぞ」と意識を高めていきます。テスト開始からPart 1のDirectionsが終わるまで約1分30秒ありますが，写真をチェックした後は目を閉じ，問題の開始を心静かに待ちましょう。この間にPart 3やPart 4の先読みをすると，始めから慌しいスタートを切ることになり，全体のペースが乱れます。Part 1は近年かなり難化傾向にあり，上級者でさえ2問前後，戸惑う問題が出てきます。よけいなタスクは増やさず，落ち着いた気持ちで目の前の課題に取り組むようにしましょう。

※ リスニングの間にリーディングの問題を見る行為は禁止されています。

満点ポイント3

「定番表現」をおさえる

Part 1では，写真のテーマごとに同じ語句や表現が繰り返し使われます。こうした「定番表現」を知っていれば，放送が流れる前に正解となりえる描写文を予測することができ，解答が楽になります。またそれにより，Part 1の後半に控える難問に対して最大限の集中力を残しておくこともできます。本書や公式問題集を利用して頻出表現をおさえ，写真から描写文がすぐに思い浮かぶようにしておきましょう。

次の2枚は，どちらもPart 1定番の写真です。放送が流れる前に正解を予測してみてください。

1.

Ⓐ Ⓑ Ⓒ Ⓓ

2.

Ⓐ Ⓑ Ⓒ Ⓓ

1

(A) A basket is mounted on a wheelbarrow.	(A) カゴが手押し車の上に載っている。
(B) A bicyclist is stopped beside the path.	(B) サイクリストが道のそばで呼び止められている。
(C) A container is being raised off the ground.	(C) 容器が地面から持ち上げられているところだ。
(D) A bicycle is propped up against the pole.	(D) 自転車が柱に立てかけられている。

正答 propped up against ...(〜に立てかけられている)は Part 1 の定番表現で，これを含む (D) が自転車の状態を的確に表している。誤答 (A) の wheelbarrow（〔土などを運ぶ〕手押し車）も Part 1 に頻出する。(B) は，bicyclist と bicycle を聞き間違えないように注意。(C) の container は背後に写っているが，持ち上げられている最中ではない。

重要語句 □ mounted on ...「〜の上に載せられている，取り付けられている」 □ bicyclist「サイクリスト」 □ path「小道」 □ pole「柱」

2

(A) Bushes are being trimmed in the yard.	(A) 低木が庭で剪定されているところだ。
(B) Potted plants are casting shadows on the grass.	(B) 鉢植えの植物が芝に影を落としている。
(C) Merchandise has been set up in a row.	(C) 商品が一列に並べられている。
(D) Tree branches overhang the building.	(D) 木の枝が建物を覆っている。

正答 植物が影を落としている様子を言い表した (B) が正解。casting a shadow on [over] ...(〜の上に影を落としている)は Part 1 頻出の表現で，影が写っていたらこの表現を思い浮かべたい。誤答 (C) の set up in a row（一列に並べられている）も頻出表現だが，写真からは鉢植えが販売用とは考えにくいので不適切。

重要語句 □ bush「低木」(= shrub) □ trim「〜を刈り込む，剪定する」 □ potted plant「鉢植え植物」 □ overhang「〜の上に突き出る」(= stick out over ...)

▶名詞

□ broom	「ほうき」	□ lane	「車線道路」
□ ladder	「ハシゴ」	□ shelter	「雨よけ，風よけ」
□ barn	「納屋」	□ dock	「船着場」
□ lawnmower	「芝刈り機」	□ pier	「桟橋」
□ heavy machinery	「重機」	□ lighthouse	「灯台」
□ courtyard	「(四方の囲まれた) 中庭」	□ ripple	「さざ波，波紋」
□ patio/terrace	「テラス，中庭」	□ pots and pans	「鍋類」
□ archway	「アーチ型の入り口，通路」	□ cupboard	「食器棚」
□ pillar/column	「柱，支柱」		※[kʌ́bərd] という発音に注意
□ brick wall	「レンガの壁」	□ produce	「農産物」
□ windowsill	「出窓，窓台」	□ crate	「(運搬用の) 箱，ケース」
□ window pane	「窓ガラス」	□ garment	「衣服」
□ light fixture	「照明効果」	□ platform	「台 (演台，車台など)」
□ doorway	「戸口」	□ podium	「演台」
□ hallway/corridor	「(建物内の) 通路，廊下」	□ spectator	「観客」
□ walkway	「歩道」	□ microscope	「顕微鏡」
□ curb	「縁石」		

▶表現

□ strolling along ...	「～をゆっくり歩いている」
□ glancing at ...	「～をさっと見ている」
□ gazing at ...	「～を見つめている」
□ paging through ...	「～をさっと読んでいる」
□ grasping .../gripping .../holding onto ...	「～をつかんでいる」
□ waiting on ...	「～に接客している」
□ staffing .../stationed at ...	「～で働いている」
□ hovering above[over] ...	「～の上空に浮かんでいる」
□ crowded together	「集まっている」
□ placed[positioned] against ...	「～に背を寄せて置かれている」
□ secured to ...	「～に固定されている」
□ bordered by ...	「～が境になっている」
□ overlook ...	「(場所から) ～を見渡せる」
□ wind through ...	「曲がりくねって～を通っている」
□ patterned	「模様のある」
□ slanted	「傾斜のある」

進行形の受動態を確実に聞き分ける

集中力が切れ始める後半の写真に登場するのが，現在完了形の受動態《have [has] been -ed》と現在進行形の受動態《is [are] being -ed》の聞き分けを試すパターンです。発音が似ているため，気を緩めていると誤答に誘われます。been は [bín] と短く発音される（1音節）のに対し，being は [bíːiŋ] とやや長めの発音になる（2音節）ので，一度慣れれば聞き分けはそれほど難しくはありません。ここで，それぞれの受動表現が写真と一致するかどうかを確実に判断できるようにトレーニングしておきましょう。

---

❶ 現在完了形の受動態「〜されている（状態）」

▶ Books **have been stacked** on the table.

　　　　　　↓

テーブルに積まれた状態を表す

= Books are stacked on the table.

❷ 現在進行形の受動態「今〜されているところだ」

1）動作を表す動詞

▶ Books **are being stacked** on the table.

　　　　　　↓

今積み上げられている最中を表す

　　　　　　↓

人（または機械）がその動作をしている必要がある

≠ Books are stacked on the table.

2）状態を表す動詞

▶ Books **are being displayed** on the table.

　　　　　　↓

今展示されている状態を表す

　　　　　　↓

その場に人がいる必要はない

= Books are displayed on the table.

= Books have been displayed on the table.

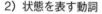

3.

Ⓐ Ⓑ Ⓒ Ⓓ

4.

Ⓐ Ⓑ Ⓒ Ⓓ

3

正解 ➤ (C)

(A) A notice is being posted on a bulletin board.	(A) 通知が掲示板に張られているところだ。
(B) Papers are being scattered over the desk.	(B) 書類がデスクの上にばらまかれているところだ。
(C) Some monitors have been turned on in the workstation.	(C) パソコンデスクにあるいくつかのモニターの電源がついている。
(D) Office equipment is being positioned in front of the man.	(D) オフィス機器が男性の前に置かれているところだ。

正答 2つのモニターの電源がついている状態を Some monitors have been turned on と現在完了形で言い表した (C) が適切。誤答 (A) は A notice is posted [has been posted], (B) は Papers are scattered [have been scattered], (D) は Office equipment is positioned [has been positioned] であればいずれも正解となる。今回のように,人が中心に写っていても,その人の動作ではなく周りのモノを描写した文が選択肢に並ぶ場合があるので注意しよう。

重要語句 □ bulletin board「掲示板」(= notice board)　□ scatter「〜をばらまく,ちらかす」　□ workstation「パソコン作業ができるスペース」

4

正解 ➤ (D)

(A) The room is being set up for an event.	(A) 部屋がイベント用にセッティングされているところだ。
(B) Concrete tiles are being laid on the floor.	(B) コンクリートのタイルが床に敷かれているところだ。
(C) Chairs are being arranged around each table.	(C) イスが各テーブルの周りに並べられているところだ。
(D) Vehicles are being exhibited indoors.	(D) 乗り物が屋内に展示されている。

正答 動詞 exhibit（〜を展示する）は,are being exhibited という現在進行形で「展示中」の状態を表せるので,(D) が正解。Vehicles are exhibited [have been exhibited] のように現在形や現在完了形でももちろんよい。誤答 他の描写にはいずれも人が伴うので,その動作をしている人が写っている必要がある。(A)は The room is set up [has been set up], (B)は Concrete tiles are laid [have been laid], (C) は Chairs are arranged [have been arranged] であればいずれも正解。

7 現在進行形と現在完了形の聞き分けトレーニング

音声を聞き，発音の違いを聞き比べてみましょう。その後，各文を音読し，自分で意識的に使い分けられるようにしてください。

1.

(A) A notice **is being posted** on a bulletin board.
   A notice **has been posted** on a bulletin board.

(B) Papers **are being scattered** over the desk.
   Papers **have been scattered** over the desk.

(C) Some monitors **are being turned** on in the workstation.
   Some monitors **have been turned** on in the workstation.

(D) Office equipment **is being positioned** in front of the man.
   Office equipment **has been positioned** in front of the man.

2.

(A) The room **is being set up** for an event.
   The room **has been set up** for an event.

(B) Concrete tiles **are being laid** on the floor.
   Concrete tiles **have been laid** on the floor.

(C) Chairs **are being arranged** around each table.
   Chairs **have been arranged** around each table.

(D) Vehicles **are being exhibited** indoors.
   Vehicles **have been exhibited** indoors.

満点ポイント5
風景描写を極める *Part 1*

　Part 1 の難関が，モノの位置関係や景色を言い表した文が正解になる「風景描写」の問題です。人の動作を説明する場合と異なり，「風景描写」は学習者にとって馴染みのない表現が出てくることもあり，描写文が予測しづらいからです。また，いわゆる「風景写真」だけでなく，人の写った「人物写真」においても，奥の目立たない景色を描写したものが正解になる意表を突いたパターンも登場します。どんな写真であっても，道路のうねりや後方に小さく写る山など，写真のあらゆる細部まで必ず目を通しておきましょう。

Disc 1
8 - 9

5.

6.

Ⓐ Ⓑ Ⓒ Ⓓ　　　　　　　　　　　　　　　　　　Ⓐ Ⓑ Ⓒ Ⓓ

(A) A boat is being lowered into the water.	(A) ボートが海に下ろされているところだ。
(B) The mountaintop is reflected in the ocean.	(B) 山頂が海面に映っている。
(C) A canoe is tipped to one side.	(C) カヌーが片側に傾いている。
(D) A paddle is creating ripples in the water.	(D) パドルが水面にさざ波を起こしている。

正答 カヌーを漕いで波紋ができている様子を適切に言い表した (D) が正解。ripples（さざ波，波紋）は Part 1 の重要語。誤答 (A) は，A boat is being rowed（ボートが〔人によって〕漕がれている）と発音が似ているので注意。(B) の reflected in the ocean [water]（～が海面〔水面〕に映っている）は Part 1 頻出の表現で，正答になることも多い。

重要語句 □ tipped「傾いている」(= tilted) □ paddle「(カヌーを漕ぐ)櫂，パドル」※大きめのボートを漕ぐ櫂は oar（オール）と呼ばれる。

(A) A vehicle has been parked in a garage.	(A) 乗り物がガレージに駐車されている。
(B) A shade has partially covered a window pane.	(B) ブラインドが窓ガラスを一部覆っている。
(C) The porch of the house is patterned with stripes.	(C) 家のポーチに縞模様が描かれている。
(D) The lawn has been mown in the courtyard.	(D) 中庭の芝が刈り取られている。

正答 手前に見える一階の窓にブラインドが少しかかっているので，(B) が適切。語彙レベルも高く，車など目立つ特徴にとらわれていると一文まるごと聞き逃してしまう難問である。誤答 (A) は garage（車庫）ではなく driveway（道路から家に通じる私道）であれば正解。(C) の porch は写真に写っていないが，(B) を聞いて動揺した結果 (C) の冒頭を聞き逃す，ということはよくあるので気をつけよう。(D) は，courtyard（中庭）ではなく単に yard であればよい。

重要語句 □ shade「ブラインド」(= window shade; blind) □ window pane「窓ガラス」 □ porch「ポーチ（玄関口にある屋根つきのスペース）」 □ patterned with ...「～の模様が描かれた」

Part 1
まとめの練習

それではまとめとして，Part 1 の難問パターンを 6 問一気に解いてみましょう。

Disc 1
10-13

7.

Ⓐ Ⓑ Ⓒ Ⓓ

8.

Ⓐ Ⓑ Ⓒ Ⓓ

9.

Ⓐ Ⓑ Ⓒ Ⓓ

10.

Ⓐ Ⓑ Ⓒ Ⓓ

11.

Ⓐ Ⓑ Ⓒ Ⓓ

12.

Ⓐ Ⓑ Ⓒ Ⓓ

7

(A) Music is being played on a platform.	(A) 音楽が壇上で演奏されているところだ。
(B) Instruments are being assembled on a stage.	(B) 楽器がステージ上で組み立てられているところだ。
(C) Light fixtures are being installed above the performers.	(C) 照明器具が演奏者の頭上に設置されているところだ。
(D) Spectators are being shown to a stand.	(D) 観客が売り場に案内されているところだ。

正答 ステージ自体は見えないが，壇上で音楽演奏をしているのは写真から明確なので，(A) が描写文として正しい。platform は「一段高くなった台」のことで，「演台」や「(車を上下に動かす) 車台」などを幅広く意味する重要語。**誤答** (C) の light fixtures のように目立たないモノが主語に来た場合も，後ろに続く動詞が are being installed なのか have been installed なのかを聞き逃さないよう注意しよう。

重要語句 □ instrument「楽器」(= musical instrument) □ spectator「観客」 □ stand「売り場」(= stall)

8

(A) A balcony has been constructed above the archway.	(A) ベランダがアーチ形の入り口の上部に建設されている。
(B) The entrance opens onto a flight of steps.	(B) 入り口が一続きの階段に通じている。
(C) A vehicle is being parked outside the building.	(C) 乗り物が建物の外に駐車されているところだ。
(D) Some items are being placed on the windowsill.	(D) 物がいくつか窓台に置かれているところだ。

正答 入口がそのまま階段に通じている様子を言い表した (B) が適切。open onto ...(～に通じている)という表現は過去に一度登場したことがあるので，ぜひ覚えておきたい。**誤答** (A) は，balcony らしいモノが写っていないので不適切。また，難易度の高い (B) の描写文が聞き取れなくても，すぐに気持ちを切り替え (C) や (D) の is [are] being -ed を聞き逃さないようにしよう。

重要語句 □ a flight of steps「一続きの階段」(= a set of steps) □ windowsill「窓台 (窓の下部にあるモノを置けるスペース)」 ※ 窓の外側に設置する「植木箱」は window box と呼ばれる。

(A) A cargo ship is docked along the shore.

(A) 貨物船が岸辺に停められている。

(B) The man is moving through the waterway.

(B) 男性が水路を進んでいる。

(C) Railings line either side of the pier.

(C) 柵が桟橋の両側に沿って設置されている。

(D) A bridge is being built with planks of wood.

(D) 橋が木の板で作られているところだ。

正答 桟橋の両側に柵があるので，(C) が正解。pier（桟橋）は絶対に覚えておこう。また，either side は「どちら側も」(= each side) という意味で，one side（片側）ではないことに注意。**誤答** (A) は，桟橋の奥にあるモノが何かハッキリしないが，岸辺ではないので不適切。(B) は waterway（水路）ではなく walkway（通路），(D) は is built/has been built であれば正解になる。

重要語句 □waterway「（ボートなどで運行できる）水路」 □railing「柵」 □line「〜に沿う」 □pier「桟橋」 □plank「（細長い）木の板」

(A) A jacket is being draped over a chair.

(A) ジャケットがイスの上にかけられているところだ。

(B) One of the chairs is being positioned against the wall.

(B) イスのひとつが壁に背がつくように置かれているところだ。

(C) Eating utensils have been arranged beside each plate.

(C) ナイフ・フォーク類が各皿のそばに並べられている。

(D) Tableware has been put on top of the cloth.

(D) 食卓食器が布の上に置かれている。

正答 テーブルクロスの上に食器類が置かれている状態を言い表した (D) が正解。**誤答** (A) と (B) はそれぞれ，is draped/has been draped や is positioned/has been positioned であれば正解になる。(C) の eating utensils は一部の皿の上に載せてあるだけなので不適切。

重要語句 □drape *A* over *B*「A を B にたらして掛ける」 □eating utensils「食べ物を口に運ぶ食器（ナイフ・フォーク・箸など）」 ※silverware/cutlery「ナイフ・フォーク類」，kitchen utensils「台所用具」(= kitchenware)，cooking utensils「料理器具」(= cookware) も重要語。□tableware「食卓食器」 □on top of ...「〜の上に」

11

(A) Pebbles are being collected into piles.

(B) A structure is being supported on posts.

(C) The man is strolling along the side of a ramp.

(D) Glass is being fitted into the window frame.

(A) 小石が山積みにされているところだ。

(B) 建物が支柱で支えられている。

(C) 男性がスロープのそばをゆっくり歩いている。

(D) ガラスが窓の枠にはめ込まれているところだ。

正答 建物の中を柱が通っているので, (B) が適切な描写文である。is being supported という現在進行形で「支えられている状態」を表せるので, is supported や has been supported と同じ意味になる。**誤答** (C) の ramp (〔段差をつなぐ〕スロープ) は lamp (ランプ) との発音の違い [rǽmp]-[lǽmp] に注意。ちなみに,「街灯柱」は lamppost と呼ばれる。

重要語句 □ pebble「(海岸などにある) 丸い小石」 □ post「柱, 支柱」 □ fit *A* into *B*「*A* を *B* にはめ込む, 入れる」

12

(A) Some diners are being seated outdoors.

(B) The attic window overlooks the pedestrian walkway.

(C) Some furniture has been arranged under the awning.

(D) An open-air café is decorated with flowers in vases.

(A) 食事客が外で席を案内されている。

(B) 屋根裏部屋の窓から歩行者通路が見渡せる。

(C) テーブル・イス類が日よけの下に並べられている。

(D) 屋外カフェが花瓶の花で飾られている。

正答 日よけの下に座席が用意されている状態を, (C) が適切に言い表している。awning を知らなくても, has been arranged という現在完了形を絶対に聞き逃さないようにし, 消去法で正解を残したい。furniture は tables や chairs など「動かせる家具類」を幅広く指す。**誤答** (A) は are seated や have been seated であれば座っている状態を表せるが, 進行形にすると「(席に座らせられている最中=)席を案内されている」という意味になるため不適切。(B) は attic window らしいモノが写っていない。(D) の vase は, アメリカ英語では [véis] と発音されるが, イギリス英語では [vάːz] となり, TOEIC のカナダ人男性ナレーターも [vάːz] と発音するので注意。

重要語句 □ attic「屋根裏部屋」 □ overlook「(場所から) ～が見渡せる, 見下ろせる」 □ pedestrian walkway「歩行者通路」 □ awning「日よけ, 天幕」 □ vase「花びん」 ※ 写真に映っているのは planter。

Part 2

応答問題

満点ポイント 6

Directionsの間に気持ちをリセットする

Part 2

Part 2 の Directions は約 1 分あります。この間にゆっくり深呼吸しながら，Part 1 で乱れたペースを取り戻し，気持ちをリフレッシュして Question 11 を迎えましょう。質問（発言）と応答のみが 30 問淡々と繰り返される Part 2 は，リスニング・セクションの中でもっとも集中力を要するパートです。Directions の間に Part 3 の先読みをする受験者も多いですが，30 問を解いた後にはすべて忘れてしまうもの。Part 1 同様，目の前のタスクへと意識を高め，Part 2 を全問確実に正解しましょう。

満点ポイント 7

場面を瞬時にイメージする

Part 2 の難問は，「when に対して時を答える」というお決まりの応答ではなく，あくまでその場面に合った自然な受け答えを選ばせるものです。日常的に英語を話す機会がなくても，海外ドラマやインターネット動画など英会話を「疑似体験」できる素材は山ほどありますので，視覚イメージとともに日頃から会話を吸収しておきましょう。そのうち，質問文とドラマの一場面が重なったり，間違いの応答が場違いすぎておもしろかったり（How are you going to the airport? に対して By e-mail. など）と，力を抜いて問題に臨めるようになります。単調な Part 2 をこのように「楽しみながら解く」ことが，適度な集中力を保つ最大のテクニックです。

ここで，「イメージ力」を試す 5 問に挑戦しましょう。

| 1. | Mark your answer on your answer sheet. | Ⓐ Ⓑ Ⓒ |
| 2. | Mark your answer on your answer sheet. | Ⓐ Ⓑ Ⓒ |

3. Mark your answer on your answer sheet. Ⓐ Ⓑ Ⓒ
4. Mark your answer on your answer sheet. Ⓐ Ⓑ Ⓒ
5. Mark your answer on your answer sheet. Ⓐ Ⓑ Ⓒ

1

正解 ➤ (A)

When's Anita planning to book our accommodations for the next convention?

(A) She's waiting to confirm who's going.

(B) Earlier this week, I heard.

(C) It's in Pittsburgh again this year.

アニータは次の会議の際の宿泊をいつ予約する予定ですか。

(A) 誰が行くか確定するのを待っているところです。

(B) 今週のことだったと聞きました。

(C) 今年もまたピッツバーグです。

正答 (A) には「参加者が確定してから予約する」という意味合いが含まれるので、いつ予約するかを尋ねる質問に合っている。誤答 (B) は Later this week（今週これから）であれば応答が成立するが、Earlier this week は「今週のうちすでに過ぎた日」を指すため不適切。(C) は where に対する応答。

2

正解 ➤ (C)

Do consumers prefer our coffee or tea?

(A) Either one will be fine.

(B) Let's ask them when they get here.

(C) Tea's selling better in our region.

消費者は当社のコーヒーと紅茶のどちらを好んでいますか。

(A) どちらでも大丈夫ですよ。

(B) ここに着いたら聞いてみましょう。

(C) 我々の地区では紅茶のほうが売れています。

正答 一般消費者の好みを尋ねているのに対し、(C) は「tea の売上が高い」、つまり「tea を好んでいる」と適切に答えている。誤答 (A) と (B) はどちらも、Do our clients prefer coffee or tea?（クライアントはコーヒーと紅茶のどちらを好むでしょうか）のように、来訪客に関する質問であれば応答として成立するので、あくまで「場面」を見極められるようにしたい。

重要語句 □ sell better は sell well（よく売れる）という表現を比較級にした形。

31

3

正解 ➤ (A)

Do you know how I should address this letter?

(A) To Ms. Barbara Lyndberg.

(B) Have someone double-check it.

(C) By express mail.

この手紙を誰宛てにすればいいか知っていますか。

(A) バーバラ・リンドバーグさん宛てです。

(B) 誰かに再確認してもらってください。

(C) 速達です。

正答 address a letter は「手紙の宛名を書く」という意味で，宛名をどうするかを尋ねている。したがって，名前を答えている (A) が正解。**誤答** (B) は What should I do with the letter I wrote?, (C) は How should I send this letter? に対する応答。

重要語句 □ have *someone do* ...「人に~させる，してもらう」

4

正解 ➤ (B)

Where did Mr. Nakamura go with that proposal?

(A) He would always read in the meeting room.

(B) He wanted some feedback from Ms. Fields.

(C) I think it was presented by the board.

ナカムラさんはあの企画書を持ってどこに行きましたか。

(A) 彼はいつも会議室で読書をしていました。

(B) フィールズさんからの意見が欲しかったのです。

(C) 取締役会によって提案されたものだと思います。

正答 企画書を持って行った「場所」を尋ねているのに対し，(B) は直接「場所」を答えてはいないが，意見をもらうため Ms. Fields のところに行ったことがわかるので，自然な応答が成り立っている。**誤答** (A) の《would ＋頻度の副詞》は「昔はよく~したものだ」と回想する表現。場所を示す語句だけにとらわれず，あくまで「自然な応答か」を瞬時に感じ取ろう。(C) は I think it was presented <u>to</u> the board. であれば正解。

5

正解 ➤ (C)

How would you like to transfer to the New York branch permanently?

(A) I'm really looking forward to it.

(B) I'd prefer a flight in the early morning.

(C) That's something I would consider.

ニューヨーク支社に永久に転属するのはいかがですか。

(A) 本当に楽しみにしています。

(B) 早朝の便がいいです。

(C) それは検討する価値がありますね。

正答 How would you like to ...? には，「どのように~したいか」と手段を尋ねる場合と，「(~したい気持ちはどれくらいあるか＝) ~するのはいかがですか」と「意思」を尋ねる場合があり，ここでは後者の意味。一時的に New York 支社に来た従業員に「永久に異動してくるのはどうか」と尋ねている。したがって，「検討する価値がある」と気持ちを伝えている (C) が適切。**誤答** (A) は How do you feel about your transfer to New York?, (B) は When would you like to leave for New York? などに対する応答。

重要語句 □ permanently「永久に，ずっと」(＝ for good)

「発言」問題を極める Part2

Part 2 では，I think the printer is broken. に対して It's not plugged in. が正解になるといった，「発言→応答」のパターンが3問前後登場します。このタイプの問題は応答をあらかじめ予測しづらいため，質問文に答えるよりも高い英語力が求められます。ただ，発言がなされる場面がイメージできていれば，他の選択肢が明らかに間違いだと気づけるケースがほとんどです。ここで，「発言」問題を連続して解き，難度の高いこのパターンを確実にマスターしましょう。

Disc 1
21-30

6.　　Mark your answer on your answer sheet.　　Ⓐ Ⓑ Ⓒ

7.　　Mark your answer on your answer sheet.　　Ⓐ Ⓑ Ⓒ

8.　　Mark your answer on your answer sheet.　　Ⓐ Ⓑ Ⓒ

9.　　Mark your answer on your answer sheet.　　Ⓐ Ⓑ Ⓒ

10.　Mark your answer on your answer sheet.　　Ⓐ Ⓑ Ⓒ

11.　Mark your answer on your answer sheet.　　Ⓐ Ⓑ Ⓒ

12.　Mark your answer on your answer sheet.　　Ⓐ Ⓑ Ⓒ

13.　Mark your answer on your answer sheet.　　Ⓐ Ⓑ Ⓒ

14.　Mark your answer on your answer sheet.　　Ⓐ Ⓑ Ⓒ

15.　Mark your answer on your answer sheet.　　Ⓐ Ⓑ Ⓒ

6

Many of our clients are having trouble finding our place.	顧客の多くが当社の場所を見つけるのに苦労しています。
(A) No, there haven't been any problems.	(A) いいえ，何も問題はありません。
(B) We've just updated our map.	(B) ちょうど地図を更新したところですよ。
(C) It must have been misplaced.	(C) それを置き違えたに違いありません。

正答 「顧客が会社の場所を見つけられない」という問題に対し，(B) が「map を更新したところだ（だから大丈夫）」という適切な応答になっている。誤答 (A) は There weren't any problems before.（以前は問題がなかったのですが）であればよい。(C) は finding と misplaced という関連語による混乱をねらった選択肢。

重要語句 □ have trouble *doing*「～するのに苦労する」 □ misplace「～を置き違える，紛失する」

7

We were asked to specify a date for the reception.	祝賀会の日取りを明記するよう依頼されました。
(A) I think it'll be 15.	(A) 15 人だと思います。
(B) Do we have to decide right away?	(B) 今すぐに決めなくてはいけませんか。
(C) I'd intended to go on Wednesday.	(C) 水曜日に行く予定でした。

正答 日取りを明記することについて，(B) は今すぐに決める必要があるかを問い返しており，自然な応答が成り立っている。このように，「発言」に「質問」で返すパターンも頻出。誤答 (A) は，「15 日」であれば it'll (= the reception will) be on the 15th となる。(C) は Wednesday という曜日があるが，質問の答えにはなっていない。

重要語句 □ specify「～を明記する」(= state ... exactly)

8

The deal with Pennsky Manufacturing has fallen through.	ペンスキー・マニュファクチャリング社との取引は成立しませんでした。
(A) It's all thanks to your support.	(A) すべてあなたの助けがあったからです。
(B) Oh, that's a shame.	(B) そうですか，それは残念です。
(C) It's only decreased slightly.	(C) 少し下がっただけです。

正答 fall through は「失敗に終わる」という表現。取引の失敗に関して「残念だ」という気持ちを伝えている (B) が適切。誤答 (A) は，発言が The deal went through.（取引が成立した）であれば適切な応答になる。(C) は fallen と decreased という関連語を用いているが，発言内容にはまったく関係がない。なお，実際のテストでも，6 ～ 8 の問題のように同じ正答（ここでは B）が 3 つ続く場合があるが，それに気をとられないようにしよう。

重要語句 □ thanks to ...「～のおかげで」

9

We could use a few more pieces of furniture for the hotel lobby.

(A) Well, each room has one couch.

(B) I used some of it yesterday.

(C) What kind do you have in mind?

ホテルのロビーにもう少し家具があるといいんですが。

(A) ええと，各部屋に1つ長イスがあります。

(B) 昨日いくつか使用しました。

(C) どのようなものを考えていますか。

正答 「家具がもう少しあれば」という意見に対し，具体的に何がよいと考えているかを尋ね返している (C) が適切。could use は「〜があるとよい，ありがたい」という慣用表現で，I could use some help.（助けがあればありがたい）のように会話でよく用いられる。誤答 (A) は客室の情報を伝えているので不適切。(B) は，use という同じ語を使ったひっかけの選択肢。

10

I was told we're starting a new recruitment drive.

(A) It's because the department is expanding.

(B) Yes, but it's just a short trip from here.

(C) It only applies to our part-time employees.

新たに採用活動を始める予定だと聞きました。

(A) 部署が大きくなっているからです。

(B) はい，でもここから少し行くだけです。

(C) パートタイムの従業員にのみ適用されます。

正答 採用活動に関して，(A) がその理由を話すことで自然な応答になっている。we're starting という現在進行形は，ここでは「確定した予定」を表す。誤答 (B) は drive と trip という関連語によるひっかけの選択肢。(C) の applies (apply) to ... は「（規則などが）〜に適用される」という意味。

重要語句 □ drive「（組織的な）活動, 取り組み」(= planned effort) ※ 他にも, a charity drive（チャリティ活動）や an economy drive（節約運動）などの形で用いられる。

11

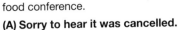

I was looking forward to attending the food conference.

(A) Sorry to hear it was cancelled.

(B) I didn't know you were there.

(C) I've been considering it for a while.

食品会議に参加するのを楽しみにしていたのですが。

(A) 中止になって残念ですね。

(B) あなたがそこにいるとは知りませんでした。

(C) しばらくそれについて検討していました。

正答 I was looking forward という過去形を用いることで，「楽しみにしていた（のに行けなくなった）」という隠れた文意をくみ取れるかを試す難問。発言だけでは行けなくなった理由はわからないが，相手の気持ちを感じ取っている (A) が自然な応答である。

誤答 (B) は I attended the food conference, (C) は I heard you are leaving the company. などに対する応答。

正解 ► (C)

Let me know if you can drop by the office any time soon.

(A) I'll drop it off as soon as possible.

(B) Sure, just come in at your convenience.

(C) Will it be all right to stop by at lunchtime?

近々オフィスに立ち寄れるか知らせてください。

(A) できるだけ早く届けます。

(B) もちろんです。都合のよいときに来てください。

(C) ランチの時間に立ち寄ってもいいですか。

 drop by は「立ち寄る」(= stop by) という意味。「オフィスに来られるか」と尋ねているのに対し、「lunchtime に行ってもいいか」と聞き返している (C) が自然な応答。誤答 (A) の drop ... off は「〜を車で届ける」(= take ... to a place by car) という意味で、drop by とのサウンドトリックによる誤答。(B) は、Can I drop by your office? であれば自然な応答になる。

重要語句 □ at *one's* convenience「都合の良いときに」※at *one's* earliest convenience は「できるだけ早急に」(= as soon as possible) の意味。

正解 ► (B)

It was a very long telephone survey I participated in yesterday.

(A) I attended the same one, actually.

(B) It'd be more convenient online, wouldn't it?

(C) I thought you've already finalized it.

昨日受けた電話アンケート調査は本当に長かったです。

(A) 私もじつは同じものに出席しました。

(B) ネット上で行えばもっと便利ですよね。

(C) すでに仕上げたと思っていました。

正答 「telephone survey が長かった」という発言に対し、(B) では「online のほうが (電話よりも) 便利ですよね」と意見を述べているので、応答が成立している。誤答 (A) の attend は be present at や go to の意味なので、attend a telephone survey とは言えないことに注意。(C) は、発言が I need more time to get this report done. などであれば応答として成り立つ。

重要語句 □ It'd be more convenient online は It would be more convenient (if the survey were conducted) online. という仮定法の表現。 □ finalize「〜を仕上げる、最終版を出す」(= finish the last part of ...)

14

正解 ➤ (A)

It's never occurred to me that the company would relocate.

(A) Management's been talking about it for months.

(B) I wonder who was chosen.

(C) It could have happened anywhere.

会社が移転になるとは思いませんでした。

(A) 経営陣が何か月もその話をしていましたよ。

(B) 誰が選ばれたのでしょうか。

(C) どこでも起こりえたことです。

正答 occur to *someone* は「〜の心に思い浮かぶ」(= come into *someone's* mind) という表現。「会社が relocate すると思わなかった」というつぶやきに対し,「経営陣がずっと話していた」と事実を伝えている (A) が適切。**誤答** (B) は I wonder why., (C) は It could have happened anytime. であれば応答として成り立つ。

重要語句 □ management「経営陣」(= people in charge of a company)

15

正解 ➤ (B)

I think we need to buy a new microscope for our laboratory.

(A) The experiments weren't conducted properly.

(B) AcePro down the street is a great place.

(C) It'll be a little cheaper to get an assistant.

研究室用に新しく顕微鏡を買う必要があると思います。

(A) 実験が適切に行われませんでした。

(B) 通りを進んだところにあるエイスプロがいいですよ。

(C) アシスタントを雇ったほうがやや安上がりです。

正答「new microscope が必要だ」という発言に対して,(B) が AcePro ... is a great place (to buy one). と店を紹介しているので,これが応答として適切。**誤答** (A) は experiments という質問に関連する語を用いているが,応答になっていない。(C) は,文尾の assistant まで集中して聞かないと正解に聞こえてしまうので注意。

重要語句 □ microscope「顕微鏡」

一瞬たりとも聞き逃さない

Part 2

正解のヒントが質問の一文に集約されている Part 2 では,「一瞬の聞き逃し」が致命的になります。判断に迷う問題があっても,"Number ..."という読み上げが始まるまでに必ずマークをして意識を切り替え,次の質問文を絶対に聞き逃さないことが鉄則です。ここで,疑問文の中でも聞き取りに注意を要する「付加疑問文」「否定疑問文」「選択疑問文」の3パターンを実際よりも速いペースで解き,「瞬発力」と「集中力」を鍛えましょう。

Disc 1
31-40

16.	Mark your answer on your answer sheet.	Ⓐ Ⓑ Ⓒ
17.	Mark your answer on your answer sheet.	Ⓐ Ⓑ Ⓒ
18.	Mark your answer on your answer sheet.	Ⓐ Ⓑ Ⓒ
19.	Mark your answer on your answer sheet.	Ⓐ Ⓑ Ⓒ
20.	Mark your answer on your answer sheet.	Ⓐ Ⓑ Ⓒ
21.	Mark your answer on your answer sheet.	Ⓐ Ⓑ Ⓒ
22.	Mark your answer on your answer sheet.	Ⓐ Ⓑ Ⓒ
23.	Mark your answer on your answer sheet.	Ⓐ Ⓑ Ⓒ
24.	Mark your answer on your answer sheet.	Ⓐ Ⓑ Ⓒ
25.	Mark your answer on your answer sheet.	Ⓐ Ⓑ Ⓒ

16 付加疑問文

Danielle hasn't been given the copy of the minutes, has she?

(A) She didn't have enough time.

(B) Does she know we have a meeting?

(C) She's the one who typed them up.

ダニエルは議事録をもらっていませんよね？

(A) 彼女は十分な時間がなかったのです。

(B) 彼女は会議があることを知っていますか。

(C) 彼女がそれをタイプしたのです。

正答 付加疑問文は相手に確認をとる言い方。Danielle が the minutes（議事録）をもらっていないことを確認しているのに対し，(C) は「彼女が type up した」と答えることで，「だからもらう必要がない」というメッセージになっている。**誤答** (A) は I didn't have time (to give it to her). であればよい。(B) は質問が Danielle will attend the meeting, won't she? であれば，「質問」に「質問」で返す自然なパターンが成立する。

重要語句 □ minute「議事録」（agenda「議事日程表」との違いに注意）

---

17 否定疑問文

正解 ➤ (C)

Couldn't you find the missing customer file?

(A) No, it's been on my desk.

(B) I think Ms. Kim found out about it.

(C) I haven't had a chance to look.

紛失した顧客ファイルは見つからなかったのですか。

(A) いいえ，ずっと私の机にありました。

(B) キムさんがそれについて発見したのだと思います。

(C) 探す機会がありませんでした。

正答 否定疑問文は，普通の疑問文に「驚き」や「懸念」などの感情が加わる。紛失した file を懸念する男性に対して，まだ探していないことを伝えている (C) が適切。**誤答** (A) は，No が I couldn't find it. を意味するため，後ろの部分とつながらない。(B) は，I think Ms. Kim found it. であれば正解となる。

重要語句 □ find out about ...「～（事実）を発見する」

18 選択疑問文

Will the new employee manual be available tomorrow or the day after?

(A) We've already distributed it.

(B) I'm sure she'll be available tomorrow.

(C) Actually, the offer was turned down.

新しい従業員マニュアルは明日できますか，それとも明後日ですか。

(A) もう配布していますよ。

(B) 彼女は明日ならきっと都合がつきます。

(C) じつはオファーを断られたのです。

正答 employee manual が手に入る時を尋ねているのに対し，(A) は「（明日でも明後日でもなく）すでに配布している」と適切に答えている。このように，「（A でも B でもなく）C だ」と第 3 の答えを出すものが正解になる選択疑問文のパターンは Part 2 に頻出。誤答 (B) は, she ではなく it (= the manual) であれば正解。(C) は offer に関連する内容が質問文にない。

重要語句 □ turn ... down「（申し入れや招待）を断る」（= decline; refuse）

---

19 付加疑問文

That's Matt's car in the employee parking lot, isn't it?

(A) No, he drove us home.

(B) I thought he left an hour ago.

(C) He traded it in for a newer model.

従業員駐車場にあるのはマットの車ですよね？

(A) いいえ，彼は私たちを家まで車で送ってくれました。

(B) 1 時間前に退社したものと思っていました。

(C) 彼は最新の車種に代えたと思います。

正答 向こう側に見える車を指して尋ねている場面。質問文の中に「（車があるということは）会社にいるのか」と確認する気持ちが込められていることをつかみ，「退社したと思っていた」と答えている (B) を選ぶ。ここでも，「コトバ」そのものだけでなく「場面」をイメージすることが大切。誤答 (A) の No は No, it isn't Matt's car. を意味するので，No, he drove home.（車で帰宅した）であればよい。(C) は Matt has an old car, doesn't he? に対する応答。

重要語句 □ trade A in for B「A を下取りに出して B を買う」

20 否定疑問文

正解 ➤ (A)

Won't the cost of refurbishing the break room put us over budget?

(A) The bids we received are surprisingly low.

(B) Well, that was the quoted price.

(C) It depends on how much you need it.

休憩室の修繕費用を入れると予算を超えることになりませんか。

(A) 我々が受けた提示額は驚くほど低いのです。

(B) まあ，それが見積価格だったのです。

(C) どれだけそれが必要なのかによります。

正答 修繕費用を懸念している相手に対し，(A) は「提示額が低い」，すなわち「予算をオーバーしない」ことを間接的に述べている。名詞 bid は「工事の入札（価格）」（= offer to do work for a particular price）の意味。誤答 (B) は，that が指すべき具体的な金額が質問文にない。(C) は，It depends on how much it (= the cost) will be. であれば正解。

重要語句 □ over budget「予算を上回って」 □ refurbish「〜を修繕・改装する」（= renovate） □ break room「休憩室」

21 選択疑問文

正解 ➤ (A)

Do you want me to give you a ride to the airport or would you rather take the bus there?

(A) I just bought my ticket, actually.

(B) I think we should do both.

(C) I've received one, thanks.

空港まで車で送ってほしいですか，それとも空港までバスで行きたいですか。

(A) じつはちょうどチケットを買ったところなんです。

(B) 我々は両方すべきだと思います。

(C) ひとつもらいました。ありがとうございます。

正答 「車とバスのどちらがいいか」という質問に対し，(A) は「（バスの）チケットを買った」と答えることで，バスで行くことを伝えている。誤答 (B) は，選択疑問文の答えになることもあるが，ここでは「車」と「バス」が両立できない行為なので不適切。(C) は，Would you like a newspaper? のようにモノを差し出された時の応答。

重要語句 □ give *someone* a ride to ...「人を〜まで車で送る」（= take *someone* to ... by car）

22 付加疑問文

正解 ➤ (B)

Charlotte will be attending the upcoming conference, won't she?

(A) She's expecting more time.

(B) She's delivering the opening address.

(C) I'm not sure. Do you?

シャーロットは今度の会議に参加しますよね。

(A) 彼女は時間がもっとほしいと思っています。

(B) 彼女は開演のスピーチをする予定です。

(C) わかりません。あなたは？

正答 Charlotte の予定に関して，(B) は「スピーチをする」と答えることで，彼女の参加を示唆している。誤答 (A) は，She's expecting to attend. であればよい。(C) は，Do you want to attend the conference? に対する応答。I'm not sure. だけであれば正答になるので，最後まで集中して聞くようにしよう。なお，Part 2 では，Charlotte のように「聞き取りづらい人名」をあえて登場させることがあるので注意。

重要語句 □ deliver an address「スピーチをする」(= deliver a speech)

23 否定疑問文

正解 ➤ (A)

Didn't Ms. Louise say that the venue we're using can only accommodate 30 people?

(A) What's this year's turnout projected to be?

(B) That would involve more staff.

(C) She didn't tell me either.

ルイーズさんは私たちが利用している会場では30人しか収容できないと言っていませんでしたか。

(A) 今年の参加者数はどうなる予測ですか。

(B) そうなるとスタッフがもっと必要になりますね。

(C) 私にも言っていませんでした。

正答 「30 人しか入らないと言っていたのでは」と会場の狭さを懸念しているのに対し，(A) は直接的な答えを返してはいないが，今年の参加者数を確認しているので，応答として成り立っている。この問題のように，質問文自体が長いものや，「質問返し」が正解になるパターンは難度が上がる。誤答 (B) は，Shouldn't we use a larger venue? などに対する応答。(C) は She didn't tell me. であれば正解。

重要語句 □ involve「〜を伴う」 □ turnout「参加者数」(= attendance) □ be projected to do「(現状を分析して) 〜する見込みの」

24 選択疑問文

Should we have the carpet replaced now, or would you prefer to keep it for another year?

(A) Those are very new.

(B) Let's save some for later.

(C) I think it's still usable.

カーペットを今交換すべきですか，それともも う1年使いたいですか。

(A) それらはまったく新しいものです。

(B) 後のためにいくつか取っておきましょう。

(C) まだ使えると思います。

 正答 カーペットの交換について，「まだ使える」，つまり「交換すべきではない」と答えている (C) が自然な応答。誤答 (A) は，those の受ける複数名詞が質問文になく，さらに for another year と いう部分から一年は使い続けていることがわかるので，意味も合わない。

重要語句 □ have the carpet replaced「カーペットを交換してもらう」※ 使役動詞 have を用いることで，みず から行うのではなく業者に行ってもらうという意味になる。

---

25 付加疑問文

It doesn't look like Mr. Tompkins will make it here on time, does it?

(A) It's scheduled for 7.

(B) He's just arrived in the lobby.

(C) I can help him finish it.

トンプキンスさんは間に合いそうにありません ね。

(A) 7時に予定されています。

(B) ちょうどロビーに到着したところです。

(C) 彼が終えるのを手助けできます。

正答 質問文から，Mr. Tompkins の到着を待つ場面を瞬時に思い浮かべる。ここでは，彼が間に合 うかについて「到着したところだ」と答えている (B) が正解。誤答 (A) は予定時刻を答えているだけで， 間に合うかに対する応答にはなっていない。(C) は，make it の意味合いがつかめない受験者をねらっ たひっかけ。

重要語句 □ make it「たどり着く，間に合う」

それでは，今までのトレーニングを踏まえながら，「イメージ力」「瞬発力」「集中力」をフル活用して，Part 2 の難問を 10 問を一気に解きましょう。

Disc 1
41-50

26.	Mark your answer on your answer sheet.	Ⓐ Ⓑ Ⓒ
27.	Mark your answer on your answer sheet.	Ⓐ Ⓑ Ⓒ
28.	Mark your answer on your answer sheet.	Ⓐ Ⓑ Ⓒ
29.	Mark your answer on your answer sheet.	Ⓐ Ⓑ Ⓒ
30.	Mark your answer on your answer sheet.	Ⓐ Ⓑ Ⓒ
31.	Mark your answer on your answer sheet.	Ⓐ Ⓑ Ⓒ
32.	Mark your answer on your answer sheet.	Ⓐ Ⓑ Ⓒ
33.	Mark your answer on your answer sheet.	Ⓐ Ⓑ Ⓒ
34.	Mark your answer on your answer sheet.	Ⓐ Ⓑ Ⓒ
35.	Mark your answer on your answer sheet.	Ⓐ Ⓑ Ⓒ

26

 Disc 1 41

正解 ➤ (A)

Why don't you ever fly first class for your business trips?

(A) **Because my department's on a budget.**

(B) That sounds fine to me.

(C) It was more expensive than I thought.

どうして普段出張にファーストクラスで行かないのですか。

(A) 部署の予算が限られているからです。

(B) 私はそれで構いませんよ。

(C) 思ったよりも高価でした。

正答 現在形＋ ever ...? は現在の習慣を尋ねる言い方で，first class で行かない理由を適切に答えている (A) が正解。why don't you ...?（〜したらどうか）という提案表現ではないことに注意しよう。また，why に対しこのように because で素直に答える正答も Part 2 に登場する。誤答 (B) は Why don't we fly first class?，(C) は Why didn't you fly first class? に対する応答。

重要語句 □ on a budget「少ない予算で」

27

Disc 1 42

正解 ➤ (C)

You'll finish this section of the report by the end of the day, won't you?

(A) I'll write everything down then.

(B) I've already read it in the article.

(C) **I thought you didn't need it until Monday.**

報告書のこの部分は今日中に仕上がりますよね？

(A) それではすべて書き留めることにします。

(B) すでに記事でそれを読みました。

(C) 月曜日までは必要ないと思っていました。

正答 report の今日中の完成を求めている相手に対し，「月曜まで必要ないと思っていた」と認識の違いを伝えている (C) が自然な応答。誤答 (A) の write down は「（メモなど）に書き留める」という意味なので，質問の答えになっていない。(B) は read 以下の部分が質問文とかみ合わない。

28

Disc 1 43

正解 ➤ (C)

Whose report did you think was the most informative?

(A) I believe Mr. Petersons did.

(B) I'd appreciate your input.

(C) **The one submitted by the head of sales.**

会議で誰の報告書がもっとも有益だと思いましたか。

(A) ピーターソンズさんがしたのだと思います。

(B) あなたから意見をいただければ幸いです。

(C) 営業部長が提出したものです。

正答 「誰の report がよかったか」と感想を尋ねている場面で，「the head of sales のものだ」と答えている (C) が適切。report を The one と言い換えている。誤答 (A) は，Who presented this report? のように「過去の行為」を尋ねていれば，Mr. Petersons did (= presented this report). と did で答えられる。(B) の I'd appreciate ... は，「〜があればありがたい」という間接的な依頼表現。

重要語句 □ informative「（情報の）有益な」 □ input「意見，アイデア」

29

I gather that our new legal associate is doing very well.	法務部に新しく入った社員はよくやってくれているようですね。
(A) What else did you get?	(A) 他に何を得たのですか。
(B) Mr. Jenkins has helped her a lot, though.	(B) ジェンキンスさんがかなり手助けをしましたが。
(C) Yes, it finally started working.	(C) はい，やっと動き出しました。

正答 I gather that ... は「(見聞きしたことから) ～と推察する，思う」という意味。同僚の働きぶりについて，(B) は「Mr. Jenkins の助けがあった (＝だからこそ今はよくやっている)」と適切に答えている。誤答 (A) は gather と get の混同をねらった選択肢。(C) は it を聞き逃さないように注意。

重要語句 □ associate「仲間，同僚」 □ ..., though.「(文尾に置いて) ～だけれど，～だが」

30

Shouldn't we have heard from Dr. Peters by now?	ピーターズ博士からもう連絡が来ているはずではないですか。
(A) She didn't say she would.	(A) 彼女はするとは言っていませんでした。
(B) I'm sure she's on the schedule.	(B) 彼女が予定表に入っていることは確かです。
(C) Didn't I tell you she called?	(C) 彼女から電話があったと伝えていませんでしたか。

正答 Dr. Peters からの連絡を待っている場面が思い浮かべば，電話連絡があったことを伝えている (C) が正解であるとわかる。誤答 (A) は，質問 Shouldn't Dr. Peters have called us by now? であればよいが，ここでは would の示す行為が質問文にない。(B) の on the schedule は「予定表に載っていること」を意味するので，Will Dr. Peters give a lecture today? などに対する応答。

重要語句 □ hear from ...「～から連絡が来る」

31

Would you like me to e-mail the client when we ship the order, or would you rather I call?	商品の配送時に顧客にメールを送りましょうか，それとも電話をしたほうがいいですか。
(A) I'll let you know when it arrives.	(A) 届いたらお知らせします。
(B) That went out yesterday, actually.	(B) じつは昨日発送されたのです。
(C) That would be great.	(C) それはありがたいです。

正答 配送時にすべき行動を選択疑問文で尋ねている。(B) の That は the order を指しており，それがすでに発送済みであると述べているので，今はもう何もする必要がないことがわかる。誤答 (A) はモノを受け取る側が述べる発言。(C) は選択疑問文に対する答えにならない。

重要語句 □ would rather S V「S に V してほしいと思う」(＊一種の仮定法表現で，V の位置には通例，原形か過去形が来る)

32

It's been quite a while since we last conducted a safety inspection, hasn't it?

(A) One has been arranged for the start of March.

(B) Yes, we should go there again soon.

(C) We brought it in last month.

前回安全検査を行ってからずいぶん経ちますよね？

(A) 3 月の始めに予定されていますよ。

(B) はい，また近々行きましょう。

(C) 先月持ってきました。

正答 safety inspection をしばらく行っていないと話す相手に対し，次回の予定日を答えている (A) が自然な応答。誤答 (B) は there の指す「場所」が質問文にないので不適切。(C) の bring ... in は「～を持ってくる」という意味なので，質問文に合わない。

33

正解 ➤ (C)

Disc 1 48

Weren't we supposed to bring the product samples to the presentation?

(A) They've already assembled in the room.

(B) It should have been more productive.

(C) They're being shipped by courier now.

製品サンプルをプレゼンに持って来るべきではなかったですか。

(A) 彼らはすでに部屋に集合しています。

(B) もっと実りの多いものになるはずでした。

(C) 今宅配便で配送されているところです。

正答 product samples を持って来るべきではなかったかという懸念に対し，(C) は「今配送されている」＝「持って来る必要がない」と適切に答えている。誤答 (A) のように assemble を自動詞的に用いると「集合する」（＝ get together）という意味になり，they が人を指すことになるので注意。(B) は How was the meeting? などに対する応答。

重要語句 □ productive「生産的な，実り多い」 □ courier「宅配便，宅配業者」

34

Disc 1
49

正解 ➤ (A)

I heard that Trisha will be the new assistant director as of January.	トリーシャが1月から新しいアシスタントディレクターになると聞きました。
(A) I didn't know she was under consideration.	(A) 彼女が候補に入っていたとは知りませんでした。
(B) I'm sure she'll manage it herself.	(B) 彼女ならきっと自分で何とかできると思います。
(C) I entirely agree with you.	(C) あなたにまったく同感です。

正答 Trisha が assistant director になることについて，「候補に入っていたとは知らなかった」と驚いている (A) が自然な応答。誤答 (B) の manage は「～をなんとか行う」という意味で，ここでは it の指すものが発言の中にない。(C) は相手の意見に同調する表現なので，始めの発言が I think Trisha should be the new assistant director. であれば正解。

重要語句 □ as of ...「（日付）から」 □ under consideration「考慮されている，検討中の」（= being considered）□ manage「～をなんとか行う，やりとりする」

35

Disc 1
50

正解 ➤ (B)

Are we adopting the manufacturing process that was suggested, or is the production manager happy with what we do now?	提案された製造過程を採用することになるのでしょうか，それとも製造部長は現在のやり方で満足しているのでしょうか。
(A) The new system has increased productivity.	(A) 新しいシステムで生産性が伸びました。
(B) He's still debating what to do.	(B) 彼はどうすべきかまだ検討中です。
(C) He would only work on a temporary basis.	(C) 彼は臨時で働くことになるだけです。

正答 選択疑問文の or の前後が長いので，場面を思い浮かべながら，キーとなる情報をできるだけ記憶しておこう。提案されたプロセスを採用するかどうかについて，(B) は production manager が検討中であることを伝えているので，応答が成立している。動詞 debate には「検討する」（= consider）の意味がある。誤答 (A) はプロセスを採用した後に述べること。

重要語句 □ adopt「（方法や考え）を採用する」（= accept and choose）

Part 3 & Part 4
会話問題・説明文問題

Part 3&4

Directionsの間に気持ちをリフレッシュする

　　Part 3・Part 4 の Directions が流れる 30 秒間は，それまでのパートで酷使した集中力をリフレッシュするため，まずは目を閉じて数回深呼吸しましょう。この間に心を再び落ち着かせ，自分のペースを取り戻しておくことが大切です。そして残りの時間に，はじめのセット分（1 ページ分）の設問文を先に読んでおき，これから始まる問題に対する集中力を高めていきます。次のページまで先読みをすると，かえって集中力が途切れます。「目の前のもの」に常に焦点を合わせることが重要です。

話に入り込んで場面をイメージする

　TOEIC 対策書のほとんどは，Part 3・Part 4 において「設問や選択肢の先読み」を必須テクニックとしています。さらに受験者の多くは，会話やトークを聞くと同時に答えを探す「マルチタスク型」アプローチをとっています。満点を目指す方に知っておいていただきたいのは，先読みをしなくても，また会話やトークが終わった後に設問を解く「シングルタスク型」アプローチをとっても，リスニング力があれば全問正解できるということです。その際に必要なのは，話の中に 100% 入り込み，場面や展開をイメージしながら聞く力です。「聞きながら解く」という余計なタスクがない分，慣れてくると問題を解くのが楽になります。また，「先読みしなくても話に集中すれば必ず解ける」という自信をつけておけば，本番で先読みのペースが乱れた場合でもミスをせずに切り抜けることができます。

　ここで，皆さんのリスニング力を最大限に引き上げるトレーニングを行います。問題を解く際は，「先読みをしない」，「話を聞き終えてから解く」のふたつを守ってください。また，全体の内容を理解できているかの確認として，ここでは本番よりも設問数の多い5問形式になっています。設問はいずれも話の流れがイメージできていれば解けるものです。皆さんの脳は，「コトバ」は忘れても「イメージ」は忘れません。ここで鍛えるのは，「記憶力」ではなく「イメージ力」と「集中力」です。

Part 3

1. What are the speakers discussing?
    (A) Applications for parking permits
    (B) Maintenance work on company premises
    (C) Road repairs in front of the office
    (D) Completion of a new office building

    Ⓐ Ⓑ Ⓒ Ⓓ

2. When was the work originally scheduled for completion?
    (A) Yesterday
    (B) Today
    (C) Tomorrow
    (D) In two days

    Ⓐ Ⓑ Ⓒ Ⓓ

3. What problem does the woman mention?
    (A) There are not enough workers.
    (B) There is some opposition to the plan.
    (C) The budget has been reduced.
    (D) Weather has been unfavorable.

    Ⓐ Ⓑ Ⓒ Ⓓ

4. What does the man imply he has done?
    (A) Spent a large amount of money
    (B) Made an announcement in a meeting
    (C) Found a parking space next to the office
    (D) Had his expenses reimbursed

    Ⓐ Ⓑ Ⓒ Ⓓ

5. Why did the woman miss the announcement?
    (A) She has been away from town.
    (B) She was late for work.
    (C) She has been busy with some other work.
    (D) She works in a different department.

    Ⓐ Ⓑ Ⓒ Ⓓ

6. Where most likely are the speakers?
(A) In a restaurant
(B) In a kitchenware store
(C) In a stationery shop
(D) In a furniture store
Ⓐ Ⓑ Ⓒ Ⓓ

7. What does the man say about the items?
(A) There are some in the stock room.
(B) They are no longer being made.
(C) He is expecting more soon.
(D) They are currently discounted.
Ⓐ Ⓑ Ⓒ Ⓓ

8. What is suggested about the man's store?
(A) It produces its own merchandise.
(B) It offers free delivery service.
(C) It is known for its stylish designs.
(D) It has some branches downtown.
Ⓐ Ⓑ Ⓒ Ⓓ

9. What does the woman say about her business?
(A) It was recently opened.
(B) It sells dinner plates.
(C) It is currently being renovated.
(D) It is popular with local customers.
Ⓐ Ⓑ Ⓒ Ⓓ

10. What will the man do next?
(A) Contact another store
(B) Order more merchandise
(C) Write down some information
(D) Make a call to a customer

Part 4

11. What does the speaker say about the event?
(A) It is being held for the first time.
(B) It has attracted more companies than ever before.
(C) It is funded by Nutri Foods.
(D) It is only open to current university students.

ⒶⒷⒸⒹ

12. Who is Eldrich Dilts?
(A) A university professor
(B) A local farmer
(C) An agriculture expert
(D) A hiring manager

ⒶⒷⒸⒹ

13. What will Mr. Dilts discuss?
(A) Opportunities in his area of work
(B) Networking with scientists
(C) Application procedures for research grants
(D) A recent increase in farm production

ⒶⒷⒸⒹ

14. According to the speaker, what can listeners do later this evening?
(A) Speak with the special guest
(B) Learn about training courses
(C) Tour some facilities
(D) Have job interviews

ⒶⒷⒸⒹ

15. What will listeners most likely do next?
(A) Greet a guest personally
(B) Meet representatives of different companies
(C) Sign up for a university class
(D) Listen to a presentation by another speaker

ⒶⒷⒸⒹ

16. Who most likely are the listeners?

(A) Professional designers

(B) Board members

(C) Marketing staff

(D) Store clerks

Ⓐ Ⓑ Ⓒ Ⓓ

17. What is the purpose of the speech?

(A) To request ideas for advertisements

(B) To praise staff for exceeding targets

(C) To propose changes to employee benefits

(D) To outline the results of a marketing campaign

Ⓐ Ⓑ Ⓒ Ⓓ

18. What field of business is the speaker's company in?

(A) Clothing

(B) Office equipment

(C) Advertising

(D) Automobiles

Ⓐ Ⓑ Ⓒ Ⓓ

19. According to the speaker, why has business improved?

(A) Customer surveys were effective.

(B) A new branch has opened.

(C) Prices were lowered.

(D) The advertisements were creative.

20. When will the bonuses be distributed?

(A) On Friday

(B) Next week

(C) Next month

(D) At the beginning of the year

Ⓐ Ⓑ Ⓒ Ⓓ

Questions 1 through 5 refer to the following conversation.

M: **Q1** I hope they'll finish resurfacing the office parking lot soon. It took me over twenty minutes to find a space on the street this morning. Then I had to walk several blocks to get to the office.

W: **Q2** It was supposed to be finished yesterday, but it seems to be more difficult than expected. Apparently **Q3** the bad weather we've been having has caused the delay. I heard it will take another two days at least.

M: Well, I'm glad the company announced this morning that our parking expenses will be reimbursed. **Q4** Paying the parking meter every day is costing me a lot.

W: That's good news. **Q5** I missed that announcement, because I've been tied up in a budget meeting all day. I wish you better luck tomorrow morning.

重要語句 □ resurface「～を再舗装する」 □ apparently「どうやら，見たところ」 □ reimburse「～を払い戻す」（= pay ... back） □ wish *someone* luck「人に幸運を祈る」

男性： 会社の駐車場の再舗装が早く終わるといいのですが。今朝は路上の駐車スペースを探すのに20分以上もかかりました。それからさらにオフィスまで数ブロック歩かなくてはいけなかったんです。

女性： 予定では昨日終わるはずだったのですが，予想より難しいようですね。最近の悪天候が工事の遅れの原因みたいです。最低でもあと2日はかかると聞きました。

男性： 会社が今朝，駐車料金を払い戻してくれると発表してよかったです。連日のパーキングメーター代にすごくお金がかかっていますからね。

女性： それはいいですね。今日は一日中予算会議で忙しかったので，発表を聞いていませんでした。明日の朝はもっと楽に見つかるといいですね。

1

正解 ➤ (B)

What are the speakers discussing?	2人は何について話していますか。
(A) Applications for parking permits	(A) 駐車許可証の申し込み
(B) Maintenance work on company premises	(B) 会社敷地内のメンテナンス工事
(C) Road repairs in front of the office	(C) オフィスの前の道路修繕工事
(D) Completion of a new office building	(D) 新しいオフィスビルの完成

正答 男性が始めに I hope they'll finish resurfacing the office parking lot soon. と発言しているので，会社駐車場の再舗装がテーマであることをおさえ，再舗装工事を maintenance work と言い換えた (B) を選ぶ。on company premises は「会社の敷地内で」という意味。

2

When was the work originally scheduled for completion?	作業はもともといつ終わる予定でしたか。
(A) Yesterday	(A) 昨日
(B) Today	(B) 今日
(C) Tomorrow	(C) 明日
(D) In two days	(D) 2日後

正答 女性の1回目の発言で It was supposed to be finished yesterday と述べているので，(A) が正解。yesterday は一度しか出てこないが，すでに終わっている予定だったことがイメージできていれば，(A) を選べる。

3

正解 ➤ (D)

What problem does the woman mention?	女性はどんな問題について話していますか。
(A) There are not enough workers.	(A) 作業員が足りない。
(B) There is some opposition to the plan.	(B) 計画に対して反対がある。
(C) The budget has been reduced.	(C) 予算が減らされた。
(D) Weather has been unfavorable.	(D) 天気が良くない。

正答 女性の1回目の発言で the bad weather we've been having has caused the delay とあり，悪天候によって作業が長引いているとわかるので，(D) が正解。他の選択肢については，女性が budget meeting に参加していたことを除きまったく言及していないので，確実に正解したい。

4

正解 ➤ (A)

What does the man imply he has done?	男性は何をしたと示唆していますか。
(A) Spent a large amount of money	(A) かなりのお金を使った
(B) Made an announcement in a meeting	(B) 会議で発表をした
(C) Found a parking space next to the office	(C) オフィスの隣に駐車スペースを見つけた
(D) Had his expenses reimbursed	(D) 経費を払い戻してもらった

正答 男性の2回目の発言の Paying the parking meter every day is costing me a lot. から，駐車にかなりお金がかかっていることをおさえ，(A) を選ぶ。誤答 (C) は，男性が始めに I had to walk several blocks to get to the office と発言していることから，駐車場所とオフィスが離れていたことがわかる。(D) は，our parking expenses will be reimbursed の部分から，払い戻しはこれから行われることに注意。

5

Why did the woman miss the announcement?	女性はなぜ発表を聞き逃したのですか。
(A) She has been away from town.	(A) 市外へ外出していたため。
(B) She was late for work.	(B) 会社に遅刻したため。
(C) She has been busy with some other work.	(C) 他の仕事で忙しかったため。
(D) She works in a different department.	(D) 異なる部署で働いているため。

正答 会社の発表に関する男性の話を受け，女性が I missed that announcement と述べ，その理由を because I've been tied up in a budget meeting all day と説明しているので，(C) が正解。tied up は too busy to do anything else の意味。

Questions 6 through 10 refer to the following conversation.

W: Excuse me. **Q6** I bought some of these square white dinner plates here a few weeks ago for my restaurant. At the time, you had some smaller side plates in the same style, but I don't see them now.

M: **Q7** The smaller ones are sold out at the moment, as they've been very popular with our customers. **Q7** We ordered some more last week, so I'm sure they'll be arriving any day now. **Q8** Do you want me to call one of our other branches to see if they have any in stock? The downtown stores carry more stock than we do.

W: No, I can wait. **Q9** My restaurant is being refurbished at the moment. Could you set twelve aside for me?

M: Of course. **Q10** Let me just take down your name and phone number. I'll give you a call as soon as they arrive.

重要語句 □ any day now「今日明日にでも，今すぐにでも」 □ refurbish「〜を改装する」(= renovate) □ set ... aside「〜を確保しておく」 □ take ... down「〜を書き留める」(= write ... down; note ... down)

女性： すみません。数週間前，自分のレストラン用にこちらで四角い白のディナー皿を買いました。その時，同じシリーズでもう少し小さい皿があったのですが，今日は見当たりませんね。

男性： 小さい皿はお客様にとても人気で，現在在庫切れになっています。先週追加注文をしましたので，今日明日にでも入荷すると思います。他の支店に在庫があるか電話いたしましょうか。ダウンタウンにある支店は当店よりも在庫数が多いですので。

女性： いいえ，急いではいません。私のレストランは今改装中なんです。12枚取り置きしていただけますか。

男性： もちろんです。お名前とお電話番号をお願いします。入荷次第すぐに電話でご連絡いたします。

6

Where most likely are the speakers?	2人はおそらくどこにいますか。
(A) In a restaurant	(A) レストラン
(B) In a kitchenware store	(B) キッチン用品店
(C) In a stationery shop	(C) 文房具店
(D) In a furniture store	(D) 家具店

正答 女性が始めに I bought some of these square white dinner plates here と述べ，男性店員が smaller plates の在庫状況などについて女性に説明しているので，(B) が正解であることは明らか。「場面」を問う問題は，会話がイメージできていれば後からでもすぐ解答できるはず。

7

What does the man say about the items?	男性は品物について何と言っていますか。
(A) There are some in the stock room.	(A) 倉庫にいくつか在庫がある。
(B) They are no longer being made.	(B) もう製造されていない。
(C) He is expecting more soon.	(C) もうすぐ入荷するはずだ。
(D) They are currently discounted.	(D) 現在割引中である。

正答 男性店員が side plates に関して sold out at the moment と答えた後，We ordered some more last week, so I'm sure they'll be arriving any day now. （先週注文したからすぐ入荷するはず）と説明しているので，(C) が正解。女性が取り置きを頼んでいることや，男性が入荷次第連絡すると最後に話していることも，大きなヒントになる。

8

What is suggested about the man's store?	男性の店に関して何が示唆されていますか。
(A) It produces its own merchandise.	(A) 独自で商品の製造を行っている。
(B) It offers free delivery service.	(B) 無料配送サービスを提供している。
(C) It is known for its stylish designs.	(C) おしゃれなデザインで知られている。
(D) It has some branches downtown.	(D) ダウンタウンにいくつか支店がある。

正答 男性店員が Do you want me to call one of our other branches ...? と他の支店について言及し，さらに The downtown stores と店舗の場所を述べていることから，(D) が正解であるとわかる。誤答 (C) は，男性が smaller side plates に関して they've been very popular with our customers と述べてはいるが，人気の理由が stylish designs かどうか判断できない。

59

9

What does the woman say about her business?	女性は自分のビジネスについて何と述べていますか。
(A) It was recently opened.	(A) 最近オープンした。
(B) It sells dinner plates.	(B) ディナー皿を販売している。
(C) It is currently being renovated.	(C) 現在改装中である。
(D) It is popular with local customers.	(D) 地元の客に人気がある。

正答 女性の2回目の発言に My restaurant is being refurbished at the moment. とあることから，refurbished を renovated と言い換えている (C) が正解。誤答 (B) と (D) は男性の店に関しての記述で，「女性客と男性店員」という人物関係をイメージしながら聞いていれば混同することはない。

10

正解 ➤ (C)

What will the man do next?	男性は次に何をしますか。
(A) Contact another store	(A) 他の店に連絡を取る
(B) Order more merchandise	(B) 商品を追加注文する
(C) Write down some information	(C) 情報を書き留める
(D) Make a call to a customer	(D) 客に電話をかける

正答 男性の最後の Let me just take down your name and phone number. という言葉から，name and phone number を some information と置き換えた (C) が正解であるとわかる。誤答 (A) は What does the man offer to do?, (D) は What will the man do later? に対する答えになる。(B) はすでに行ったこと。

Disc 1
55-56

Questions 11 through 15 refer to the following talk.

I'd like to thank you all for attending Garland University's job fair this year. **Q11** We are proud to welcome representatives from 37 firms, a record number for this event. Our special guest this evening is **Q12** Eldrich Dilts, the head of Research and Development at Nutri Foods and **Q12** a prominent member of the science and agriculture industry. Food and animal research is one of the fastest growing industries these days, and there is a need for more agricultural technicians to work with scientists in this industry. Mr. Dilts will speak about the importance of animal and food research, and about **Q13** career choices currently available in the field. **Q14** Afterward, I'll be back to describe some Garland University courses that can help you qualify for a job as an agricultural technician. **Q15** Now, please welcome Eldrich Dilts.

重要語句 □prominent「有名な，重要な」（= important and well-known）　□agriculture「農業」（= farming）　□qualify for ...「〜の資格を得る」

11-15 の設問は次のトークに関するものです。
今年のガーランド大学就職フェアにお越しいただきありがとうございます。今回は 37 社の担当者の方々をお迎えしておりますが，これは本イベント史上最多の数になります。今夜の特別ゲストは，ニュートリ・フーズ社の研究開発部長でもあり，農業科学の分野においても有名なエルドリック・ディルツ氏です。食品畜産研究はここ最近もっとも急成長している産業のひとつであり，この分野において科学者と共に働く農業技術者がさらに必要とされています。ディルツ氏には，食品畜産研究の重要性とともに，この分野で現在どのような職種があるかについてお話しいただきます。その後，私から農業技術者の職に就くための資格取得を目指すガーランド大学の講座に関してお話をします。それでは，エルドリック・ディルツ氏をお迎えしましょう。

11 正解 ➤ (B)

What does the speaker say about the event?	話し手はこのイベントについて何を述べていますか。
(A) It is being held for the first time.	(A) 今回初めて開催される。
(B) It has attracted more companies than ever before.	(B) 今までにない数の会社を迎えている。
(C) It is funded by Nutri Foods.	(C) ニュートリ・フーズ社が資金提供をしている。
(D) It is only open to current university students.	(D) 現役大学生のみが参加できる。

正答 スピーチの前半で We are proud to welcome representatives from 37 firms と話し，それが a record number for this event（記録的な数）と述べているので，(B) が正解。record は形容詞的に用いて「記録的な」という意味を表す重要語。**誤答** イベントは Garland University で行われているが，参加資格については言及がないので (D) は不適切。

12 正解 ➤ (C)

Who is Eldrich Dilts?	エルドリック・ディルツとは誰ですか。
(A) A university professor	(A) 大学教授
(B) A local farmer	(B) 地元の農業従事者
(C) An agriculture expert	(C) 農業の専門家
(D) A hiring manager	(D) 採用担当部長

正答 Eldrich Dilts に関して，始めに「Nutri Foods 社の研究開発部長であり，農業科学の分野においても有名」と紹介されていることや，トーク全体で agriculture がテーマになっていることから，(C) が正解とわかる。

13

What will Mr. Dilts discuss?	ディルツ氏は何について話しますか。
(A) Opportunities in his area of work	(A) 彼の分野における職の機会
(B) Networking with scientists	(B) 科学者との人脈作り
(C) Application procedures for research grants	(C) 研究補助金の申請手続き
(D) A recent increase in farm production	(D) 最近の農産物収穫高の増加

正答 Mr. Dilts の話す内容として career choices currently available in the field と述べているので，(A) が適切。誤答 (B) は，there is a need for more agricultural technicians to work with scientists とはあるが，networking（人脈作り）については述べられていない。

14

According to the speaker, what can listeners do later this evening?	話し手によれば，聞き手は今夜これから何をすることができますか。
(A) Speak with the special guest	(A) 特別ゲストと話をする
(B) Learn about training courses	(B) 研修講座について情報を得る
(C) Tour some facilities	(C) 施設を見学する
(D) Have job interviews	(D) 就職の面接をする

正答 ゲスト講演の後の予定について Afterward, I'll be back to describe ... as an agricultural technician.（農業技術者になるための資格取得を目指す講座について説明する）と述べていることをおさえ，(B) を選ぶ。誤答 他の選択肢もすべて job fair で行われる可能性はあるが，いずれもトークの中で言及されていない。

15

What will listeners most likely do next?	聞き手はおそらく次に何をしますか。
(A) Greet a guest personally	(A) ゲストと直接挨拶を交わす
(B) Meet representatives of different companies	(B) さまざまな会社の担当者に会う
(C) Sign up for a university class	(C) 大学のクラスに申し込む
(D) Listen to a presentation by another speaker	(D) 他の講演者の話を聞く

正答 スピーチの最後で Now, please welcome Eldrich Dilts. とあり，話し手に代わって彼が次に講演をすることが明確なので，確実に (D) を選べるようにしたい。このように，トーク直後の行動を問う設問は Part 4 の定番パターン。

Questions 16 through 20 refer to the following speech.

Hello, everyone. The first thing I'd like to announce **Q16** at this meeting of the board is that during the most recent quarter, **Q17** sales of **Q18** our new line of business attire have risen by 20 percent. We believe **Q17** this increase is due in large part to the efforts of the marketing staff, who have worked tirelessly since the beginning of this year to **Q19** create ads that are inventive and appeal to a wider consumer base. Because of this increase, we've decided that **Q20** next month, all the employees in the marketing department will receive a 10 percent bonus. We are considering a similar measure for **Q18** our tailors and design staff. Next, I'd like to tell you a bit about our new branch in Halifax, which has just opened on Friday.

重要語句 □ attire「服装」(= clothing) □ in large part「大部分は，主に」(= largely; mainly) □ inventive「創造的な，創意に富む」(= creative; imaginative) □ appeal to *someone*「人の心を引きつける」 □ tailor「(服の) 仕立て担当者」

16-20 の設問は次のスピーチに関するものです。

皆さん，こんにちは。この取締役会でまず始めにお知らせしたいことは，直近の四半期に当社の新しいビジネス用衣料製品の売上が 20% 上がったということです。この増加は，創造的でより広い範囲の顧客層をひきつける広告を作るため，今年の始めから辛抱強く働いてきたマーケティングスタッフの努力によるところが大きいと私たちは考えます。この増加を受けて，来月，マーケティング部の全従業員に 10% のボーナスを支給することを決めました。同様の処遇を仕立てスタッフやデザインスタッフに対しても検討しています。それでは次に，金曜日にオープンしたばかりのハリファクスの新店舗について少しお話しします。

16

正解 ➤ (B)

Who most likely are the listeners?	聞き手はおそらく誰ですか。
(A) Professional designers	(A) プロのデザイナー
(B) Board members	(B) 重役
(C) Marketing staff	(C) マーケティングスタッフ
(D) Store clerks	(D) 店員

正答 話し手が冒頭で at this meeting of the board（この取締役会で）と述べていることが決定的なヒントだが，これを聞き逃してもトーク全体で売上や各スタッフへの処遇などさまざまな話題に触れていることから，会議の参加者が (B) であると判断できる。**誤答** (C) はトークの主題ではあるが，彼ら自身に対する直接的なメッセージがないことから，聞き手ではないことに気付きたい。

17

What is the purpose of the speech?	このスピーチの目的は何ですか。
(A) To request ideas for advertisements	(A) 広告のアイデアを募ること
(B) To praise staff for exceeding targets	(B) 目標を上回ったことでスタッフを称賛すること
(C) To propose changes to employee benefits	(C) 従業員の福利厚生に対する変更を提案すること
(D) To outline the results of a marketing campaign	(D) 宣伝キャンペーンの結果について概要を伝えること

正答 目的を問う問題も，トーク全体にヒントがある。売上が 20% 伸びたことや，その理由について inventive ads（創意に富んだ広告）を挙げていることから，(D) が正解。誤答 (B) の targets については言及されていない。(C) の employee benefits は bonus を含む手当全般を指すが，そのシステム自体を変更するわけではないので不適切。

18

What field of business is the speaker's company in?	話し手の会社はどのような業種ですか。
(A) Clothing	(A) 衣料品
(B) Office equipment	(B) オフィス用品
(C) Advertising	(C) 広告
(D) Automobiles	(D) 自動車

正答 トークの前半に登場する our new line of business attire（新しいビジネス用衣料品）や，後半の our tailors（仕立て担当者）という語句から，(A) が正解であることがわかる。衣服関連の語として，他にも garment (= a piece of clothing) をぜひ覚えておきたい。

19

According to the speaker, why has business improved?	話し手によると，業績が上がったのはなぜですか。
(A) Customer surveys were effective.	(A) 顧客アンケート調査が効果的だった。
(B) A new branch has opened.	(B) 新店舗がオープンした。
(C) Prices were lowered.	(C) 価格が下げられた。
(D) The advertisements were creative.	(D) 広告が創造的だった。

正答 売上が伸びた理由について「marketing staff が創造的な ads を手掛けた」と述べていることから，inventive を creative と言い換えている (D) が適切。誤答 (A) の customer surveys や (C) の prices についての言及はない。(B) の new branch はこれから話をするテーマであり，売上が伸びた理由ではない。

When will the bonuses be distributed?	ボーナスはいつ支給されますか。
(A) On Friday	(A) 金曜日
(B) Next week	(B) 来週
(C) Next month	(C) 来月
(D) At the beginning of the year	(D) 年始

正答▶ 10 percent bonus の支給について next month と明確に述べられているので，(C) が正解。「時」を記憶に留めるのはやや難しいが，トークの中に今後の出来事として登場するのは next month だけなので，話の流れをイメージして確実に正解したい。誤答▶ (A) は新店舗が開店した日，(D) は「年始からスタッフががんばってきた」とあるのみ。

　いかがだったでしょうか。今後，公式問題集などで Part 3・Part 4 を解く際は，負荷をかけたトレーニングとしてぜひ「先読みなし」，「後から解く」を行ってみてください。

満点ポイント 12

「詳細問題」のヒントを絶対に聞き逃さない

　　Part 3・Part 4 の設問には，日時や場所など細かい情報を問う「詳細問題」が 3 問中 1 ～ 2 問あります。「詳細問題」のヒントは普通一度しか登場しないため，「先読み」自体は非常に有効な手段です。また，設問を読むだけで会話の全体像がつかめるので，リスニングも楽になります。

　　ただ，選択肢まで読むと，誤った先入観によりかえって混同する場合があるので，先読みは原則設問文だけに留め，「場面」(Where are the speakers?)，「男性の提案」(What does the man suggest the woman do?)，「女性の次の行動」(What will the woman do next?) のように 3 つのポイントを頭に入れておくだけで十分です。

　　また，聞くと同時に解答する「マルチタスク型」アプローチをとると，重要なヒントが連続する場合などに片方のヒントを聞き逃すことがあります。全問正解を目指すには，リスニングの間はリスニングに集中し，後から一気に解答することをおススメします。

　　ここでは，「先読み（設問文のみ）」⇒「リスニングに集中」⇒「速読して一気に解く」という「シングルタスク型」アプローチのトレーニングを行います。設問はすべて詳細問題です。実際の Part 3・Part 4 では設問間のポーズが約 8 秒ありますが，先読みの時間を確保するためには，遅くても 3 つ目の設問文が読み上げられるまでにすべて解答し終えるスピードが必要です。ここでは設問の間隔をあえて短くしていますので，設問文が読み上げられるタイミングですばやく解答を出すようにしてください。

Part 3

21. What is the man worried about?
    (A) Bringing a gift to a coworker
    (B) Arriving late at the event
    (C) Being able to find the event place
    (D) Carrying some breakable items

    Ⓐ Ⓑ Ⓒ Ⓓ

22. How are the speakers going to the event?
    (A) By bus
    (B) By train
    (C) By car
    (D) On foot

    Ⓐ Ⓑ Ⓒ Ⓓ

23. Where will the speakers most likely go next?
    (A) A wine shop
    (B) A bus station
    (C) A bookstore
    (D) A flower shop

    Ⓐ Ⓑ Ⓒ Ⓓ

24. When will the man most likely go to Beijing?
    (A) This month
    (B) Next month
    (C) In two months
    (D) At the end of this year

    Ⓐ Ⓑ Ⓒ Ⓓ

25. What does the woman indicate about herself?
    (A) She has worked in another country.
    (B) She has traveled extensively.
    (C) She went to school abroad.
    (D) She will be the marketing director.

    Ⓐ Ⓑ Ⓒ Ⓓ

26. What most likely is the man's concern?
    (A) Looking for a new apartment
    (B) Finding himself a good language class
    (C) Increasing his work responsibilities
    (D) Communicating with local people

    Ⓐ Ⓑ Ⓒ Ⓓ

Part 4

27. How long will the sale last?

(A) For three days

(B) For one week

(C) For two weeks

(D) For one month

Ⓐ Ⓑ Ⓒ Ⓓ

28. What will be available free of charge for a limited time?

(A) A schedule book

(B) A delivery service

(C) A book on photography

(D) A gift wrapping service

Ⓐ Ⓑ Ⓒ Ⓓ

29. What is indicated about Adonis?

(A) It offers discounts to its members.

(B) It houses a coffee shop.

(C) It is the largest bookstore in the country.

(D) It will invite a number of writers to events.

Ⓐ Ⓑ Ⓒ Ⓓ

30. What does the speaker say about the product trial?

(A) It will start on Monday.

(B) It will continue for one month.

(C) It will be held at more than one location.

(D) It will target wealthy customers.

Ⓐ Ⓑ Ⓒ Ⓓ

31. What will the head office representative do?

(A) Offer sales advice

(B) Inspect the branch

(C) Monitor the trial

(D) Interview staff

Ⓐ Ⓑ Ⓒ Ⓓ

32. What will the speaker most likely do next?

(A) Put up some posters

(B) Give a cooking demonstration

(C) Distribute promotional badges

(D) Prepare documentation for new products

Ⓐ Ⓑ Ⓒ Ⓓ

Questions 21 through 23 refer to the following conversation.

M: **Q21** I wanted to bring something to our new manager's housewarming party tonight, but my bus home got stuck in traffic. **Q21** I didn't have time to buy anything **Q22** before you picked me up.

W: **Q23** There's a florist a couple of blocks from Ms. Starr's place. It's right next to the bookstore that was opened last week. **Q23** We can stop by there on the way.

M: Good idea. Let's do that. Did you already get something for her?

W: **Q22** I have a bottle of wine back in the trunk. I hope it hasn't broken in there.

重要語句　□ housewarming「引っ越し祝い」　□ pick *someone* up「人を車で拾う，迎えに行く」

男性：今夜ある新しい部長の引越し祝いパーティに何か持っていこうと思っていたんですが，自宅までのバスが渋滞に巻き込まれてしまって。あなたに車で迎えに来てもらう前に買い物に行く時間がありませんでした。

女性：スターさんの家から数ブロック行った所に花屋がありますよ。先週オープンした本屋のちょうど隣にあるんですが。途中で寄りましょうか。

男性：それはいいアイデアですね。そうしましょう。彼女にもう何か買いましたか。

女性：ワインを1本後ろのトランクに入れてありますよ。中で割れていなければいいんですが。

21

正解 ▶ (A)

What is the man worried about?

(A) Bringing a gift to a coworker

(B) Arriving late at the event

(C) Being able to find the event place

(D) Carrying some breakable items

男性は何に関して心配していますか。

(A) 同僚にプレゼントを持っていくこと

(B) イベントに遅れること

(C) イベントが行われる場所を見つけること

(D) 壊れ物を運ぶこと

正答　男性の発言の中で，問題や懸念を示す言葉に注意。始めに I wanted to bring something ... housewarming party（部長のパーティに何か持っていきたい）と述べ，そのうえで I didn't have time to buy anything（買いに行く時間がなかった）と問題を伝えているので，(A) が適切。our new manager を a coworker に置き換えている。誤答 (D) は女性の最後の発言から，女性側の心配事であるとわかる。

22

How are the speakers going to the event?	2人はイベントまで何で行きますか。
(A) By bus	(A) バスで
(B) By train	(B) 電車で
(C) By car	(C) 車で
(D) On foot	(D) 徒歩で

正答 男性の始めの発言にある before you picked me up から，女性が男性を車で迎えに来たことがわかる。また，女性の最後の発言に I have a bottle of wine back in the trunk. とあることからも，2人が女性の車でパーティに向かうものと判断し，(C) を選択する。今回のように，1問目と2問目のヒントが同じ文に含まれる場合もあり，「マルチタスク型」で解いていると聞き逃しやすいので注意。誤答 (A) については，男性が my bus home got stuck in traffic と述べているが，女性が迎えに来る前の話なので不適切。

23

Where will the speakers most likely go next?	2人は次におそらくどこへ行くと思われますか。
(A) A wine shop	(A) ワイン販売店
(B) A bus station	(B) バス停
(C) A bookstore	(C) 本屋
(D) A flower shop	(D) 花屋

正答 女性が始めに florist（花屋）があることを伝え，さらに We can stop by there on the way. とそこに行く提案をしているので，(D) が正解。一度しか登場しない florist というヒントを絶対に聞き逃さないこと。また，今回のように，there や that といった指示語を用いてその前までの文とのつながりを把握しているかを試す難問も時々登場する。誤答 (C) は，there の直前の文に It's right next to the bookstore とあるが，あくまで florist の場所を説明しているだけなので，there が bookstore を指しているとは考えられない。

Questions 24 through 26 refer to the following conversation.

W: Tom, is it true that you are being transferred to Beijing in two months? I didn't know about it until Maria told me a few days ago.

M: Oh, I'm sorry I couldn't tell you sooner. I just received my official notice this morning. Apparently, the marketing director is resigning this month, and they need me to take over from her. **Q24** I'm actually leaving in a month to hunt for an apartment.

W: **Q25** I studied in Seoul for a year, and I enjoyed every minute of living overseas. Are you excited about the opportunity?

M: Actually, **Q26** I'm a bit worried. I don't speak much Mandarin for one thing, and I'm also not sure if I'll be able to find a good international school for my son.

重要語句 □ resign「退職する」 □ take over「他人の業務を引き継ぐ」 □ hunt for ...「〜を探す」(= look for ...; search for ...) □ Mandarin「北京語 (中国の標準語)」

女性：トム，2か月後に北京に異動になるって本当ですか。マリアが数日前に教えてくれるまで知りませんでしたよ。

男性：ああ，もっと早く言えなくてすみませんでした。今朝正式な通知をもらったばかりなんです。どうやらマーケティング部長が今月退職するみたいで，彼女の代わりに私が必要のようです。じつはアパートを探しに1か月後に行く予定なんです。

女性：私は1年間ソウルで勉強したことがありますが，海外生活を存分に楽しみましたよ。この機会は楽しみですか。

男性：じつを言うと，少し心配なんです。北京語があまり話せないことが一つと，息子に良いインターナショナルスクールが見つかるかどうかもよくわからなくて。

24

正解 ➤ (B)

When will the man most likely go to Beijing?	男性はおそらくいつ北京に行く予定ですか。
(A) This month	(A) 今月
(B) Next month	(B) 来月
(C) In two months	(C) 2か月後
(D) At the end of this year	(D) 今年の年末

正答 女性の発言の中に in two months とあるが，男性は女性の質問に対して I'm actually leaving in a month（1か月後に行く予定だ）と述べているので，(B) が正解と判断できる。このように，途中で展開が変わるパターンも難度が上がる。**誤答** (A) は the marketing director が辞任する時期。

25

What does the woman indicate about herself?	女性は自分に関して何と述べていますか。
(A) She has worked in another country.	(A) 他の国で働いたことがある。
(B) She has traveled extensively.	(B) さまざまな場所に旅行した経験がある。
(C) She went to school abroad.	(C) 外国の学校に通った。
(D) She will be the marketing director.	(D) マーケティング部長になる予定だ。

正答 女性2回目の発言から，Seoul に1年間海外留学をした経験があるとわかるので，(C) が適切。この問題も，前の問題とヒントが隣接しているので，studied を絶対に聞き逃さないよう注意しよう。誤答 (D) は男性についての記述。

26

What most likely is the man's concern?	男性の心配事はおそらく何ですか。
(A) Looking for a new apartment	(A) 新しいアパートを探すこと
(B) Finding himself a good language class	(B) 自分が言語を学ぶのに良いクラスを見つけること
(C) Increasing his work responsibilities	(C) 職務内容が増えること
(D) Communicating with local people	(D) 現地の人たちと意思疎通を図ること

正答 男性が I'm a bit worried.（心配だ）と話し，その一因として I don't speak much Mandarin と述べている。Mandarin という単語を知らなくても，speak から現地の言語であることは推測がつくので，(D) が正解と判断できる。TOEIC では言語や地理の知識がないと解けない問題は出題されないが，Mandarin は過去にも登場したことがあるのでぜひ覚えておきたい。誤答 (B) は，自分の学校探しまでは言及していない。

Disc 1
63-64

Questions 27 through 29 refer to the following advertisement.

Serving the city of Dunwich for over 30 years, Adonis has the largest selection of books and magazines in town, from fiction to fashion, from children's literature to cook books. We're pleased to announce that **Q27** we're offering 10 percent off all purchases for the next week. Also, as our New Year's gift to you, with every purchase made over the next month **Q28** we're giving away a day planner featuring photos of Dunwich's most picturesque spots. On January 20, we're holding a book signing by Fred Glenn, **Q29** the first in a series of planned appearances by renowned authors. Complimentary coffee will be served at each of these events. Visit Adonis today at 535 Innsmouth Road or at www.adonis. com.

重要語句 □ literature「文学, 書物」 □ give ... away「(景品など) を配る」 □ picturesque「(絵に描いたように) 美しい」

27-29 の設問は次の広告に関するものです。

ダンウィッチ市で 30 年以上の歴史を持つアドニスは, フィクションからファッション関係, 児童文学から料理本まで, 書籍および雑誌を町でもっとも豊富に揃えております。来週の一週間は, すべてのご購入品が 10 パーセントオフとなります。また, 新年のプレゼントとして, 来月中は各ご購入につきダンウィッチ市のもっとも美しい景色の写真を収めたスケジュール帳をひとつ差し上げます。1 月 20 日には, 著名作家が参加予定の一連のイベントにおける第 1 回目として, フレッド・グレン氏による本のサイン会を開催します。どの回もコーヒーを無料でお出しいたします。今日にでもアドニスへお越しください。住所はインズマウス通り 535 番地, ウェブサイトは www.adnois.com です。

27 正解 ➤ (B)

How long will the sale last? / セールはどれくらいの期間続きますか。

(A) For three days / (A) 3 日間
(B) **For one week** / (B) 1 週間
(C) For two weeks / (C) 2 週間
(D) For one month / (D) 1 か月

正答 10 percent off のセール期間として for the next week とあるのを絶対に聞き逃さないようにし, (B) を選ぶ。誤答 次の文では, 来月無料で提供される New Year's gift の説明があるが, セールではないので (D) は不適切。

28 正解 ➤ (A)

What will be available free of charge for a limited time? / 期間限定で無料で手に入るものは何ですか。

(A) **A schedule book** / (A) スケジュール帳
(B) A delivery service / (B) 配送サービス
(C) A book on photography / (C) 写真撮影に関する書籍
(D) A gift wrapping service / (D) ギフト包装サービス

正答 1 か月限定の New Year's gift として we're giving away a day planner と述べているので, a day planner(スケジュール帳)を a schedule book と言い換えている (A) が適切。誤答 (C) は, 「美しい写真が載っている planner」とはあるが, 写真に関する本ではない。

73

29

What is indicated about Adonis?	アドニスに関して何と述べられていますか。
(A) It offers discounts to its members.	(A) 会員割引を提供している。
(B) It houses a coffee shop.	(B) コーヒーショップが中にある。
(C) It is the largest bookstore in the country.	(C) 全国最大規模の書店である。
(D) It will invite a number of writers to events.	(D) 数々の作家をイベントに招く予定である。

正答 後半で a book signing の紹介があり，それが the first ... by renowned authors（著名作家が参加予定の一連のイベントにおける第1回目）と説明しているので，(D) が正解。a number of は「数々の」(=some) という意味。誤答 (A) の members（会員）に関する話はない。(B) は，「coffee が出される」というだけでは coffee shop があるかどうかが判断できない。(C) については，冒頭で「町でもっとも豊富な取り揃えがある」とあり，全国最大とは述べていない。

Disc 1
65-66

Questions 30 through 32 refer to the following talk.

Q30 The head office has selected our branch, along with one in Essex, to conduct a trial for a new line of vegetarian burritos starting next month. We hope that these new burritos will show that we are a healthy option for diners on a budget. As you can see, we've already put up posters around the store announcing the new products, and you'll each receive a promotional badge that should be pinned to your uniform at all times. On Monday, someone from the head office will come in to **Q31** give tips on how to encourage customers to order the new products, but **Q32** now I'm going to show you how to prepare them.

重要語句 □ on a budget「予算の少ない」 □ at all times「常時，常に」(= always)

30-32 の設問は次のトークに関するものです。

当店はエセックス支店と共に，来月から実施される新メニューのベジタリアン・ブリトーの試験販売店として本社から選ばれました。この新発売のブリトーで，当店が低予算のお客様にとっての健康的なチョイスだとアピールできることを願います。ご覧のとおり，店の周辺に新商品を紹介したポスターをすでに掲示しています。また，ユニフォームに常時着用する販促バッジを皆さんにこれから配布します。月曜日には本社から担当者が来て，お客様に新商品の注文を薦める秘訣を教えてもらいます。では，今から調理方法をお見せしましょう。

30

What does the speaker say about the product trial?

(A) It will start on Monday.

(B) It will continue for one month.

(C) It will be held at more than one location.

(D) It will target wealthy customers.

話し手は試験販売に関して何と述べていますか。

(A) 月曜日に開始になる。

(B) 1か月間続く。

(C) 複数の店舗で行われる。

(D) 富裕層の顧客を対象としている。

正答 トーク冒頭の The head office has selected ... to conduct a trial (本社が当店をエセックス支店と共に試験販売店に選んだ) という部分から, (C) が正解だと判断できる。冒頭部分は聞き逃しやすいので, 始めから意識を最大限集中させよう。誤答 (A) の on Monday は本社の担当者が来る日。(B) は,「next month から始まる」とはあるが, 期間については述べていない。また, 対象者として diners on a budget (低予算の顧客) とあるので, (D) も不適切。

31

What will the head office representative do?

(A) Offer sales advice

(B) Inspect the branch

(C) Monitor the trial

(D) Interview staff

本社の担当者は何をしますか。

(A) 販売に関するアドバイスを与える

(B) 支店を視察する

(C) 試験販売を監視する

(D) 従業員を面接する

正答 本社の担当者について, トークの後半で give tips on how to encourage customers to order the new products (客に新商品の注文を薦めるコツを教える) とあるので, tips を advice と言い換えた (A) が適切。誤答 他の選択肢はいずれもトークの中で言及されていない。

32

What will the speaker most likely do next?

(A) Put up some posters

(B) Give a cooking demonstration

(C) Distribute promotional badges

(D) Prepare documentation for new products

話し手はおそらく次に何をしますか。

(A) ポスターを貼る

(B) 料理を実演する

(C) 販促用バッジを配布する

(D) 新商品用の書類を作成する

正答 トークの最後で now I'm going to show you how to prepare them と次の行動を述べている。them はその前にある the new products, すなわちトークのテーマである vegetarian burritos という料理を指していることをおさえ, (B) を選ぶ。ここでは, prepare が cook と同じ意味。burritos を知らなくても, vegetarian や healthy option というキーワードから料理名であることを把握しよう。

「イメージしづらい会話」に注意する (Part 3)

Part 3

　Part 3 の会話は，一般的な社内会話や店の予約電話など，場面や人物関係が明確で，感情移入のしやすいものが多くを占めます。しかし，その中で 1 ～ 2 題ほど，その経験がないと場面をイメージしづらい「特殊な会話」が登場することがあります。また，同性同士の会話も展開がイメージしづらい傾向にあります。ここで，解答ペースの乱されやすい会話に慣れておきましょう。

　前のトレーニングと同様，設問文の読まれる間隔を短くしています。音声に合わせて速読して答えを出すようにし，会話の間は極力リスニングに集中してください。

Disc 1
67-70

33. Where are the speakers?
(A) At a university library
(B) At a research facility
(C) At a public garden
(D) At a medical clinic

ⒶⒷⒸⒹ

34. Who most likely is the woman?
(A) A scientist
(B) A physician
(C) A newspaper editor
(D) A lab technician

ⒶⒷⒸⒹ

35. What does the woman intend to do?
(A) Take out some books
(B) Publish a paper on plants
(C) Grow some vegetables
(D) Accompany the man into Room B

ⒶⒷⒸⒹ

36. Where do the speakers most likely work?

(A) At a repair shop
(B) At a warehouse storage service
(C) At a manufacturing facility
(D) At a mechanical parts supplier

Ⓐ Ⓑ Ⓒ Ⓓ

38. What will the speakers most likely do together?

(A) Unpack some merchandise
(B) Meet with a regular customer
(C) Go to the supply room
(D) Move items into a warehouse

Ⓐ Ⓑ Ⓒ Ⓓ

37. What happened this afternoon?

(A) A new space became available.
(B) Some equipment was replaced.
(C) An order was delivered.
(D) A fax was sent to a client.

Ⓐ Ⓑ Ⓒ Ⓓ

Disc 1
67-68

Questions 33 through 35 refer to the following conversation.

W: Good morning. An appointment was scheduled for me today. The name is Dr. Alexandria Savoski. Is this where I sign in?

M: Yes, **Q34** Dr. Savoski. We've been expecting you. Just write your name and ID number on the register. **Q33** Is this your first time accessing this lab?

W: It is. I just moved to town about a month ago. **Q34,35** I need to do some research on native vegetation as well as on the local botanical garden. It's for a journal article I'm working on.

M: Oh, we have a room here with a large collection of books on local wildlife. There's a shelf full of field guides with photos and technical data about all kinds of plants that grow in this area. It's just down the hall past Room B. Let me show you. Right this way please.

重要語句　□ register「(名前を記載した) 一覧表，名簿」(= official list of names)　□ vegetation「植生，植物」(= plants) ※ 特定の地域に自生する植物全体を指す不加算名詞。　□ botanical garden「植物園」□ field guide「図鑑，フィールドガイド」

女性：おはようございます。今日予約しているアレクサンドリア・サボスキと申します。ここが名前を記入する場所ですか。

男性：はい，サボスキ博士。お待ちしておりました。名簿に名前と ID 番号をご記入ください。この研究所をご利用になるのは今回が初めてですか。

女性：そうです。一か月前にこの町に引っ越してきました。原生植物や地元の植物園に関して調査をする必要がありまして。今書いている専門誌の論文用なのですが。

男性：それなら，ここには地元の野生生物に関する書物を多く収蔵している部屋があります。そこに，この地域に自生するあらゆる植物種の写真や専門データを掲載した図鑑で埋め尽くされている棚がありますよ。廊下をそのまま進んで Room B を過ぎたところにあります。ご案内しましょう。こちらにどうぞ。

33

Where are the speakers?	2人はどこにいますか。
(A) At a university library	(A) 大学の図書館
(B) At a research facility	(B) 研究施設
(C) At a public garden	(C) 植物園
(D) At a medical clinic	(D) 診療所

正答 男性が Is this your first time accessing this lab? と尋ねており，さらに会話の後半で専門書の説明がなされていることから，lab を言い換えている (B) が正解。Part 3 にはこのように，研究施設内での話がときどき出てくる。**誤答** lab を聞き逃して，後半の内容だけをもとに (A) を選ばないように注意。

34

Who most likely is the woman?	女性はおそらく誰でしょうか。
(A) A scientist	(A) 科学者
(B) A physician	(B) 内科医
(C) A newspaper editor	(C) 新聞編集者
(D) A lab technician	(D) 実験技師

正答 女性の名前に Dr. とあることや，女性が「a journal article を書くために調査が必要だ」と述べていることから，(A) が正解だと判断できる。**誤答** journal は「専門誌，新聞」を意味するが，彼女自身が論文を書くと話しているので，(C) の newspaper editor ではない。

35

What does the woman intend to do?	女性は何をするつもりですか。
(A) Take out some books	(A) 本を借りる
(B) Publish a paper on plants	(B) 植物に関する論文を出す
(C) Grow some vegetables	(C) 野菜を育てる
(D) Accompany the man into Room B	(D) 男性とともに Room B に行く

正答 女性が native vegetation（原生植物）や botanical garden（植物園）について調査がしたいと話し，それが journal article を書くためであるので，(B) が正解。語彙レベルが高いが，後半の男性の発言の中に plants という語も出てくるので，何とか答えを出したい。**誤答** (A) は，男性が本の話をしてはいるが，女性がそれを借りる意図があるかどうかはわからない。女性の意図は常に女性の発言にあると考えよう。

Questions 36 through 38 refer to the following conversation.

M1: Paul, could you give me a hand rearranging some inventory to free up some space in the warehouse?

M2: Of course, but I need about ten minutes. **Q36** I got an e-mail earlier this afternoon from one of our longtime clients for a particular replacement part for some factory equipment, but we've run out of stock. **Q36** I'll need to fax an order for some more. Then I can help out.

M1: Actually, I should be finished by that time, but **Q36,37** the machine parts from Tally Manufacturing arrived in the warehouse this afternoon, **Q38** and the van needs to be unloaded. Could you meet me there later?

M2: **Q38** Sure, no problem. Those boxes must be pretty heavy, so I'll get some carts from the supply room on my way to the loading dock.

（重要語句） □ inventory「在庫」(= stock) □ free up space「スペースを空ける」 □ run out of stock「在庫切れになる」 □ unload「積荷を降ろす」(↔ load「荷物を積む」) □ loading dock「積み下ろし場」

男性1： ポール，倉庫にある在庫を移し代えてスペースを空けるのを手伝ってくれませんか。

男性2： もちろんいいんですが，10分ほど必要です。今日の午後に，付き合いの長い顧客から工場機械の交換部品が欲しいとのメールが来たんですが，在庫切れなんです。その部品の注文書をファクスで送らなくてはいけないので。それからであればお手伝いできますよ。

男性1： じつのところ，そのときまでには終わっていると思います。ただ，タリー・マニュファクチャリング社の機械部品が午後に倉庫に届いたので，トラックの荷降ろしが必要なんです。そこに後で来てくれますか。

男性2： もちろんですよ。箱がかなり重いでしょうから，積み下ろし場に行く途中に備品室からカートを取ってきます。

36

正解 ▶ (D)

Where do the speakers most likely work?	2人はおそらくどこで働いていますか。
(A) At a repair shop	(A) 修理工場で
(B) At a warehouse storage service	(B) 倉庫管理サービス会社で
(C) At a manufacturing facility	(C) 製造施設で
(D) At a mechanical parts supplier	(D) 機械部品供給会社で

正答 会話の中で，工場機器部品の注文メールを受けた話や機械部品を仕入れた話などが出てくることから，(D) が正解。今回のような同性同士の会話もまれに登場し，男女の会話に比べやりとりが頭に入りにくいので，ここで慣れておこう。**誤答** (B)は倉庫スペースを提供する会社のことなので不適切。

37

What happened this afternoon?	今日の午後何がありましたか。
(A) A new space became available.	(A) 新しいスペースが使えるようになった。
(B) Some equipment was replaced.	(B) 備品が取り替えられた。
(C) An order was delivered.	(C) 注文品が届いた。
(D) A fax was sent to a client.	(D) ファクスが顧客に送られた。

正答 this afternoon の話は 2 度登場するが，その中で男性 1 の 2 回目の発言 the machine parts ... in the warehouse this afternoon（タリー・マニュファクチャリング社の機械部品が倉庫に届いた）の内容と一致する (C) を選ぶ。誤答 男性 2 の発言に I'll need to fax an order とあるが，client に対してではなくこれから行うことなので (D) は不適切。

38

What will the speakers most likely do together?	2 人はおそらく一緒に何をすることになりますか。
(A) Unpack some merchandise	(A) 商品を箱から取り出す
(B) Meet with a regular customer	(B) 常連の顧客と会う
(C) Go to the supply room	(C) 備品室に行く
(D) Move items into a warehouse	(D) 商品を倉庫内に移す

正答 男性 1 が「倉庫に届いた部品の荷降ろしが必要だから来てもらえるか」と尋ね，男性 2 がそれに対して Sure と答えているので，(D) が適切。there が前の文の in the warehouse を指していることを記憶しておく必要のある難問。誤答 (A) の unpack は「（箱などを開けて）物を取り出す」という意味で，unload（荷物を降ろろ）との違いに注意。(C) は男性 2 が一人で行うこと。

「ネイティブスピード」に慣れる (Part 4)

Part 3・Part 4 の会話やトークは，いわゆる「自然」なスピードで話されます。また，TOEIC のオーストラリア英語の男性ナレーターは，他のナレーターに比べやや速めに話す傾向にあります。ただ，実際のネイティブの会話や本場のニュース番組と比べると，TOEIC のスピードははるかに聞き取りやすいものです。日頃から生の英語を含むインターネット動画や DVD などを利用し，「ネイティブスピード」に慣れ親しんでおいてください。

以下の問題は，実際の TOEIC よりも速く，本場のニュース番組やラジオ放送とほぼ同じスピードです。また，前のトレーニング同様，設問の読まれる感覚を短くしています。設問文を先読みした後は，リスニングに最大限集中し，後から一気に解答してください。

Disc 1
71-72

39. When did the first event take place?
(A) Last year
(B) Five years ago
(C) Twelve years ago
(D) Twenty years ago

Ⓐ Ⓑ Ⓒ Ⓓ

40. Who most likely is Mark Connors?
(A) An owner of a movie theater
(B) A journalist for a movie magazine
(C) A manager of a film distribution company
(D) The founder of the event

Ⓐ Ⓑ Ⓒ Ⓓ

41. According to the speaker, what happened at the first event?
(A) Local theaters declined the offer to be involved.
(B) Attendance was very low.
(C) Some of the showings were postponed.
(D) Only a small number of movies were shown.

Ⓐ Ⓑ Ⓒ Ⓓ

42. What is mentioned about the festival?

(A) It takes place every year.

(B) It has completely blocked Main Street.

(C) It started one hour ago.

(D) It is being held by a river.

Ⓐ Ⓑ Ⓒ Ⓓ

43. Where is construction work taking place?

(A) On Riverside Drive

(B) On the Azura River Bridge

(C) On Highway 12

(D) On Maple Boulevard

Ⓐ Ⓑ Ⓒ Ⓓ

44. What will the listeners most likely hear next?

(A) The national news

(B) An update on the weather

(C) More traffic information

(D) Some music

Ⓐ Ⓑ Ⓒ Ⓓ

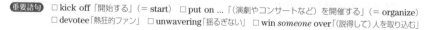

Questions 39 through 41 refer to the following radio broadcast.

And now, here is *Cinema World*. Tonight we'll be discussing **Q39** the 12th annual Ditchford Film Festival which kicks off on April 24. I'd like to introduce **Q40** the person who, more than anyone, is responsible for making this event possible. For the first ever festival, **Q40** Mark Connors managed to convince five film distributors and the city's two movie theaters to put on a three-day series of movies. **Q41** Each showing drew only a few movie devotees, and most of us in the local press declared the event a failure. But his determination and unwavering energy won over everyone involved, and each year since then the event has attracted more distributors, more fans and more journalists from all over the world. Mr. Connors is joining us here today and will talk about this year's line up.

重要語句 □ kick off「開始する」(= start) □ put on ...「(演劇やコンサートなど) を開催する」(= organize)
□ devotee「熱狂的ファン」 □ unwavering「揺るぎない」 □ win *someone* over「(説得して) 人を取り込む」

39-41 の設問は次のラジオ放送に関するものです。

それでは，シネマ・ワールドの時間です。今夜は，4 月 24 日に幕を開ける毎年恒例の第 12 回ディッチフォード映画祭についてです。他の誰よりもこのイベントの実現に尽力してきた方をご紹介します。この映画祭の第 1 回の開催のとき，マーク・コナーズ氏は 5 社の映画配給会社と市の 2 つの映画館を説得し，3 日間にわたる映画の上映にこぎつけました。どの上映にもひとにぎりの映画ファンしか集まらず，私たち地元報道陣の大半はこのイベントを失敗と伝えました。しかし，彼の決意と揺るぎないエネルギーは関係者すべてを取り込み，その後年を重ねるたびに，このイベントは世界中からより多くの配給会社，より多くのファンと，より多くのジャーナリストを動員しています。今日はコナーズ氏がこの番組に出演し，今年の映画ラインナップについてお話しくださいます。

39

When did the first event take place?	イベントの第 1 回目はいつ開催されましたか。
(A) Last year	(A) 去年
(B) Five years ago	(B) 5 年前
(C) Twelve years ago	(C) 12 年前
(D) Twenty years ago	(D) 20 年前

正答 冒頭にある the 12th annual Ditchford Film Festival（今年で第 12 回目のディッチフォード 映画祭）から，初回の開催は (C) だとわかる。冒頭に登場する数字は聞き逃しやすいので注意。実際 の Part 4 では，次の文以降に再びヒントが出てくることもあるので，最後まで集中して聞こう。

40

Who most likely is Mark Connors?	マーク・コナーズとはおそらく誰ですか。
(A) An owner of a movie theater	(A) 映画館のオーナー
(B) A journalist for a movie magazine	(B) 映画雑誌の記者
(C) A manager of a film distribution company	(C) 映画配給会社の部長
(D) The founder of the event	(D) イベント創設者

正答 Mark Connors に関してまず the person ... making this event possible（このイベントの 実現に尽力してきた人）と紹介し，さらに Mark Connors managed to convince ... to put on a three-day series of movies.（映画配給会社や映画館を説得し映画の上映にこぎつけた）とあるこ とから (D) が正解とわかる。誤答 (A) や (C) は彼が働きかけた相手であり，彼自身のことではない。

41

According to the speaker, what happened at the first event?	話し手によれば，最初のイベントで何がありま したか。
(A) Local theaters declined the offer to be involved.	(A) 地元の映画館が参加の申し出を断った。
(B) Attendance was very low.	(B) 観客数が少なかった。
(C) Some of the showings were postponed.	(C) 上映のいくつかが延期された。
(D) Only a small number of movies were shown.	(D) ごくわずかな映画しか上映されなかった。

正答 初回イベントに関する説明の中で Each showing drew only a few movie devotees とあるこ とを聞き取り，(B) を選ぶ。only a few は only a small number of の意味。誤答 (D) は，トークの 中で a three-day series of movies とあるだけなので，映画の本数は判断できない。

Questions 42 through 44 refer to the following radio broadcast.

For KLR Radio News, this is Rob Benson with the latest traffic report. The Maple Boulevard Street Fair has slowed traffic as **Q42** the festival has now been underway for an hour. The parade down Main Street has led to the closure of both northbound lanes. There appears to be no impact on southbound travel. We've received several reports of stop-and-go traffic on all westbound lanes of Highway 12. Commuters heading west from downtown are advised to take the Riverside Drive instead, to avoid the congestion from the festival crowd. Our traffic copter has just sent us word from above **Q43** the Azura River Bridge, where construction work has closed all northbound lanes but one. **Q44** Stay tuned for the national news, followed by the weather forecast and another traffic update in 30 minutes.

重要語句 □ underway「行われている，進行中の」(= in progress)　□ stop-and-go「のろのろ運転の」※stop-and-go traffic で「交通渋滞」の意味。　□ copter = helicopter の略。　□ all but ...「～を除くすべて」※ この but は except を意味する前置詞。

42-44 の設問は次のラジオ放送に関するものです。
KLR ラジオニュースでロブ・ベンソンが最新の交通情報をお届けします。メイプル大通りストリートフェアが始まって 1 時間が経った現在，車の流れが悪くなっています。メイン通りを進むパレードにより，北行き両車線が通行止めとなっています。南行きに影響はない模様です。また，幹線道路 12 号線の西行き全車線で渋滞が報告されています。ダウンタウンから西に向かう方は，フェスティバルの人ごみによる渋滞を避けるためリバーサイド通りを利用されたほうがいいでしょう。また，アズラ川橋の上空から交通ヘリコプターによる報告があり，アズラ川橋では工事のため北行き車線が 1 車線を除いて通行止めとなっている模様です。それでは引き続き全国ニュースと，天気予報をお聞きください。30 分後に再び最新の交通情報をお伝えします。

42

正解 ➤ (C)

What is mentioned about the festival?	フェスティバルに関して何が述べられていますか。
(A) It takes place every year.	(A) 毎年開催されている。
(B) It has completely blocked Main Street.	(B) メイン通りを完全に遮断している。
(C) It started one hour ago.	(C) 1 時間前に開始された。
(D) It is being held by a river.	(D) 川の近くで行われている。

正答 フェスティバルに関して has now been underway for an hour と述べているので，この内容を言い換えた (C) が正解。**誤答** Main Street に関して，次の 2 文に「northbound lanes は通行止めだが southbound travel には影響がない」とあるので，(B) は不適切。(A) や (D) に関しては言及していない。

43

Where is construction work taking place?	工事が行われているのはどこですか。
(A) On Riverside Drive	(A) リバーサイド通り
(B) On the Azura River Bridge	(B) アズラ川橋
(C) On Highway 12	(C) 幹線道路 12 号線
(D) On Maple Boulevard	(D) メイプル大通り

正答 construction work という語句に注意して聞いていれば，その直前にある (B) の the Azura River Bridge での出来事だとわかる。誤答 (A) は通行が薦められている通り，(C) は west bound lanes が渋滞している通り，(D) はストリートフェアが行われている大通り。

44

What will the listeners most likely hear next?	聞き手はおそらく次に何を聞きますか。
(A) The national news	(A) 全国ニュース
(B) An update on the weather	(B) 最新の天気予報
(C) More traffic information	(C) 最新の交通情報
(D) Some music	(D) 音楽

正答 Stay tuned for ... （引き続き〜をお聞きください）はラジオの定番表現。後ろの the national news を絶対に聞き逃さないようにし，(A) を選ぶ。radio broadcast の問題は，次の番組に関する設問が 3 問目に登場することがよくあるので，特に最後の一文に集中しよう。誤答 followed by ... は「〜が後に続いて」という意味で，the national news の後に (B) や (C) が放送されることに注意。

リスニングのオススメ教材

● 『CNN English Express』（朝日出版社）

　　最新の CNN ニュースを学習しやすいようにアレンジした月刊誌です。毎回興味深いトピックを多く取り上げており，本場のニュースに触れる絶好の機会です。私も毎日一時間，本誌を利用して音読トレーニングをした経験があります。

まとめの練習

最後に，Part 3・Part 4 のまとめの問題を解きます。ここでは，「シングルタスク型」，「マルチタスク型」のどちらのアプローチでも構いません。今までのトレーニングを踏まえ，自分に合うと思うやり方で問題を解いてください。

Part 3

45. What does the man say about Ms. Kim?

(A) She needs to make some handouts.

(B) She informed him of the problem.

(C) She will contact a technician.

(D) She has a meeting with a client.

ⒶⒷⒸⒹ

46. What does the man offer to do?

(A) Inspect the copier personally

(B) Go to a print shop

(C) Prepare materials for the presentation

(D) Have the machine repaired

ⒶⒷⒸⒹ

47. When most likely is the woman's presentation?

(A) This morning

(B) This afternoon

(C) Tomorrow morning

(D) Tomorrow afternoon

ⒶⒷⒸⒹ

48. Who most likely is the man?

(A) A taxi driver

(B) A call center operator

(C) A passenger

(D) A computer programmer

ⒶⒷⒸⒹ

49. What is the problem?

(A) The man misplaced his business card.

(B) A computer system is inaccessible.

(C) A handbook was left behind.

(D) A customer made a complaint.

ⒶⒷⒸⒹ

50. What will the man most likely do next?

(A) Turn onto Dresden Avenue

(B) Visit a company

(C) Drop off a client

(D) Call for technical support

ⒶⒷⒸⒹ

Part 4

51. How long did the speaker work at Seki Research Institute?
    (A) For three years
    (B) For six years
    (C) For ten years
    (D) For twenty years
    Ⓐ Ⓑ Ⓒ Ⓓ

52. Why did the speaker leave her job at Seki Research Institute?
    (A) To do more extensive research
    (B) To start a company
    (C) To design equipment
    (D) To work in a pharmacy
    Ⓐ Ⓑ Ⓒ Ⓓ

53. What did the speaker most likely do today?
    (A) Met with science graduates
    (B) Discussed employment opportunities
    (C) Accepted a new position
    (D) Toured the facility's grounds
    Ⓐ Ⓑ Ⓒ Ⓓ

54. What is the news report about?
    (A) An official celebration
    (B) Construction of new ships
    (C) A recent acquisition
    (C) The launch of a new service
    Ⓐ Ⓑ Ⓒ Ⓓ

55. How will the decision affect King Cruises?
    (A) Its number of luxury ships will increase.
    (B) It will be the third-largest company in the industry.
    (C) Its headquarters will relocate.
    (D) It will be able to cut operating costs.
    Ⓐ Ⓑ Ⓒ Ⓓ

56. According to the report, what will King executives do?
    (A) Reduce the entire workforce
    (B) Ask for approval from shareholders
    (C) Leave Porto the way it is
    (D) Replace older ships
    Ⓐ Ⓑ Ⓒ Ⓓ

Questions 45 through 47 refer to the following conversation.

W: Rob, do you know what's wrong with the copier? All my copies are coming out with a big black streak down the middle.

M: **Q45** Ms. Kim was just telling me that she noticed the same thing this morning. **Q46** I'll call the service center and get a technician over here.

W: I hope they'll send someone this afternoon. I need all the materials prepared for my sales presentation by tomorrow morning at the latest. **Q47** A prospective client will visit us here at 1.

M: Well, if it doesn't get fixed in time, I'd go to the print shop down the street.

重要語句 □ streak「線，筋」 □ need ... prepared「〜を揃える必要がある」(= need ... to be prepared)

女性：ロブ，コピー機のどこが悪いかわかりますか。コピーするとすべて用紙の真ん中に黒い線が入るんです。

男性：今朝キムさんが同じことに気付いたと言っていました。サービスセンターに電話して，修理に来てもらいましょう。

女性：今日の午後に来てもらいたいんですが。遅くても明日の午前中までに販売プレゼン用の資料をすべて揃えなくてはいけないので。見込み客が1時に来る予定なんです。

男性：もし修理が間に合わなかったら，私なら通りにあるコピーショップに行きます。

45

正解 ▶ **(B)**

What does the man say about Ms. Kim?	男性はキムさんについて何と言っていますか。
(A) She needs to make some handouts.	(A) 配付物を作成する必要がある。
(B) She informed him of the problem.	(B) 彼に問題について知らせた。
(C) She will contact a technician.	(C) 技術者に連絡をとる予定である。
(D) She has a meeting with a client.	(D) 顧客との打ち合わせがある。

正答 男性の発言に注目。女性がコピー機の不調を伝えた後，男性が Ms. Kim was just telling me ... this morning. (キムさんが今朝同じことに気付いたと言っていた) と話しているので，(B) を確実に選びたい。**誤答** (A) と (D) は話し手の女性に関する記述。(C) は男性が自分で行うこと。

46

What does the man offer to do?	男性は何をすることを申し出ていますか。
(A) Inspect the copier personally	(A) コピー機をみずから点検する
(B) Go to a print shop	(B) コピーショップへ行く
(C) Prepare materials for the presentation	(C) プレゼンテーション資料の準備をする
(D) Have the machine repaired	(D) 機器の修理の手配をする

正答 同じく男性の発言の中で，offer の表現に注意。すると，I'll call the service center and get a technician over here. とあることから，(D) が正解。前の設問とヒントが隣り合わせなので，絶対に聞き逃さないようにしよう。誤答 男性みずから修理をするわけではないので，(A) は不適切。また，男性が最後に I'd (＝ I would) go to the print shop と述べているが，この I'd は「もし私だったら～する」と提案をする仮定法の表現なので，(B) は不適切。男性がオファーをしているのであれば I'll go to the print shop for you. となる。

47

When most likely is the woman's presentation?	女性のプレゼンはおそらくいつですか。
(A) This morning	(A) 今朝
(B) This afternoon	(B) 今日の午後
(C) Tomorrow morning	(C) 明日の午前中
(D) Tomorrow afternoon	(D) 明日の午後

正答 presentation に関して，女性がまず「tomorrow morning までに準備が必要」と述べた後，「顧客が 1 時に来る」と時刻を伝えているので，(D) が適切と判断する。語句だけを聞き取ろうとするのではなく，常に文脈の流れをイメージしながら聞くことが大切。

Disc 1
77 - 78

Questions 48 through 50 refer to the following conversation.

M: Hello, it's Richard Henderson. **Q49** I found some kind of programming guide in the back of **Q48** my cab. Has anyone phoned the call center to claim it? A business card was inserted into it as a bookmark. It says Alta Technologies on Dresden Avenue.

W: **Q49** We did, in fact, receive a call a while ago from a woman at Alta missing a technical manual. She was very concerned about it because it has information about a computer program that's still in the developmental phase. Do you have time to bring it to the call center later?

M: Oh, that won't be necessary. I'm on Dresden Avenue now, and the address is right down the street. **Q50** I'll just take it to Alta directly and drop it off there.

重要語句 □ claim「〜を（自分のものだと）主張する」　□ phase「段階」（＝ stage）　□ drop ... off「〜を車で届ける」

男性：もしもし，リチャード・ヘンダソンです。タクシーの後部座席にプログラミング・ガイドのようなものを見つけたんです。誰かコールセンターに問い合わせの電話をしてきませんでしたか。名刺がしおり代わりに挟まっていました。ドレスデン通りのアルタ・テクノロジズ社と書かれています。

女性：じつはちょっと前にアルタ社の女性から技術マニュアルを紛失したとの電話がありましたよ。まだ開発段階のコンピュータ・プログラムに関する情報が含まれているようで，とても心配している様子でした。後でコールセンターまで届けにくる時間はありますか。

男性：ええと，その必要はありませんよ。今ドレスデン通りにいて，住所は通りを進んだところなので。直接アルタ社に行って届けてくることにします。

48

正解 ➤ (A)

Who most likely is the man?	男性はおそらく誰ですか。
(A) A taxi driver	(A) タクシー運転手
(B) A call center operator	(B) コールセンターのオペレーター
(C) A passenger	(C) 乗客
(D) A computer programmer	(D) コンピュータ・プログラマー

正答 男性の始めの発言で my cab とあることや，call center の女性と確認を取り合っていることなどから，(A) が正解であることを見抜きたい。今回のように，始めの発言が 4 〜 5 文にわたって長い場合，2 人目の人物がいつ話を始めるかがつかみにくく，集中力が下がりやすいので注意。誤答 (B) は女性のこと。

49

正解 ➤ (C)

What is the problem?	問題は何ですか。
(A) The man misplaced his business card.	(A) 男性が名刺を紛失した。
(B) A computer system is inaccessible.	(B) コンピュータシステムが利用できない。
(C) A handbook was left behind.	(C) 手引書が置き忘れてあった。
(D) A customer made a complaint.	(D) 客から苦情がきた。

正答 男性が「タクシーの中に programming guide のようなものを見つけた」と述べていることや，女性が「a technical manual をなくしたという人から電話が来た」と話していることから，(C) が正解と判断できる。誤答 Part 3 の設問や選択肢にある the man や the woman は常に話し手を指し，また紛失したのは a woman at Alta であることからも，(A) を選ばないように注意。

50

What will the man most likely do next? | 男性はおそらく次に何をしますか。
(A) Turn onto Dresden Avenue | (A) ドレスデン通りに曲がる
(B) Visit a company | (B) 会社を訪問する
(C) Drop off a client | (C) 顧客を降ろす
(D) Call for technical support | (D) 技術サポートを得るために電話をする

正答 男性の最後の発言に I'll just take it to Alta directly とあるので，(B) が適切。**誤答** (A) については，男性が I'm on Dresden Avenue now と述べていることから，すでにその通りにいることがわかる。

Disc 1
79-80

Questions 51 through 53 refer to the following excerpt from a speech.

I'd like to start off by thanking Dr. Calvin for that wonderful introduction. As he said, I was a student at Seki Research Institute for six years before becoming a member of the science faculty. **Q51** This was a position I held for a decade **Q52** before leaving to found HobbAid Pharmaceuticals. In fact, this is my first time back here in over twenty years. It's amazing to see how much this place has grown in that time. **Q53** I counted three new science buildings alone, and the quality of the equipment in the laboratories I saw today was top-notch. I'm glad, because more than ever there is a need for qualified, capable chemistry and science graduates in a variety of fields. I'd like to tell you now about some of the wonderful work opportunities available to you in the pharmaceutical industry.

重要語句 □ faculty「教員陣，講師陣」(= all the teachers) □ top-notch「一流の」(= of the highest quality) □ pharmaceutical「製薬の」

51-53 の設問は次のスピーチの一部に関するものです。

まずは，すばらしい紹介をしてくださったカルビン博士に感謝します。彼がおっしゃったように，私はセキ・リサーチ・インスティテュートの理学部教員になる前，6 年間学生として在籍していました。教員職は，ホブエイド製薬を設立するために退職するまで 10 年間勤めていました。じつは，今日ここに訪ねてきたのは，20 年以上ぶりです。その期間のこの学校の成長ぶりには目を見張るものがあります。理学部の新しい建物だけで 3 つありますし，研究室にある機器は一流品ばかりです。多くの分野において，資格のある有能な化学および理学の卒業生を求める声が今までにないほど多いことを，とても嬉しく思います。ここで，製薬業界におけるすばらしい雇用機会について話したいと思います。

51

How long did the speaker work at Seki Research Institute?	話し手はセキ・リサーチ・インスティテュートで何年間勤務しましたか。
(A) For three years	(A) 3 年間
(B) For six years	(B) 6 年間
(C) For ten years	(C) 10 年間
(D) For twenty years	(D) 20 年間

正答 Seki Research Institute で a member of the science faculty（理学部の教員）になったことについて，This was a position I held for a decade と述べているので，a decade を ten years に言い換えた (C) が正解。誤答 (B) は学生としての在籍期間。

52

Why did the speaker leave her job at Seki Research Institute?	なぜ話し手はセキ・リサーチ・インスティテュートでの職を辞めたのですか。
(A) To do more extensive research	(A) より幅広い研究を行うため
(B) To start a company	(B) 会社を始めるため
(C) To design equipment	(C) 機器をデザインするため
(D) To work in a pharmacy	(D) 薬局で働くため

正答 前の設問と同じ一文で before leaving to found HobbAid Pharmaceuticals（ホブエイド製薬を設立するために退職するまで）とあることから，退職の目的は (B) であるとわかる。一文の中に 2 つの設問の情報が連続して登場するので，ヒントを聞き逃さないよう注意。誤答 (D) の pharmacy は「薬局」の意味で，製薬会社の名前によく使われる pharmaceuticals（もとは「医薬品」の意味）と混同しないようにしよう。

53

What did the speaker most likely do today?	話し手はおそらく今日何をしましたか。
(A) Met with science graduates	(A) 理学の卒業生と会った
(B) Discussed employment opportunities	(B) 雇用機会に関して話をした
(C) Accepted a new position	(C) 新しい職を引き受けた
(D) Toured the facility's grounds	(D) 施設の敷地内を見学した

正答 I counted three new science buildings alone（新しい建物だけでも 3 つ数えて回った）とあり，さらに the quality ... I saw today was top-notch の部分から研究室内も見て回ったことがわかるので，(D) が適切。動詞 tour は「〜を見て回る」（＝ go around）の意味。誤答 (B) はこれから話をするテーマ。

Questions 54 through 56 refer to the following news report.

Q54 The directors of King Cruises, the world's largest cruise company, were in a festive mood, after their company became even bigger by purchasing Lisbon-based Porto Cruises and its ships. King completed the 8.4 billion dollar deal Wednesday after gaining approval from shareholders of both companies. The addition of Porto, currently the third-largest company in the industry, gives King a total fleet of 62 vessels. More importantly, **Q55** King will have more upscale cruise ships to complement its lower-end cruise ships and its mid-priced line. **Q56** King executives said that they don't intend to make any changes to the Porto service, and that they don't plan any lay-offs of Porto employees.

重要語句 □ festive「お祝い（気分）の」※ 名詞の festivity「お祭り事」も重要語。 □ fleet「（会社の保有する）全車両，全船」 □ vessel「船」（＝ ship） □ upscale「高所得者向けの」 □ complement「〜を補足・補完する」（＝ add to ...）

54-56 の設問は次のニュース報道に関するものです。
世界最大のクルーズ会社であるキング・クルージズ社の役員らは，リスボンを拠点におくポルト・クルージズ社とその船を買収したことでさらに大きな企業となり，お祝い気分に包まれたようです。両社の株主の賛同を得た後，キング社は水曜日に 84 億ドルで取引を完了しました。現在世界第 3 位の企業であるポルト社を傘下に入れることにより，キング社は合計で 62 隻もの船を所有することになります。さらに重要なことに，キング社は従来の低価格なクルーズ船と中価格帯の船に加え，高級クルーズ船をより多く保有することになります。キング社の幹部らは，ポルト社のサービスを変更する予定や，ポルト社の従業員を解雇する計画はないと述べています。

54

正解 ➤ (C)

What is the news report about?	これは何に関するニュース報道ですか。
(A) An official celebration	(A) 公式の祝賀会
(B) Construction of new ships	(B) 新しい船の製造
(C) A recent acquisition	(C) 最近行われた企業買収
(D) The launch of a new service	(D) 新サービスの開始

正答 report の冒頭文で「King Cruises 社が Porto Cruises 社を買収してお祝い気分に包まれた」とあるので，(C) の acquisition（買収）に関するニュースだとわかる。**誤答** (A) の celebration は可算名詞として用いた場合「祝賀会」を意味することに注意。

55

How will the decision affect King Cruises?	今回の決定はキング・クルージズ社にどのような影響を与えますか。
(A) Its number of luxury ships will increase.	(A) 豪華船の数が増えることになる。
(B) It will be the third-largest company in the industry.	(B) 業界第3位の規模の会社になる。
(C) Its headquarters will relocate.	(C) 本社が移転になる。
(D) It will be able to cut operating costs.	(D) 運営費を削減できるようになる。

正答 買収後の話として，King will have more upscale cruise ships と述べていることから，upscale cruise ships を luxury ships と言い換えている (A) が正解である。upscale は「高級志向の，高所得者向けの」という意味。誤答 (B) の third-largest company は Port 社のこと。(C) や (D) に関しては言及がない。

56

According to the report, what will King executives do?	報道によると，キング社の幹部らは何をする予定ですか。
(A) Reduce the entire workforce	(A) 従業員数を減らす
(B) Ask for approval from shareholders	(B) 株主からの賛同を得る
(C) Leave Porto the way it is	(C) ポルト社を現状のままにしておく
(D) Replace older ships	(D) 古い船を取り替える

正答 最後の King executives said ... any lay-offs of Porto employees. という一文から，Porto 社に対する変更は行われないことをおさえ，(C) を選ぶ。誤答 (B) はすでに行われたこと。

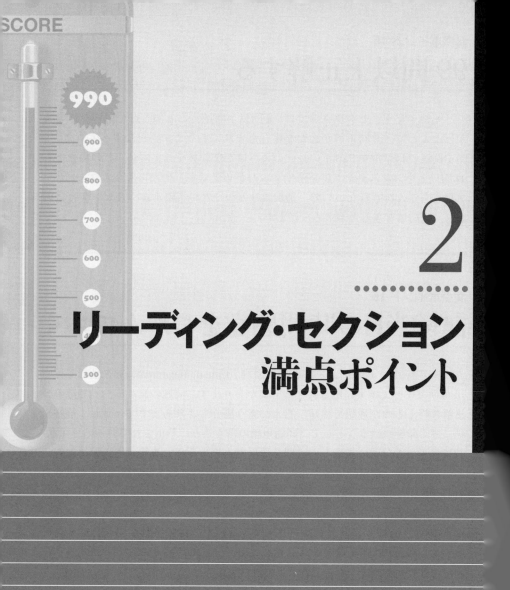

SCORE

990

900

800

700

600

500

300

リーディング・セクション
満点ポイント

2
・・・・・・・・・・・

99 問以上正解する

リーディング・セクションでは，2 問以上間違えると 495 点をとれない場合がほとんどで，全問正解が必要な場合もまれにあります。回によって，文法・語彙問題のレベルや Part 7 の長文の長さはかなり異なりますが，どの場合でも 99 問以上をコンスタントに正解できる力が必要です。ケアレスミスやマークミスはもちろん許されないので，選択肢ひとつひとつを慎重かつスピーディに検討し，全問解ききる力が求められます。

試験当日の時間感覚をつかんでおく

リーディング・セクションでは，時間管理（time management）を徹底して行い，75 分間ですべて確実に解き終える必要があります。問題の流れに沿ってそのまま解き終えるのが理想ですが，答えに迷う場合もとりあえずマークし，解答用紙に薄く印をつけるなどして（問題用紙の書き込みは禁止されているので注意），試験終了の 5 分前に見直しの時間を確保できるようにしましょう。始めは答えが出なくても，最後の最後で正解がひらめく場合もあります。Part 5・Part 6 を合わせて 15 ～ 20 分（Part 5 は 1 問 5 ～ 20 秒，Part 6 は 1 セット 1 分 30 秒）で終え，Part 7 に最低でも 50 分は残す必要があります。試験当日は 13 時 46 分※から 15 時 1 分までがリーディングの時間なので，14 時 5 分までに Part 6 を終わらせ，14 時 30 分までにシングルパッセージを終わらせるなど，試験当日に通用する時間感覚をつかんでおいてください。

当日の時間配分の目安

※ 回によりリスニングは 45 ～ 47 分を前後しますが，46 分の場合がほとんどです。

（13:00 ～ 13:46 リスニング）		14:05 ～ 14:30	Part 7 シングルパッセージ
13:46 ～ 13:59	Part 5	14:30 ～ 14:56	Part 7 ダブルパッセージ
13:59 ～ 14:05	Part 6	14:56 ～ 15:01	見直し

Part 5

短文穴埋め問題

品詞問題も文頭からアプローチする *Part 5*

　Part 5 の一般的な解答アプローチは「空所前後で速答しろ」というものですが，このやり方には 2 つワナがあります。ひとつは，空所前後で判断がつかなければ文頭から読み直すという二度手間になること。もうひとつは，空所前後に視野を狭めると誤答が正解に見えてしまう場合があることです。確実に満点を取るには，たとえ「品詞」の問題であっても，文頭から速読して全体の構文をつかみ，総合的な視野で答えを即決するスキルが不可欠です。ここでまず，品詞問題の難問パターンを見ていきましょう。

複合名詞を問うもの

　複合名詞は application form など「名詞 1 + 名詞 2」の形をとるもので，form for application のように「名詞 2 for 名詞 1」の形で言い換えられるのが基本です。（renovation/renovated）project のように「空所 + 名詞」の場合と，safety（regulations/regularly）のように「名詞 + 空所」の場合がありますが，最近は後者のパターンが多い傾向にあります。

Part 5 に登場する複合名詞の代表例

❶ 「規則・基準」関連（rule, regulation, policy, standard, guideline など）

> hiring policy（雇用規定）　quality control standard（品質管理基準）

❷ 「計画・策略」関連（plan, strategy, initiative, measure, project など）

> a growth initiative（成長戦略）
> a business expansion strategy（ビジネス拡大戦略）

❸ 「契約・書類」関連（contract, agreement, application, permit など）

> an employment contract（雇用契約）
> a construction permit（建設許可証）

名詞の可算・不可算を問うもの

　名詞が複数形で使えるかどうかを試す品詞問題も難度が上がります。purchase（購入品）や advance（進歩）など，動詞と名詞が同形のものが選択肢に並びます。

▶ The discovery led to **advances** in technology.
└──▶ advance は可算名詞（単数形の advance は ×）
（その発見が科学の進歩につながった）

▶ All **purchases** made online will be delivered free of charge.
└──▶ purchase は可算名詞（all purchase は ×）
（インターネット上で購入した全商品は無料配送されます）

形容詞の後置修飾を問うもの

　形容詞句が名詞を修飾する場合は，「名詞＋形容詞句」という後置修飾の形をとります。また，以下の形容詞（過去分詞）は，1語で後置修飾する用法があります。

responsible（責任者の）	available（利用できる）
applicable（適用される）	present（その場にいる）
involved/concerned（関与した）	questioned/interviewed/surveyed
	（質問を受けた）

▶ Please review the terms and conditions **applicable** (to this offer).
名詞句　　　　　　　　　　　　　　　　形容詞(句)
（この特典に適用される条件をご確認ください）

▶ Many people (who were) **surveyed** indicated that they drink coffee every day.
名詞句　　過去分詞
（アンケートを受けた人の多くは，毎日コーヒーを飲むとのことだった）

動詞の語法を問うもの

品詞問題の中には，以下の語法パターンが正解のカギを握る場合があります。

❶ 補語をとる動詞：be 動詞（SVC）型

seem/appear（～のようだ）	look（～に見える）
sound（～に聞こえる）	remain/stay（～のままだ）
get/become/turn/grow（～になる）	

▶ He seemed hesitant to make a decision.
　 S　　V　　　C

（彼は決断を躊躇しているようだった）

❷ 目的語を 2 つとる動詞：give（SVO$_1$O$_2$）型

offer（差し出す）	assign（任せる）
guarantee（約束する）	grant（与える）
win（獲得させる）	deny/refuse（認めない）
allow/permit（認める）	

▶ The store guarantees each customer delivery within 24 hours.
　 S　　　　V　　　　　O$_1$　　　　O$_2$

（その店には客に 24 時間以内の配達を保証している）

❸ 「目的語＋補語」をとる動詞：SVOC 型

make OC（O を C にする）	keep OC（O を C に保つ）
leave OC（O を C のままにする）	find OC（O が C だと思う）
consider [deem] OC（O が C だと考える）	hold OC（O が C だとみなす）
declare OC（O が C だと宣言する）	

▶ The inspector declared the working conditions acceptable.
　 S　　　　　　V　　　　　　O　　　　　　　　　C

（検査員は労働環境が条件を満たしているとした）

1. The company worked out a deal that would allow all employees ------- to the newly opened municipal art museum.
   (A) admission
   (B) to admit
   (C) admitted
   (D) admittedly

   Ⓐ Ⓑ Ⓒ Ⓓ

2. Only one of the candidates interviewed possessed prior work experience ------- to that required for the job opening.
   (A) compared
   (B) comparably
   (C) comparable
   (D) comparing

   Ⓐ Ⓑ Ⓒ Ⓓ

3. The sensitive nature of the project for Metatech, Inc., necessitates that all those concerned must act in keeping with the client confidentiality -------.
   (A) agreeably
   (B) agreement
   (C) agreeable
   (D) to agree

   Ⓐ Ⓑ Ⓒ Ⓓ

4. Ms. Sun Li's efforts have helped the firm make significant ------- in its pursuit of a larger market share.
   (A) progresses
   (B) progression
   (C) progress
   (D) progressing

   Ⓐ Ⓑ Ⓒ Ⓓ

5. As the illustrated character closely resembles a controversial politician, the marketing committee deemed the proposed logo design -------.
   (A) objectively
   (B) objective
   (C) to object
   (D) objectionable

   Ⓐ Ⓑ Ⓒ Ⓓ

6. The company policy changes will partially be shaped by what each of the employees ------- is important to them on their survey forms.
   (A) indicatively
   (B) indicates
   (C) indicating
   (D) indication

   Ⓐ Ⓑ Ⓒ Ⓓ

1 動詞の語法 正解 ➤ (A)

The company worked out a deal that would <u>allow</u> <u>all employees</u> **admission** to the
newly opened municipal art museum.
V O₁   O₂

会社は，新しくオープンした市立美術館に全従業員が入場できるようになる取引を何とか成立させた。

正解 動詞 allow は《allow O to *do*》（O が〜できるようにする）の語法が一般的だが，不定詞の (B) to admit を入れると admit to …（〔自分の非〕を認める）という表現になり文意を成さない。そこで，もうひとつの語法である《allow O₁ O₂》（O₁ に O₂ を認める）を当てはめ，目的語 O₂ になる名詞の (A) admission（入場）を入れれば前後が適切につながる。**誤答** (C) admitted は過去形・過去分詞，(D) admittedly（確かに）は副詞。

重要語句 □ work out「〜をうまく成立させる」 □ municipal「市営の」

2 形容詞の後置修飾 正解 ➤ (C)

Only one of the candidates interviewed possessed <u>prior work experience</u> **comparable** to
that required for the job opening.
名詞

面接を受けた応募者のうち一人だけが，求人職の必要条件に見合った職歴があった。

正解 空所前で文が完成しており，直後に to that（that = prior work experience）が続いていることから，comparable to …（〜と同等の）の形で名詞を後置修飾できる形容詞の (C) comparable を入れる。**誤答** 過去分詞の (A) も compared to …（〜と比較して）の形で用いられるが，ここでは文意が成立しないことに注意。副詞の (B) comparably（同等に）は直後の to とつながらない。(D) comparing は動詞 compare の動名詞・現在分詞。

重要語句 □ candidates interviewed「面接を受けた応募者」（= candidates who were interviewed） □ possess「〜を所有する，持つ」（= have; own）

3 複合名詞 正解 ➤ (B)

The sensitive nature of the project for Metatech, Inc., necessitates that all those
concerned must act in keeping with the client <u>confidentiality</u> **agreement**.
名詞   名詞

メタテック社とのプロジェクトは厳重に取り扱うべき問題を含むため，関係者は全員，顧客情報の秘密保持契約に従って行動する必要がある。

正解 空所前の in keeping with は「〜に従って」（= in accordance with）という意味なので，後ろには「従うべきモノ」が必要。そこで名詞の (B) agreement（合意，契約）を入れれば，(client) confidentiality agreement（〔顧客情報の〕機密保持契約）という複合名詞が完成し，文意も通る。**誤答** (A) agreeably（快く）は副詞，(C) agreeable（心地よい，合っている）は形容詞，(D) to agree は不定詞。

重要語句 □ sensitive「厳重に扱うべき」 □ nature「性質」 □ necessitate that SV「〜を必要とする」（= require） □ those concerned「関係者」 □ confidentiality「機密保持」※形容詞形は confidential（機密の）。

4 可算名詞 vs. 不加算名詞 　　　　　　　　　　　　　　　　　正解 ➤ (C)

Ms. Sun Li's efforts have helped the firm <u>make</u> significant **progress** in its pursuit of a larger market share.

スン・リさんの努力は，会社が市場占有率を大幅に伸ばすことにつながった。

正解 動詞 make の目的語になる名詞が求められているので，名詞の (C) を入れ make progress（前進する）という表現を完成させる。progress は不加算名詞なので，複数形で用いないことに注意。**誤答** (A) progresses は動詞 progress の 3 人称単数現在形。名詞の (B) progression（〔状況の〕進行）は，make とともに用いない。(D) progressing は動名詞・現在分詞。

重要語句 □ pursuit「追い求めること」※ 動詞形は pursue（〜を追い求める＝ chase; try to obtain）。

5 動詞の語法 　　　　　　　　　　　　　　　　　　　　　　　　正解 ➤ (D)

As the illustrated character closely resembles a controversial politician, the marketing committee <u>deemed</u> <u>the proposed logo design</u> **objectionable**.
　　　　　　　　　　　　　　　　　　　　　V　　　　　O　　　　　　　　　　　　C

キャラクターの絵が問題のある政治家に酷似しているため，マーケティング委員会は提案されたロゴのデザインを不快なものと見なした。

正解 動詞 deem には《deem OC》（O を C と見なす＝ consider）という語法がある。目的語 the proposed logo design を説明する補語 C として適切なのは，形容詞の (D) objectionable（不快にさせる＝ offensive）。**誤答** (B) objective は「目標」という名詞の意味のほか，「客観的な」という形容詞の意味もあるが，文意に合わない。(A) objectively（客観的に）は副詞, (C) to object は不定詞。

重要語句 □ resemble「〜に似ている」　□ controversial「問題のある，物議を醸す」

6 複雑な構文 　　　　　　　　　　　　　　　　　　　　　　　　正解 ➤ (B)

The company policy changes will partially be shaped by what (<u>each of the employees</u>
　　　　　　　　　　　　　　　　　　　　　　　　　　　　　　　　　　　S'
indicates) is important to them on their survey forms.
　 V'

社則は，アンケート用紙で従業員一人ひとりが自分にとって重要だと記載した内容を一部もとにして変更される。

正解 what（each of the employees ------- ）is important のカッコ部分を省いても文が成り立つことから，主語 each of the employees と，それに呼応する動詞の (B) indicates が挿入された形であることを見極める。関係詞の後ろではこのように，「主語＋発言や考えを示す動詞（say/indicate/think/hope など）」が挿入されることがよくある。**誤答** 空所だけをとっても文が成立しないので，副詞の (A) indicatively（暗示的に）は不適切。(C) indicating は動名詞・現在分詞。(D) indication（印，示し）は名詞。

重要語句 □ partially「一部」（= partly, in part）　□ shape「〜を形成する」

前置詞 vs. 接続詞を極める

Part 5

　前置詞は名詞（句）を，接続詞は節（主語〔S〕＋動詞〔V〕）をつなぐというのが基本ですが，その見極めに注意が必要なものや，慣用的な語法が問われる場合もあります。ここで，前置詞 vs. 接続詞の注意すべきパターンを確認しましょう。

---

❶ -ed 形がある場合は，過去形か過去分詞かに注意する。

　　Because the ad **appeared** online, we received many responses.
　　　接続詞　　　　S　　　　　V　　➡ appeared は過去形
　　　　　　　　　　　　（広告がインターネットに出たので）

　　Because of the ad (**posted** online), we received many responses.
　　　前置詞　　　　　　　　　　└➡ posted は ad を修飾する過去分詞
　　　　　　　　　　　　　（インターネットに掲載された広告によって）

❷ 接続詞のうち，「時」を示す when/while/once/until，「条件」を示す if/unless，「譲歩・逆説」を示す although/though は，後ろに分詞 (-ing/-ed) を直接とる場合や，「代名詞の主語＋ be 動詞」が省略される場合がある。

　　▶ Ms. Jones visited many temples **when** (she was) in Japan.
　　　　　　　　　　　　　　　　　　　　　　　　➡ 時（日本にいた時）

　　▶ Applications will not be accepted **unless** (they are) **submitted** with a
　　　letter of reference.　　　　　　　　　　　　　　　　　　過去分詞
　　　　　　　　　　　　　➡ 条件（推薦状を添えて提出されなければ）

❸ 前置詞と接続詞両方の機能をもつ before/after/since の後ろでは「代名詞の主語＋ be 動詞」の省略が起こらない。一方，前置詞として後ろに動名詞 (-ing) をとることはできる。

　　▶ **Since joining** the company, Mr. Brown has made numerous contributions.
　　　　前置詞
　　　= Since he joined the company（会社に入って以来）

　　▶ The article was revised several times **before being published**.
　　　　　　　　　　　　　　　　　　　　　　前置詞
　　　　　　　　　　　　　　　= before it was published（出版される前に）
　　　　　　　　　　　　　　　（before published は ×）

❹「特定の期間」を示す前置詞の during/throughout/over は，後ろに動名詞をとらない。

▶ Ms. Jones visited many temples **during her stay** in Japan.
前置詞

= **while** (she was) staying in Japan
(during staying は ×)

⏱ 制限時間：6問　2分

7. ------- the poor service received during his last stay, Mr. Garner will be upset that the Hotel Sun Juan is the only available accommodation option.
(A) Given
(B) So that
(C) Since
(D) Provided

Ⓐ Ⓑ Ⓒ Ⓓ

8. ------- implemented next week, the procedural changes are expected to improve communication and work efficiency.
(A) Upon
(B) After
(C) Once
(D) As

Ⓐ Ⓑ Ⓒ Ⓓ

9. ------- formerly a local theater actress, Ms. Flugstaad has established and currently hosts a popular radio talk show.
(A) Despite
(B) Other than
(C) Besides
(D) Although

Ⓐ Ⓑ Ⓒ Ⓓ

10. Motorists should allow time for delays caused by traffic congestion ------- commuting into the downtown area.
(A) from
(B) if
(C) during
(D) thereafter

Ⓐ Ⓑ Ⓒ Ⓓ

11. ------- an audience of over 200 people anticipated at the event, the annual film festival was moved to another venue.
(A) Because
(B) Whereas
(C) With
(D) Before

Ⓐ Ⓑ Ⓒ Ⓓ

12. ------- much-needed renovations to the historic city library building have been postponed for another year was disappointing news to Mayor Feingold and her staff.
(A) Whether
(B) That
(C) Even
(D) What

Ⓐ Ⓑ Ⓒ Ⓓ

7 前置詞

正解 ➤ (A)

Given <u>the poor service</u> (<u>received</u> during his last stay), Mr. Garner will be upset that
名詞句
the Hotel Sun Juan is the only available accommodation option.

前回滞在した際に受けたサービスがひどかったので，ガーナー氏はサン・ホアンホテルが宿泊できる
唯一の場所であることにがっかりするだろう。

正解 名詞句 the poor service の後ろに続く received (during his last stay) はこれを修飾する過
去分詞句。よって，名詞句をつなぐ前置詞である (A) Given (〜を考えると= considering) が入る。
誤答 (B) の So that (〜できるように= in order that) と (D) の Provided (that) (〜であれば= if;
on condition that) は接続詞なので，後ろに節が必要。(C) Since を前置詞として用いる場合は「〜
(過去の時点) 以来」という意味なので，文意が通らない。

重要語句 □ accommodation「宿泊 (施設)」(= lodging)

---

8 接続詞＋分詞

正解 ➤ (C)

Once <u>implemented</u> next week, the procedural changes are expected to improve
communication and work efficiency.

手順の変更が来週実行に移されれば，意思伝達や仕事の効率が改善されることが期待される。

正解 過去分詞 implemented をつなぐ用法があるのは，接続詞の (C) Once (いったん〜したら) と
(D) As (〜のとおり) だが，文意を成すのは (C) Once。Once (they are) implemented の they (=
procedural changes) are が省略された形と考えるとよい。**誤答** (A) Upon (〜次第) と (B) After
は, upon [after] being implemented のように動名詞を用いれば可。(D) の As は, as requested (要
望どおり) や as specified (記載どおり) といった表現でよく用いられる。

重要語句 □ implement「〜を実行に移す，導入する」(= put ... into effect)

---

9 「代名詞の主語＋ be 動詞」の省略

正解 ➤ (D)

Although <u>formerly a local theater actress</u>, Ms. Flugstaad has established and
currently hosts a popular radio talk show.

フラグスタッドさんは，以前は地元の舞台女優だったが，人気のラジオ番組を立ち上げ，今では司会
進行役をしている。

正解 空所の後ろにある (formerly) a local theater actress は，主語 Ms. Flugstaad とイコールの
関係にあることに注目。接続詞の (D) Although を入れることで，Although (she was) formerly ...
actress という節の she was が省略された形ができあがる。**誤答** 前置詞の (A) Despite (〜に関わ
らず= in spite of) は，Despite formerly <u>being</u> a ... actress (女優で<u>あった</u>にもかかわらず) とす
ればよい。(B) Other than は「〜のほかには」(= apart from, aside from)，(C) Besides は「〜
に加えて」(= in addition to) という意味の前置詞。

重要語句 □ establish「〜を始める，立ち上げる」(= make *something* start to exist)

10 接続詞+分詞 正解 ➤ (B)

Motorists should allow time for delays caused by traffic congestion **if** <u>commuting</u>
   s
into the downtown area.

ダウンタウン地区に通勤する場合，ドライバーの方は交通渋滞による遅れの時間を考慮する必要があ
ります。

正解 主節の主語は Motorists で，空所の直後に現在分詞 commuting がある。接続詞の (B) if を
入れれば，if (they are) commuting という「接続詞+分詞」の形が完成する。**誤答** 前置詞の (A)
from は文法上動名詞を後ろにつなぐことはできるが，ここでは文意を成さない。(C) during は動名
詞をとらない前置詞なので，during their commute とすれば OK。(D) thereafter（その後= after
that）は副詞。

重要語句 □ allow「〜を見込む，取っておく」(= set aside)

11 前置詞 正解 ➤ (C)

With <u>an audience of over 200 people</u> (<u>anticipated</u> at the event), the annual film
              名詞句   過去分詞
festival was moved to another venue.

200 人以上の観客の来場が見込まれたため，毎年恒例の映画祭は別の会場に移された。

正解 空所の後ろにある anticipated が過去分詞であることをおさえる。前置詞の (C) With には，
《with +名詞+過去分詞》の形で「名詞が〜されて」と状況を補足説明する用法（付帯状況の with）
があり，これがあてはまる。**誤答** (A) Because は接続詞なので，Because an audience ... was
anticipated のように後ろを節 (SV) にする必要がある。(B) Whereas（〜の一方で）も接続詞。(D)
を入れて Before an audience とすると「観客の前で」という意味になり，文意を成さない。

12 接続詞 正解 ➤ (B)

[**That** much-needed renovations to the historic city library building have been
postponed for another year] was disappointing news to Mayor Feingold and her
                             v
staff.

急務とされる歴史市立図書館の改修工事がもう 1 年延期になったのは，フェインゴールド市長やス
タッフにとって残念な知らせとなった。

正解 一文の動詞が was であり，空所から was までの節全体が主語になっている構造をとら
え，名詞節を作る接続詞の (B) That（〜であること= the fact that）を入れる。**誤答** 接続詞の (A)
Whether が名詞節を作る場合は「〜かどうか」という不確定の意味を表すため，文意が通らない。(C)
Even は副詞。(D) What は関係代名詞で，後ろの節に名詞の要素（主語や目的語）が欠けることになる。

重要語句 □ postpone「〜を延期する」(= put off ...) □ mayor「市長」

動詞は語法を見極める

　選択肢に異なる動詞が4つ並ぶ問題は，後ろに目的語をとるかとらないか（他動詞か自動詞か）や，どの前置詞を後ろに伴うかといった語法が問われることがよくあります。身近な動詞ほど表現の幅は広いもので，動詞自体の意味を知っていても正解に迷うケースは上級者でもよくあります。満点取得者に求められるのは，確信をもって正解を選び，かつ確信をもって他の選択肢を消去できる力です。英英辞書をこまめにチェックし，豊富な表現力を身につけておきましょう。

他動詞	自動詞＋前置詞
*attend（～に出席する，行く）	participate in（～に参加する）
*answer（～に答える）	reply to/respond to/react to 　　　　　　　　　　（～に反応・返答する）
seek（～を探し求める）	look for/search for（～を探す）
address/handle/*manage 　　　　　　　　　（～に対処する）	deal with/cope with（～に対処する）
follow/obey/observe/honor 　　　　　　　（～に従う，～を守る）	adhere to/comply with/ conform to/abide by　　　（～に従う）
oppose（～に反対する）	object to（～に異議を唱える）
	comment on/remark on 　　　　　　（～についてコメントする） specialize in（～を専門とする） proceed with（～を進める）

（ * は自動詞として用いることもあります）

「動詞＋that節」型
state（述べる） indicate（示す） specify（明示する） confirm（確認する） verify（確認・実証する） ensure（確実にする） require（要求する） suggest（提案する・示唆する） recommend（勧める）

「動詞＋人＋that節」型
inform（知らせる） notify（通知する） assure（確信を与える・保証する） remind（念を押す） convince（納得させる・説得する） persuade（納得させる・説得する）

13. The computer skills session was well ------- by the staff, so management has arranged for it to be conducted again as early as next month.

(A) participated
(B) received
(C) succeeded
(D) commented

Ⓐ Ⓑ Ⓒ Ⓓ

14. A discount voucher for a future workshop is presented in gratitude if an attendee ------- a friend or acquaintance to the cooking seminar.

(A) mentions
(B) refers
(C) persuades
(D) addresses

Ⓐ Ⓑ Ⓒ Ⓓ

15. The speaker was asked to ------- on some of the points he had mentioned during the presentation.

(A) elaborate
(B) itemize
(C) identify
(D) summarize

Ⓐ Ⓑ Ⓒ Ⓓ

16. Dr. Morrissey ------- to be the first cardiologist in the region to make use of the cutting-edge scanning equipment at a private practice.

(A) believes
(B) claims
(C) declares
(D) contends

Ⓐ Ⓑ Ⓒ Ⓓ

17. After years of clinical trials, the pharmaceutical company's research ------- that the new medication was both a safe and effective treatment for the illness.

(A) founded
(B) represented
(C) convinced
(D) established

Ⓐ Ⓑ Ⓒ Ⓓ

18. Management was impressed with the level of service that was offered by DynaPass Corporation and decided to ------- into another two-year contract.

(A) agree
(B) reach
(C) extend
(D) enter

Ⓐ Ⓑ Ⓒ Ⓓ

13 自動詞 vs. 他動詞 　　　　　　　　　　　　　　正解 ➤ (B)

The computer skills session was <u>well</u> **received** by the staff, so management has arranged for it to be conducted again as early as next month.

パソコンスキルアップ研修が社員に好評だったので，経営陣は来月にも再度行えるよう手配した。

正解 1語で受動態にできるのは他動詞のみ。直前の副詞 well とともに用いて文意を成す他動詞は (B) received である。well received で「受けがよい，好評の」という意味になる。**誤答** 自動詞の (A) participate(d) は受動態で用いない（出席者が多い場合は well attended）。(C) の succeed(ed) は「成功する」という意味では自動詞。他動詞として「〜の地位を引き継ぐ」という意味もあるが，文意が成立しない。(D) comment(ed) は，comment on [upon] ...（〜についてコメントする）の形で用いる自動詞で，The seminar was positively commented on. のように，前置詞とともに受動態で用いることは可能。

重要語句 □ arrange for ... to *do*「…が〜するよう手配する」 □ as early as「早くも〜には（時期の早さを強調する）」

14 動詞 *A to B* の語法 　　　　　　　　　　　　　　正解 ➤ (B)

A discount voucher for a future workshop is presented in gratitude if an attendee **refers** a friend or acquaintance to the cooking seminar.

ご友人かお知り合いの方を料理セミナーにご紹介いただきますと，感謝の印として今後行われるワークショップに使用できる割引券を差し上げます。

正解 空所の後ろが人 to ... の形になっていることに着目。(B) refers を入れれば，《refer *someone* to ...》（人を〜に差し向ける，紹介する）という語法があてはまり，文意にも合う。**誤答** (A) は《mention ... to *someone*》で「〜について人に話す」，(C) は《persuade *someone* to *do*》で「人に〜するよう説得する」という意味。(D) は《address ... to *someone*》で「（質問など）を人に向ける」（= direct ... to *someone*）という意味を表す。動詞 address はほかにも，address a problem で「問題に対処する」（= deal with），address an audience で「観客にスピーチをする」（= speak to）という意味を表す TOEIC 頻出の動詞。

重要語句 □ in gratitude「感謝の意を込めて」（= in appreciation）

15 自動詞 vs. 他動詞 　　　　　　　　　　　　　　正解 ➤ (A)

The speaker was asked to **elaborate** <u>on</u> some of the points he had mentioned during the presentation.

プレゼンを行った人は，プレゼン中に述べたいくつかの点をより詳しく説明するよう求められた。

正解 空所直後の前置詞 on とともに用いるのは自動詞の (A) elaborate が正解。elaborate on で「〜を詳しく述べる」（= give more details on）という意味を表す。同形の形容詞 elaborate（きめ細かい，精巧の= detailed; intricate）も重要語。**誤答** (B) itemize（〜を項目別に分ける），(D) summarize（〜を要約する= outline）は他動詞。(C) identify は「〜を特定する」という他動詞の用法のほか，identify with ... の形で「〜に共感する」という自動詞の用法もある。

16 動詞＋ to 不定詞　　　　　　　　　　　　　　正解 ➤ (B)

Dr. Morrissey **claims** to be the first cardiologist in the region to make use of the cutting-edge scanning equipment at a private practice.

モリッシィ博士はみずからを，地域で初めて最新鋭の CT スキャン装置を診療所で使用する心臓医だと主張している。

正解 空所直後の to be という不定詞を目的語にとる語法があるのは，(B) claims のみ。claim to be ... で「〜であると（根拠なく）主張する」という意味を表し，He claims that he is the first cardiologist のように that 節でも言い換えられる。**誤答** (A) believes は，He is believed to be the first cardiologist のように受動態であれば可。(C) declares（宣言する）は He declares himself (to be) the first cardiologist のように declare *A* (to be) *B* の形で用いることはできる。(D) contends は contends that SV の形で「〜を主張する」（＝ claim; argue）の意味。

重要語句 □ cardiologist「心臓医」　□ cutting-edge「最新鋭の」（＝ most advanced）　□ practice「診療所，診療業務」※practice は動詞として work as a doctor or lawyer という意味も表す。

17 動詞＋ that 節　　　　　　　　　　　　　　　正解 ➤ (D)

After years of clinical trials, the pharmaceutical company's research **established** that the new medication was both a safe and effective treatment for the illness.

長年の臨床実験により，その製薬会社は新薬がその病に安全かつ有効な治療法であることを立証した。

正解 選択肢に並ぶ動詞のうち，直後に that 節をとる語法をもつのは (D) established のみ。establish that SV で「〜を立証する，はっきりさせる」（＝ discover; prove）という意味を表せるのは上級者が見落としがちな語法ではないだろうか。**誤答** (C) は人を目的語にとった《convince *someone* that SV》（人に〜を納得させる）の形で用いる。(A) found(ed)（〜を設立する＝ establish）や (B) represent(ed)（〜を示す）には that 節をとる語法がない。

重要語句 □ clinical trial「臨床実験」　□ pharmaceutical company「製薬会社」

18 動詞＋ into ... の語法　　　　　　　　　　　　正解 ➤ (D)

Management was impressed with the level of service that was offered by DynaPass Corporation and decided to **enter** into another two-year contract.

経営陣は，ダイナパス・コーポレーション社が提供するサービスに感銘を受け，さらに 2 年の契約を結ぶことにした。

正解 空所直後に前置詞 into があり，その後ろに名詞 contract があることをおさえ，enter into a contract（契約を結ぶ）という表現を完成させる (D) enter を選ぶ。「場所に入る」意味の enter は他動詞だが，「活動に参入する」という意味合いでは enter into の形を用いる。**誤答** (A) は agree to a contract で「契約に同意する」という意味。(B) reach は「〜に達する」の意味では他動詞。(C) extend は他動詞として extend a contract（契約を延長する）のように用いるほか，extend into ... の形で「〜にまで及ぶ」（The project will extend into next year.）という意味を表す。

単語力ではなく語彙力を高める

Part 5 に毎回 10 ～ 12 問出題される語彙問題のうち，上級者を迷わせる難問が 1 ～ 2 問登場することがあります。ただ，語彙レベルそのものが高いことはあまりなく，むしろ単語自体を知っていても，コロケーション（語句の相性）がわからないケースがほとんどです。つまり，「単語をどれだけ知っているか」ではなく，自然な文意を成す語をすばやくアウトプットできる「実践的な語彙力」が求められているわけです。語彙問題を全問確実に正解するためには，日頃から自然な英語に多く触れ，英語の「感覚」に磨きをかけておくことが不可欠です。

語彙問題の特徴として，不正解の選択肢の中に英検一級レベルの難しい単語が「意図的に」含まれていることがあります。参考までに，過去の公開テストで語彙問題の選択肢に並んでいた単語のうち，語彙レベルの高いものを挙げておきます。

正解になった語

pursue（追求する）	consolidate（統合する）	amendment（改正）
justification（正当な理由）	speculation（憶測）	delegation（代表団）
shortcoming（欠点）	insistence（強い要求）	integral（不可欠の）
subsequent（次の）	lengthy（長々とした）	strikingly（著しく）
candidly（率直に）	indefinitely（無期限に）	meticulously（入念に）

不正解だった語

premonition（予感）	mutation（変形）	deprivation（剥奪）
deployment（配備）	fixative（固定剤）	compliant（従順の）
rightful（しかるべき）	dismayed（落胆した）	secluded（人里離れた）

19. Advance tickets for Jason Grant's limited ------- at the City Performing Arts Center have already nearly sold out.
(A) schedule
(B) reservation
(C) engagement
(D) seating

Ⓐ Ⓑ Ⓒ Ⓓ

20. It is hoped that an exhaustive inspection of the equipment will bring the cause of the problem to -------.
(A) focus
(B) light
(C) attention
(D) view

Ⓐ Ⓑ Ⓒ Ⓓ

21. A new musical directed by ------- choreographer Mia Li-Sung was performed for the first time to the delight of the audience last night at the Carroll Theater.
(A) excelled
(B) familiarized
(C) improvised
(D) celebrated

Ⓐ Ⓑ Ⓒ Ⓓ

22. The company will have to decide whether to strive to be the industry leader in quality or in price, as the two are mutually ------- goals.
(A) exclusive
(B) distinguished
(C) arbitrary
(D) ultimate

Ⓐ Ⓑ Ⓒ Ⓓ

23. The clients appeared to be ------- impressed with the advertising agency's proposed brochure design.
(A) suitably
(B) candidly
(C) steadily
(D) institutionally

Ⓐ Ⓑ Ⓒ Ⓓ

24. Willingness to listen to customers and adapt to their changing needs is a key ------- of success in business.
(A) procedure
(B) combination
(C) ingredient
(D) conduct

Ⓐ Ⓑ Ⓒ Ⓓ

25. The survey from the historical architecture tour showed that the information given by the guide was only of ------- interest to those participating.

(A) restrictive

(B) vast

(C) marginal

(D) articulate

ⒶⒷⒸⒹ

26. The department director held the project team ------- accountable for the missed deadline.

(A) unanimously

(B) sharply

(C) collectively

(D) meticulously

ⒶⒷⒸⒹ

27. The artwork is on loan and displayed in the museum gallery by ------- of the National Historical Society.

(A) legacy

(B) token

(C) means

(D) courtesy

ⒶⒷⒸⒹ

28. The company president is generally hesitant to ------- authority over the supervisors regarding matters that relate to their specific departments.

(A) transmit

(B) exercise

(C) manipulate

(D) influence

ⒶⒷⒸⒹ

19 名詞   正解 ➤ (C)

Advance tickets for Jason Grant's limited **engagement** at the City Performing Arts Center have already nearly sold out.

市演劇芸術センターで行われるジェイソン・グラントの限定公演の前売券は，すでにほぼ完売状態だ。

正解 冒頭に Advance tickets for ...（～の前売チケット）とあり，Jason Grant's と人名が続くことから，この人物が行うイベントを表す語が空所に入ると考える。(C) engagement は「固い約束」「従事」のイメージをもち，limited engagement の形で「限定公演（契約）」という意味を表すので，これが文脈に合う。prior engagement（先約）の形もおさえておこう。**誤答** (A) schedule（予定），(B) reservation（予約），(D) seating（席〔の総数〕）は，いずれもここでは文意を成さない。

重要語句 □ advance「事前の」 □ sell out「完売する」

20 慣用表現   正解 ➤ (B)

It is hoped that an exhaustive inspection of the equipment will bring the cause of the problem to **light**.

その機器を徹底的に点検することで，問題の原因が明らかになるだろうと期待されている。

正解 文脈と bring the cause of the problem to という形に着目し，(B) light を入れて bring ... to light（～を明るみに出す＝ reveal）という慣用表現を完成させる。**誤答** (A) focus は bring ... into focus の形で「～に焦点を合わせる，～を明確にする」（＝ make ... clear），(C) attention は bring ... to one's attention の形で「～を人に知らせる」（＝ make someone notice），(D) view は bring ... into view で「～が見えるようにする」（＝ make ... visible）という意味を表す。

重要語句 □ exhaustive「徹底的な」（＝ thorough）

21 過去分詞   正解 ➤ (D)

A new musical directed by **celebrated** choreographer Mia Li-Sung was performed for the first time to the delight of the audience last night at the Carroll Theater.

振付師として名高いミア・リ・サンによる新作ミュージカルが，昨夜，キャロル劇場で初めて上演され，観客が歓喜の声に沸いた。

正解 空所直後の choreographer Mia Li-Sung という「人」を一語で限定修飾できるのは，「有名な」という意味を持つ(D) celebrated（＝ well-known; renowned）。**誤答** (A)の原形 excel は excel at [in] ...（～に秀でる）の形で用いられる自動詞。名詞を修飾できる自動詞出身の過去分詞は，retired（引退している）や agreed（合意済みの）など，「完了している状態」を明確に表せるものに限られる。(B) は be familiarized with ...（～を熟知している）の形では用いられるが，何を熟知しているかを示す必要があるため，一語で限定修飾する用法はない。(C) の原形 improvise は「～を即興で作る」という意味で，improvised speech（即興スピーチ）のように用いる。

重要語句 □ choreographer「振付師」 □ to the delight of ...「～が喜んだことに」

22 形容詞　　　　　　　　　　　　　　　　　　　　　　　正解 ➤ (A)

The company will have to decide whether to strive to be the industry leader in quality or in price, as the two are <u>mutually</u> **exclusive** <u>goals</u>.

会社は，品質と価格どちらの面で業界トップを目指していくのかを決断しなければならないが，これは両者が相容れない目標だからだ。

正解 空所前にある副詞 mutually（相互に）とともに用いて名詞 goals を適切に修飾できるのは，「他を締め出す」イメージをもつ形容詞の (A) exclusive。mutually exclusive goals で「相容れない目標」という意味になる。**誤答** (B) distinguished は「（人の成功などが）目覚しい」という意味で，形の似た distinguishable（区別できる）との違いにも注意。(C) arbitrary（気まぐれの，思いに任せた）は an arbitrary decision（任意で下した決定）の形でよく用いられる。(D) ultimate（最終的な＝final）は ultimate goal（最終目標）とは言えるが，mutually と合わない。

重要語句 □ strive to *do*「〜しようと努める」

23 副詞　　　　　　　　　　　　　　　　　　　　　　　　正解 ➤ (A)

The clients appeared to be **suitably** impressed with the advertising agency's proposed brochure design.

顧客は，広告代理店が提案したパンフレットのデザインに対し，期待どおり感銘を受けたようだった。

正解 impressed（感銘を受けた）という人の反応に対して用いられる副詞として，(A) の suitably「（反応が）期待どおり，やはり」が入る。suitably には「適切に」（He is suitably qualified for the position.）という意味もある。**誤答** (B) candidly は「（話が）率直に」（= frankly; honestly），(D) institutionally は「組織的に」という意味。(C) steadily（着実に，一定のペースで）は steadily increased など，主に変化を示す動詞とともに用いる。

24 名詞　　　　　　　　　　　　　　　　　　　　　　　　正解 ➤ (C)

Willingness (to listen to customers and adapt to their changing needs) is a <u>key</u> **ingredient** of success in business.

顧客に耳を傾け，移り変わる要望に対応しようとする意思が，ビジネスの成功に欠かせない要素だ。

正解 willingness（進んで行おうとする意思）という主語を説明し，かつ a key ------- of success という前後の語句に合うのは，(C) の ingredient（構成要素＝ element; component）である。a key [vital/essential] ingredient of ...（〜に欠かせない要素）の形でおさえておこう。ingredient はほかにも，「（料理の）具材」の意味で TOEIC に頻出。**誤答** (A) procedure（手順），(B) combination（組み合わせ），(D) conduct（行為）は，いずれも willingness を説明する名詞として不適切。

重要語句 □ adapt to ...「〜に対応する」（= accommodate）

25 形容詞　　　　　　　　　　　　　　　　　正解 ➤ (C)

The survey from the historical architecture tour showed that the information given by the guide was only of **marginal** interest to those participating.

歴史建造物ツアーのアンケート調査により，ガイドが伝えた情報は，参加者たちにとってほとんど興味の沸かないような内容だったことがわかった。

正解 空所直後にある名詞 interest の程度を示すのに適切な形容詞として，(C) marginal（わずかな = very small）を選択する。margin は「余白」を意味し，「余白にあるもの＝取るに足らないもの」というイメージにつながった語。誤答 (A) restrictive は「制限の多い，厳しい」（= limiting），(B) vast は「（範囲が）広大な，（量が）膨大な」（= extremely large），(D) articulate は「（言葉や考えが）明瞭な」という意味で，いずれも名詞 interest を修飾するのには用いない。

26 副詞　　　　　　　　　　　　　　　　　　正解 ➤ (C)

The department director held the project team **collectively** accountable for the missed deadline.

部長は，締め切りに間に合わなかったことに対して，プロジェクトチーム全員に説明責任を負わせた。

正解 空所直後の形容詞 accountable を適切に修飾する副詞として，「まとめて，合わせて」という意味を補足する (C) collectively（= as a group）が入る。誤答 (A) unanimously は「（親が）全員一致で」の意味で，unanimously agreed [decided] といった組み合わせで用いられる。(B) sharply は「（変化が）急に」（= suddenly and quickly），(D) meticulously は「入念に，細部まで」（= thoroughly）という意味。

重要語句 □ hold *someone* accountable「（人）に説明責任を負わせる」※accountable のほか，responsible や liable も同じ形でよく用いられる。

27 名詞　　　　　　　　　　　　　　　　　　正解 ➤ (D)

The artwork is on loan and displayed in the museum gallery by **courtesy** of the National Historical Society.

全国歴史協会の厚意により，美術品が貸し出され美術館のギャラリーに展示されている。

正解 空所前後の by ------- of とつながり，かつ文意に合うのは，by courtesy of ... で「〜の厚意により」という意味を表せる (D)。courtesy は「親切さ」や「礼儀正しさ」を意味する名詞で，形容詞の courteous（親切な，礼儀正しい）と合わせておさえておこう。誤答 (A) legacy は「遺産」（= inheritance）。(B) token（印）は，as a token of appreciation（感謝の印として）の形でよく用いられる。(C) means（手段）は by means of ... で「〜の手段を用いて」という意味。

重要語句 □ on loan「貸し出されて」（= being borrowed or lent）

The company president is generally hesitant to **exercise** <u>authority</u> over the supervisors regarding matters that relate to their specific departments.

社長は，各部門に関わる事柄に関しては，一般に部長たちに権力を行使するのをためらいがちだ。

正解 後ろの名詞 authority を目的語にとることができるのは，(B) の exercise（〜を行使する＝ use）のみ。ほかにも，exercise caution（〔注意力を使う＝〕注意する）という組み合わせを覚えておきたい。**誤答** (A) transmit（〜を送信・伝達する）（= send out; pass）は，人から人へ伝わっていくイメージを持ち，signals/diseases/information などを目的語に取る。(C) manipulate は「（人や情報）をうまく操る」（= control skillfully），(D) influence は「影響を及ぼす」（= affect）という意味で，The president manipulated [influenced] the supervisor. とは言える。

重要語句　□ relate to ...「〜に関連する」（= pertain to ...）

オススメ文法書

● *Practical English Usage*　Michael Swan 著（Oxford University Press）

　日本語の文法書ではつかめない「ネイティブ感覚」が身につく優れた文法書です。学習者にとって目からウロコの内容が多くあります。私は留学中，読み物として毎日ページをめくっていました。

⏱ 制限時間：12問　5分

29. The owner of the resort hotel pays for insurance coverage ------- against financial loss caused by storm damage.
    (A) protection
    (B) protected
    (C) protectively
    (D) to protect

    Ⓐ Ⓑ Ⓒ Ⓓ

30. Under the new compensation system, employee ------- has risen considerably and productivity has increased to correspondingly higher levels.
    (A) motive
    (B) ethic
    (C) incentive
    (D) morale

    Ⓐ Ⓑ Ⓒ Ⓓ

31. Of the two venues considered for the seminar, the Ahmanson Civic Center had the ------- facilities.
    (A) most impressed
    (B) impressing
    (C) more impressive
    (D) impression

    Ⓐ Ⓑ Ⓒ Ⓓ

32. The Springfield Inn has a concierge on duty 24 hours a day whose role is to ------- to the specific needs of all guests.
    (A) attend
    (B) dedicate
    (C) correspond
    (D) tailor

    Ⓐ Ⓑ Ⓒ Ⓓ

33. After ------- consideration, the board of directors has decided to accept the budgetary revisions requested by Ms. Chin.
    (A) numerous
    (B) due
    (C) successive
    (D) participatory

    Ⓐ Ⓑ Ⓒ Ⓓ

34. The worker had misplaced his identification card and was denied ------- to the laboratory facility.
    (A) accesses
    (B) accessible
    (C) access
    (D) to access

    Ⓐ Ⓑ Ⓒ Ⓓ

35. Ms. Bioche ------- to the team members of the project that she had not kept track of her expenses closely enough.
(A) suspected
(B) instructed
(C) notified
(D) admitted

Ⓐ Ⓑ Ⓒ Ⓓ

36. Please bear in mind that personal savings accounts ------- balances of one hundred dollars or less are subject to a monthly service charge.
(A) whose
(B) with
(C) which
(D) when

Ⓐ Ⓑ Ⓒ Ⓓ

37. The manager cautioned employees that failure to fulfill obligations to the client in a punctual manner could ------- a breach of contract.
(A) interpret
(B) constitute
(C) impose
(D) preclude

Ⓐ Ⓑ Ⓒ Ⓓ

38. The meeting to take place between the heads of the marketing and sales departments has been ------- scheduled for Tuesday, August 21 at 3 P.M.
(A) provisionally
(B) indefinitely
(C) virtually
(D) readily

Ⓐ Ⓑ Ⓒ Ⓓ

39. This year's revenue figures were higher than those of previous years, as ------- by the marketing consultant.
(A) being projected
(B) had been projected
(C) to project
(D) projection

Ⓐ Ⓑ Ⓒ Ⓓ

40. In response to the problems experienced last month, all employees have been asked to take ------- precautions to avoid disclosing any sensitive information.
(A) securely
(B) securing
(C) secured
(D) security

Ⓐ Ⓑ Ⓒ Ⓓ

29 満点ポイント！ 品詞 正解 ▶ (D)

The owner of the resort hotel pays for insurance coverage **to protect** against financial loss caused by storm damage.

リゾートホテルの所有者は，暴風雨の被害による金銭的な損失を防ぐため，保険に加入している。

正解 The owner ... insurance coverage までで文が完成することを見極める。ここで，動詞 protect には protect against ...（～から守る，～を防ぐ）という語法があることから，不定詞の (D) to protect を入れれば目的を補足する構文ができあがる。**誤答** 名詞の (A) は insurance protection（保険による補償＝ insurance coverage）という複合名詞を作ることはできるが，ここでは同じ意味の coverage がすでにあるため不適切。過去分詞の (B) protected（～から守られている）を入れると，直前の insurance coverage を修飾することになり，意味を成さない。副詞の (C) protectively（守るように，かばうように）も文法的には空所に入るが，やはり文意に合わない。

30 満点ポイント！ 語彙 正解 ▶ (D)

Under the new compensation system, employee **morale** has risen considerably and productivity has increased to correspondingly higher levels.

新しい報酬制度の下で社員の士気が著しく向上し，それに伴って生産性も伸びた。

正解 直後に has risen とあるので，選択肢に並ぶ名詞のうち唯一「上下する」イメージでとらえることのできる (D) morale（士気，やる気）を選ぶ。「やる気を高める」という場合は, raise [improve/boost] morale と言える。**誤答** (A) motive は「動機」（＝ reason），(B) ethic は「（行動を決定する）信念」，(C) incentive は「やる気を起こさせるもの，奨励策」という意味。

重要語句 □ correspondingly「それに伴って」

31 満点ポイント！ 品詞 正解 ▶ (C)

Of the two venues considered for the seminar, the Ahmanson Civic Center had the **more impressive** facilities.

セミナー用に検討した 2 つの会場のうち，アーマンソン市民センターがよりすばらしい設備を有していた。

正解 冒頭の Of the two ... s（ふたつの～のうち）という比較級を導く表現をとらえ，(C) more impressive（よりすばらしい）を入れる。**誤答** impressed は「感銘を受けている」という《人の気持ち》を表すので，(A) は more impressed であっても文意を成さないことに注意。現在分詞の (B) impressing は，直後の名詞を修飾するのに用いない。(D) impression（印象）は名詞。

重要語句 □ venue「会場」（＝ event site）

32

The Springfield Inn has a concierge on duty 24 hours a day whose role is to **attend** to the specific needs of all guests.

スプリングフィールド・インには，全宿泊客の細かな要望に対応するのが仕事である案内係が 24 時間体制で勤務している。

正解 空所直後の前置詞 to とともに用いる語法をもち，かつ後ろの the specific needs と意味のつながる動詞は，attend to ... の形で「～に対応する」（= deal with）という意味を表せる (A) attend。**誤答** (B) dedicate と (D) tailor はどちらも他動詞で，dedicate A to B（A を B に捧げる）（= devote），tailor A to B（A を B〔要望など〕に合わせる）の形で用いる。tailor は Your trip can be tailored to your needs. のように特に受動態の形で頻出。(C) を入れた correspond to ... は「～と一致する」という意味で，ここでは文意が通らない。

重要語句 □ concierge「（ホテルの）案内係，コンシェルジュ」

33

After **due** consideration, the board of directors has decided to accept the budgetary revisions requested by Ms. Chin.

十分に検討した結果，取締役会はチン氏が要請した修正予算案を採用することに決めた。

正解 空所直後にある単数名詞 consideration を適切に修飾できる形容詞として，(B) due（十分な，適切な = proper）が入る。due には expected の意味が基本にあり，「支払われるべき」（Payment is due upon delivery.）や「予定の」（The store is due to open next month.）などさまざまな用法がある。**誤答** (A) numerous（数多くの）は many と同じ意味で，after numerous discussions のように後ろに複数名詞が来る。(C) successive（連続する = consecutive）は，for four successive years/for the forth successive year（4 年連続で）のフレーズを覚えておこう。(D) participatory（参加型の）は，participatory media（〔ブログなどの〕参加型メディア）のように用いる。

34

The worker had misplaced his identification card and was denied **access** to the
(O₁)　　　　　　　　　　　　　　　　　　　　　　　(V)　(O₂)
laboratory facility.

その従業員は ID カードを紛失してしまい，研究施設に入ることを拒否された。

正解 空所前にある動詞 deny (denied) は，《deny O_1O_2》で「O_1 に O_2 を認めない」（= not allow）という語法をもつ。ここでは O_1（= the worker）が主語の位置に移動し受動態になった形であることをおさえ，目的語 O_2 になる名詞の (C) access（入場 = entrance）を入れる。access は不加算名詞なので，(A) accesses を複数名詞として用いないことに注意。**誤答** 形容詞の (B) accessible（アクセスできる）は形容詞，(D) to access は不定詞。ちなみに，動詞 access は他動詞で，He was not allowed to access the facility. と言い換えることはできる。

重要語句 □ misplace「～を置き違える，紛失する」（= lose）

35

Ms. Bioche **admitted** to her team members of the project that she had not kept track of her expenses closely enough.

ビオチェさんは，経費をきちんと記録していなかったことをチームのメンバーに対して認めた。

正解 空所の後ろに続く to 人 that SV の形に着目し，《admit (to *someone*) that SV》で「(人に) that 以下の事実を認める」(= confess) という意味になる (D) を入れる。**誤答** (A) は《suspect that SV》で「〜ではないかと思う」(= guess)，(B) は《instruct *someone* to do ...》で「人に〜するよう指示する」(= tell)，(C) は《notify *someone* that SV》で「人に that 以下のことを通知する」(= inform) という意味。

重要語句 □ keep track of ...「〜の跡をたどる，記録をつける」(↔ lose track of)

36

Please bear in mind that personal savings accounts **with** balances of one hundred
　　　　　　　　　　　　　　S　　　　　　　　　　　　　　　　　　　　名詞句
dollars or less are subject to a monthly service charge.
　　　　　　　　V

残高が 100 ドル以下の個人預金口座には，毎月口座維持手数料がかかりますのでご注意ください。

正解 that 節内の主語 S は personal savings accounts，動詞 V は are。そこで，この SV の間にある名詞句 balances of ... or less（100 ドル以下の残高）をつなぐ前置詞の (B) with を入れる。この with は「〜のある」という付加・含有の意味。**誤答** (A) whose, (C) which, (D) when は関係詞（または接続詞）で，いずれも名詞句をつなぐことはできない。常に一文全体の構造をとらえよう。

重要語句 □ bear in mind that SV「〜を心に留めておく」(= keep in mind that SV; remember that SV)
□ subject to ...「〜の影響を受ける，対象となる」(= likely to be affected by)

37

The manager cautioned employees that failure to fulfill obligations to the client in a
　　　　　　　　　　　　　　　　　　　　S
punctual manner could **constitute** a breach of contract.
　　　　　　　　　　　　　V

部長は従業員に対し，クライアントに対する義務を期日どおりに果たせない場合は契約違反になると注意を促した。

正解 主語 failure to fulfill obligations（義務の不履行）と目的語 a breach of contract（契約違反）を適切につなぐ動詞は，「〜（の構成要素）となる」という意味の (B) constitute。動詞 constitute は，Business people constitute 20 percent of the students. のように用いて「〜を構成する」(= form; make up; consist of) という意味も表せる。**誤答** (A) interpret（〜を解釈する）は，受動態（Failure ... could be interpreted as a breach of contract.）にすれば文意が通る。(C) impose は impose *A* on *B* で「A（義務など）を B に課す」，(D) preclude は「（可能性を排除して）〜を防ぐ（= prevent）」という意味。

重要語句 □ caution *someone* that SV「人に〜と注意する」(= warn)　□ in a punctual manner「時間通りに」
(= punctually; on time; in a timely manner)　□ breach「（契約・規則の）違反」

38 満点ポイント！ 語彙　　　　　　　　　　　　　　　　　　　正解 ➤ (A)

The meeting to take place between the heads of the marketing and sales departments has been **provisionally** scheduled for Tuesday, August 21 at 3 P.M.

マーケティング部と営業部の部長で行う会議は，8月21日火曜日の午後3時に仮設定されている。

正解 (A) provisionally には「仮に，暫定的に」（= tentatively）という意味があり，これが文脈に合致する。もとの動詞 provide の持つ「pro-（前もって）-vide（見る）＝あらかじめ整えておく」というニュアンスと結び付けておこう。**誤答** (B) indefinitely は「無期限に」，(C) virtually は「事実上，ほとんど」（= almost; practically）の意味。(D) readily（たやすく＝ easily and quickly）は readily available（たやすく手に入る）の形でよく用いる。

39 満点ポイント！ 品詞　　　　　　　　　　　　　　　　　　　正解 ➤ (B)

This year's revenue figures were higher than those of previous years, as **had been projected** by the marketing consultant.

マーケティングコンサルタントの推定どおり，今年の収益は去年までと比べて大きかった。

正解 接続詞 as の後ろに置くのに適切な動詞の形として，(B) を入れて as had been projected（〔主節の内容が〕推定されたとおり＝ as projected）とする。as にはこのように，主節全体の内容を受けながら，後ろの節で主語の働きを兼ねる用法がある。**誤答**「接続詞 as ＋現在分詞」の用法はないため，(A) being projected は不適切。前置詞の as は主に「～として」という意味なので，名詞の (D) projection（見積もり）を入れても文意を成さない。(C) to project は不定詞。

重要語句 □ revenue「収益」※revenue から cost を差し引いたものが profit。

40 満点ポイント！ 品詞　　　　　　　　　　　　　　　　　　　正解 ➤ (D)

In response to the problems experienced last month, all employees have been asked to take **security** precautions to avoid disclosing any sensitive information.

先月起きた問題を受け，全従業員は機密情報を開示しないようセキュリティ対策を講じることを求められている。

正解 空所直後の名詞 precautions（予防策）を適切に修飾する語として，名詞の (D) security を入れれば security precautions「セキュリティ対策」という複合名詞が完成する。**誤答** 普通なら形容詞を選びたくなるところだが，(A) securely（安全に，しっかりと）は副詞。(B) securing は他動詞 secure（～を確保する，守る）の現在分詞。他動詞出身の現在分詞は，感情を表すもの（surprising, interesting など）を除き，原則一語で名詞を修飾するのに用いない。過去分詞の (C) secured も，precautions と secure の間に受身の関係が成り立たないため不適切。

重要語句 □ in response to ...「～に応えて」 □ disclose「～を開示する」（= reveal）

Part 6
長文穴埋め問題

空所のない文もすべて読む

　Part 6 には，空所を含む一文だけで答えの出る「一文完結型」の問題と，前後の文脈が手がかりになる「文脈依存型」の問題があります。Part 6 は 1 文書 1 分 30 秒を平均ペースとして，すべて迷わず即答したいパートです。「空所のある文だけを先に読み，わからなければ前後に戻る」という解き方はかえって時間がかかり，ミスにもつながります。文脈の流れのまますべて読み進め，空所にたどり着いた時点でそのつど答えを判断しましょう。

「文脈依存型」の代表 4 パターン

❶　語彙　同じ品詞の単語（特に名詞）が並んでおり，文書のテーマに合うものを選ぶもの。

Thank you for your recent -------. We still have a few tickets available for the date you mentioned in your previous e-mail.

(A) purchase
(B) inquiry
(C) visit
(D) stay

❷　時制　文書の日付や前後の文から時制を判断するもの。

Over 100 people ------- the workshop. Most of the participants reported great satisfaction about the instructor.

(A) attend
(B) will be attending
(C) attended
(D) would attend

❸ 接続副詞　therefore や however など，前後の文脈を適切につなぐ副詞を選ぶ
もの。

> I hope you will like this new product. -------, please return your item to
> receive a full refund.
> (A) However
> (B) Otherwise
> (C) Formerly
> (D) Accordingly

正解　① inquiry「問い合わせ」
② attended「参加した」過去形
③ Otherwise「そうでなければ」= if not

代表的な接続副詞（句）

❶ 結論・結果

> Therefore（それゆえに）　Accordingly（したがって）
> Consequently/As a result（その結果）

❷ 逆接・対照

> However（しかし）　Nevertheless/Still/Yet（それでも）
> Conversely/In contrast（逆に，対照的に）　On the other hand（一方）

❸ 例示

> For example/For instance（例えば）
> Specifically/In particular（特に，具体的には）

❹ その他

> Otherwise（さもなければ）　Instead/Rather（むしろ，そのかわり）
> Alternatively（あるいは）　Indeed/In fact（実のところ）

⏱ 制限時間：1分30秒

Questions 1-3 refer to the following notice.

In line with the announcement at last month's general meeting, the human resources department ------- a series of mandatory training

1. (A) conducted
(B) has been conducting
(C) is conducting
(D) will have conducted

Ⓐ Ⓑ Ⓒ Ⓓ

workshops from November 3 to 9. These classes have already been taught in our other plants, and cover measures to take in the event of equipment malfunctions, power outages and other contingencies that may pose a risk of injury.

Each factory worker will be assigned to a specific session. Whoever is absent from their sessions due to illness or other reasons will be required to meet with a training instructor on an individual basis to go over ------- procedures. The company must keep regular production

2. (A) manufacturing
(B) reimbursement
(C) maintenance
(D) emergency

Ⓐ Ⓑ Ⓒ Ⓓ

schedules while the training is underway. Accordingly, human resources will authorize overtime hours ------- needed during the

3. (A) that
(B) as
(C) upon
(D) for

Ⓐ Ⓑ Ⓒ Ⓓ

week of the workshops.

1-3 の設問は次の通知に関するものです。

先月の総会で行われた発表に従いまして，11月3日から9日まで，人事部が参加必須の研修会を行います。この研修会は，当社の他の工場ではすでに行われたもので，機械の故障や停電，その他ケガの危険性を引き起こす不測の事態が起きた場合にとるべき措置を確認します。

工場の各従業員に特定のセッションが割り当てられることになります。病気やその他の理由で研修会を欠席される方は，個別に研修担当講師に会い，緊急時の手順を必ず確認してください。会社は，研修中も通常の製造スケジュールを維持する必要があります。従いまして，研修会が行われる週の間，人事部は必要に応じて残業を許可する予定です。

重要語句 □ in line with ...「〜 に 沿 っ て，従 っ て」(＝ in keeping with ...; in accordance with ...) □ mandatory「必須の」(＝ required) □ in the event of ...「〜の場合に」(＝ in case of ...) □ contingency「不測の事態」 □ pose「〜を引き起こす」(＝ cause; present) □ authorize「〜を承認する」(＝ officially approve)

---

1 ［文脈依存型］時制 　　　　　　　　　　　　　　　　　　　正解 ➤ (C)

In line with the announcement at last month's general meeting, the human resources department **is conducting** a series of mandatory training workshops from November 3 to 9.

正解 動詞 conduct の時制を判断する問題。次の文で These classes have already been taught とあるが，これは他の工場での話なので，そのまま読み進めていく。すると，次の段落の Each factory worker will be assigned to a specific session. の部分でワークショップがこれから行われるとわかるので，確定した予定を表せる現在進行形の (C) を選ぶ。**誤答** (A) は過去形，(B) は現在完了進行形。未来完了形の (D) は，未来のある1点（by November 9 など）を文中に明示したうえで，その時までの完了・継続を示す形。

---

2 ［文脈依存型］語彙 　　　　　　　　　　　　　　　　　　　正解 ➤ (D)

Whoever is absent from their sessions due to illness or other reasons will be required to meet with a training instructor on an individual basis to go over **emergency** procedures.

正解 workshops の内容として，第1段落で「機械の故障や停電，その他不測の事態が起こった場合にとるべき措置を確認する」とあるので，(D) emergency を入れて emergency procedures（緊急時の手順）とすれば文脈に合う。**誤答** (A) manufacturing（製造），(B) reimbursement（払い戻し），(C) maintenance（メンテナンス）は，空所付近だけを見るといずれも正解に見えるので，全体の文脈をとらえながら速読することが重要。

Accordingly, human resources will authorize overtime hours **as** needed during the week of the workshops.

正解 選択肢に前置詞と接続詞が混在しているので，一文の構造をすばやく見極める。ここでは，空所直後の過去分詞 needed をつなぐ働きをもつ接続詞の (B) as が正解。as needed で「必要に応じて」(= as necessary) という意味を表す。誤答 関係代名詞の (A) that は overtime hours that are needed とは言える。(C) upon と (D) for は前置詞。

「文脈依存型」を極める

Part 6

　「文脈依存型」の問題は，1文書につき普通1〜2問含まれており，まれに3問すべてという場合もあります。シンプルな問題も多いですが，テーマをつかんでいないと誤答に誘われる語彙問題や，前後の文だけでは判断しづらい時制問題が出てくることもあります。次の3セットは設問がすべて「文脈依存型」です。ここで，文全体をスピーディに読み進めながら，かつ正確に答えを出す力を鍛えましょう。

Questions 4-6 refer to the following article.

NEW YORK, January 5—Company shareholders of Victory Limo and Red Line Transit voted today in favor of ------- the two companies.

4. (A) closing
   (B) acquiring
   (C) consolidating
   (D) establishing

Ⓐ Ⓑ Ⓒ Ⓓ

The idea was originally proposed in response to the stagnant sales experienced by the companies over the past two years. The merger ------- one of New York's largest transportation services.

5. (A) has created
   (B) will create
   (C) was to create
   (D) would have created

Ⓐ Ⓑ Ⓒ Ⓓ

At a press conference conducted afterward, Mr. Trent, who will be president of the unified company, said he anticipated support in this matter. "Our ------- recognize that this move will help enhance

6. (A) customers
   (B) employees
   (C) citizens
   (D) investors

Ⓐ Ⓑ Ⓒ Ⓓ

efficiency and provide better services in New York and other surrounding areas. Moreover, it will help sustain the long-term value of their shares."

Questions 7-9 refer to the following letter.

Dear Mr. Rodriguez,

I am writing to tender my resignation as director of sales, effective on Friday, January 23. This decision was not an easy one to make, as Jacobi International has provided me with over five years of enjoyable employment. ------- , I have received and accepted an offer to join

    7. (A) Indeed
       (B) Nevertheless
       (C) In so far
       (D) Consequently
           Ⓐ Ⓑ Ⓒ Ⓓ

senior management with a financial firm. I am convinced -------

    8. (A) next
       (B) either
       (C) neither
       (D) this
           Ⓐ Ⓑ Ⓒ Ⓓ

position will represent a chance to put my educational background to greater use and to expand my career horizons.

I am happy to provide you with a list of suitable candidates as my replacement from within my department. I hope you will be able to announce the ------- prior to my leaving. In that case, I would also be

    9. (A) appointment
       (B) opening
       (C) interview
       (D) application
           Ⓐ Ⓑ Ⓒ Ⓓ

available to take part in the initial training process. Please let me know how I can be of any assistance in this regard.

Sincerely,

Gail Kim

Questions 10-12 refer to the following excerpt from a magazine.

Upbridge Weekly

May 15 issue

The *Upbridge Weekly* is pleased to announce that Middleton Tech, the country's leading manufacturer of computer components, has been short-listed for our Best Local Employer Award. As its name suggests, the company ------- in the northern city of Middleton. Its recent

     10. (A) is based
         (B) will base
         (C) has based
         (D) was based

             Ⓐ Ⓑ Ⓒ Ⓓ

relocation to Upbridge makes the company eligible for the accolade for the first year ever.

Middleton Tech was nominated due to its excellent working conditions reported by employees. Our online poll indicates that its workers are among the most highly ------- in the region. The competitive salary and

     11. (A) praised
         (B) contented
         (C) skilled
         (D) compensated

             Ⓐ Ⓑ Ⓒ Ⓓ

a complete range of benefits the company offers are cited as reasons for this level of satisfaction.

The recipient of the award will be announced on June 28. ------- , you

         12. (A) For example
            (B) Then
            (C) In the meantime
            (D) Specifically

             Ⓐ Ⓑ Ⓒ Ⓓ

can check each issue of the *Upbridge Weekly* for profiles of other local businesses that have been selected for this year.

ニューヨーク，1月5日―ビクトリー・リモ社とレッドライン・トランジット社の株主は今日，2社の統合に賛成票を投じた。統合のアイデアはもともと，過去2年間に両社が経験した業績不振を受けて提案されたものであった。合併により，ニューヨーク最大の交通サービスとなる新しい会社が誕生することになる。

その後行われた記者会見で，統合される会社の社長となるトレント氏は，この件に関して支持を得られることを予期していたと語った。「投資家の方々は，この決断によって効率性が高まり，ニューヨークや他の周辺地域によりよいサービスを提供できるようになると認識しています。さらには，株価が長期的に安定することにもつながることでしょう」

重要語句 □ vote in favor of ...「～に賛成票を投じる」(↔ vote against ...) □ in response to ...「～を受けて」 □ stagnant「停滞している」(= not changing) □ unified「統合された」 □ anticipate「～を予期する」 (= expect) □ enhance「～を向上させる」(= improve) □ sustain「～を維持する」(= keep; maintain)

語彙 正解 ➤ (C)

Company shareholders of Victory Limo and Red Line Transit voted today in favor of **consolidating** the two companies.

正解 次の文で「業績不振を受けて提案された」とあり，さらに The merger（この合併が）と続いていることから，「統合する」という意味の (C) consolidating (= combining) が文脈に合うと判断できる。文章の後半にある the unified company という表現も，2社が統合することの裏づけになる。**誤答** (A) closing（閉鎖する），(B) acquiring（買収する），(D) establishing（設立する）は，いずれも両社が合意した内容として文脈上不適切。

時制 正解 ➤ (B)

The merger **will create** one of New York's largest transportation services.

正解 それまでの文脈から，merger は今日可決されたばかりであるとわかる。また，次の文で Mr. Trent, who will be president と will があることからも，両社はこれから正式に統合されるものと判断し，未来を表す (B) will create を選ぶ。それまでの文章で過去形が用いられている中で，あくまで文脈のつながる時制を選べるかが試される。**誤答** 現在完了形の (A) has created は，現時点までの完了行為を表す。(C) was to create は，必然的な未来を表す《be to ＋原形動詞》を過去形にしたもので，「～することになっていた（がしなかった）」という意味。(D) would have created は「（もし ... であれば）～だっただろう」と過去の事実に反する仮定をする仮定法過去完了の形。

6 語彙 正解 ▶ (D)

Our **investors** recognize that this move will help enhance efficiency and provide better services in New York and other surrounding areas.

正解 前の文で「この件（合併）に関して支持を得られると思っていた」とあり、さらに次の文で their shares（彼らの持ち株）とあることから、their が指す名詞として (D) investors（投資家）が適切。**誤答** (A) customers（顧客）、(B) employees（従業員）、(C) citizens（市民、住民）は、いずれも記事の文脈に合致しない。

7-9 の設問は次の手紙に関するものです。

ロドリゲス様、

1月23日の金曜日付けで、営業部長の職を辞任させていただきたく、お知らせ申し上げます。ジャコビ・インターナショナル社には、5年以上もの間楽しい仕事の機会を提供していただいたので、この決断は容易なものではありませんでした。しかしながら、私はとある金融会社の上級管理職として働くオファーを受け、これを受諾いたしました。この新しい職は、これまでの学歴をより有効に生かし、かつ今後のキャリアの可能性を広げてくれるチャンスとなるものです。

営業部の中で私の後任にふさわしい候補者のリストを提出いたします。1月23日までに後任の任命が発表されれば幸いです。その場合は、始めの研修過程に私も参加することができます。この件に関して、どのようにお手伝いさせていただければよいかご連絡ください。

敬具

ゲイル・キム

重要語句 □ tender「（正式に）〜を差し出す」(= offer) □ effective + 時「〜付けで、〜から」(= as of ...; starting from ...) □ be convinced (that) SV「〜であると確信している」(= be certain that SV) □ put ... to use「〜を利用する、生かす」(= make use of ...) □ expand *one's* horizons「視野を広げる」(= broaden[widen] *one's* horizons) □ replacement「後任」 □ prior to ...「〜より前に」(= before) □ in this regard「この点で、この件で」(= in this matter)

---

7 接続副詞 正解 ▶ (B)

Nevertheless, I have received and accepted an offer to join senior management with a financial firm.

正解 前の文で「辞職する決断は容易ではなかった」と述べているのに対し、空所を含む文では他社のオファーを受諾したと伝えていることから、逆接的な内容をつなぐ (B) Nevertheless（それでも、しかし）が適切。**誤答** (A) Indeed（じつのところ= In fact）は、前に述べた内容を強調・補足する表現。(C) In so far は、《in so far as SV》（または insofar as SV）の形で「あくまで〜の範囲で」(= to the degree that) という意味を表す（The product has been successful, in so far as it is suggested by Mr. Kato's report.「新商品は成功しているが、あくまでカトウさんの報告からわかる限りでのことだ」）。「今のところ」という意味の so far と混同しないように注意しよう。(D) Consequently（したがって、その結果）は結論・結果を導く副詞。

8 指示語　　　　　　　　　　　　　　　　　正解 ➤ (D)

I am convinced **this** position will represent a chance to put my educational background to greater use and to expand my career horizons.

正解 空所の前で新しい仕事について述べているので，(D) を入れて this position will represent a chance ...（この仕事が〜のチャンスとなる）とすれば文脈がつながる。動詞 represent が「〜となる」という意味で be 動詞的に用いられることもおさえよう。誤答 (A) next（次の）は形容詞なので，the next position のように冠詞が必要。(B) either（どちらの〜も）と (C) neither（どちらの〜もない）は文脈に合わない。

9 語彙　　　　　　　　　　　　　　　　　　正解 ➤ (A)

I hope you will be able to announce the **appointment** prior to my leaving.

正解 次の文の冒頭に In that case（その場合は）とあるので，どの場合なら研修に参加できるかを考える。「任命」の意味をもつ (A) appointment を入れれば，「辞職前に後任の任命が発表されれば研修に参加できる」という自然な文脈が完成する。誤答 (B) opening（仕事の空き），(C) interview（面接），(D) application（申込）は一見いずれも正解に見えるが，in that case 以降とつながらない。

10-12 の設問は次の雑誌の一部に関するものです。

アップブリッジ・ウィークリー

5月15日号

『アップブリッジ・ウィークリー』は，国内大手のパソコン部品メーカーであるミドルトンテック社が，弊誌のベスト・ローカル・エンポロイヤ賞の最終選考に残ったことを喜んでお伝えします。その名が示すとおり，同社は北部にあるミドルトン市に拠点を構えていました。最近アップブリッジに移転したことで，今年になり初めてこの賞の対象となったのです。

ミドルトンテック社は，従業員が伝えたすばらしい勤務環境によりノミネートされました。オンライン調査によると，同社の従業員の満足度は地域でもっとも高いことがわかっています。高い給与と，提供される福利厚生が充実していることが，これほどまで満足度の高い理由として挙げられています。

受賞企業は6月28日に発表となる予定です。その間，『アップブリッジ・ウィークリー』の各号で今年選考されたほかの企業のプロフィールをご覧いただけます。

重要語句 □ component「部品」(= part) □ short-listed「最終選考に残る」 □ suggest「示す」(= indicate) □ accolade「賞」(= award) □ poll「意見調査」(= survey) □ cite A as B「A を B の例として挙げる」

10 態・時制 正解 ➤ (D)

As its name suggests, the company **was based** in the northern city of Middleton.

正解 動詞 base は「～に拠点を置く」という意味の他動詞で，ここでは目的語となる名詞が後ろにないことから，受動態の (A) is based と (D) was based のふたつに絞れる。ここで，次の文の Its recent relocation to Upbridge から，現在は Middleton に所在していないことを見極め，過去形の (D) を選ぶ。be based in は「～に拠点・本社のある」という意味の頻出表現。誤答 (B) will base と (C) has based は能動態になるので，後ろに目的語が必要。

11 語彙 正解 ➤ (B)

Our online poll indicates that its workers are among the most highly **contented** in the region.

正解 次の一文で for this level of satisfaction（これほどの満足度）と述べているので，online poll によってわかったことは「満足している」という意味の (B) contented だと判断できる。ここでは，among the most highly contented (workers) の workers が省略された形になっている。
誤答 (A) praised（賞賛されている），(C) skilled（能力の高い），(D) compensated（給与を得ている＝ paid）はいずれも一見正解に見えるので，空所を含む文と次の文とのつながりを的確にとらえよう。

12 接続副詞 正解 ➤ (C)

In the meantime, you can check each issue of the *Upbridge Weekly* for profiles of other local businesses that have been selected for this year.

正解 前の文の「受賞企業が 6 月 28 日に発表される」と，空所を含む文の「選考された他の企業を各号でチェックする」という内容を文脈上適切につなぐのは，「それまでの間」という意味を表す (C) In the meantime（＝ meanwhile）。誤答 (B) Then（＝ after that time）を入れると，発表以降に出版になる号を毎回チェックすることになるので，文脈上不自然である。(A) For example（例えば）と (D) Specifically（特に，具体的に）は，ともに具体例を示す表現。

Questions 13-15 refer to the following advertisement.

Jacobs, Schmidt & Associates is currently seeking technicians to join our winning team. Be part of one of the nation's most rapidly growing companies, and learn to ------- in a fast-paced working environment.

      13. (A) pursue
            (B) specialize
            (C) commit
            (D) thrive

                  Ⓐ Ⓑ Ⓒ Ⓓ

Members of our team will work closely with many of the nation's top hospital administrators and physicians, providing them with training and support for our state-of-the-art technological gear. Successful candidates must have a degree in medical laboratory science -------

                 14. (A) qualified
                       (B) qualification
                       (C) to qualify
                       (D) qualifying

                                Ⓐ Ⓑ Ⓒ Ⓓ

for the position. No hands-on experience is required. However, those who have a background working with high-tech medical devices will receive ------- .

      15. (A) exception
            (B) advantage
            (C) consideration
            (D) preference

                Ⓐ Ⓑ Ⓒ Ⓓ

Please send your résumé along with a cover letter detailing what would make you a perfect fit for the position to career@jsa.com.

Questions 16-18 refer to the following e-mail.

To: Elaine Flint <eflint@riverton.com>
From: Laurence Halbee <lhalbee@riverton.com>
Sent: Monday, September 8
Subject: Mia Young

Dear Elaine,

As discussed on the telephone last week, head office ------- one of its

                      16. (A) will be sending
                              (B) has sent
                              (C) sends
                              (D) would send

Ⓐ Ⓑ Ⓒ Ⓓ

junior executives to our division to act as the advisor in our talks with
Garrison & Associates. Her name is Mia Young. You and I are scheduled
to meet with her at our office for an initial information exchange when she
first arrives on the morning of September 25.

Ms. Young has worked with directors of Garrison & Associates on several
occasions over the last ten years. I assume that her familiarity with -------

                      17. (A) our
                              (B) its
                              (C) their
                              (D) her

Ⓐ Ⓑ Ⓒ Ⓓ

company is the main reason she was chosen to do this job.

After our meeting, she will be introduced to the remainder of the -------

                      18. (A) recruiting
                              (B) consultation
                              (C) management
                              (D) negotiation

Ⓐ Ⓑ Ⓒ Ⓓ

specialists later in the afternoon. Please let me know before the end of the
week if you can attend this meeting as well.

Best regards,
Laurence

13-15 の設問は次の広告に関するものです。

ジェイコブズ・シュミット・アンド・アソシエイツ社は，優秀な当社のチームに加わっていただける技術者を探しています。全国でもっとも急成長を遂げている会社である当社の一員になって，テンポの速い仕事環境で成功する術を身につけませんか。チームで働く従業員は，全国有数の病院に勤務する理事長や医師の多くと密接に働きながら，当社の最先端機器を使用するための研修やその他の支援を提供していきます。応募を希望される方は，この職の条件として，医療検査学の学位を有している必要があります。実務経験は必須ではありませんが，ハイテク医療機器を扱った経験がある方は優遇いたします。

履歴書と，あなたがこの職に適任である理由を記したカバーレターを，career@jsa.com までご送付ください。

(重要語句) □ seek「〜を探し求める」(= look for ..., search for ...) □ state-of-the-art「最先端の」(= most advanced) □ gear「機器」(= equipment) □ hands-on「実践的な」(= practical) □ a perfect fit「適任者」

13 一文完結型（自動詞 vs. 他動詞） 正解 ➤ (D)

Be part of one of the nation's most rapidly growing companies, and learn to **thrive** in a fast-paced working environment.

正解 空所の後ろに目的語がないことから，自動詞が必要。選択肢のうち，後ろの in a fast-paced working environment と文意のつながる自動詞は，「成功する，うまくやる」(= be successful) という意味の (D) thrive である。誤答 (A) pursue は「〜を追い求める」(= chase; try to achieve) という意味の他動詞で，pursue a goal や pursue a career の形でよく用いる。(B) specialize は specialize in ...（〔分野〕を専門とする）の形で用いられる自動詞で，ここでは in の後ろと意味がつながらない。(C) commit は他動詞・自動詞両方の働きがあるが，自動詞としては commit to ...（〜に専念する）の形で用いる。

14 一文完結型（品詞） 正解 ➤ (C)

Successful candidates must have a degree in medical laboratory science **to qualify** for the position.

正解 空所の前までで文が完成しているので，目的を補足する不定詞の (C) to qualify を入れて，to qualify for the position（この職の応募対象となるために）とすれば，文意も通る。qualify for ... で「〜の資格がある，対象となる」という意味。誤答 形容詞（過去分詞）の (A) は qualified for ... で「〜にふさわしい」という意味を表し，candidates qualified for the position（その職にふさわしい候補者）のように普通人を修飾する。現在分詞の (D) qualifying（対象となっている）はその前にある名詞（degree や medical laboratory science）を修飾することになり，意味を成さない。また，前置詞 in の後ろには degree の「分野」を示す語句が必要なので，名詞の (B) qualification（資格）も不適切。

No hands-on experience is required. However, those who have a background working with high-tech medical devices will receive **preference**.

正解 前の文で「実務経験は必要ない」とあり，空所を含む一文で「しかし経験があれば〜を受ける」と続いているので，(D) preference（優先）を入れて receive preference（優先される）とすれば文脈がつながる。誤答 (A) exception（例外）や (C) consideration（考慮，検討）では文意が通らない。(B) advantage（有利，強み）は他者から受け取るものではないため，receive の目的語として用いない（have an advantage であれば OK）。

16-18 の設問は次のメールに関するものです。
受信者：イレイン・フリント <eflint@riverton.com>
送信者：ローレンス・ハルビー <lhalbee@riverton.com>
送信日：9月8日(月)
件名：ミア・ヤング

イレインさん

先週電話でお話ししたとおり，ギャリソン・アンド・アソシエイツ社との交渉におけるアドバイザーとして，幹部補佐の一人が本社から一時的に私たちの部門に送られてきます。彼女の名前はミア・ヤングさんで，あなたと私は，9月25日の朝に彼女が初めてオフィスに来るときに彼女とミーティングを行い，最初の情報交換をする予定になっています。
ヤングさんはさまざまな機会において，ここ10年間ギャリソン・アンド・アソシエイツ社の幹部との仕事を担当してきました。彼女が先方の会社をよく知っているので，今回の仕事に抜擢されたのだと思います。
私たちのミーティングの後，午後には交渉チームの残りのメンバーたちに彼女を紹介することになります。そのミーティングにも出席できるようであれば，今週末までにご連絡ください。

敬具
ローレンス

重要語句 □ act as ...「〜としての役割を務める」(= serve as ...)　□ the remainder of ...「〜の残り」(= the rest of ...)

16 文脈依存型（時制）　　　　　　　　　　　　　　　　　正解 ➤ (A)

As discussed on the telephone last week, head office **will be sending** one of its junior executives to our division to act as the advisor in our talks with Garrison & Associates.

正解 空所直後にある one of its junior executives は，次の文に出てくる Mia Young のこと。彼女に会う時期として段落の後半に when she first arrives on the morning of September 25 とあることから，まだ 2 人の職場に派遣されていないことをおさえ，未来を表す (A) will be sending を入れる。誤答 (B) has sent は現在完了形。現在形の (C) sends が未来を示す場合は，日常的なスケジュールを述べる場合に限られる。また，彼女との会議の予定がすでに立てられているため，仮定法の (D) would send は使えない。

17 文脈依存型（指示語）　　　　　　　　　　　　　　　　正解 ➤ (C)

I assume that her familiarity with **their** company is the main reason she was chosen to do this job.

正解 前の文で，Mia Young に関して「directors of Garrison & Associates との仕事を過去 10 年間担当してきた」と述べており，この会社はメールの 1 文目にある our talks with Garrison & Associates の部分から他社であるとわかる。したがって，(C) を入れて their company とするのが適切。誤答 (B) its を入れると「Garrison & Associates 社の（保有する）会社」を指すことになり，意味を成さない。

18 文脈依存型（語彙）　　　　　　　　　　　　　　　　　正解 ➤ (D)

After our meeting, she will be introduced to the remainder of the **negotiation** specialists later in the afternoon.

正解 空所を含む一文で「私たちと会った後，彼女が残りの specialists に紹介される」とある。ここで Garrison & Associates 社との talks（交渉）が全体のテーマになっていることから，talks の言い換えとなる (D) を入れて negotiation specialists（交渉のスペシャリスト）とすれば文意が成立する。誤答 Ms. Young の役割が advisor であるため，(B) consultation（相談）も入れたくなるが，the advisor という表現から advisor はひとりしかいないことがわかる。(A) recruiting（人材採用）と (C) management（経営管理）も文脈に関連しない。

Part 7

読解問題

文章をすべて「先読み」する

　一般に普及している Part 7 のテクニックは「設問を先読みしてから関連箇所だけ読む」というものです。しかし，読み飛ばす部分が多いほど，重要な情報を見落とすリスクも当然高まります。また，文脈の流れをつかむ前に設問を先読みしても，答えの場所が見つからず結局すべて読まされることになり，かえって時間の浪費につながります。満点を目指すのであれば，設問に移る前に文章をすべて速読しましょう。シングルパッセージにも，異なる箇所にある複数の情報を組み合わせてひとつの答えを導く「クロスリファレンス型」の問題が登場することがあります。全文を先に読んでおいたほうがはるかに解答もしやすくなり，また他の選択肢が明らかに間違いであることにも気付けます。

① リテンショントレーニング

　文章をすべて読み，かつ時間内に解き終えるためには，速いリーディングスピード
を身につけることが不可欠です。ただし，速読ができても内容が頭に入っていなけれ
ば，結局本文を何度も読み返すことになってしまうので，あくまで内容を把握しなが
ら読める「自然なスピード」を意識的に高めていくことが重要です。ここでまず，文
書全部を先に読み,その後文書に戻らずに設問を解く「リテンション（記憶保持）トレー
ニング」を行います。1つ目は設問が4つ，2つ目は長めの文章で設問が6つ用意さ
れています。学習成果を高めるため，守っていただきたいポイントが4つあります。

　　1. 内容をくみ取れる範囲で速読すること。
　　2. 知らない単語があっても目を止めず，全体の流れをつかむよう努めること。
　　3. 文書を読み終える時間をタイマーで計っておくこと。
　　4. 設問に答える際は，正解があやふやでも文書に戻らないこと。

　それでは，始めましょう。

Questions 1-4 refer to the following article.

While many major airlines have begun charging for in-flight meals, seasoned travelers know that Skylark Airlines has held on to the tradition of offering complimentary meal service. Effective November 1, however, the carrier will join its competitors in charging for meals aboard its domestic flights.

Skylark representatives have announced that its future menu will offer a diverse selection of nutritious entrées and snacks, comparable to those served in casual-dining establishments. Menu offerings will include spinach lasagna, Asian-style rice dishes, and even bacon cheeseburgers.

"The decision to expand our in-flight menu is in direct response to customer feedback. Our passengers have made it abundantly clear that they would prefer a greater array of fare on our flights," says Gerard Han, Skylark's director of food services. "In view of these requests, we looked into trends in the restaurant industry and conducted taste trials on a vast range of prospective menu items. We are striving to provide food options that reflect modern consumer preferences."

Skylark's new program is to be implemented in lieu of the formerly complimentary meal service provided on most routes, although soft drinks and other non-alcoholic beverages will still be provided for free. Food and beverage service on international routes and domestic flights longer than 5 hours will continue to be offered at no additional charge. Meals, snacks and alcoholic beverages will remain free for first-class and business-class travelers on all routes.

1. What does Skylark Airlines intend to do on November 1?
   (A) Partner with a major food distributor
   (B) Begin charging for meals on certain flights
   (C) Increase its fares for domestic routes
   (D) Discontinue serving alcoholic beverages on certain flights

2. To what type of businesses does Skylark Airlines compare its menu selection?
   (A) Fast-food restaurants
   (B) Gourmet restaurants
   (C) Casual restaurants
   (D) Buffet-style restaurants
   Ⓐ Ⓑ Ⓒ Ⓓ

3. According to Gerald Han, why did Skylark Airlines decide to change its menu?
   (A) Because customers requested a greater variety of choices
   (B) In order to comply with new industry regulations regarding nutrition
   (C) To ensure its food compares favorably to that of its competitors
   (D) In response to passenger complaints about the quality of its food
   Ⓐ Ⓑ Ⓒ Ⓓ

4. According to the article, what has Skylark Airlines done?
   (A) Consulted nutrition experts
   (B) Interviewed noted chefs
   (C) Hired additional food service staff
   (D) Investigated industry trends
   Ⓐ Ⓑ Ⓒ Ⓓ

Once Marina Ponchez, her mother, and her two older sisters emigrated to America and joined her father in California, he blocked access to television channels that broadcast in Spanish. Ricardo Ponchez, a native of Columbia, told his daughters that in order to succeed in their new home, they would need to learn to speak English. By the time a fourth daughter was born two years later, the Ponchez household affairs were conducted exclusively in English.

The strict upbringing paid off for Marina, who was born and raised in Peru prior to coming to the U.S. In a ceremony last week at Inverness Valley High School, she was officially named a winner of the prestigious Tanner-Mayhew Scholarship. The scholarship will cover the cost of four years of university education, including her tuition and books. Tens of thousands of high school students apply and submit the required seven essays, many also including letters of recommendation from their teachers, but the Tanner-Mayhew Scholarship is awarded to only 100 students across the country every year. "I was flabbergasted when I heard I won,"

said Marina. She said she had anticipated a whole lot of competition and doubted her chances of winning would be very good. When asked who deserved the most credit for motivating her as a student, Marina told stories of how her father would take her and her sisters to the library every week. "He would ask us a lot of questions about the books we were reading, and occasionally even made us write book reports."

Impressed by her intelligence, Mark Pennington, Marina's debate coach and teacher, decided to nominate her for the scholarship. Not only would she answer almost every question he asked in class, but she had no fear of engaging him in debate. This made him feel certain that she was an exceptional student.

Marina's father is now encouraging her to study law and become an attorney, but her real desire is to become a teacher. She said she has had some truly remarkable mentors, and wants to do for other students what these exceptional educators have done for her.

5. What can be understood about Marina Ponchez?

(A) She lived in Columbia as a child.

(B) She is the youngest child in her family.

(C) She emigrated to America from Peru.

(D) She appeared on television.

Ⓐ Ⓑ Ⓒ Ⓓ

6. What are all candidates for the scholarship required to do?

(A) Take part in a group discussion

(B) Provide letters of recommendation

(C) Make an oral presentation

(D) Write multiple essays

Ⓐ Ⓑ Ⓒ Ⓓ

7. How many students per year are awarded the Tanner-Mayhew Scholarship?

(A) 1

(B) 10

(C) 100

(D) 1000

Ⓐ Ⓑ Ⓒ Ⓓ

8. How did Marina Ponchez say she felt before winning the scholarship?

(A) She was confident that she would win.

(B) She was afraid she might not be eligible.

(C) She thought she was unlikely to win.

(D) She thought there would be more competition.

Ⓐ Ⓑ Ⓒ Ⓓ

9. According to Marina Ponchez, who has had the most influence on her as a student?

(A) Her sisters

(B) Her debate instructor

(C) Her father

(D) Her classmates

Ⓐ Ⓑ Ⓒ Ⓓ

10. According to the article, what does Marina Ponchez want to do in the future?

(A) Become an educator

(B) Practice as a lawyer

(C) Write books about her life

(D) Attend a graduate school

Ⓐ Ⓑ Ⓒ Ⓓ

Questions 1-4 （語数：232 語）

While many major airlines have begun charging for in-flight meals, seasoned travelers know that Skylark Airlines has held on to the tradition of offering complimentary meal service. **Q1** Effective November 1, however, the carrier will join its competitors in charging for meals aboard its domestic flights.

Skylark representatives have announced that **Q2** its future menu will offer a diverse selection of nutritious entrées and snacks, comparable to those served in casual-dining establishments. Menu offerings will include spinach lasagna, Asian-style rice dishes, and even bacon cheeseburgers.

Q3 "The decision to expand our in-flight menu is in direct response to customer feedback. Our passengers have made it abundantly clear that they would prefer a greater array of fare on our flights," says Gerard Han, Skylark's director of food services. "In view of these requests, **Q4** we looked into trends in the restaurant industry and conducted taste trials on a vast range of prospective menu items. We are striving to provide food options that reflect modern consumer preferences."

Skylark's new program is to be implemented in lieu of the formerly complimentary meal service provided on most routes, although soft drinks and other non-alcoholic beverages will still be provided for free. Food and beverage service on international routes and domestic flights longer than 5 hours will continue to be offered at no additional charge. Meals, snacks and alcoholic beverages will remain free for first-class and business-class travelers on all routes.

重要語句 □ seasoned 「経験豊富な」（= experienced）　□ hold on to ... 「～を手放さないでいる」（= stick to ...）　□ effective＋日付 「～から」　□ carrier 「航空会社」　□ entrée 「（コース料理の）メインディッシュ」（= main dish）※「前菜」の意味で用いるのは主にイギリス英語。　□ abundantly clear 「きわめて明確な」　□ a great array of ... 「多種多様な～」（= a wide range of ...）　□ fare 「食べ物，料理」（= food）　□ in view of ... 「～を踏まえて」（= after considering ..., in light of ...）　□ in lieu of ... 「～の代わりに」（= instead of ...）

1-4 の設問は次の記事に関するものです。

多くの大手航空会社が機内食の有料化を始めた一方で，旅行経験の豊富な人はスカイラーク航空が無料で食事を提供するという伝統を貫いてきたことをご存知だろう。しかし，11 月 1 日から，スカイラーク航空も国内線の食事を有料にしている他社の仲間入りをすることになる。

スカイラーク航空広報担当者は，今後のメニューにはカジュアルなレストランに匹敵するほどの栄養価の高いメインディッシュや軽食を豊富に取り揃えると発表した。提供することになるメニューの内容には，ほうれん草ラザニアやアジアスタイルのご飯料理，さらにはベーコンチーズバーガーも含まれることになる。

「機内食のメニューを増やすという決断は，お客様からの意見に直接対応したものです。弊社を利用される乗客の方々は，機内でより豊富な種類の食事をとりたいとの意見を極めて明確にしました」と話すのは，スカイラーク航空の食事サービス部長であるジェラルド・ハン氏だ。「こうした要望を踏まえて，弊社はレストラン業界の動向を調査し，提供できる可能性のある幅広いメニューに対して飲食テストを実施いたしました。私たちは，今日のお客様の好みを反映する食事を提供することに尽力しています」

スカイラーク航空の新たなプログラムは，それまで多くの便で無料で提供されていた食事サービスに代わって導入されることになるが，ソフトドリンクや他のアルコールを含まない飲み物はそれまで同様無料で提供される。同社によれば，国際線と飛行時間が 5 時間以上の国内線においては，飲食サービスは追加料金なしで引き続き提供されるとのことである。食事や軽食，アルコール飲料は，ファーストクラスとビジネスクラスの全便で引き続き無料となる。

1
正解 ▶ (B)

スカイラーク航空は 11 月 1 日に何を行う計画ですか。
(A) 大手の食品販売会社と提携する
(B) 一部の便で食事の有料化を始める
(C) 国内線の運賃を上げる
(D) 一部の便でアルコール飲料の提供を中止する

正解 第 1 段落 2 文目の the carrier will join ... its domestic flights（国内線の食事を有料にしている他社の仲間入りをする）とあるので，(B) が正解。記事全体のテーマでもあるので，確実に正解したい。

2

スカイラーク航空は自社のメニューの取り揃えをどの種類の会社と比較していますか。

(A) ファーストフードレストラン

(B) グルメレストラン

(C) カジュアルレストラン

(D) バイキングレストラン

正解 第2段落冒頭で，future menu に関して comparable to those served in casual-dining establishments（カジュアルレストランで出されるものに匹敵する）とあるので，(C) が正解。comparable to ... は「～に匹敵する，～と同等の」という意味。

3

ジェラルド・ハン氏によれば，スカイラーク航空はなぜメニューを変更することに決めましたか。

(A) 顧客がより豊富なメニューの取り揃えを要望したから

(B) 栄養価に関する新しい業界規制に従うため

(C) 提供する食事が競合他社のものよりも優れたものにするため

(D) 食事の質に対する乗客からの不満に対応するため

正解 第3段落1～2文目で，決断の理由として in direct response to customer feedback（顧客からの意見に直接対応して）や they would prefer a greater array of fare（より種類の豊富な食事を望んでいる）と述べているので，(A) が適切。array や fare という単語自体の意味がつかめなくても，前後の文脈から推測できるようにしたい。

4

この記事によれば，スカイラーク航空は何を行いましたか。

(A) 栄養士の意見を聞いた

(B) 著名なシェフから話を聞いた

(C) 食事サービススタッフを追加で雇った

(D) 業界の動向を調査した

正解 第3段落の3文目に we looked into trends in the restaurant industry とあるので，(D) が正解。look into（～を調査する）は investigate のほか，research，examine，explore などとも言い換えられる重要表現。

Questions 5-10　(語数：351 語)

Once **Q5** Marina Ponchez, her mother, and her two older sisters emigrated to America and joined her father in California, he blocked access to television channels that broadcast in Spanish. Ricardo Ponchez, a native of Columbia, told his daughters that in order to succeed in their new home, they would need to learn to speak English. By the time a fourth daughter was born two years later, the Ponchez household affairs were conducted exclusively in English.

The strict upbringing paid off for **Q5** Marina, who was born and raised in Peru prior to coming to the U.S. In a ceremony last week at Inverness Valley High School, she was officially named a winner of the prestigious Tanner-Mayhew Scholarship. The scholarship will cover the cost of four years of university education, including her tuition and books. **Q6** Tens of thousands of high school students apply and submit the required seven essays, many also including letters of recommendation from their teachers, but **Q7** the Tanner-Mayhew Scholarship is awarded to only 100 students across the country every year. "I was flabbergasted when I heard I won," said Marina. **Q8** She said she had anticipated a whole lot of competition and doubted her chances of winning would be very good. **Q9** When asked who deserved the most credit for motivating her as a student, Marina told stories of how her father would take her and her sisters to the library every week. "He would ask us a lot of questions about the books we were reading, and occasionally even made us write book reports."

Impressed by her intelligence, Mark Pennington, Marina's debate coach and teacher, decided to nominate her for the scholarship. Not only would she answer almost every question he asked in class, but she had no fear of engaging him in debate. This made him feel certain that she was an exceptional student.

Marina's father is now encouraging her to study law and become an attorney, but **Q10** her real desire is to become a teacher. She said she has had some truly remarkable mentors, and wants to do for other students what these exceptional educators have done for her.

重要語句 □ household affairs「家の中で行われること，家事」 □ upbringing「しつけ，育て方」 □ pay off「功を奏す，うまくいく」 □ prestigious「栄誉ある」(= important and respected) □ flabbergasted「慌てふためく」(= stunned; astonished; astounded) □ a whole lot of ...「じつに多くの～」 □ deserve the most credit for ...「～に対する功績がある」※credit は「功績を認めること」を意味する。 □ engage *someone* in ...「人を～に引き込む」(= involve) □ remarkable「特筆すべき，すばらしい」(= impressive; exceptional) □ mentor「師」

マリナ・ポンチェスと母親と二人の姉が，アメリカに移住してカリフォルニアにいる父親と住み始めてまもなく，父親はスペイン語放送のテレビ番組を見られないようにした。コロンビア出身である父親のリカルド・ポンチェスは娘に対し，新しい土地で成功するためには英語を話せるようにならなくてはいけないと諭した。4人目の娘が2年後に生まれる頃には，ポンチェス家での一切が英語だけで行われた。

アメリカに来る前にペルーで生まれ育ったマリナにとって，この厳しいしつけが功を奏した。インバーネス・バリー高校で先週行われた式で，彼女は栄誉あるタナー・メイヒュー奨学金の受賞者として正式に選ばれたのだ。この奨学金は，授業料やテキスト代を含む大学4年間の教育費をまかなうというものだ。何万人という高校生が応募をし，7種類の小論文を提出することが必須となっており，応募者の多くは教師からの推薦状も送る。しかし，その中でタナー・メイヒュー奨学金が与えられるのは，全国でたった100人に限られる。「私が受賞したと聞いたときは本当に驚きました」とマリナは話した。競争が非常に激しいとあらかじめ予想していたため，自分が受賞する可能性は低いと思っていたと彼女は語った。学生としての彼女の意欲をもっとも高めてくれたのは誰かと尋ねられると，マリナは父親が毎週姉妹を図書館に連れて行ってくれたと言い「父は，私たちが読んでいる本に関して多くの質問をしたり，時には感想文を書かせたりもしました」と話した。

マリナのディベートコーチであり教師でもあるマーク・ペニントンは，彼女の賢さに感銘を受け，奨学金への推薦を決めた。彼女は，彼が授業中に投げかける質問に対しほとんどすべて答えることができただけでなく，何の恐れもなく彼を議論に引き込んだりもした。このことが，マリナが並外れた生徒であるという確信につながったとのことだ。

マリナの父親は今，彼女に法律を学んで弁護士になるよう勧めているが，彼女の本当の夢は教師になることだ。彼女は，今まで実に優れた師に巡り会えたため，こうしたすばらしい先生たちが自分のためにしてくれたことを他の生徒たちに返していきたいと話した。

 5

正解 ➤ (C)

マリナ・ポンチェスに関して何がわかりますか。

(A) 子どもの頃コロンビアに住んでいた。

(B) 家族で一番年下である。

(C) ペルーからアメリカに移住した。

(D) テレビに出演した。

正解 第1段落冒頭で Marina Ponchez, her mother, and her two older sisters emigrated to America と述べ，さらに第2段落の冒頭部分で Marina に関して born and raised in Peru prior to coming to the U.S.（アメリカに来る前はペルーで生まれ育った）とあるので，(C) が正解。emigrate to ... は「（国外）へ移住する」という意味。

6

奨学金の応募者は皆何をすることが求められますか。
(A) グループ討論に参加する
(B) 推薦状を提出する
(C) 口頭で発表を行う
(D) 複数の小論文を書く

正解 第2段落4文目に the required seven essays とあるので，(D) が正解。形容詞 multiple は more than one の意味。誤答 (B) は，many (students) also including letters of recommendation from their teachers から，多くの学生がそうしているだけで，必須ではないことがわかる。

7

年間何人の生徒がタナー・メイヒュー奨学金を与えられますか。
(A) 1 人
(B) 10 人
(C) 100 人
(D) 1000 人

正解 第2段落4文目に the Tanner-Mayhew Scholarship is awarded to only 100 students とあるので，(C) が正解。他の数字が記事に出てこないことや，「全国でたったの100人」という明確な記述があることから，本文に戻らなくても正解できるようにしたい。

8

マリナ・ポンチェスは，奨学金を受賞する前にどのように感じたと話しましたか。
(A) 受賞することを確信していた。
(B) 受賞資格がないのではと思っていた。
(C) 受賞する可能性は低いと思っていた。
(D) もっと競争率が激しいものと思っていた。

正解 第2段落6文目で，she ... doubted her chances of winning would be very good（受賞できるチャンスはあまり高くないと思った）と感想を述べているので，この内容を言い換えた (C) が正解。doubt that SV で「～であることを疑う，～ではないと思う」（= not think that SV）という意味。混同しがちな表現として，suspect that SV（～ではないかと思う= think that SV）との違いにも注意。

9

マリナ・ポンチェスによれば，学生としての彼女にもっとも大きな影響を与えたのは誰ですか。

(A) 姉妹

(B) ディベートのコーチ

(C) 父親

(D) 同級生

正解 第2段落7文目の When asked ... as a student（学生としての彼女の意欲を誰がもっとも高めてくれたかと尋ねられたとき）の後ろで，父親の話を引き合いに出していることから，(C) が正解であるとわかる。He would ask us ... の would は回想を表し，「あの頃はよく〜したものだった」と思い出話をするときに用いられる。

10

正解 ➤ (A)

記事によれば，マリナ・ポンチェスは将来何をしたいと思っていますか。

(A) 教育者になる

(B) 弁護士として開業する

(C) 自分の人生について本を書く

(D) 大学院に通う

正解 最終段落で her real desire is to become a teacher と述べていることから，(A) が正解。同じ段落の中に mentor や educator といった teacher の類語が出てくることからも，確実に正解を選べるようにしたい。

② 速読実感トレーニング

ここで，自分のリーディングスピードを，以下のように算出してください。

> **（記事の語数 ÷ 読み終えるのにかかった秒数）× 60 ＝ 1 分間に読める速度**
> [wpm (words per minute)]
>
> Question 1 ～ 4：232 語
> Question 5 ～ 10：351 語

　Part 7 で全問正解を目指すためには，文章をすべて読んで，選択肢をミスのないよう入念にチェックし，さらに必要に応じて本文を読み返す時間が必要なので，最低でも 180 wpm 以上は必要になります。当然，読む文章の種類や内容により，wpm はかなり前後するので，あくまでも目安としてとらえてください。ここで，以下のステップを行い，求められるスピード感覚をつかんでおきましょう。

1. 文章中の表現を確認し，すべて内容が理解できるようにする。
2. CD の音声に合わせて目を動かし，スピードをつかむ（ふつう：160 wpm/速め：180 wpm）。
3. 文章を繰り返し音読する。慣れてきたら，CD のスピードに挑戦する。
4. CD を使わずに黙読し，さらにスピードを上げる。このとき，一字一句頭の中で発音しないようにする（内容を目で吸収していくイメージ）。
5. 最後にもう一度「自然な速度」で黙読し，wpm を算出する。

　すでに繰り返し読んでいる文章ですから，始めとは比較にならないほど速く読めるはずです。「文章に読まされる」重苦しい感覚ではなく，目が自動的に動き，内容が頭にスッと入っていくのではないでしょうか。この「ネイティブ感覚」をしっかりつかんでください。ちなみに，一般的なネイティブスピーカーのリーディングスピードは，文章の内容や読む目的にもよりますが，平均300wpm と言われています。

③ 多読習慣トレーニング

　自分のリーディングの感覚を普段から「ネイティブ感覚」に近づけるのに必要なのは，後はただひとつ。「生の英語」を多読する習慣を身につけることです。題材は，小説・アニメ・ノンフィクション・雑誌・映画のスクリプトなど，「楽しんで読めるもの」であれば何でも OK です。

　多読の際には，注意点がひとつあります。それは，「辞書を原則ひかないこと」です。生の英語には，上級者でも知らない単語が山ほど登場しますので，ひとつひとつ気にしていると，ほぼ確実に挫折することになるからです。2 度 3 度繰り返し出てくる語

（テーマに関連する語）に関しては，まずは意味を推測し，最低でも読んでいるセクションが終わった後に調べるようにしてください。「どうしても知りたい！」と好奇心を高めたうえで調べた単語は，自然と記憶に深く刻み込まれます。

リーディングスピードは，日頃の習慣によって自然に上がっていくものです。楽しんで読める本に一度でも出会えたら，英語の可能性はそこから無限大に広がっていきます。

それでは，次ページから TOEIC に特化した実践練習に入りましょう。

オススメの洋書

参考までに，私がもっとも感動した洋書を 2 冊紹介します。

● *Tuesdays with Morrie* Mitch Albom 著（Broadway）
（邦題『モリー先生との火曜日』NHK 出版）

病を患った大学時代の恩師から「人生の意味」についてレッスンを受ける著者の実話。英語もわかりやすいので，どの方にも読んでいただきたい感動の一冊です。映画版も出ています。

● *Grandfather* Tom Brown Jr. 著 (Berkley)
（邦題『グランドファーザー』徳間書店）

アメリカ先住民の古老ストーキング・ウルフ（グランドファーザー）が，すべての人に通じる大地の技術と哲学を後世に残すという使命のために生涯を捧げた実話。英語は難しめですが，自然が好きな方や環境問題に関心のある方は，自然に対する見方が 180 度変わります。

5問つきシングルパッセージを極める

シングルパッセージ（SP）には，設問が5つある250 〜 300語程度（まれに350語前後）の長文が毎回ひとつ含まれます。この5問付きSPは，すでに疲労している脳にさらに追い討ちをかけるかのようにダブルパッセージ（DP）の直前に登場します。ここで，長いパッセージの情報をすばやくかつ正確にとらえるスピードとタフさを身につけましょう。

トレーニングのため，全文を先に読んでから設問に答えるようにしてください。

API

11336 Route 244 North, Spearhead, South Dakota 57799

September 10

Ms.Crystal McCormick
100 Capital Avenue
Pierre, SD 56403

Dear Ms. McCormick:

I am writing on behalf of API to ask for your assistance in resolving a problem our company is experiencing, which concerns the State Transportation Bureau's plan to construct a barrier on Route 244 near our manufacturing facility. We have contacted the head of the bureau ourselves to ask him to reconsider the plan, but he has since denied our request. I have enclosed copies of both letters for your review.

The barrier is intended to prevent congestion caused by drivers waiting to make left turns into the API building complex from the southbound lane of Route 244. However, the barrier will force delivery trucks, commercial vehicles and factory employees to travel another 2 kilometers south to Delphi Avenue. They are then to be rerouted through the Forest Pines neighborhood and eventually onto an overpass to reverse direction, and head back north on Route 244. Beyond the unnecessary disturbance to residents, the extra driving distance, over time, will amount to a substantial waste of fuel. This runs counter to our ongoing companywide efforts to reduce energy consumption.

We are planning a follow-up letter to the bureau, in which we will offer to donate a strip of our property along Route 244 to allow for its expansion and the creation of a turning lane, eliminating the need for the barrier. We will also volunteer to cover the cost of installing a traffic signal, preventing any need for a traffic officer to be stationed at our intersection during peak traffic hours.

We would appreciate your contacting the State Transportation Bureau in regard to our offer. As a State Representative, your support could be the determining factor in persuading the bureau to adopt our proposal as an alternative to the aforementioned barrier.

Please do not hesitate to call me anytime should you wish to discuss this matter.

Sincerely,

Jeffery Glover
Jeffery Glover
President
API

11. Why was this letter written?

(A) To offer help for an upcoming campaign

(B) To inquire about a construction project

(C) To solicit support from a government official

(D) To explain a new company policy

Ⓐ Ⓑ Ⓒ Ⓓ

12. What is indicated about Forest Pines?

(A) Its residents will be inconvenienced by the Transportation Bureau's plan.

(B) It is a proposed real estate development along Route 244.

(C) Many API employees live in that neighborhood.

(D) API operates a manufacturing facility there.

Ⓐ Ⓑ Ⓒ Ⓓ

13. What is the purpose of the construction plan?

(A) To protect pedestrians on the sidewalk

(B) To facilitate the flow of traffic along Route 244

(C) To prevent unauthorized access into a building complex

(D) To protect a neighborhood from noise

Ⓐ Ⓑ Ⓒ Ⓓ

14. According to the letter, what is API prepared to do?

(A) Implement a new measure to reduce energy consumption

(B) Help hire an employee to direct traffic

(C) Cover the cost of any additional traffic signs

(D) Waive ownership of some real estate

Ⓐ Ⓑ Ⓒ Ⓓ

15. What does Mr. Glover want Ms. McCormick to do?

(A) Help persuade local residents to support his ideas

(B) Encourage the Transportation Bureau to make road repairs more promptly

(C) Convince the Transportation Bureau to accept API's suggestions

(D) Determine the cost of a proposed road construction project

Ⓐ Ⓑ Ⓒ Ⓓ

MEMORANDUM

From: Cassandra Tomlinson, Office Manager
To: All Staff
Date: Wednesday, March 14

As you are all aware, in the week immediately following the end of the fiscal year, Pettigrew Consolidated will transfer our headquarters to Granite Heights. As part of this move, inactive customer account files will be shipped to Docu-Depot, a storage facility in nearby Rutherford. Any business records or other important paper documents more than two years old will go into storage as well, except those relating to ongoing projects. A crew from Docu-Depot will arrive between 9 A.M. and 10 A.M. on Thursday, March 29 to collect these records and files. Therefore, we ask staff to have these items ready for pickup before the office closes at 6 P.M. the previous day.

Sorting and packing of documents and files will begin a week from today, when Docu-Depot will drop off some gray storage containers to be used exclusively for this purpose. At that time, each staff member will also be given a yellow plastic storage crate, in which active files and recent documents that must remain immediately accessible should be placed. These crates will be shipped to Granite Heights simultaneously with our furniture, machinery, office supplies and personal items. If a single crate is insufficient, please contact Anna Nowotny, who can provide you with as many as you need. Additional green recycling bins will be placed in each department for any unnecessary duplicates or other paperwork that no longer needs to be kept.

Furthermore, our IT technicians will begin disconnecting the computers and office equipment starting at 2 P.M. on Friday, March 30. All desks must be empty of any supplies and personal property by that time (cardboard boxes of various sizes and labels for itemizing contents are available in the supply room). Axis Transport will take everything to Granite Heights the following morning.

16. What is the purpose of the memo?

(A) To prepare for the transfer of supplies to a warehouse

(B) To notify staff of information security procedures

(C) To outline a plan for the relocation of an office

(D) To describe a method for dealing with old equipment

Ⓐ Ⓑ Ⓒ Ⓓ

17. What are office employees asked to do?

(A) Place all important paperwork into yellow plastic crates

(B) Make hard copies of computer files

(C) Ask Anna Nowotny for boxes to store personal belongings

(D) Determine whether certain documents can be disposed of

Ⓐ Ⓑ Ⓒ Ⓓ

18. What will Pettigrew Consolidated most likely do next Wednesday?

(A) Review its business records for accuracy

(B) Receive a delivery from Docu-Depot

(C) Acquire office furniture for its staff

(D) Open a new branch in Granite Heights

Ⓐ Ⓑ Ⓒ Ⓓ

19. When should Pettigrew employees have items ready for transport to Rutherford?

(A) March 28

(B) March 29

(C) March 30

(D) March 31

Ⓐ Ⓑ Ⓒ Ⓓ

20. What would most likely NOT be delivered by Axis Transport?

(A) Financial records accumulated over the past year

(B) Office computers that were purchased more than five years ago

(C) An employee's family photograph

(D) Files for customers who no longer use Pettigrew's service

Ⓐ Ⓑ Ⓒ Ⓓ

11-15 の設問は次の手紙に関するものです。（語数：303 語）

API

11336 ルート 244 ノース，スペアヘッド，サウスダコタ 57799

9 月 10 日

クリスタル・マコーミック様
100 キャピタル・アベニュー
ピエール，サウスダコタ 56403

マコーミック様

API 社を代表しまして，当社の抱える問題を解決するためのお力添えをいただきたくご連絡申し上げます。その問題とは，当社の製造施設付近にある 244 番線に防壁を建てるという州交通局の計画についてです。交通局長には直接連絡を取り，この計画について再検討していただくよう要請しましたが，その後当社の要望は拒否されました。その際に交わしたお互いの手紙のコピーを同封いたしますので，ご一読ください。

244 番線の南行き車線から API 社の施設に入るのにドライバーが左折待ちをすることで起こる渋滞を防ぐことが，この防壁の意図のようです。しかし，防壁ができれば，配送トラックや商品輸送車，そして工場従業員がデルファイ通りまでさらに 2 キロ南に進まなくてはならなくなります。そして，フォレスト・パインズ地区を通って経路を変更し，その後方向転換のために陸橋を渡って，244 番線を北向きに戻ることになります。本来なくていいはずの迷惑を地元住民にかけてしまうこともさることながら，運転距離が長くなることで，長期的にはかなりの燃料を浪費することになります。これは，当社全体で現在行っているエネルギー消費削減活動に逆行するものです。

現在，再度交通局に手紙を書き，防壁を建てる必要がないように 244 番線沿いにある当社の土地の一画を差し出し，244 番線を拡張して左折可能な車線を作るよう提案するつもりでおります。また，交通量のピーク時に交通整理官が交差点に立たなくて済むように，信号機の設置費用も当社で負担することを提案する予定です。

当社のこの申し出に関しまして，マコーミック様から州交通局にご連絡いただければ幸いです。州議会議員として，あなたのお力添えが，交通局を説得し，当社の提案を上記の防壁に代わる代替案として採択していただく決定要因になりえるからです。

この件に関しまして話し合いの機会をご希望であれば，いつでもお気軽にお電話ください。

敬具
ジェフリー・グローバー
API 社 社長

重要語句 □ State Transportation Bureau「州交通局」 □ barrier「防壁」 □ since「その後」(= after that) ※ここでは副詞として用いられている。 □ rerouted「行き先の変更を余儀なくされる」(= redirected) □ overpass「陸橋」 □ amount to ...「(合計で)に達する」(= total) □ run [go] counter to ...「〜に逆行する」(= be the opposite of ...) □ a strip of ...「(土地)の一画」(= a piece of ...; a plot of ...) □ allow for ...「〜を可能にする」(= make ... possible to happen) □ be stationed「駐留する, 配置に就く」 □ determining factor「決定要因」 □ aforementioned「前述の」 □ should you wish「ご希望であれば」※if you should wishの倒置形。 □ solicit「〜を募る」(= ask for ...) □ inconvenience「〜に迷惑をかける」(= cause inconvenience to ...) □ determine「〜を判断する, 見極める」(= find out ...; judge ...)

11
正解 ➤ (C)

この手紙が書かれた理由は何ですか。
(A) 今度のキャンペーン活動に対する支援を申し出るため
(B) 建設工事について問い合わせるため
(C) 役人から援助を募るため
(D) 会社の新しい方針について説明するため

正解 冒頭の I am writing on behalf of API to ask for your assistance から, 助けを求めている手紙であることは明白。さらに, 手紙の相手である Ms. McCormick に関して, 第 4 段落 2 文目で As a State Representative (州議会議員として) と述べていることから, これを government official と言い表した (C) が正解。誤答 (A) の upcoming campaign や (D) の new company policy については言及がない。(B) も問い合わせはしていないので不適切。

12
正解 ➤ (A)

フォレスト・パインズについて何が述べられていますか。
(A) 交通局の計画がそこの住民の迷惑になる。
(B) 不動産開発が予定されている 244 番線沿いの地区である。
(C) API 社の多くの従業員がその地域に住んでいる。
(D) API 社がそこで製造施設を運営している。

正解 Forest Pines という固有名詞が出てくる第 2 段落 3 文目に注目。交通局の計画の影響として, They (= delivery trucks, commercial vehicles and factory employees) are then to be rerouted through the Forest Pines neighborhood と述べ, さらに次の文で unnecessary disturbance to residents (住民にとって本来なくていいはずの迷惑だ) と表現していることから, (A) が正解。誤答 real estate development (不動産開発) の計画や, 従業員の住所については記述がないので, (B) と (C) はすぐ消去したい。Forest Pines は製造施設より 2 キロ先にある地区なので (D) も不適切。

13

建設計画の目的は何ですか。

(A) 歩道にいる歩行者を守ること

(B) 244 番線の交通の流れをスムーズにすること

(C) ビルに無許可で侵入するのを防ぐこと

(D) 近隣区域を騒音の被害から守ること

正解 construction plan とは，手紙のテーマになっている第 1 段落 1 文目の the State Transportation Bureau's plan to construct a barrier のこと。この barrier に関して，第 2 段落の冒頭で The barrier is intended to prevent congestion ... of Route 244. と目的が明示されているので，(B) が合致する。動詞 facilitate は「～を円滑にする」(= make *something* go smoothly)の意味。全体の文脈をあらかじめつかんでいれば，文書に戻らなくても解答できるはず。

14

この手紙によれば，API 社は何をする準備ができていますか。

(A) エネルギー消費削減策を新たに実施する

(B) 交通整理員を雇う手助けをする

(C) 追加で必要になる交通標識の費用をまかなう

(D) 土地の一部の所有権を放棄する

正解 API の今後の行動として，第 3 段落 1 文目で we will offer to donate a strip of our property along Route 244 と申し出ていることから，この内容を言い換えている (D) が適切。動詞 waive は「(権利など) を手放す」という意味で，waive fees（料金を免除する）の形でも頻出する。誤答 (A) の measure to reduce energy consumption は，第 2 段落最終文の ongoing からすでに行っているものであるとわかる。(C) は，第 3 段落 2 文目に cover the cost of installing a traffic signal（信号機の設置費用を負担する）と書かれているが，選択肢にある traffic signs は「交通標識」であることに注意。

15

グローバーさんはマコーミックさんに何をしてもらいたいですか。

(A) 地元の住民が彼の考えを支持するよう説得する

(B) 交通局が道路の修繕をもっと迅速に行うよう促す

(C) 交通局が API 社の提案を受け入れるよう説得する

(D) 予定されている道路建設工事の費用を見積もる

正解 第 4 段落冒頭に，We would appreciate your contacting the State Transportation Bureau という依頼表現がある。ここで，your support ... persuading the bureau to adopt our proposal（交通局に当社の提案を受け入れてもらう決定要因になる）と述べているので，これを言い換えた (C) が正解。convince [persuade] *someone* to do は「人を説得して～させる」という表現。誤答 local residents からの支持を得ることについては言及していないので，(A) は選べない。

16-20 の設問は次の社内連絡に関するものです。（語数：295 語）

連絡

差出人：カッサンドラ・トムリンソン 業務部長

宛先：全従業員

日付：3 月 14 日（水）

皆さんご存知のとおり，営業年度が終了する直後の週に，ペティグルー・コンソリデイティット社は本社をグラナイト・ハイツに移転する予定です。この移転作業の一環として，現在使われていない顧客情報ファイルを近くのラザーフォードにある倉庫会社のドキュ・ディーポに送ることになります。現在進行中のプロジェクトに関連するものを除き，2 年以上経過した業務記録やその他の重要文書もそこに保管されることになります。ドキュ・ディーポの作業員は，3 月 29 日（木）の午前 9 時から 10 時の間に，こうした記録やファイルの集荷に来る予定です。したがいまして，従業員の皆さんは，その前日の，オフィスが閉まる午後 6 時までに，これらの荷物を集荷できる準備を整えておいてください。

書類やファイルの分類・梱包作業は今日からちょうど一週間後に開始しますが，そのときにドキュ・ディーポの作業員がこれらの荷物専用として灰色の収納箱を届けにきます。また，各従業員に対して，プラスチック製の黄色い収納箱がそのときに 1 つずつ配布されます。すぐに見られるようにしておく必要がある使用中のファイルや最近使用した書類は，その箱の中に入れてください。これらの収納箱は，オフィス内の家具類や機器，オフィス用品や従業員私物と一緒にグラナイト・ハイツに配送する予定です。もし箱が 1 つで足りなければ，アナ・ノウォトニーさんに連絡して，必要な数だけもらってください。また，もう保存する必要のないコピーや書類を入れるのに，各部門に追加で緑色のリサイクルボックスを設置いたします。

さらに，3 月 30 日（金）の午後 2 時より，当社の IT 担当者がパソコンとオフィス機器の接続を外していきます。そのときまでには，どのデスクにも，オフィス用品や私物がないようにしておいてください（各種サイズの段ボール箱，および箱の中身を記入するためのラベルは備品室にあります）。その翌朝には，アクシス・トランスポートがすべての荷物をグラナイト・ハイツに配送する予定になっています。

重要語句 □ fiscal year「（決算の区切りとなる）営業年度」 □ as part of ...「～の一環として」 □ inactive「（文書などが）使用されていない」 □ a crew「作業員たち」※crew は作業員全員を指す集合名詞。作業員一人であれば a crew member となることに注意。 □ crate「（木製やプラスチック製の）箱」 □ simultaneously「同時に」（= at the same time; concurrently） □ duplicate「複製，コピー」（= copy） □ itemize「～を項目ごとに分ける」 □ hard copy「（プリントアウトした）コピー」

16

正解 ► (C)

この社内連絡の目的は何ですか。
(A) 日用品を倉庫に移す準備をすること
(B) スタッフに情報セキュリティの手順について通知すること
(C)オフィスの移転計画の概要を伝えること
(D) 古くなった機器の対処法を説明すること

正解 第1段落の冒頭でまず Pettigrew Consolidated will transfer our headquarters to Granite Heights と本社の移転について話し，それ以降の文章全体で従業員がすべきことについて述べていることから，(C) が正解と判断できる。誤答 (A) は，倉庫会社の Docu-Depot に移すのは documents のみなので不適切。(D) equipment は documents に置き換えれば正解になるので注意。Part 7 では，選択肢の細部の情報を読み違えて誤答を選んでしまうことが意外と多い。

17

正解 ► (D)

オフィスの従業員は何をするよう依頼されていますか。
(A) 重要書類をすべてプラスチック製の黄色い箱に入れること
(B) パソコン上のファイルをプリントアウトすること
(C) アナ・ノウォトニーに私物を保管するための箱をもらうこと
(D)ある特定の書類が処分できるかどうかを判断すること

正解 文書全体で細かい指示をしているので，各選択肢を慎重に検討していこう。第2段落最終文で必要のないコピーや書類を recycling bins に入れるよう促されていることから，(D) がこの内容の言い換えとして適切。誤答 (A) の yellow plastic crates に関しては2段落2文目で「すぐ必要な書類を入れる」とあるが，第1段落3文目にある important paper documents more than two years old については第2段落冒頭で gray storage container に入れる指示があるので，(A) を消去する。(B) の hard copies（プリントアウトしたコピー）については触れられていない。(C) の Anna Nowotny は書類を入れる crate をくれる人物であり，私物については第3段落2文目で cardboard boxes ... are available in the supply room と述べているので，これも合致しない。

18

両文参照型

正解 ► (B)

ペティグルー・コンソリデイティット社は来週水曜日に何をすると思われますか。
(A) 業務記録が正しいかどうかを確認する
(B) ドキュ・ディーポが届ける物を受け取る
(C) 従業員が使用するオフィス家具を購入する
(D) グラナイト・ハイツに新しく支社をオープンする

正解 社内連絡の日付が Wednesday, March 14 なので，来週水曜日は第2段落冒頭にある a week from today のこと。この文で Docu-Depot will drop off some gray storage containers とあることから，(B) が正しいことを見極める。誤答 同じ文に Sorting and packing of documents とあるので，(A) は for accuracy の部分がなければ正解になることに注意。

ペティグルー社の従業員は，ラザーフォードに荷物を運ぶ準備をいつ整える必要がありますか。

(A) 3 月 28 日
(B) 3 月 29 日
(C) 3 月 30 日
(D) 3 月 31 日

正解 第 1 段落 2 文目から，Rutherford は Docu-Depot のある場所であることをまずおさえる。こ
こで，同段落 4 文目に A crew from Docu-Depot ... March 29 と作業員が荷物を取りに来る日
を述べ，さらに準備を整えるタイミングとして，次の文に before the office closes at 6 P.M. the
previous day.（その前日のオフィスが閉まる午後 6 時までに）とあることから，(A) March 28 が適
切。誤答 (C) は，第 3 段落 1 文目にパソコンやオフィス機器を外す日付として登場する。(D) は最
終文の Axis Transport will ... the following morning. の部分から，Granite Heights に荷物を運ぶ
日であることがわかる。

アクシス・トランスポート社によって配送されないと思われるものはどれですか。
(A) 過去一年間にとった財務記録
(B) 5 年以上前に購入したオフィス用パソコン
(C) 従業員の家族写真
(D) ペティグルー社のサービスをもう利用していない顧客のファイル

誤答 NOT 問題は消去法が基本。Axis Transport が本社に荷物を送る業者であることを最終文でお
さえたら，各選択肢を落ち着いて検討する。(A) は，第 1 段落 3 文目で Docu-Depot に送るものと
して挙げられている business records ... more than two years old に該当しないので，本社に送
られるもの。(B) と (C) は，第 2 段落 3 文目の These crates（= yellow plastic storage crates）
will be shipped ... office supplies and personal items. に該当するので，同じく本社に配送される。
正解 (D) は，第 1 段落 2 文目にある inactive customer account files（使われていない顧客情報ファ
イル）に該当し，その後ろで will be shipped to Docu-Depot と述べているので，これだけが本社
に送られないものであるとわかる。

「記事」を恐れない

　多くの受験者が苦手意識を感じるのは「記事」問題です。記事は，シングルパッセージに1題前後出題され，使われる語彙レベルもやや高めです。また，記事は2段組の場合がほとんどで，慣れていないとレイアウト的にも読みづらさを感じます。ただ，問題自体はシンプルな場合もあるので，必要以上に記事を恐れることはありません。日頃から英字新聞などを読み，記事に対する苦手意識をなくしておくことが大切です。ここでは，長い記事問題を2題続けて解くことで，苦手意識を払拭しましょう。

Questions 21-25 refer to the following article.　⏱ 制限時間：2セット　12分

While other companies are cutting jobs in order to survive in the current economic climate, the circumstances differ substantially at the Santa Brenda based firm Turner Rigby. Employees play video game consoles in the company break room, whose cabinets are stuffed with free candy, soda and snacks. Furthermore, when sales quotas are surpassed, staffers are treated to cruises and flights to exotic locales.

According to company president Andrew Purdell, these types of perks are commonplace in other high-tech firms throughout the country. Mr. Purdell contends that because the company relies on intelligent programmers who are in high demand throughout the industry, it is a necessity to keep them content in order to retain them. Turnover at the firm is well below eight percent annually.

Turner Rigby is one of myriad small tech firms in the city, although most residents are not familiar with it. Leaders of area tech firms feel the city needs to do more to draw attention to the industry in order to attract talented university graduates as well as venture capitalists to invest in these small yet growing companies.

Turner Rigby creates software for saving and storing digital images, primarily for saving scanned paper documents as computer files. The company recently devised an application that erases unwanted marks from documents such as those left by staples and punched holes in the original paper versions. From January, the company will initiate work on a follow-up to its commercially successful suite of office software.

Mr. Purdell and some colleagues founded the firm as Turner Imaging twelve years ago and purchased a competing firm called Rigby Technologies eight years ago, merging the two names. Sales dropped last year with the economic downturn, but the firm has yet to lose money in any individual year. A recent rebound has led company directors to forecast total revenues approaching $38 million this year.

21. According to the article, why does Turner Rigby allow employees to use video game consoles?

(A) To make employees more productive while working

(B) To update employees on recent advances in computer technology

(C) To keep employees motivated to work for the company for a long time

(D) To test sample products that are created by the company

22. What is indicated about Santa Brenda?

(A) Many of its residents have benefited from the service Turner Rigby provides.

(B) A majority of its citizens are employed in the technology field.

(C) Quite a few university students in the city are interested in working for technology firms.

(D) A variety of technology companies are situated in the city.

23. According to the article, what has Turner Rigby developed?

(A) A machine that removes staples from paper documents

(B) Software for scanning oversized documents

(C) A device that modifies and prints digital images

(D) A set of computer programs for business purposes

24. What can be understood about Rigby Technologies?

(A) It was founded by Andrew Purdell.

(B) It was located outside of Santa Barbara.

(C) It purchased a competitor eight years ago.

(D) It was formerly a rival of Turner Imaging.

Ⓐ Ⓑ Ⓒ Ⓓ

25. What is NOT indicated about Turner Rigby?

(A) It provides vacation travel to employees when they exceed sales targets.

(B) The number of employees who leave the company has remained low.

(C) It has been officially recognized for technological innovation.

(D) It is expected to earn more money this year than last year.

Ⓐ Ⓑ Ⓒ Ⓓ

With two of the city's three public libraries scheduled to close next month, there is growing concern that residents of the suburbs, especially the elderly, will have difficulty accessing books. Although the library downtown will be unaffected, the council's decision is expected to deter some from using its services due to the distances and costs involved in traveling there.

The Collette Beamish Foundation announced yesterday that it is planning to combat this problem by providing a mobile library service. The foundation plans to use a converted truck to take books to both the outskirts of the city and the outlying villages. Dubbed the "Book Bus," this vehicle will house a collection generously contributed by the city council. Patrons of the new service will be able to use an inter-library loan system, which will allow them to order books stocked by any of the other lending facilities in the state. A local commercial vehicle dealership, Wheel Good, has already agreed to donate a truck to the program. Michelle Trenchfoot, the project leader and the manager at one of the two facilities slated for closure, said yesterday, "We already have people offering their time to drive the vehicle for us. However, we will still need funds to cover the day-to-day expenses of operating the program."

On the other hand, the news has done little to alleviate the disappointment felt by some citizens. Travis Jackson, newly elected leader of the Drabton Citizens Association, said on local radio, "The council's decision is simply unacceptable. A city the size of Drabton needs more than one library. Once you factor in the people living in the surrounding villages, one facility will be providing a service to over 100,000 people. The mobile service is of course welcome, but the city council should not make decisions like this without consulting the public."

The foundation is planning a series of fundraising events over the next few months, starting with a book fair to be held at Drabton Municipal Hall next Saturday, November 17. Admission is $2, and the event will feature readings by local poet Brian Norris. Full details can be found at www.collettebeamish. co.wa.

26. What can be understood from the article?

(A) A new bus service will operate between downtown and the surrounding villages.

(B) All public libraries within the city are scheduled to shut down.

(C) The library in the city center will remain open to the public.

(D) Area libraries are used mainly by elderly people.

Ⓐ Ⓑ Ⓒ Ⓓ

27. Who is Michelle Trenchfoot?

(A) The head of the Collette Beamish Foundation

(B) An employee at a public library

(C) The owner of an automobile dealership

(D) A member of the city council

Ⓐ Ⓑ Ⓒ Ⓓ

28. How will money raised by the Collette Beamish Foundation most likely be used?

(A) To purchase a new vehicle

(B) To advertise for drivers

(C) To acquire books for the project

(D) To pay fuel and maintenance costs

Ⓐ Ⓑ Ⓒ Ⓓ

29. What is indicated about Travis Jackson?

(A) He is opposed to the Collette Beamish Foundation's plan.

(B) He works as a presenter on a local radio station.

(C) He believes that city officials should have spoken to residents.

(D) He recently relocated to the area.

Ⓐ Ⓑ Ⓒ Ⓓ

30. According to the article, what will happen in December?

(A) A book fair will be held.

(B) Some new library services will be introduced.

(C) Some public institutions will be closed.

(D) A new Web site will be launched.

Ⓐ Ⓑ Ⓒ Ⓓ

21-25 の設問は次の記事に関するものです。（語数：310 語）

他の会社が現在の経済状況の中生き残りをかけて人員削減を実施している一方で，サンタ・ブレンダに拠点を置くターナー・リグビー社の状況は著しく異なっているようだ。従業員は会社の休憩室でゲーム機で遊び，休憩室は無料のキャンディや炭酸飲料・お菓子でいっぱいになっている。さらには，販売ノルマを上回った場合，従業員は異国情緒あふれる地へ船や飛行機で旅行に行くことができる。

社長のアンドレ・バーデル氏によれば，こうした手当は，国内の他のハイテク企業では一般的なようだ。バーデル氏は，社が業界で需要の高い聡明なプログラマーに頼っているため，彼らを会社に留めておくために満足度を維持させる必要があると主張する。会社の離職率は，毎年 8 パーセントをはるかに下回るという。

ターナー・リグビー社は，市内に数え切れないほどあるハイテク小企業のうちのひとつだが，市民のほとんどは同社についてよく知らないという。地元のハイテク企業のトップたちは，才能ある大卒者や，こうした小さいながらも成長を遂げている会社に投資してくれる投資家を引き寄せるためにも，この業界を市がもっとアピールする必要があると感じている。

ターナー・リグビー社はデジタル画像を保存・記録するソフトを製造しており，主に読み込んだ紙の文書をパソコンファイルに保存するものだ。同社は近年，読み込んだ文書から，もとの原稿にあるホッチキスやパンチ穴によって付いてしまう不要な点を消すことのできるソフトを開発した。また，同社は 1 月から，高い売上を誇ったオフィス用ソフトの後継版の開発に着手する予定だ。

バーデル氏は 12 年前に，同僚とともにターナー・イメージング社の名称で会社を設立した後，競合会社のリグビー・テクノロジズ社を 8 年前に買収し，両社の名称を組み合わせた。会社の売上は経済の低迷とともに昨年落ち込んだが，今までどの年も赤字になったことはない。最近売上が回復していることを受け，取締役会は，今年の総収益はほぼ 3800 万ドルに達するだろうと予測している。

重要語句　□ stuffed with ...「～でいっぱいになっている」（= filled with ...）　□ quota「ノルマ」　□ surpass「～を上回る」（= exceed; go beyond ...）　□ staffer「従業員」（= staff member）　□ treat *someone* to ...「人を～でもてなす」　□ locale「場所」（= place）　□ perks「手当，特典」（= benefits）　□ contend that SV「～であると主張する」（= argue that SV）　□ content「満足している」（= satisfied）　□ well below ...「～をはるかに下回って」　□ myriad「数え切れないほどの」（= very many; countless）　□ draw attention to ...「～に注目を向けさせる」（= call attention to ...; make people notice ...）　□ venture capitalist「（ベンチャー企業に投資する）投資家」　□ yet「それでも」（= but）　□ primarily「主に」（= mainly; mostly; predominantly）　□ devise「～を開発する」（= create; invent）　□ initiate「～を開始する」（= start）　□ a suite of ...「一揃えの～」（= a set of ...）※a suite of software または a software suite は「さまざまな用途のソフトウェアがセットになった製品」を指す。　□ merge「～を組み合わせる」（= combine）　□ have yet to *do* ...「まだ～していない」（= have not yet *done* ...）

21

この記事によれば，ターナー・リグビー社はなぜ従業員がゲーム機を使えるようにしているのですか。

(A) 勤務中の従業員の生産性を高めるため

(B) 従業員にコンピュータ技術の最近の進歩を伝えるため

(C) 従業員が会社に長く働く意欲を保つため

(D) 会社が製造するサンプル製品を試すため

正解 Tuner Rigby 社に関して，第 1 段落 2 文目で Employees play video game consoles in the company break room と述べているのを受け，第 2 段落 2 文目ではその理由として it is a necessity to keep them（= programmers）content in order to retain them（プログラマーを会社に留めるには満足度を維持させる必要がある）という社長（Mr. Purdell）の主張が紹介されていることから，(C) が一致する。次の文にある turnover（離職率）もテーマをつかむ重要なキーワード。他の選択肢はいずれもこのテーマに関連していないので，すばやくかつ確実に正解したい。

22

サンタ・ブレンダ市に関して何が述べられていますか。

(A) 住民の多くがターナー・リグビー社の提供するサービスに恩恵を受けてきた。

(B) 市民のほとんどがテクノロジーの分野で働いている。

(C) 市内のかなりの大学生がハイテク企業で働くことに関心がある。

(D) さまざまなハイテク企業が市内にある。

正解 Santa Brenda は，第 1 段落冒頭文の the Santa Brenda based firm Turner Rigby から，Turner Rigby の所在地であることをおさえる。さらに，第 3 段落冒頭文で Turner Rigby is one of myriad（= very many）small tech firms in the city とあることから，この情報を言い換えた (D) を選ぶ。**誤答** (C) の quite a few（かなり多くの= many）を only a few（ごくわずかの）と混同しないように注意。

23

記事によると，ターナー・リグビー社は最近何を開発しましたか。

(A) 紙の文書からホッチキスの針を取り外す機械

(B) サイズが規定以上の書類を読み込むソフト

(C) デジタル画像を修正・印刷する機器

(D) ビジネス目的のパソコンプログラム一式

正解 Turner Rigby の開発製品に関しての記述があるのは第 4 段落全体。その最終文で a follow-up to its commercially successful suite of office software（よく売れたオフィス用ソフト一式の後継版）の開発に着手する予定とあることから，suite of office software をすでに開発していることがわかるので，(D) が正解。**誤答** (C) は，段落中に「読み込んだ文書から不要なマークを消すソフトを開発した」とはあるが，print（印刷）もできるわけではない。

リグビー・テクノロジズ社に関して何がわかりますか。

(A) アンドリュー・パーデルによって設立された。

(B) サンタ・バーバラ市外にあった。

(C) 8年前に競合会社を買収した。

(D) かつてターナー・イメジング社の競合会社だった。

正解 Rigby Technologies の名称は第5段落に登場する。冒頭で，Mr. Purdell and some colleagues founded the firm as Turner Imaging twelve years ago（パーデル氏と同僚がターナー・イメジングを12年前に設立した）と purchased a competing firm called Rigby Technologies eight years ago（8年前にリグビー・テクノロジズという競合会社を買収した）というふたつの情報を合致させ，両社が競合会社だったと述べている (D) を選ぶ。誤答 (A) は，Andrew Purdell が設立したのは Turner Imaging 社であることに注意。Part 7 ではこのように，類似した会社名や人名を複数登場させ，受験者の混乱を誘う設問がときどき登場する。

ターナー・リグビー社に関して何が述べられていませんか。

(A) 販売目標を上回った場合，会社は従業員を旅行に連れて行く。

(B) 会社をやめる従業員の数は低いままだ。

(C) 斬新な技術に関して受賞歴がある。

(D) 今年は去年よりも売上が高くなると見込まれている。

誤答 (A) は第1段落最終文の when sales quotas are surpassed, staffers are treated to cruises and flights to exotic locales と，(B) は，第2段落最終文の Turnover at the firm is well below eight percent annually. とそれぞれ情報が一致している。(D) は，第5段落3文目で Sales dropped last year とあり，次の文で A recent rebound ... approaching a $38 million this year. と売上が回復していることが述べられているので，これも本文の内容に合う。正解 (C) の受賞歴に関する記述はどこにもないので，これが正解。NOT 問題では，「述べられている」選択肢を誤って選んでしまうことがよくあるので注意しよう。

26-30 の設問は次の記事に関するものです。（語数：355 語）

市の 3 つの公立図書館のうち 2 つが来月閉館する予定であるため，郊外に住む市民，特に高齢者がなかなか図書館の本を利用できなくなるという懸念が高まっている。市の中心部にある図書館は従来どおり開館するが，今回の市議会の決定により，図書館まで行く距離と費用を考慮して図書館サービスの利用を思いとどまる人もいるだろう。

昨日，コレット・ビーミッシュ財団は，移動図書館のサービスを提供することによってこの問題に対処しようとしていることを発表した。当財団はトラックを図書館に改造して，市の郊外や市の中心部から離れた村に本を届けることを計画している。「ブック・バス」と呼ばれるこのトラックには，市議会から寄付された本が搭載される。また，この新しいサービスでは図書館相互貸出システムを利用でき，これによって州内にあるほかのどの貸出図書館に収蔵されている本も注文できるようになる。地元の営業車の販売代理店であるウィール・グッド社は，すでにこのプログラムのためにトラックを一台寄付することに同意している。このプロジェクトのリーダーであり，閉館予定の 2 つの図書館のうち 1 つの図書館の館長であるミシェル・トレンチフット氏は，「私達のために車を運転してくれるボランティアの方々はすでに集まりましたが，このプログラムを日々運営していく費用を賄う資金がまだ必要なのです」と昨日語った。

一方で，この知らせは，一部の市民の落胆を軽減することにはほとんどつながっていない。ドラブトン市民協会会長として新しく選出されたトラビス・ジャクソン氏は，地元のラジオ番組の中で，「市議会の決断はとうてい受け入れ難いものです。ドラブトンほど規模のある市には，2 つ以上の図書館は必要です。周辺の村に住む人たちを計算に入れれば，ひとつの図書館が 10 万人以上もの人たちにサービスを提供することになるのです。移動図書館サービスは確かに歓迎できるものですが，市議会は一般市民から意見を聞くことなく今回のような決断をすべきではありません」と述べた。

コレット・ビーミッシュ財団は，今後数か月にわたって一連の資金集めのイベントを計画しており，最初のイベントは来週 11 月 17 日（土）にドラブトン公会堂で開催されるブックフェアである。入場料は 2 ドルで，イベントでは地元の詩人ブライアン・ノリスによる朗読会が催される。詳細は www.collettebeamish.co.wa に掲載されている。

重要語句 □ With two（of the city's three public libraries）scheduled to close next month《with ＋名詞＋過去分詞（名詞が〜されて）》という付帯状況 with の構文。deter *A* from *doing B*「A が B するのを思いとどまらせる」（＝ discourage） □ converted truck「改造トラック」 □ the outskirts of ...「〜の外れ」 □ outlying「中心地から離れた」（＝ far from the center） □ dubbed「ニックネームの付いた」（＝ named） □ lending facilities「貸出施設」※ ここでは libraries のこと。 □ slated for ...「〜が予定されている」（＝ planned for ...） □ alleviate「〜を軽減する」 □ factor in ...「〜を計算に入れる」（＝ take ... into account）

179

26

この記事から何がわかりますか。

(A) バスの新しい便が，市の中心部と周辺の村との間を運行する予定である。

(B) 市内のすべての公立図書館が閉館する予定である。

(C) 市の中心部にある図書館は，今までどおり一般の人が利用できる。

(D) 地域の図書館は主に高齢者によって利用されている。

正解 記事全体に関する設問なので，選択肢をひとつひとつ慎重に検討する。第1段落冒頭に With two of the city's three public libraries scheduled to close とあるのに対し，次の文で the library downtown will be unaffected（中心部の図書館は影響を受けない〔＝そのまま開館する〕）と述べているので，(C) が正解。**誤答** (A) は，第2段落3文目に "Book Bus" の記述はあるが，これは mobile library service に使用されるトラックの名称なので不適切。(D) は，第1段落冒頭文で especially the elderly, will have difficulty accessing books とはあるが，利用者の大半が elderly people であることの根拠にはならない。

27

ミシェル・トレンチフットさんはどんな人物ですか。

(A) コレット・ビーミッシュ財団の会長

(B) 公立図書館の職員

(C) 自動車の販売代理店のオーナー

(D) 市議会議員

正解 Michelle Trenchfoot の名前が登場する第2段落6文目に，the project leader and the manager at one of the two facilities slated for closure とある。ここで，第1段落冒頭の文脈から，facilities は public libraries のことだと判断し，(B) を選択する。「給与を得て働く人」であれば manager でも employee（＝ worker）と表現できることをおさえよう。**誤答** あくまでこの project のリーダーであるだけなので，(A) は選べないことに注意。

28

コレット・ビーミッシュ財団が集めた資金は何のために利用されると思われますか。

(A) 新しい車を購入するため

(B) 運転手の募集をするため

(C) プロジェクトに用いる本を入手するため

(D) 燃料費や維持費の支払いに充てるため

正解 第2段落後半にある Michelle Trenchfoot の発言内容に着目。最終文で「day-to-day expenses（日々かかる経費）をまかなう資金が必要だ」と資金の用途を説明していることから，day-to-day expenses と見なせる (D) を選ぶ。**誤答** (A) は，同段落5文目の A local commercial vehicle dealership ... donate a truck to the program. と，(B) は6文目の We already have people ... to drive the vehicle for us. と，(C) は3文目の this vehicle will house a collection (of

books）generously contributed by the city council と合わない。most likely を含む設問は，答え
が直接的に述べられないので，ほかの選択肢が不正解である根拠を，必ず本文から突き止めよう。

29　　　　　　　　　　　　　　　　　　　　　　　　正解 ➤ (C)

トラビス・ジャクソンに関して何が述べられていますか。
(A) コレット・ビーミッシュ財団の計画に反対している。
(B) 地元のラジオ局のパーソナリティを務めている。
(C) 市が住民と話をすべきだったと考えている。
(D) 最近この地域に引っ越してきた。

正解　Travis Jackson の話は第 3 段落に登場する。彼の発言の最後にある the city council should
not ... consulting the public（一般市民から意見を聞くことなく決断すべきではない）という部分
と内容の一致する (C) が正解。誤答 彼は，the council's decision（to close libraries）には反対し
ているが，Collete Beamish 財団の「移動図書館サービス」については of course welcome と述べ
ているので，(A) は不適切。

30　　　　　　　　　　　　　　　　　　　　　　　　正解 ➤ (C)

この記事によれば，12 月に何が起こりますか。
(A) ブックフェアが開催される。
(B) 新しい図書館のサービスが導入される。
(C) いくつかの公共施設が閉鎖になる。
(D) 新しいウェブサイトが開設される。

正解　第 4 段落にある next Saturday, November 17 に着目し，December が来月であることを
おさえる。ここで，記事の冒頭に With two of the ... public libraries scheduled to close next
moth とあることを確認し，(C) を選択する。誤答 (A) は最終段落で「資金集めのイベントのひとつ
が November 17 の book fair だ」とあるだけで，来月も同じ book fair があるとは述べていない。

　全文読んでいるとどうしても時間が足りなくなる場合や，疲れて内容が頭に入らなくなる場合は，段落の冒頭部分のみ先に読んでいく「パラグラフリーディング」をオススメします。英語では，文書全体の主旨は第1段落にあり，各段落の主旨はその段落の冒頭部分にあるのが普通です。したがって，その部分を先に読むことにより，文書全体のテーマをすばやくつかむことができ，かつ時間や体力を節約できます。具体的には，第1段落はすべて読み，第2段落以降は主旨がつかめるまで読んで次の段落に進むようにします。

例　Questions 26-30 の記事の問題

第1段落

With two of the city's three public libraries scheduled to close next month, there is growing concern that residents of the suburbs, especially the elderly, will have difficulty accessing books. Although the library downtown will be unaffected, the council's decision is expected to deter some from using its services due to the distances and costs involved in traveling there.

[主旨]　ダウンタウンの図書館を除く公立図書館が来月閉館されるため，本を利用しづらくなるという懸念が高まっている。▶問題提起

第2段落

The Collette Beamish Foundation announced yesterday that it is planning to combat this problem by providing a mobile library service. The foundation plans to use a converted truck to take books to both the outskirts of the city and the outlying villages.

[主旨]　The Collette Beamish Foundation は移動図書館サービスを開始し，郊外に本を届ける計画だ。▶解決策

第３段落

On the other hand, the news has done little to alleviate the disappointment felt by some citizens. Travis Jackson, newly elected leader of the Drabton Citizens Association, said on local radio, "The council's decision is simply unacceptable. A city the size of Drabton needs more than one library.

[主旨]　Drabton Citizens Association の代表者 Travis Jackson は，移動図書館サービスが開始されても問題解決にはならず，図書館を閉館するという市議会の決断がそもそも受け入れられないものだと述べる。▶さらなる問題提起

第４段落

The foundation is planning a series of fundraising events over the next few months, starting with a book fair to be held at Drabton Municipal Hall next Saturday, November 17.

[主旨]　The Collette Beamish Foundation は今後資金集めのイベントを行っていく予定だ。▶今後の予定

　ただし，先に読み飛ばす部分が多ければ多いほど，重要な情報を見逃す可能性も高まります。満点を取るのに必要なのは，全文をしっかり読んでも時間内に解き終わるリーディング力です。日頃から多読を習慣にして，長い文章を読み続ける体力を身につけておいてください。

990 点への道のり

　私がはじめて TOEIC に出会ったのは，大学一年生の夏です。偶然立ち寄った本屋で TOEIC の問題集を目にした私は，こう直感しました。「TOEIC は英語圏での生活をテストにしているから，これを極めれば英語が使えるようになる！」と。この妄想（？）に浸りながら，まずは 730 点対策本を一式買い揃えました。そして帰宅後，受験日を決め，当日までに行うべきタスクをスケジュール帳に書き出しました。予定通りこなせば目標に届くと信じ，最初に受けた TOEIC では，目標スコアを上回る 765 点（L350 点，R415 点）でした。

　目標をクリアすることにゲーム感覚を覚え，半年後に受けた TOEIC ではさらに 840 点（LR ともに 420 点）に跳ね上がりました。しかし，その後は 15 点しかアップせず，また，スコアの割に英語を「使えない」自分に危機感を感じ始めました。そこで，ネイティブ並みに英語が使える自分をイメージしながら，日常生活をできるかぎり英語モードに切り替えました。具体的には，洋書や英字新聞を読む，海外ニュースを聴く，英会話のスクリプトを音読して丸ごと暗記する，などです。気づいた頃には英語で日記をつけるようになり，夢も英語で見るようになりました。バンクーバーの留学中は，授業以外にボランティアをして会話の機会を増やしたり，トーストマスターズ・クラブ（スピーチを訓練する団体）に入ってネイティブの前で即興スピーチをしたりと，できることはなんでもしました。留学生活も終わりに近づいた頃，現地にあった TOEIC 模試を解きあさって弱点を埋め，帰国直前に 970 点（L495 点，R475 点），帰国後に 990 点をとりました。

　方法論はわかっていても，なかなか実行に移せない方は多いと思います。私が常に追求したのは，「何をすれば楽しいか」です。どれほど効果的に見える勉強法でも，楽しくなければ続かず，自分にとっての価値はありません。楽しさを追求すれば，英語を使うチャンスにも自然とめぐり合えます。

　山頂への道のりは人それぞれ違います。自分の心を信じて，突き進んでください。

Believe and follow the compass of your heart ...
（Tokyo Disney Sea Sinbad's Storybook Voyage より）

ダブルパッセージも「全文先読み」が基本

ダブルパッセージには，上下2つの文書の情報を組み合わせて正解を導き出す「両文書参照型」（クロスリファレンス型）の問題が，1セットに1〜2問（まれに3問）含まれています。正解に必要な複数の情報を逃さないためには，両文書ともに全部読むことが不可欠です。ただ，文章が長い場合は，先にすべて一気読みするとかなり疲労し，内容が頭に入らないケースもあります。したがって，上の文書は全文先読みし，下の文書も短ければ先にすべて読む，長ければ「パラグラフリーディング」で主旨だけは先につかんでおく，などと必要に応じてストラテジーを切り替えてもよいと思います。「両文書参照型」を確実に正解するためには，どのみち全文読まなくてはならないので，「時間がないから読みとばして解く」ことだけは絶対に避けるようにしましょう。

Questions 31-35 refer to the following e-mail and excerpt from a magazine.

E-Mail Message

From: lynda@powernet.com
To: customerservices@slumberwellhotels.com
Date: October 2
Subject: My recent stay at Slumberwell

To whom it may concern,

I want to start by saying that I generally enjoyed my stay at the newest Slumberwell branch in the city of Henderson on September 20. However, while reviewing my invoice, I noticed a discrepancy between the advertised room rate and the actual price I was charged. In your advertisement, you quoted a price of $105 per night, but I was charged a rate of $145 per night for my standard room. Please find attached the scanned copy of the bill.

Additionally, there were some other aspects of my stay that fell short of my expectations, compared to the usual high level of service at Slumberwell. Your janitorial crew did not seem to do an adequate job with my room. More disturbingly though, I also seem to have been billed for having an Internet connection I never used.

Thanks for your attention to this matter. Please note that I have completed and returned the feedback form I was previously sent along with this e-mail.

Best regards,
Lynda Mellors

Letter from the Editor

Dear Customer:

Welcome to the November edition of *Getaway*, the magazine for Slumberwell Gold Club members. Inside this month's issue, you will find a feature on our most recently opened branch, which features a fitness center with a sauna, a business center with a full range of office equipment, and in-room Internet availability. You will find stunning pictures and in-depth interviews with the staff on pages 60-67. Also in this issue is a look into the workings of our main office in Gilbert, Arizona, and a report on the nightlife around our Spokane branch.

It has been brought to our attention that the special offer advertised in last month's issue of our member's magazine could be misleading. We regret any misunderstanding and would like to take this opportunity to clarify the situation.

The special offer celebrates the tenth anniversary of the opening of our first branch in Bakersfield, and is valid at any of our establishments. The offer only applies to stays between September 4 and December 16, and suites and junior suites are not part of the promotion. The offer is only good for stays on weekdays and may not be used for weekends, when all rooms are offered at our regular rates.

Finally, with cold weather just around the corner, we are pleased to be able to announce this year's winter breakfast specials. Details and photographs of these dishes can be found on pages 21-24.

31. What does Ms. Mellors indicate about her experience at the hotel?

(A) She was charged a cancellation fee for a certain service.

(B) The hotel staff did not respond to her requests in a timely manner.

(C) She received unsatisfactory cleaning service.

(D) The information provided on the hotel's Web site was inaccurate.

Ⓐ Ⓑ Ⓒ Ⓓ

32. What is attached to the e-mail?

(A) A customer satisfaction survey

(B) An itemized list of all the hotel services and rates

(C) A copy of a hotel advertisement

(D) A proof of club membership

Ⓐ Ⓑ Ⓒ Ⓓ

33. What can be understood about Ms. Mellors?

(A) She claimed a discount at a location where it did not apply.

(B) She tried to seek a special offer after it had ended.

(C) She visited the hotel on a weekend in September.

(D) She booked a type of room that was not covered by the offer.

Ⓐ Ⓑ Ⓒ Ⓓ

34. What is NOT listed as a feature of the November issue of *Getaway*?

(A) A photo of a company's branch

(B) A preview of seasonal offerings

(C) A promotion for a special rate

(D) A description of entertainment options in a city

Ⓐ Ⓑ Ⓒ Ⓓ

35. What is available at the hotel's branch in Henderson?

(A) Laundry service

(B) Free Internet access

(C) A conference room

(D) Exercise facilities

Ⓐ Ⓑ Ⓒ Ⓓ

31-35 番は次のメールと記事の一部に関するものです。(語数:163 語+ 235 語)

差出人:lynda@powernet.com
宛先:customerservices@slumberwellhotels.com
日付:10 月 2 日
件名:スランバーウェルでの最近の宿泊

ご担当者様

ヘンダーソン市にあるもっとも新しいスランバーウェルホテルの支店に 9 月 20 日に宿泊し、概して楽しい時間を過ごせたことをまず申し上げたいと思います。もっとも、請求書をチェックしたところ、広告に掲載されていた室料と実際の請求額が異なることに気付きました。貴社の広告では、1 泊当たりの室料は 105 ドルと掲載されていましたが、私はスタンダードルームの料金として 1 泊当たり 145 ドルを請求されました。請求書をスキャンしたものを添付いたしましたのでご確認ください。

また、スランバーウェルホテルで通常提供される高いサービスの質を考えると期待外れであった点がほかにもいくつかありました。清掃スタッフは、私の宿泊した部屋を適切に掃除していないようでした。ただ、さらに困惑したのは、私が一度も利用していないインターネット接続の料金も請求されていたことです。

この件につき、ご確認いただければと思います。以前送られてきたアンケートに記入し、このメールに添付して返送いたしましたので、ご確認ください。
敬具
リンダ・メローズ

編集長より

お客様各位:
スランバーウェルゴールド・クラブ会員様向けの雑誌『ゲッタウェイ』の 11 月号をお読みいただき、ありがとうございます。今月号では、当社のもっとも新しくオープンしたホテルを特集しています。このホテルには、サウナ付きのフィットネスセンター、そしてあらゆるオフィス機器を備えたビジネスセンターがあり、客室内にはインターネットの使用環境が整っております。60-67 ページにはすばらしい写真とスタッフの詳しいインタビュー記事が掲載されています。また、今月号には、アリゾナ州ギルバートにある本社がどのように運営されているかに関する記事や、スポンケインにある当社のホテル周辺のナイトライフについてのレポートも掲載されています。

この会員様向けの雑誌の先月号に掲載されていた特別割引に関する広告において、誤解を招く可能性のある記載があった旨の指摘がありました。誤解を招いてしまったことをお詫びいたしますとともに、この機会を利用してご説明したいと思います。

この特別割引は当社が最初に開設したベイカーズフィールドのホテルの 10 周年を記念したもので、当社のどの支店においてもご利用いただけます。この割引は、9 月 4 日から 12 月 16 日までのご宿泊にのみ適用され、スイートルームおよびジュニアスイートルームは適用外となります。また、この特別割引は平日のご宿泊のみを対象とするもので、全客室が通常料金となります週末にはご利用いただけません。

最後になりましたが、もうすぐ寒くなるこの時期に、今年の冬の特別朝食メニューついてお知らせできることをうれしく思います。朝食メニューに関する詳細および料理の写真が 21-24 ページに掲載されていますのでご覧ください。

□ discrepancy「食い違い，不一致」（= difference; inconsistency）　□ quote a price「価格を提示する」　□ fall short of ...「〜に及ばない」（= fail to meet or reach）　□ janitorial crew「清掃スタッフ」※「清掃員」を意味する名詞 janitor から派生した表現。　□ stunning「驚くほど見事な」（= very impressive）　□ in-depth「徹底的な，深く掘り下げた」（= detailed; through）　□ workings「運営」　□ bring ... to *one's* attention「〜を（人）に知らせる」※It has been brought to *one's* attention that SV（〜という報告があった）の形でよく用いられる。　□ misleading「誤解を招きうる」　□ around the corner「間近に迫って」（= coming very soon）

31
正解 ➤ **(C)**

メローズさんはこのホテルでの経験に関して何と述べていますか。

(A) あるサービスのキャンセル料金を請求された。

(B) ホテルのスタッフが要望に対して迅速に対応しなかった。

(C) 受けた清掃サービスが満足のいくものではなかった。

(D) ホテルのウェブサイトに掲載されていた情報が正確ではなかった。

正解 メールの第2段落2文目で，janitorial crew（清掃スタッフ）に関して did not seem to do an adequate job with my room と述べているので，(C) が正解。janitorial のように，学習者にとって馴染みのない単語が正解を導くカギになることがまれにあるが，消去法を駆使して正解を残せるようにしたい。誤答 (A) は，第2段落後半で「使用していないインターネット料金を請求された」とあるが，キャンセルしたとは述べていない。(D) は，「広告の料金と請求金額が違っていた」というのが Ms. Mellors の主張だが，ウェブの広告ではないので不適切。

32
正解 ➤ **(A)**

メールに何が添付されていますか。

(A) 顧客満足度を調査するアンケート

(B) ホテルの全サービスと室料を項目ごとに記載したリスト

(C) ホテルの広告のコピー

(D) クラブ会員であることの証明

正解 第1段落最終文にある Please find attached the scanned copy of the bill. にすぐ着目したいところだが，the bill の言い換えとなる選択肢がない。ここで，第3段落最後に I have completed and returned the feedback form ... along with this e-mail. とあることから，feedback form（アンケート用紙）も一緒に添付されていることをおさえ，(A) を選択する。誤答 (B) はホテルのサービス兼料金表を意味するので，bill の言い換えにはならない。

両文書参照型　　　　　　　　　　　　　　　　　　　　　　　　　正解 ▶ (C)

メローズさんに関して何がわかりますか。

(A) 割引が適用されないホテルで割引の要求をした。

(B) 特典が終了した後に特典を利用しようとした。

(C) 9月の週末にホテルに訪れた。

(D) 特別割引の対象にならない部屋を予約した。

正解　Ms. Mellors のメールだけでは選択肢が絞れないので，下の文書で足りない情報を補う「両文書参照型」だとわかる。上のメールでは滞在日が September 20 であり，「広告よりも料金が高かった」と話している一方，下の文書の第3段落2文目にオファーの期間として between September 4 and December 16，さらに第3段落3文目で The offer ... may not be used for weekends とあることから，(C) が適切。誤答 location に関する (A) は，下の文書の第3段落に valid at any of our establishments とあるので不適切。滞在日と special offer の時期は重なっているので，(B) も該当しない。room に関する (D) は，下の文書の同段落2文目で suites and junior suites are not part of the promotion とあるのに対し，上の文書では standard room に宿泊したことがわかるので，これも割引を受けられなかった理由ではない。

　　　　　　　　　　　　　　　　　　　　　　　　　　　　　　　正解 ▶ (C)

『ゲッタウェイ』誌の11月号の特集として述べられていないのは何ですか。

(A) 会社の店舗の写真

(B) 季節限定で提供されるサービスの事前情報

(C) 特別料金の宣伝

(D) ある市で利用できる娯楽に関する記述

誤答　November issue of *Getaway* の抜粋である下の文書の中から，各選択肢の該当箇所を確実に突き止めていく。(A) は第1段落3文目の stunning pictures と，(B) は第4段落の this year's winter breakfast specials と，(D) は第1段落最終文の a report on the nightlife around our Spokane branch と一致する。正解 (C) は，第2段落に the special offer advertised in last month's issue とあり，本文ではその内容の補足説明が書かれているだけで，今月号の特集ではないので，(C) が正解。また，名詞 rate は hotel rate や telephone rate のように「単位（時間や距離など）を基準に定める料金」を指すので，breakfast specials とは関係ないことにも注意しよう。

ヘンダーソン市内にあるホテルの支店では何が利用できますか。

(A) 洗濯サービス

(B) 無料のインターネット接続

(C) 会議室

(D) エクササイズ設備

正解 メール冒頭に the newest Slumberwell branch in the city of Henderson とあることから，下の文書の第 1 段落 2 文目にある our most recently opened branch と同じ店舗を指すことを見極める。その後ろに a fitness center とあるので，(D) が正解。名詞 facility は「施設」の意味のほか，facilities の形で「設備」（＝ equipment）を意味することをおさえておこう。

誤答 文中には in-room Internet availability とあるが，上のメールの「インターネット接続料金を請求された」という記述からもうかがえるとおり free ではないので，(B) を選ばないように注意。business center はパソコンやプリンターなど個人が仕事のできる設備を整えたもので，必ずしも会議室があるわけではないので，(C) も選べない。

満点ポイント27
同義語問題を極める

　Part 7 に 2 問前後出題される同義語問題は，address や represent など多義語の用法を試すものがその多くを占め，あくまで文脈上その語に意味の近い選択肢を見極めます。まれに, forge a relationship の forge を create で言い換えるなど,ハイレベルな単語が問われることもありますが，それでも前後の文脈で推測できるケースがほとんどです。日頃から英英辞書を積極的に活用し，和訳ではなく「英語のまま言い換える力」を磨いておきましょう。

　ここで，ハイレベルな同義語問題を 10 問一気に解いてみましょう。まずは枠内の文章を速読し，その後に言い換えとしてふさわしい語（句）を選んでください。

⏱ **制限時間：8 分**

36.

> Jacob Huntwick is one of the city's most respected business proprietors. He has a solid reputation for his values of commitment and service to the local community.

　The word "values" in line 2 is closest in meaning to

(A) honors

(B) prices

(C) principles

(D) judgments　　　　　　　　　　　　　　　　　Ⓐ Ⓑ Ⓒ Ⓓ

37.

> The accounting department is pleased to announce that sales topped $10 million in the previous quarter. As the marketing team leader, you are to be commended for your efforts in achieving this impressive milestone.

　The word "commended" in line 2 is closest in meaning to

(A) complimented

(B) rewarded

(C) endorsed

(D) assigned　　　　　　　　　　　　　　　　　　Ⓐ Ⓑ Ⓒ Ⓓ

38.

Companies employing drivers must comply with standards set by the Department of Transportation. Employers are reminded to take out insurance policies for any employees who operate company vehicles.

The word "policies" in line 2 is closest in meaning to

(A) claims

(B) guidelines

(C) contracts

(D) procedures Ⓐ Ⓑ Ⓒ Ⓓ

39.

It has come to the attention of management that several patrons were disturbed last night by the noise coming from room 708. In fact, a formal complaint has been filed at the hotel service desk.

The word "filed" in line 2 is closest in meaning to

(A) dealt with

(B) kept in

(C) lined up

(D) turned in Ⓐ Ⓑ Ⓒ Ⓓ

40.

The recent merger has resulted in a noticeable shift in corporate culture. Needless to say, It will take a while for our employees to adapt to the new working conditions.

The phrase "adapt to" in line 2 is closest in meaning to

(A) get accustomed to

(B) adhere to

(C) make modifications to

(D) dramatize Ⓐ Ⓑ Ⓒ Ⓓ

41.

Thank you for the service you provided at our reception last week. All of your hotel staff were very obliging whenever our guests made special requests.

The word "obliging" in line 2 is closest in meaning to

(A) accommodating

(B) responsible

(C) compelling

(D) grateful   Ⓐ Ⓑ Ⓒ Ⓓ

42.

I appreciate your taking the time to stop by my office and discuss the matter. Your input has been valuable in helping me to make this important decision.

The word "valuable" in line 2 is closest in meaning to

(A) cherished

(B) expensive

(C) worthwhile

(D) beneficial   Ⓐ Ⓑ Ⓒ Ⓓ

43.

Folk artist Garth Medford has finally returned to the studio after a long absence. His new album gracefully combines a variety of musical styles, and has commanded attention from both the domestic and international entertainment media.

The word "commanded" in line 2 is closest in meaning to

(A) directed

(B) gained

(C) overlooked

(D) recovered   Ⓐ Ⓑ Ⓒ Ⓓ

44.

Ms. Patel, who is known for her uncanny foresight, has pointed out some problems that could put the success of the project at risk. These matters merit careful consideration and a committee meeting has been planned to address them.

The word "merit" in line 2 is closest in meaning to

(A) call for
(B) benefit
(C) lead to
(D) represent   Ⓐ Ⓑ Ⓒ Ⓓ

45.

We are planning to improve our corporate image, and Janelle Trent has mentioned your name as a commercial designer who consistently produces top-quality work. Based on her recommendation, we would like to invite you to our offices so that we can take a look at your portfolio.

The word "portfolio" in line 4 is closest in meaning to

(A) statement summarizing a career background
(B) combination of financial investments
(C) folder for storing business documents
(D) collection of professional works   Ⓐ Ⓑ Ⓒ Ⓓ

36

ジェイコブ・ハントウィックは市でもっとも尊敬を集めている事業主のひとりである。彼は，地域社会に対する献身と奉仕の価値観により，確固たる評判を得ている。

正解 名詞 value は，values と複数形で用いると「(人の) 価値観，(組織の) 基本理念」(= ideas that influence your behavior) を意味するので，ここでは「信念，信条」を意味する (C) principles (= basic rules or beliefs) が適切。**誤答** market value など value を「価格」の意味で用いれば (B) prices で言い換えられる。名詞 value に (A) honors (名誉，賞) や (D) judgments (判断) の意味はない。

重要語句 □ proprietor「事業主，オーナー」(= business owner)

37

経理部では，前四半期の売上が 1000 万ドルを越えたことを喜んでお伝えします。マーケティングチームのリーダーとして，あなたがたがこの見事な成果を成し遂げるために費やした努力に対し，称賛の意を贈ります。

正解 動詞 commend は「〜を称賛する」(= praise officially) という意味なので，(A) の compliment(ed) (〜を褒める= praise) が正解。ほかに類義語として，acclaim (= praise publicly) も TOEIC 頻出語。**誤答** (B) reward(ed) は「〜に報酬を与える」，(C) endorse(d) は「〜を支持する，推奨する」(= support publicly or officially)，(D) assign(ed) は「〜に任せる」(= give a task to ...) という意味。

重要語句 □ top「〜を上回る」(= exceed) □ milestone「(人生や歴史の) 節目」

38

車の運転手のいる会社は，交通局の定めた基準に従う必要があります。雇用主の方は，社用車を運転する従業員がいれば必ず保険に加入するようにしてください。

正解 take out insurance policies は「保険契約に加入する」という意味を表す表現なので，(C) contracts が言い換えとしてふさわしい。take out a subscription (購読契約に加入する) もぜひ覚えておきたい。**誤答** (A) claims (請求) は insurance claims で「保険金の請求」を意味するが，policies の意味はない。policy は「規則，方針」(= a set of rules or actions) を意味することも多く，その場合は (B) guidelines (方針，指針= rules or official instructions) や (D) procedures (〔従うべき〕手順，やり方= a correct way of doing something) の意味に近くなる。

重要語句 □ comply with ...「〜に従う」(= obey; adhere to ...)

39

経営陣は，宿泊客の数人が昨晩 708 号室から聞こえる音に悩まされたとの報告を受けました。実際，ホテルのサービス担当デスクに正式な苦情届が出されたとのことです。

正解 file a complaint で「（正式な書面で）苦情を出す」という意味を表すので，ここでは turn in （〜を提出する＝ submit）の過去分詞である (D) turned in が正解。**誤答** A complaint has been addressed. であれば (A) dealt with（対処される）に，Documents are filed in the cabinet. であれば (B) kept in（保管される）に言い換えられる。また，file には「列になって進む」という意味もあるので，New employees filed into the meeting room. と言えば (C) lined up（並んだ）と言い換えになる。

40

最近行われた合併により，社風が大幅に変わりました。言うまでもなく，従業員がこの新しい勤務環境に慣れるには多少の時間がかかると思われます。

正解 adapt (*oneself*) to ... は「〜に順応する」（= adjust to ...）という意味なので，(A) の get accustomed to（〜に慣れる = get used to）が正解。**誤答** adapt methods for the new working environment のように adapt A for B（A を B に適合させる）の形で用いた場合は，(C) make modifications to（〜を修正する）に言い換えられる。(B) adhere to は「（規則など）に従う」という意味。また adapt the novel for a film だと「〜を脚色する」の意味合いになり，(D) dramatize の言い換えになる。

41

先週弊社の祝賀会ですばらしいサービスを提供いただきありがとうございます。会の参加者が特別なお願いをしたときにも，ホテルのスタッフの皆様が常に寛大に対応してくださいました。

正解 形容詞 obliging は「助けになる，親身に対応する」（= willing to help）という意味を表し，(A) accommodating も同じ意味で用いられる。**誤答** (B) responsible は「責任感のある」，(C) compelling は「心をつかんで離さない」（= very interesting）の意味。obliged の形では I'm much obliged to you.（大変感謝いたします）のように (D) grateful（感謝している）を意味する場合もあるが，非常にフォーマルな言い方。

42

このたびはオフィスに足をお運びいただき，また問題について話し合う時間を割いていただきありがとうございました。あなたのご意見は，今回の重要な決定をするにあたりに大変有益なものとなっています。

正解▶ valuable input は「有益な意見」を意味するので，(D) beneficial（有益な，役立つ＝ useful）が言い換えとして適切。誤答▶ valuable memories であれば「大事にしている」という意味の (A) cherished に，valuable painting であれば「高価な」という意味の (B) expensive に言い換えられる。(C) worthwhile は「時間を費やす価値のある，やりがいのある」という意味なので，valuable experience であれば worthwhile に近い。

43

フォークシンガーのガース・メドフォードは，長いブランク期間を経てようやくスタジオに戻ってきた。彼の最新アルバムは，さまざまな音楽スタイルが優雅に融合したもので，国内外の芸能メディアから注目を集めている。

正解▶ command は command attention の形で「（注目など）を引きつける」という意味を表すので，ここでは (B) gain(ed)（獲得する＝ get）が適切。garner attention（注目を集める）という表現も Part 7 の文書の中に出てきたことがある。誤答▶ command が「命令・指揮する」（＝ order or control officially）の意味で用いられる場合は (A) direct(ed)（指示する）に言い換えられる。また，command a view of ... の形で「（場所が）〜を一望する」という意味を表すので，その場合は (C) overlook(ed)（〜を見下ろす）に近い。(D) recover(ed) は「（損失などを）取り戻す」という意味。

重要語句 □ gracefully「優雅に，上品に」

44

人並み外れた先見の明があることで知られているパテルさんが，プロジェクトの成功が危ぶまれる可能性のある問題を指摘しました。これらの問題は慎重に検討する必要がありますので，話し合いのため委員会会議が予定されています。

正解▶ 動詞 merit は「〜に値する，〜を得るべき」（＝ deserve; warrant）という意味を表し，merit consideration で「検討の必要がある」という意味になる。よって (A) call for（〜を必要とする＝ demand; necessitate）が言い換えとしてふさわしい。誤答▶ (B) benefit は「〜の利益になる」という意味。名詞 merit は「（称賛に値する）価値・長所」を意味するので，名詞 benefit（利点）に近い。(C) lead to は「〜につながる」（＝ cause; result in）という意味で，一見文意は通りそうだが，merit の言い換えとして不適切。(D) represent は「〜を示す」（＝ show; be a sign of）の意味。

重要語句 □ uncanny「人智を超えた，説明できない」（＝ strange and mysterious）　□ foresight「先見の明」
□ address「〜に対処する，〜を扱う」（＝ deal with; cover）

当社は企業イメージの向上を計画しており，極めて質の高い作品を常に生み出す CM デザイナーとしてジャネット・トレントがあなたの名前を挙げました。彼女の推薦に基づき，当社オフィスにお越しいただき，あなたの作品を拝見したいと思っております。

正解 portfolio には (B)(C)(D) のいずれの意味もあるが，この文脈に合うのは (D) collection of professional works（〔自分の能力を示す〕作品サンプル集）。誤答 (B) combination of financial investments（〔個人や会社の〕保有資産）や (C) folder for storing business documents（書類ケース）では文脈に合わない。(A) statement summarizing a career background は résumé（履歴書）のこと。このように，選択肢に「辞書的な定義」が並ぶパターンもまれに登場する。

⏱ 制限時間：4セット　21分
音声はダウンロード

Questions 46-49 refer to the following e-mail.

E-Mail Message

From: janehawthorn@globenet.com
To: acastillo@peppermilheights.com
Subject: Available units

Dear Mr. Adam Castillo,

Thank you for sending the application form along with the lease agreement for the unit in which I had expressed interest. I enjoyed talking to you in person last week, and I appreciate your taking the time to show me around the Peppermill Heights in Hudson City and its various available units. I am actually writing about a few concerns I have about the lease.

Paragraph sixteen of the lease states that the building manager can raise the rent at any time within thirty days of providing written notice. Although I am completely willing to commit to the agreed-upon monthly rate for the entire twelve months of the lease, I am a bit hesitant to sign anything that would contractually obligate me to pay you an indefinite price. Would it be possible to specify a fixed monthly rent throughout the term of the rental agreement?

Also, the paragraph that immediately follows asserts that I would be held financially liable for damage caused by frozen plumbing. I acknowledge my responsibility to maintain the appropriate heat level in the apartment's water system, and intend to do so. However, I would prefer that this section of the lease be edited so that it would exclude cases where frozen pipes are the result of failure of the heating system.

I hope you do not mind my bringing up these points. I can tell you are quite particular in determining the suitability of potential residents of your complex. Likewise, my prior experience as a tenant leads me to pay close attention to details before entering into a rental agreement.

Best regards,
Jane Hawthorn

46. What is the main purpose of the e-mail?

(A) To inquire about an application form

(B) To confirm receipt of a finalized rental contract

(C) To look into a possibility of altering a lease agreement

(D) To request a reduction of the monthly payment

Ⓐ Ⓑ Ⓒ Ⓓ

47. Why had Mr. Castillo met Ms. Hawthorn previously?

(A) To give some paperwork to her

(B) To inspect some damage in the unit

(C) To set up an interview to find a suitable tenant for the unit

(D) To give a tour around vacant apartments within a complex

Ⓐ Ⓑ Ⓒ Ⓓ

48. What part of the contract is Ms. Hawthorn concerned about?

(A) A condition pertaining to the types of acceptable heating appliances

(B) A provision that allows for increases to the monthly rent when the lease is renewed

(C) A statement that prevents canceling the lease before the term expires

(D) A clause that requires tenants to cover damages caused by malfunctioning equipment

Ⓐ Ⓑ Ⓒ Ⓓ

49. According to the e-mail, what do Mr. Castillo and Ms. Hawthorn have in common?

(A) They both have concerns about the rental agreement.

(B) They have both lived in Hudson City.

(C) They are both very cautious when making a contract.

(D) They both have similar career backgrounds.

Ⓐ Ⓑ Ⓒ Ⓓ

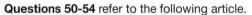

June 5, London—According to a government survey published in April, the number of graduates applying for jobs in the IT sector reached a record high last year. Applications also increased for positions in other technology-related fields such as engineering, as well as for openings in the service industry. However, the news for employers is not uniformly good, with the number of young people entering manual trades dropping to an all-time low.

Although this was not intended to be the primary focus of the General Union of Manual Workers conference, which concluded yesterday, it quickly became so. Supposedly, the theme of the event was how to safeguard the jobs of those workers in industries where automation is eroding job security. This was quickly overshadowed by the opening address of Lisa Polton, who appeared before an audience numbering almost a thousand. Ms. Polton outlined the country's new initiative which is designed to encourage young people to train for manual trades. Under the new plan, which was prompted by the April study, young people will be offered cash incentives to enter training programs for skilled manual jobs. "Within ten years, the country is going to face a serious shortage of carpenters, plumbers, welders and other skilled labor," said Ms. Polton. She finished by promising to speak on behalf of the government about the progress of the scheme at the second of the two conferences planned for this year.

The reception of her speech was positive, and the new scheme became a talking point throughout the rest of the conference. Regardless, some industry analysts remain skeptical, pointing out that the financial benefit being offered is minuscule. "The money that the government is distributing in these grants is not even sufficient to cover one year's tuition," noted Bernard Simpson of *Economics Review*.

50. What most likely was the intended topic of the conference?

(A) Ways of promoting an industry

(B) Measures to improve workplace safety

(C) Fields of work which appeal to recent graduates

(D) Methods for protecting current jobs

Ⓐ Ⓑ Ⓒ Ⓓ

51. According to the article, why was the initiative introduced?

(A) To respond to some recent research findings

(B) To provide assistance to university graduates

(C) To encourage people to join a union

(D) To support companies in the IT sector

Ⓐ Ⓑ Ⓒ Ⓓ

52. Who most likely is Lisa Polton?

(A) A public official

(B) A company representative

(C) An industry professional

(D) A facilitator at the conference

Ⓐ Ⓑ Ⓒ Ⓓ

53. What is NOT indicated about the conference?

(A) It took place in June.

(B) It will meet again later this year.

(C) Ms. Polton has spoken at it before.

(D) About a thousand people attended.

Ⓐ Ⓑ Ⓒ Ⓓ

54. What is mentioned about the new plan?

(A) It has been supported by the majority of citizens.

(B) It covers an insufficient number of training courses.

(C) It does not compensate students highly enough.

(D) It will cost the government too much money.

Ⓐ Ⓑ Ⓒ Ⓓ

Questions 55-59 refer to the following memo and e-mail.

MEMORANDUM

To: All department heads

From: Penny Arp, CEO

Subject: General Assembly Meeting

We have set the date for this year's general assembly meeting. The event will take place on Friday July 15 from 9:00 A.M. until 5:00 P.M. The main order of business will be a discussion of the changes to the company's pay structure, which will take effect in August. As the meeting hall at our head office is currently under renovation, this year's venue will be the Norbert Business Center. Lunch will be provided by Goodtime Catering. As always, all branch managers and assistant managers have been asked to attend.

Jessica Portbury is stepping down as human resources director the week before the meeting. Her successor is not due to join us until the following month, so members of her department will have to do some supplementary work in order to cover her duties in the meantime. In light of this, I would like to suggest that someone from the marketing department take care of making final arrangements for the general assembly. Ajay, could I get you to find someone from within your department to do this? To keep the work involved to a minimum, Ms. Portbury will do as much as possible before she leaves us. Please meet with her to confirm the status of the preparations before making your choice.

╔══════════════════════ E-Mail Message ══════════════════════╗

To: Molly Lee

From: Ajay Duvall

Date: May 21

Ms. Lee,

I have been asked by our CEO to find someone to assume responsibility for running this year's general assembly meeting. As your background is in event planning, I immediately thought of asking you to do this task.

The lineup of speakers has already been finalized and the catering company hired. In addition, all materials will be printed and compiled by the first week of July. However, there are often last-minute changes and problems with events of this nature. Your duties would entail dealing with such issues, as well as organizing the employees who will be staffing the event. While we cannot offer any extra remuneration for undertaking this task, it would almost certainly benefit your long-term prospects for job promotion.

55. What will mostly likely happen in August?
(A) All departments will be restructured.
(B) A department supervisor will retire.
(C) A new employee will begin work.
(D) Renovation work will end.
Ⓐ Ⓑ Ⓒ Ⓓ

56. In the e-mail, the word "assume" in paragraph 1, line 1, is closest in meaning to
(A) pretend
(B) consider
(C) incur
(D) accept
Ⓐ Ⓑ Ⓒ Ⓓ

57. What did Mr. Duvall most likely do before May 21?
(A) He agreed to set up a conference.
(B) He spoke to a human resources director.
(C) He hired a catering company for a meeting.
(D) He suggested a way to improve an event.
Ⓐ Ⓑ Ⓒ Ⓓ

58. What can be understood about Ms. Lee?
(A) She has worked in a catering business before.
(B) She is currently planning the general assembly meeting.
(C) She is an employee of the marketing department.
(D) She has worked with Mr. Duvall for many years.
Ⓐ Ⓑ Ⓒ Ⓓ

59. What is stated about the temporary role given by the CEO?
(A) No extra pay is being offered for accepting it.
(B) It will involve finding speakers for the meeting.
(C) Any employee in the company may apply for it.
(D) It will involve hiring staff to help organize the event.
Ⓐ Ⓑ Ⓒ Ⓓ

Questions 60-64 refer to the following letter and article.

January 8

Dear Sirs and/or Madams,

On behalf of the Donner Park Community Association (DPCA), I am pleased to announce the details of the upcoming Community Action Challenge. The theme we have chosen is the natural environment. All entries should be projects that have in some way made your organization, or the local area, a greener place. Entries are accepted from any non-profit organization within Reed County, including but not limited to clubs, environmental groups and local charities. Multiple submissions from one organization are permissible. Full submission guidelines and eligibility requirements, along with an entry form, are attached to this letter.

A panel of judges comprising officers of the DPCA as well as those of the Reed County Environmental Coalition will choose the three best entries and award prizes to each. Prizes for our Community Action Challenge are typically donated by local businesses and very occasionally by private individuals. The first prize will be $5,000 in store credit from Office Stop Furniture & Supply. Second prize is a $1,000 voucher from Donner Electronics, and third prize is a complete 22-volume set of the newest edition of Smith's Encyclopedia from the Book Nook. There will also be a commemorative plaque awarded for the best presentation of a project.

Details on past winners, as well as tips on how to present your project, are available on request from the DPCA, 51 Main Street, Donner Park.

Best wishes,

Jupiter Jones
Jupiter Jones
DPCA Communications Officer

Donner Park, Oct 27—Three local organizations were awarded prizes at the DPCA Community Action Challenge yesterday, but the big winner was the environment. First place was awarded to the Whole Earth Coalition for its cleanup project at Garfield Pond. Members of the group have, over the past six months, worked hard to not only remove all garbage from this site, but to restock it with fish. The pond, whose scenic surroundings and plentiful wildlife had once made it popular with nature enthusiasts, ceased to be so as it became increasingly polluted. The pond is now once more open to tour groups and other visitors.

The runner-up was the Oakwood Arboricultural Club for its work in planting a variety of trees around the city of Alchester. Willard Snow, the club's president, estimates that the project has resulted in an increase of 15 percent in the diversity of trees within the city limits. The project has not only helped to beautify Alchester and improve its air quality, but has also provided new habitats that have drawn new species into the city.

The final prize went to Reed County Residents Association (RCRA), which presented its newspaper-recycling project. Members transformed old newspapers into usable items such as envelopes and coasters. These artistically created and aesthetically pleasing craft items have in turn been sold locally to raise money for an RCRA-led anti-littering campaign in September. The organization was also recognized for its riveting presentation.

Green Team, a local environmental group, received an honorary mention for its posters featuring adorable characters that encourage people to take better care of the environment.

---

60. What is NOT stated in the letter?

(A) Organizations can enter more than one project for the competition.

(B) The competition takes place every year.

(C) More than one organization will participate in selecting winners.

(D) Private citizens rarely contribute items for prizes.

Ⓐ Ⓑ Ⓒ Ⓓ

61. According to the letter, why should someone contact the DPCA?

(A) To receive a directory of organizations who previously participated

(B) To ask for an additional copy of an entry form

(C) To request details on the contest guidelines

(D) To obtain ideas for improving presentation methods

Ⓐ Ⓑ Ⓒ Ⓓ

62. What can be understood from the results of the competition?

(A) The Whole Earth Coalition was given store credit from a home electronics store.

(B) The Oakwood Arboricultural Club received a set of books.

(C) Reed County Residents Association was presented with a commemorative plaque.

(D) Green Team was awarded for the best presentation.

Ⓐ Ⓑ Ⓒ Ⓓ

63. Who helped restore a local sightseeing attraction?

(A) The people who encouraged wildlife to come to the local area

(B) The organization that came up with an impressive poster design

(C) The group that used paper items for its project

(D) The people who spent half a year on their project

Ⓐ Ⓑ Ⓒ Ⓓ

64. What has happened in Reed County this year?

(A) The competition has been featured in several magazines.

(B) An urban area has been made more attractive.

(C) Proceeds collected from local residents have been used to hold the DPCA event.

(D) Posters have been distributed to local non-profit organizations.

Ⓐ Ⓑ Ⓒ Ⓓ

46-49 の設問は次のメールに関するものです。（語数：264 語）

送信者：janehawthorn@globenet.com
宛先：acastillo@peppermilheights.com
件名：入居可能なアパート

アダム・カスティロ様,

先日入居希望とお伝えしたアパートの賃貸借契約書と申込書をお送りいただきありがとうございました。先週は直接お話することができ楽しい時間を過ごせました。ハドソン・シティにあるペッパーミル・ハイツをご案内いただき，また入居可能なアパートをいくつか見せていただきありがとうございました。じつは，契約についていくつか気になる点がありましたのでご連絡差し上げた次第です。

契約書の16条には，ビル管理人が書面による通知後30日以内にいつでも家賃を上げることができると書かれております。契約の全12か月間，取り決められた家賃を支払うことはもちろんお約束いたしますが，定まっていない賃料の支払いを義務づける契約書にサインをすることには少し抵抗があります。賃貸借契約期間を通じて一定の家賃を明記していただくことはできますでしょうか。

また，その直後の条項では，凍結してしまった水道管によって起こる損害についてその支払い責任を負うと書かれています。アパートの給水装置を適切な温度に保つ責任があることは承知しておりますし，そうするつもりでおります。しかしながら，契約書の当該箇所を，暖房装置の故障により水道管の凍結が起こった場合を除くように修正していただければ幸いです。

上記の点について，ご理解いただければと思います。あなたがビルの居住者にふさわしい人物を判断するのに細心の注意を払っておられることはよくわかります。それと同様に，私も居住者としてこれまでの経験から，賃貸借契約を結ぶ前には細部まで確認するようにしていることをご理解ください。

敬具
ジェーン・ホーソン

重要語句 □ unit「アパートの一室」(= apartment) □ commit to ...「〜に対する責任を果たす」 □ contractually「契約上」 □ obligate *someone* to *do*「(人) が〜する義務を負わせる」(= oblige) □ indefinite「定まっていない」(↔ fixed) □ assert that SV「〜を主張する，述べる」(= state) □ hold *someone* liable for ...「人に〜に対する法的責任を負わせる」 □ I would prefer that SV「〜になればと思います」※that 節で be 動詞が原形になっているのは，まだ現実になっていない内容を述べる仮定法現在の用法によるもの。 □ particular「慎重に選ぶ，好みにうるさい」 □ complex「(総合) ビル施設」 □ likewise「同様に」(= similarly) □ enter into an agreement「契約を結ぶ」 □ vacant「空いている」(= empty) ※動詞形は vacate（〔アパートなど〕を空ける］）。 □ pertaining to ...「〜に関する」(= regarding) □ provision「(契約書などの) 条項」(= clause, condition)

正解 ➤ (C)

このメールの主な目的は何ですか。
(A) 申込書について問い合わせること
(B) 最終決定した賃貸借契約書の受領を伝えること
(C) 賃貸借契約の内容を変更できないかを探ること
(D) 毎月の支払い額の値下げを求めること

正解 第 1 段落の最後で「契約について懸念がある」と述べ，第 2 段落で家賃について，3 段落で水道管の凍結による損害についてそれぞれ契約内容の修正を求めていることから，(C) を確実に正解したい。誤答 (B) は，finalized（最終決定した）という語を見落とさないように注意しよう。

正解 ➤ (D)

カスティロさんがホーソンさんに以前会ったのはなぜですか。
(A) 書類を渡すため
(B) アパートの損傷を確認するため
(C) アパートにふさわしい居住者を探す面接の日時を設定するため
(D) ビル内のアパートの空き室を案内するため

正解 Mr. Castillo がメールの宛先で，Ms. Hawthorn が送信者であることをまずおさえる。Ms. Hawthorn は，第 1 段落 2 文目の I appreciate your ... various available units の部分で，居住可能なアパートを案内してくれたことに感謝しているので，(D) がこの内容に一致する。誤答 (A) は，第 1 段落冒頭で Thank you for sending ... とあるので，会って手渡されたものではない。

正解 ➤ (D)

ホーソンさんは契約書のどの箇所に関して懸念がありますか。
(A) 使用可能な暖房器具の種類に関する条項
(B) 契約の更新時に月々の家賃の値上げができるようにする条項
(C) 契約期間の満了前に解約できないようにする記載
(D) 故障した機器によって起こる損害費用の支払いを居住者に義務付ける条項

正解 第 3 段落で述べている「凍結した水道管によって起こる損害費用の支払い責任を負う」という条項に関して，同段落の最終文で I would prefer that ... the heating system（凍結が暖房装置の故障により起こった場合を除くように修正してほしい）と要求していることから，(D) が正解であるとわかる。誤答 (B) は，第 2 段落で「契約期間中いつでも家賃を上げられる」という条項について修正を求めており，更新時については触れていない。

メールによれば，カスティロさんとホーソンさんはどのような共通点がありますか。

(A) ふたりともこの賃貸借契約について懸念がある。

(B) ふたりともハドソン・シティに住んだことがある。

(C) ふたりとも契約を結ぶ際には非常に慎重になる。

(D) ふたりとも経歴が似ている。

正解 最終段落1行目でまず you are quite particular ... of your complex（あなたは居住者を選ぶ際に細心の注意を払っている）と述べており，さらに，次の文で Likewise（同様に）と共通点を示唆し，自分に関しても my prior experience ... before entering into a rental agreement（契約を結ぶ前は細部まで確認するようにしている）と話しているので，ふたりとも cautious（慎重）だと述べている (C) が正解。誤答 (A) は，懸念を伝えているのは送信者の Ms. Hawthorn だけ。(B) は，第1段落の the Peppermill Heights in Hudson City からアパートの所在地であることしかわからない。(D) は，Mr. Hawthorn のキャリアについて言及がない。

50-54 の設問は次の記事に関するものです。（語数：298 語）

6月5日，ロンドン―4月に公表された政府の調査によると，昨年，IT業界への就職を希望する大卒者の数が過去最高に達した。また，エンジニアリングなどその他の科学技術関連分野の仕事やサービス業の求人への応募も増加した。しかし，雇用者にとって一様に良いニュースばかりではない。手に職をもった職人の仲間入りをする若者の数は過去最低にまで落ち込んだ。

これは昨日閉会した職人一般労働組合会議の主要な議題となる予定ではなかったが，実際にはすぐにそうなった。当初の会議のテーマは作業の自動化によって職の安定が脅かされている産業の労働者の雇用をどのように守るかということであったと思われるが，ほぼ1000人におよび聴衆の前に立ったリサ・ポルトン氏の開会のスピーチがあると，この議題はすぐに影を薄くしてしまった。ポルトン氏は，若者に職人としての訓練を受けることを奨励するために発案された新しい政府の計画の概要を述べた。4月の調査結果によって実施が決定したこの新しい計画の下では，熟練した職人の仕事を学ぶ職業訓練プログラムに参加するため若者には奨励金が支給される。ポルトン氏は「10年以内に，この国において大工，配管工，溶接工などの職人が大幅に不足することになるでしょう」と話した。彼女は，今年2回の開催が予定されている会議の第2回目で，この計画の進捗状況について政府を代表して話すことを約束し，スピーチを締めくくった。

彼女のスピーチは好評であり，会議の残りの期間はその新構想が議題となった。しかし，一部の産業アナリストは，この計画への疑念をいまだ持っており，提供される金額はごくわずかなものであることを指摘している。「政府が支給しようとしている奨励金の額は1年間の授業料にも満たないものです」と，『エコノミクス・レビュー』誌のバーナード・シンプソンは述べた。

□ reach a record high「最高記録に達する」 □ uniformly「一様に，均一に」(= evenly) □ manual trade「手を使う職業」 □ an all-time low「史上最低（史上最高は an all-time high)」 □ supposedly「（推測するところでは）おそらく」 □ safeguard「～を守る」(= protect) □ those workers in industries where ... この those は，後ろに具体的な説明を加えるときに用いられるもの。前の文で述べられた人たちを受けているわけではないことに注意。(例：those people who work for manual trades「手を使った職業に就く人たち」) □ erode「～を侵食する，徐々にむしばむ」(= gradually reduce or destroy; undermine) □ be overshadowed「影が薄くなる，目立たなくなる」 □ number「～の数に達する」 □ plumber「配管工」 □ welder「溶接工」 □ reception「反応，反響」(= reaction) □ talking point「話題，議題」(= topic) □ skeptical「懐疑的な」(= having doubts) □ minuscule「非常に小さい」(= extremely small)

50

正解 ➤ (D)

会議の予定されていたテーマはおそらく何でしたか。

(A) ある産業を発展させるための方策
(B) 労働環境の安全性を改善する対策
(C) 最近の大卒者が魅力を感じる職種
(D) 今就いている職を守るための方策

正解 第1段落にある government survey の内容を受け，第2段落冒頭で this was not intended to be the primary focus と述べているので，もともと予定されていた topic は何だったのかを考える。すると，次の文で the theme of the event was ... eroding job security（作業の自動化によって職の安定が脅かされている労働者の雇用をどのように守るかがテーマだった）とあることから，この部分を言い換えた (D) が正解。誤答 job security は「雇用の確保」のことなので，(B) の workplace safety には関連しない。(A) と (C) はどちらも，Ms. Polton の発表によって当日の主要なテーマに変わったものであることに注意。

51

正解 ➤ (A)

記事によると，なぜこの計画が出されましたか。

(A) 最近行われた調査の結果に対応するため
(B) 大卒者を支援するため
(C) 労働組合への加入を奨励するため
(D) IT 業界の企業を支援するため

正解 the initiative に関して，第2段落5文目で prompted by the April study（4月に行われた調査が発案につながった）と説明していることから，(A) が一致する。この prompt は，「(行動など) を引き起こす，誘発する」(= cause; provoke) の意味。誤答 (C) は，a union ではなく manual trades であれば正解。

211

52 両文参照型　　　　　　　　　　　　　　　　　　　　　　　　正解 ➤ (A)

リサ・ポルトンはおそらくどのような人物ですか。

(A) 役人

(B) 会社の代表者

(C) 産業アナリスト

(D) 会議の進行役

> 正解 Lisa Polton が最初に登場するのは第 2 段落 3 文目の the opening address of Lisa Polton だが、これだけでは正解が絞れない。そこで、もうひとつのヒントである同段落最終文の on behalf of the government に着目。on behalf of ... は「(団体) を代表して」(= representing ...) という 意味を表すことから、(A) の A public official (= A government official) が正解であると判断する。 人物問題は、人名の直前か直後の語句で正解が定まることも多いが、複数の箇所を参照させる問題も まれにあるので、正解につながる決定的な根拠を見逃さないようにしよう。

53 　　　　　　　　　　　　　　　　　　　　　　　　　　　　　　正解 ➤ (C)

会議に関して何が述べられていませんか。

(A) 6 月に開催された。

(B) 年内に再び開催される予定である。

(C) ポルトン氏は以前会議でスピーチをしたことがある。

(D) 約 1000 人の人が出席した。

> 誤答 (A) は、第 2 段落 1 文目に which concluded yesterday とあり、記事の日付が June 5 であ ることから、正しい記述であるとわかる。(B) は、第 2 段落最後の promising to speak ... at the second of the two conferences planned for this year、(D) は、第 2 段落 3 文目の an audience numbering almost a thousand と、それぞれ内容が一致する。正解 (C) は、Ms. Polton がこれま で演説をしたことを示す記述がどこにもないため、これが正解。

54 　　　　　　　　　　　　　　　　　　　　　　　　　　　　　　正解 ➤ (C)

新しい計画に関して何が述べられていますか。

(A) 過半数の市民の支持を得ている。

(B) 適用対象となる訓練コースの数が十分にない。

(C) 訓練生への支給額が不十分である。

(D) 政府にとって金銭的負担があまりに大きい。

> 正解 計画に対する批判的な意見が述べられている第 3 段落に注目。2 文目の the financial benefit ... is minuscule、次の "The money ... is not even sufficient to cover one year's tuition," で、提 供される金額が不十分だという意見が示されているので、(C) が適切。the new plan が記事の中で the initiative や the new scheme と言い換えられていることもおさえておこう。誤答 (A) は、同段 落冒頭で The reception of her speech was positive (スピーチは好評だった) とあるが、これは 会議における反応なので、citizens ではなく conference attendees であればよい。

55-59 の設問は次の社内連絡とメールに関するものです。（語数：212 語＋ 120 語）

連絡

宛先：各部長

差出人：ベニー・アーブ　CEO（最高経営責任者）

件名：総会

今年の総会の日時が決定しましたのでお知らせします。総会は 7 月 15 日，金曜日の午前 9 時から午後 5 時まで開催されます。主要なテーマは，8 月から実施になる会社の給与体系変更についての話し合いになる予定です。本社の会議ホールは現在工事中であるため，今年の会場はノーベルト・ビジネス・センターになります。昼食はグッドタイム・ケータリング社により提供されます。従来どおり，支店長と副支店長は全員出席してください。

人事部長のジェシカ・ポートベリーさんが総会が開催される前の週に退職されます。彼女の後任者は翌月まで当社での勤務を開始しない予定なので，その間彼女の担当業務を行うため，人事部の社員は通常より多く仕事をする必要があります。このような事情を踏まえて，マーケティング部の誰かに総会の最終的な手はずを整える仕事をして欲しいと考えています。エイジェイさん，あなたの部門の中からこの仕事をする人を見つけてもらえますか。仕事の負担を最小限に抑えるため，ポートベリーさんも退職するまでできるだけのことをしてくれます。仕事を行ってくれる人を決定する前に，彼女に会って，準備がどこまで進んでいるか確認してください。

宛先：モリー・リー

差出人：エイジェイ・デュバル

日付：5 月 21 日

リーさん

今年の総会運営の仕事を引き受ける人を探して欲しいという依頼を CEO から受けました。あなたはこれまでイベント企画の仕事をしてきたので，この仕事を頼もうとすぐに思いました。

総会で話をする人はすでに最終確定し，ケータリング業者の手配も済んでいます。さらに，7 月の初週までにすべての必要な資料の印刷および編集が終わる予定です。しかし，この種のイベントには最終段階での変更や問題が生じることがよくあります。あなたの仕事は，このような問題に対処し，総会の運営を手伝う従業員を効率よく行動させることです。この仕事を引き受けていただくことに対する報酬は支払われませんが，長期的に見れば，昇進にほぼ確実にプラスになるでしょう。

重要語句　□ order of business「対処すべき課題」※the first order of business は「最優先して行うべき仕事」を表す。　□ take effect「実施になる，効力を発する」（＝ go [come] into effect; be implemented）　□ step down as ...「～の職を下りる」（＝ resign as ...）　□ successor「後任者」（＝ replacement）　□ be due to *do*「～することになっている」（＝ be expected to *do*）　□ in light of ...「～を踏まえて」（＝ in consideration of ...）　□ ... the catering company hired: the catering company（has been）hired の has been が省略された形。　□ catering company「ケータリング会社（イベント等に出張して料理の手配・配膳を行う会社）」　□ compile「～を編集する，まとめる」（＝ put together）　□ last-minute「土壇場の，直前の」　□ nature「種類」（＝ type; kind）　□ entail「～を伴う」（＝ involve）　□ staff「（ある場所や行事）で働く」（＝ work in/at ...）　□ undertake「～を引き受ける」（＝ agree to *do*; take on ...）　□ prospects「（成功の）チャンス，見込み」　□ set up ...「～を設定する，予定を組む」（＝ arrange; schedule）

55

おそらく 8 月に何が起こると思われますか。

(A) 全部門が再編成される。

(B) ある部長が退職する。

(C) 新入社員が勤務を開始する。

(D) 改装工事が終了する。

正解 meeting の開催日は July 15。これを受け，第 2 段落冒頭で the week before the meeting（会議の前の週）に Jessica Portbury が人事部長の職を辞任すると書かれている。さらに，次の文で Her successor is ... until the following month とあることから，その翌月の 8 月から後任者が新しく会社に加わることをおさえ，(C) を選択する。誤答 (A) は，第 1 段落で the company's pay structure について述べているが，部門そのものが restructure されるわけではないので不適切。(B) は 7 月のこと。(D) の renovation の話は第 1 段落にあるが，いつ終わるかは明示されていない。

56

メールの第 1 段落 1 行目にある "assume" にもっとも意味の近い語は

(A) ふりをする

(B) 検討する

(C) こうむる

(D) 引き受ける

正解 assume responsibility は「責任を引き受ける，担う」（= take on; undertake）という意味を表すので，ここでは (D) accept が言い換えとして適切。他にも，assume the position（職に就く），assume control（実権を握る）をおさえておきたい。誤答 assume possibilities といった場合の assume は「想定する」（= presume）の意味になり，(B) consider に近くなる。(C) incur は，incur costs（費用を負担する）のように，「費用や損害などを負う」という意味合いで用いられる。

---

57 両文書参照型

デュバルさんは 5 月 21 日より前におそらく何をしましたか。

(A) 会議の開催を設定する仕事を引き受けた。

(B) 人事部長と話をした。

(C) 会議のためにケータリング業者を手配した。

(D) イベントをより良いものにする方法を提案した。

正解 May 21 は Mr. Duvall のメールの日付なので，メールの送信前にすでに行っていることを見極める。まず，社内連絡の最終文で Ajay（= Mr. Duvall）に対し，Please meet with her（= Ms. Portbury）to confirm the status of the preparations と依頼していることを把握。さらに，メールの第 2 段落冒頭で彼が準備の進行状況を説明していることをおさえる。これらの情報から，彼が human resource director である Ms. Portbury に会って状況を確認したことがわかるので，(B) が正解と判断する。上の文書を全文読んでいないと正解を見出せない難問である。誤答 (C) は，メー

ルの第2段落で the catering company (has been) hired と述べているので，人事部がすでに行った仕事であるとわかる。

58 両文書参照型 正解 ➤ (C)

リーさんに関して何がわかりますか。
(A) ケータリング業者で働いたことがある。
(B) 現在総会の企画をしている。
(C) マーケティング部に所属している。
(D) デュバルさんと長年一緒に働いてきた。

正解 Ms. Lee はメールの宛先。社内連絡の第2段落3〜4文目に I would like to ... to do this?（マーケティング部の誰かに手はずを整えてほしいので，あなたの部門の中から人を見つけてもらえるか）とあるのを受け，メールの中で Mr. Duvall が Ms. Lee に仕事の担当を勧めていることから，ふたりとも marketing department の従業員であることをおさえ，(C) を選択する。誤答 (A) は，メールの中で your background is in event planning とあるので，catering business での経験ではない。

59 正解 ➤ (A)

CEO から任せられた臨時の仕事に関して何が述べられていますか。
(A) 引き受けたことに対する報酬は支払われない。
(B) 会議で話をする人を見つけることも仕事内容に含まれる。
(C) 会社の従業員は誰でもその仕事に応募することができる。
(D) イベントの準備を手伝う従業員を雇うことも仕事内容に含まれる。

正解 メールの最終文で，we cannot offer any extra remuneration for undertaking this task（この仕事を引き受けたことによる報酬を与えることはできない）と述べていることから，(A) がこの内容に合致する。remuneration は「（勤務に対する）報酬」（= compensation）の意味。誤答 (B) は，第2段落冒頭の The lineup of speakers has already been finalized の部分から，すでに対処済みであるとわかる。(C) は，社内連絡の中で CEO が marketing department の従業員に限定しているので不適切。(D) は，メールの第2段落で organizing the employees who will be staffing the event（イベントを運営する従業員をまとめる）とあるが，スタッフを新しく hire するわけではない。

60-64 の設問は次の手紙と記事に関するものです。（語数：226 語＋266 語）

1月8日

ご担当者各位

ドナー・パークコミュニティ協会（DPCA）を代表して，来たる地域活動コンテストの詳細をお知らせいたします。当協会が選んだテーマは自然環境です。応募対象となるのは，所属団体や周辺地域を何らかの形でより環境に優しい場所にしたプロジェクトに限ります。リード・カウンティ内で活動する同好会や環境保護団体，地域の慈善団体，その他非営利団体であればどんな団体でも応募を受け付けます。一団体からの複数応募も認められます。プロジェクトの提出に関する指針と応募条件，応募用紙は本状に添付されております。

DPCA 役員とリード・カウンティ環境保護会会員で構成される審査委員会により，上位３位のプロジェクトを選出し，それぞれに賞品を贈呈します。この地域活動コンテストの賞品は，主として地域の企業からの寄付によるもので，ごく一部個人による寄付も含まれます。１等賞はオフィス・ストップ・ファニチャ＆サプライ社による 5000 ドル相当のクーポン券です。２等賞はドナー・エレクトロニクス社による 1000 ドル相当の商品券，３等賞はブック・ヌック社によるスミス百科事典の最新版全 22 巻となります。さらに，もっとも優れたプロジェクトのプレゼンテーションに対しては記念の額が贈呈されます。

過去の受賞団体に関する情報，およびプロジェクトのプレゼンテーション方法に関するアドバイスをご希望の方は，DPCA（メイン通り 51，ドナー・パーク）宛てにご連絡ください。

敬具

ジュピター・ジョーンズ

DPCA 広報担当

ドナー・パーク，10月27日―DPCA 地域活動コンテストにおいて昨日，地域の３団体が賞を授与されたが，このコンテストでもっとも恩恵を受けたのは環境そのものだった。優勝に輝いたのは，ガーフィールド池の清掃プロジェクトを行ったホール・アース連合会だった。この半年間にわたり，同団体の会員は懸命に努力して池のゴミをすべて撤去し，池に魚を放流した。ガーフィールド池は，周辺の景色のよさや野生生物の豊富さによって，かつては自然愛好家に人気があったが，日に日に汚染されていき人気の影はひそめていた。現在，ガーフィールド池は，団体の観光客やその他の訪問者たちに再び公開されている。

第２位となったのは，アルチェスター市の随所に多種多様な木々を植える活動を行ったオークウッド植樹同好会だ。会長のウィラード・スノウ氏は，このプロジェクトの結果として，市内の木の種類が 15 パーセント増えたと見積もっている。このプロジェクトで，アルチェスター市の環境をきれいにし空気の質が改善されただけでなく，それまで市内に見られなかった生物が生息できるような場所を提供することにもなった。

第３位は，新聞紙のリサイクルプロジェクトを発表したリード・カウンティ住民自治会 (RCRA) だった。自治会の会員たちは古い新聞紙を封筒やコースターなど使用可能な物に作り変えた。芸術的に作られ，かつ見栄えも美しいこれらの作品は，9月に RCRA 主催で行われたポイ捨て反対キャンペーンの資金集めのために地元で販売された。また，RCRA は，見事なプレゼンテーションをしたこと対する賞も受賞した。

地域の環境保護団体であるグリーン・チームは，環境保護を人々に促す愛くるしいキャラクターをあしらったポスターを作成し，選外佳作に選ばれた。

（重要語句）□ including but not limited to ...「〜を含むがそれだけに限定されない」 □ very occasionally「ご くまれに」(= rarely) □ store credit「クーポン券」 □ commemorative plaque「記念の額」※ commemorate（〜を記念する）という動詞とともにおさえておこう。 □ on request「要求に応じて」 (= on demand) □ restock *A* with *B*「A に B を補充する。（魚などを）放流する」 □ cease to *do* 「〜しなくなる」(= stop *doing*) □ once more「もう一度」(= once again) □ arboricultural「植 林・植樹の」 □ habitat「生息地」(= living place) □ transform *A* into *B*「A を B に変形させる」 □ aesthetically pleasing「美的にも優れた」 □ in turn「その後、その結果」(= as a result) □ riveting「心を奪われるほどの」(= extremely interesting; fascinating; absorbing) □ mention 「表彰」(honorary mention で「選外佳作」の意味) □ adorable「愛くるしい」

60　　　　　　　　　　　　　　　　　　　　　　　　　　　正解 ➤ (B)

手紙で述べられていないことは何ですか。

(A) 団体はコンテストに複数のプロジェクトを応募できる。

(B) コンテストは毎年行われている。

(C) 複数の団体が受賞団体の選考に関わっている。

(D) 一個人による賞品の寄付はまれである。

誤答 手紙の中から、各選択肢の該当箇所を確実に突き止める。(A) は第 1 段落 5 文目の Multiple submissions from one organization are permissible. と一致する。(C) は、第 2 段落冒頭で A panel of judges（審査委員会）について officers of the DPCA と those (= officers) of the Reed County Environmental Coalition というふたつの団体が述べられていることから、これも一致して いる。(D) は、第 2 段落 2 文目の Prizes ... very occasionally by private individuals. の部分と一致 する。**正解** (B) は、every year であることを示すヒントがどこにもないので、これが正解。ちなみに、 毎年開催であれば、annual という語がほぼ必ず登場する。

61　　　　　　　　　　　　　　　　　　　　　　　　　　　正解 ➤ (D)

手紙によれば、どのような場合に DPCA に連絡すべきですか。

(A) 以前参加した団体の名簿を受け取る場合

(B) 応募用紙を追加で請求する場合

(C) コンテストの指針に関する詳細を請求する場合

(D) プレゼンテーションの改善方法に関するアイデアを得る場合

正解 手紙の最終段落で、tips on how to present your project について available on request（要 望があれば入手できる）とあることに着目し、この内容（プレゼン方法のコツ）に一致する (D) を選ぶ。 **誤答** (A) は、同じ文で past winners（過去の受賞団体）と限定していること、また directory（名簿） をもらえるとまでは書いていないことから不適切。

62 両文書参照型　　　　　　　　　　　　　　　　　　　　　　　正解 ➤ (C)

コンテストの結果から何がわかりますか。

(A) ホール・アース連合会が家電販売店で使用できるクーポン券を授与された。

(B) オークウッド植樹同好会が本のセットをもらった。

(C) リード・カウンティ住民自治会が記念の額を授与された。

(D) グリーン・チームがもっとも優れたプレゼンテーションを行ったことで受賞した。

> **正解** コンテスト結果が述べられている記事の第3段落冒頭に Reed County Residents Association が The final prize（〔最後の賞＝〕3等賞）をとり，さらに同段落最終文の recognized for its riveting presentation からプレゼンテーションに関しても受賞したことがわかる。ここで，手紙の第2段落最終文に commemorative plaque awarded for the best presentation とあることから，(C) が正解。**誤答** The whole Earth Coalition は First Place（1等賞）だったとあるが，1 等賞品は手紙の第2段落に store credit from Office Stop Furniture & Supply と書かれているので，a home electronics store（家電販売店）とある (A) は不適切。

63　　　　　　　　　　　　　　　　　　　　　　　　　　　　　　正解 ➤ (D)

地元の観光地を復活させる手助けをしたのはどの人たちですか。

(A) 野生生物が地域に来るように促した人たち

(B) 見事なポスターのデザインを考案した団体

(C) プロジェクトに紙製の物を使用したグループ

(D) プロジェクトに半年間を費やした人たち

> **正解** 記事の第1段落最終文にある The pond is now once more open to tour groups and other visitors. が設問内容と関連していることを見極め，このプロジェクトを行った Whole Earth Coalition に関する記述を選択肢から選ぶ。同段落に Members of the group have, over the past six months, worked hard と書かれているので，(D) が正しい。**誤答** (A) は Oakwood Arboricultural Club, (B) は Green Team, (C) は Reed County Residents Association に関する記述。

64 両文書参照型　　　　　　　　　　　　　　　　　　　　　　　正解 ➤ (B)

リード・カウンティで今年何が起こりましたか。

(A) コンテストがいくつかの雑誌に掲載された。

(B) 都市がより魅力的になった。

(C) 地元住民から集めた収益金が，DPCA 主催のイベントを開催するために使用された。

(D) ポスターが地元の非営利団体に配布された。

> **正解** 手紙の第1段落4文目に Entries are accepted ... within Reed County とあるので，記事にある出来事はすべて Reed County でのこと。記事の第2段落で木が Alchester 市内に植えられ，それが「市内を美化し空気の質を向上させ，市内で見られなかった生物もやってきた」とあることから，city を urban area と言い換えた (B) が一致することがわかる。**誤答** (C) は，第3段落に an RCRA-led anti-littering campaign のためのお金が集められたとはあるが，選択肢にある DPCA はコンテストを開催している団体なので不適切。

SCORE

990

900

800

700

600

500

400

300

3

実戦模試
200問

LISTENING TEST

In the Listening test, you will be asked to demonstrate how well you understand spoken English. The entire Listening test will last approximately 45 minutes. There are four parts, and directions are given for each part. You must mark your answers on the separate answer sheet. Do not write your answers in your test book.

PART 1

Directions: For each question in this part, you will hear four statements about a picture in your test book. When you hear the statements, you must select the one statement that best describes what you see in the picture. Then find the number of the question on your answer sheet and mark your answer. The statements will not be printed in your test book and will be spoken only one time.

Sample Answer

Example   Ⓐ   Ⓑ   ●   Ⓓ

Statement (C), "They're standing near the table," is the best description of the picture, so you should select answer (C) and mark it on your answer sheet.

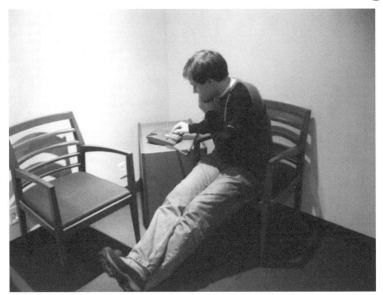

1.

2.

GO ON TO THE NEXT PAGE

3.

4.

5.

6.

GO ON TO THE NEXT PAGE

7.

8.

9.

10.

GO ON TO THE NEXT PAGE

PART 2

Directions: You will hear a question or statement and three responses spoken in English. They will not be printed in your test book and will be spoken only one time. Select the best response to the question or statement and mark the letter (A), (B), or (C) on your answer sheet.

Sample Answer

Example   Ⓐ ● Ⓒ

You will hear: Where is the meeting room?

You will also hear: (A)   To meet the new director.
                                 (B)   It's the first room on the right.
                                 (C)   Yes, at two o'clock.

The best response to the question "Where is the meeting room?" is choice (B), "It's the first room on the right," so (B) is the correct answer. You should mark answer (B) on your answer sheet.

11. Mark your answer on your answer sheet.   26. Mark your answer on your answer sheet.

12. Mark your answer on your answer sheet.   27. Mark your answer on your answer sheet.

13. Mark your answer on your answer sheet.   28. Mark your answer on your answer sheet.

14. Mark your answer on your answer sheet.   29. Mark your answer on your answer sheet.

15. Mark your answer on your answer sheet.   30. Mark your answer on your answer sheet.

16. Mark your answer on your answer sheet.   31. Mark your answer on your answer sheet.

17. Mark your answer on your answer sheet.   32. Mark your answer on your answer sheet.

18. Mark your answer on your answer sheet.   33. Mark your answer on your answer sheet.

19. Mark your answer on your answer sheet.   34. Mark your answer on your answer sheet.

20. Mark your answer on your answer sheet.   35. Mark your answer on your answer sheet.

21. Mark your answer on your answer sheet.   36. Mark your answer on your answer sheet.

22. Mark your answer on your answer sheet.   37. Mark your answer on your answer sheet.

23. Mark your answer on your answer sheet.   38. Mark your answer on your answer sheet.

24. Mark your answer on your answer sheet.   39. Mark your answer on your answer sheet.

25. Mark your answer on your answer sheet.   40. Mark your answer on your answer sheet.

PART 3

Directions: You will hear some conversations between two people. You will be asked to answer three questions about what the speakers say in each conversation. Select the best response to each question and mark the letter (A), (B), (C), or (D) on your answer sheet. The conversations will not be printed in your test book and will be spoken only one time.

41. What does the man want to do?

(A) Receive a driver's license
(B) Apply for a resident visa
(C) Open a bank account
(D) Obtain health insurance

42. How long must the man live in the country before applying?

(A) Two weeks
(B) Three weeks
(C) Two months
(D) Three months

43. How should the man submit his application?

(A) Through a Web site
(B) By mail
(C) By fax
(D) In person

44. Why is the man calling?

(A) To inquire about an express delivery
(B) To request a hotel service
(C) To reschedule an appointment
(D) To ask for a replacement part

45. What does the woman say about the express service?

(A) It is only available after 12 P.M.
(B) It is more expensive.
(C) It is not being offered today.
(D) It takes up to 48 hours.

46. What does the woman offer to do?

(A) Send over a technician
(B) Transfer the man's call
(C) Change the man's room
(D) Have an item picked up

GO ON TO THE NEXT PAGE

47. What is the woman looking for?

(A) Her briefcase

(B) Her gloves

(C) Her books

(D) Her eyeglasses

48. Where most likely are the speakers?

(A) At a bookstore

(B) At a hotel

(C) At a library

(D) At a doctor's office

49. According to the man, what should the woman do?

(A) Go to the security office

(B) Ask a clerk upstairs

(C) Listen for an announcement

(D) Wait in the lobby

50. According to the woman, what happened last year?

(A) She participated in a sales campaign.

(B) Some merchandise was released overseas.

(C) A campaign for new phones was started.

(D) The man worked with Target Electronics.

51. In what department does the woman most likely work?

(A) Production

(B) Sales

(C) Marketing

(D) Public Relations

52. What is mentioned about Jeff Barkley?

(A) He designed a mobile phone.

(B) He is the woman's supervisor.

(C) He praised the man's work.

(D) He is coordinating an upcoming campaign.

53. What are the speakers discussing?

(A) Proposed topics for a conference
(B) The launch of a publication
(C) The man's public speaking skills
(D) Attendance at the recent event

54. Who most likely is David Reese?

(A) A conference attendee
(B) An author
(C) The speakers' colleague
(D) A film maker

55. What will the man do tomorrow?

(A) Visit a factory
(B) Give a speech
(C) Read a book
(D) Work in his office

56. What problem is mentioned?

(A) A product is sold out.
(B) A delivery has been delayed.
(C) Sales have decreased.
(D) The merchandise is overpriced.

57. What does the woman recommend?

(A) Ordering a different brand
(B) Placing a larger order
(C) Offering a discount
(D) Rearranging the display

58. What is the man's concern?

(A) He received complaints from customers.
(B) Customers might go to competing stores.
(C) The purchasing manager is absent.
(D) Betafix is no longer being produced.

GO ON TO THE NEXT PAGE

59. What is the woman worried about?

(A) Having a bid rejected
(B) Finishing tasks before the next meeting
(C) Approving a schedule change
(D) Meeting project requirements

60. What has the woman's department done recently?

(A) Hired more accountants
(B) Completed a joint project
(C) Received several new contracts
(D) Relocated to a new office

61. What does the man offer to do?

(A) Train newly hired employees
(B) Prepare documents for the board meeting
(C) Assign people to work for the woman's department
(D) Organize a special event

62. Who most likely is the woman?

(A) A recruitment agency representative
(C) An airport security officer
(B) An employee of an airline
(D) An owner of a store

63. What does Mr. Garrett lack?

(A) Customer service skills
(B) Professional references
(C) Education credentials
(D) Experience in the industry

64. According to the woman, what is a requirement of the job?

(A) Frequent travel
(B) Owning a car
(C) Regular overtime
(D) Managerial skills

65. Who most likely are the speakers?

(A) Restaurant servers
(B) Store clerks
(C) Hotel receptionists
(D) Event coordinators

66. What most likely is the problem?

(A) There are insufficient flowers.
(B) An order was not placed in time.
(C) The room is not large enough.
(D) Attendance is higher than expected.

67. What is Bob currently doing?

(A) Purchasing flowers
(B) Picking up some plates
(C) Borrowing a few chairs
(D) Collecting some food

68. What kind of company do the speakers work for?

(A) An accounting firm
(B) A computer manufacturer
(C) An electronics store
(D) A software developer

69. What is suggested about EZBooks?

(A) It is currently less popular than AccountTec.
(B) Its price has recently been reduced.
(C) It runs faster than programs of rival companies.
(D) It is as powerful as AccountTec.

70. What will the woman do next?

(A) Start work on a new product
(B) Go over some figures
(C) Contact her supervisor
(D) Read reviews from customers

GO ON TO THE NEXT PAGE

PART 4

Directions: You will hear some talks given by a single speaker. You will be asked to answer three questions about what the speaker says in each talk. Select the best response to each question and mark the letter (A), (B), (C), or (D) on your answer sheet. The talks will not be printed in your test book and will be spoken only one time.

71. Where does the speaker work?

(A) At a sports store
(B) At a travel agency
(C) At an airport
(D) At a restaurant

72. What does the speaker want Susan to do?

(A) Take some time off work
(B) Call back as soon as possible
(C) Substitute for him
(D) Reserve a ticket by the end of the week

73. When will the speaker most likely meet Susan next?

(A) Tomorrow
(B) Tuesday
(C) Thursday
(D) Friday

74. What will happen tomorrow?

(A) Some machinery will be inspected.
(B) Production will be suspended.
(C) New equipment will be installed.
(D) The employees will be evaluated.

75. When is the earliest time that the elevator will be accessible?

(A) At 8 A.M.
(B) At 11 A.M.
(C) At noon
(D) At 11 A.M.

76. What are listeners told to do with the boxes?

(A) Leave them in the elevator
(B) Carry them down the stairs
(C) Pile them next to the wall
(D) Show them to an inspector

77. Who most likely is Benn Monroe?

(A) A founder of a school
(B) A graduate of a local college
(C) A renowned architect
(D) A curriculum developer

78. What is mentioned about the college?

(A) It is situated in a coastal town.
(B) It has closed down completely.
(C) It is currently located in the suburbs.
(D) It is the most important college in the area.

79. What will listeners most likely do next?

(A) Tour an educational center
(B) Explore the city in groups
(C) Visit a popular art gallery
(D) View exhibits of historical importance

80. What item's listing has an incorrect photograph?

(A) The printer
(B) The air conditioner
(C) The ceiling fan
(D) The portable heater

81. What does the speaker say about the A-70 model?

(A) It was launched a year ago.
(B) It has been discounted.
(C) It appears on a Web site.
(D) It is no longer being sold.

82. According to the message, what is the speaker going to do now?

(A) Send out the brochures
(B) Contact a printing company
(C) Wait for Josh to return a call
(D) Update the company Web site

GO ON TO THE NEXT PAGE

83. What is the purpose of the talk?

(A) To present an analysis

(B) To train staff members

(C) To promote a company

(D) To announce a new schedule

84. According to the speaker, what needs to be improved?

(A) Office communications

(B) Staff compensation

(C) Work environment

(D) Data confidentiality

85. What does the speaker suggest?

(A) Installing a new computer system

(B) Hiring additional employees

(C) Holding meetings more often

(D) Instituting a new policy

86. What does the speaker say about the survey?

(A) It was started in April.

(B) It cost more than expected.

(C) It targeted people nationwide.

(D) It was conducted by a local company.

87. According to the report, what do people spend the most money on?

(A) Home improvements

(B) Vacation Travel

(C) Dining out

(D) Entertainment

88. According to the report, what kind of business is becoming more popular?

(A) Family restaurants

(B) Hardware stores

(C) Holiday resorts

(D) Shopping malls

89. Who is the intended audience for the talk?

(A) Technical consultants
(B) Business executives
(C) Software developers
(D) Self-employed workers

90. According to the speaker, what are many people doing?

(A) Launching new Web sites
(B) Creating their own software applications
(C) Operating office equipment inefficiently
(D) Applying for technology-related jobs

91. What does the speaker say is available at a reasonable price?

(A) Memory upgrades
(B) Regular maintenance work
(C) New office software
(D) Private consultation

92. Who most likely is Batima Attam?

(A) A singer
(B) A concert promoter
(C) A dancer
(D) A guitar player

93. What does the speaker say about the brothers?

(A) They started to play last year.
(B) They will not appear at the concert.
(C) They will perform live on the radio show.
(D) They released an album this year.

94. What will listeners most likely do next?

(A) Hear a radio advertisement
(B) Ask questions to special guests
(C) Learn more about a director
(D) Listen to some music

GO ON TO THE NEXT PAGE

95. Who is the speaker introducing?

(A) A novelist

(B) A poet

(C) A researcher

(D) A journalist

96. What did Ms. Kawamura do while attending university?

(A) She published a book.

(B) She changed her major.

(C) She met a famous author.

(D) She received a degree in biology.

97. When did Ms. Kawamura receive an award?

(A) Earlier this year

(B) One year ago

(C) Five years ago

(D) Eight years ago

98. What is one purpose of the talk?

(A) To start a training workshop

(B) To recognize everyone's accomplishments

(C) To ask employees for feedback

(D) To outline a schedule of events

99. What will be covered in the new program?

(A) Business planning

(B) Training techniques

(C) Sales strategies

(D) Project development

100. What is being given to listeners by the speaker?

(A) Performance evaluation sheets

(B) Course material packages

(C) Workshop registration forms

(D) Details about the upcoming events

READING TEST

In the Reading test, you will read a variety of texts and answer several different types of reading comprehension questions. The entire Reading test will last 75 minutes. There are three parts, and directions are given for each part. You are encouraged to answer as many questions as possible within the time allowed.

You must mark your answers on the separate answer sheet. Do not write your answers in your test book.

PART 5

Directions: A word or phrase is missing in each of the sentences below. Four answer choices are given below each sentence. Select the best answer to complete the sentence. Then mark the letter (A), (B), (C), or (D) on your answer sheet.

---

101. *Fields of Clover*, Gilda Vern's second novel, helped distinguish ------- as one of the country's brightest new authors.

(A) hers
(B) she
(C) herself
(D) her

102. Diamaz Jewelry offers free engraving services for customers who want to have their purchases ------- with their initials.

(A) personally
(B) personal
(C) personalized
(D) to personalize

103. The keynote speech at the international trade conference lasted ------- over two hours.

(A) well
(B) more
(C) all
(D) ever

104. If the suggested policy change ------- with the supervisor's approval, it will be adopted as the new standard.

(A) meets
(B) complies
(C) satisfies
(D) consents

GO ON TO THE NEXT PAGE

105. Although the new software seems exceptionally technical and complex, the fully illustrated user manual will give customers peace of -------.

(A) advice
(B) rationale
(C) mind
(D) reliability

106. While attending the convention in Lisbon, Mr. Burka will try to remain ------- with headquarters via e-mail.

(A) contacts
(B) to contact
(C) contacting
(D) in contact

107. As Manaluga Airways offers two dining options for its in-flight meal, passengers may choose ------- a chicken dish and a vegetarian entrée.

(A) both
(B) either
(C) between
(D) rather

108. ------- to park in the employee garage, which is on the basement level, are obtainable from Ms. Lee in reception.

(A) Permission
(B) Permitted
(C) Permits
(D) Permitting

109. While Banner Bridge is under repair, city officials plan to ------- traffic to the Sanger Tunnel.

(A) divert
(B) replace
(C) alternate
(D) facilitate

110. The magazine decided to expand next year's summertime price promotion so that new subscribers would also be entitled to discounts ------- spring.

(A) within
(B) every
(C) since
(D) during

111. There is pressure on authors of fiction to publish ------- to ensure that they keep a large readership.

(A) regular
(B) regulation
(C) regulates
(D) regularly

112. Artisan traditions that date back hundreds of years have been ------- to make each replica of ancient handicraft displayed in the gallery as authentic as possible.

(A) delegated
(B) employed
(C) conformed
(D) emerged

113. Ms. Mapston is ideally suited for the management opening, in ------- she has extensive experience as a production supervisor.

(A) that
(B) which
(C) itself
(D) as much

114. Appearing as a guest instructor, local entrepreneur Alfred Peterson told workshop attendees very ------- stories about business management.

(A) advance
(B) gainful
(C) engaging
(D) resourceful

115. The board is planning to hold a special event as a ------- to the outgoing director after his thirty-year career at the firm.

(A) tribute
(B) respect
(C) celebration
(D) caliber

116. Careful strategic planning prior to the relocation will ensure as ------ a transition as possible.

(A) easy
(B) easing
(C) ease
(D) easily

117. Mr. Banks argued that the firm would be better off enlarging its existing production facilities, ------- constructing any new factories.

(A) in contrast
(B) other than
(C) as opposed to
(D) whereas

118. Having surpassed his sales targets by a wide margin, Mr. En expects that his achievements will have a positive impact on his performance ------- this year.

(A) appraising
(B) appraisal
(C) appraisingly
(D) to appraise

119. After ------- to manager three years ago, Mr. Rodriguez went on to become the head of the eastern sales division of Maxiwell Corporation.

(A) promoting
(B) having promoted
(C) promoted
(D) being promoted

120. In his popular television program, renowned chef Justin Duval draws ------- 15 years of culinary experience to show viewers how to prepare gourmet food at home.

(A) back
(B) upon
(C) over
(D) aside

121. George Ortega has served the citizens of Brownsville for twenty years in his ------- as the leader of the town council.

(A) capacity
(B) integrity
(C) authenticity
(D) majority

122. Recent declines in sales revenue and corresponding budget reductions make it likely that the company's expansion plans will have to wait for ------- another year.

(A) yet
(B) one
(C) again
(D) until

123. Only the applicants showing the most ------- will be called back for the second screening process held at the firm's head office.

(A) promising
(B) promises
(C) promisingly
(D) promise

124. Mr. Navari won ------- support by presenting a very persuasive case for his proposal to company directors.

(A) himself
(B) them
(C) its
(D) theirs

125. Economic indicators suggest that worldwide demand for consumer electronics ------- exponentially in the year ahead.

(A) increase
(B) will be increasing
(C) has been increased
(D) to increase

126. Traffic congestion was expected on Fifth Avenue from 3 P.M. to 5 P.M. on Wednesday, but Ms. Petrelli had to use that road -------.

(A) otherwise
(B) nevertheless
(C) likewise
(D) meanwhile

127. While many felt that the suggestion was a reasonably ------- solution to the problem, the president opposed it vigorously.

(A) soundly
(B) sounded
(C) sound
(D) sounding

128. ------- the ten sales representatives enrolled in the company's online negotiating techniques workshop, Mr. Durand was the only one who completed the course within the specified period.

(A) Out of
(B) Notwithstanding
(C) As soon as
(D) Altogether

129. Decisions regarding promotions within the department are left to the ------- of the supervisor.

(A) discretion
(B) perspective
(C) liability
(D) insistence

130. Despite being created by the same architect, there are some ------- differences in the design of the two buildings.

(A) oblivious
(B) enduring
(C) attentive
(D) marked

131. Owing to his hard work in the past year, Mr. Bernard ------- a prominent role on the design team.

(A) assigned
(B) was assigned
(C) has been assigning
(D) assigning

132. A variety of artists performed commendably at the annual concert this past weekend, the last of ------- was by far the most well-known in the country.

(A) which
(B) whose
(C) all
(D) whom

133. Several of the items reported missing from the warehouse have yet to be -------.

(A) shown up
(B) looked into
(C) turned out
(D) accounted for

134. The proposal for expansion of the entire ground floor of the building has been rejected, as such an undertaking would have ------- high costs.

(A) prohibited
(B) prohibitively
(C) prohibiting
(D) prohibitive

135. The executive committee ------- the success of the promotional campaign to the hard work of the marketing staff.

(A) credited
(B) appreciated
(C) rewarded
(D) acknowledged

136. Due to predicted inclement weather, there is a ------- possibility that the organizers will have to move tomorrow's event to an indoor venue.

(A) decisive
(B) distinct
(C) profuse
(D) dependent

GO ON TO THE NEXT PAGE

137. MGO Travel promises to deliver vacations that are both reasonably priced and -------.

(A) memories
(B) memorized
(C) memorable
(D) memorably

138. Duplication or redistribution of this film or any of its content without the written consent of Globoflix Entertainment, Inc., is ------- forbidden.

(A) expressly
(B) vastly
(C) adamantly
(D) exclusively

139. Although numerous proposals have been submitted from the research and development staff, ------- have been discussed at recent committee meetings.

(A) little
(B) much
(D) neither
(D) none

140. When Mr. Phelps summarized the research findings, he inadvertently left out some ------- details.

(A) apparent
(B) contingent
(C) pertinent
(D) subsequent

PART 6

Directions: Read the texts that follow. A word or phrase is missing in some of the sentences. Four answer choices are given below each of the sentences. Select the best answer to complete the text. Then mark the letter (A), (B), (C), or (D) on your answer sheet.

Questions 141-143 refer to the following article.

The Canberra Museum of Natural History will soon begin extensive renovations in order to create a brighter, more spacious environment. The curator of the museum announced yesterday that the initial phase of the project, ------- to continue

141. (A) expecting
(B) which expected
(C) having been expected
(D) expected

for the next three months, will entail an overhaul of the Goldberg Wing of the museum. All exhibits of the wing will be ------- while the work is in progress.

142. (A) displayed
(B) replaced
(C) inspected
(D) stored

Following the renovations, the Goldberg Wing will offer a much-improved experience to museum visitors. All artwork will be reclaimed from the warehouse facility and reinstalled in a way that takes full advantage of the renovated area. ------- the inconvenience to patrons, during the renovation period the regular

143. (A) So as to
(B) As part of
(C) In accordance with
(D) In light of

admission price of $5 will be waived.

GO ON TO THE NEXT PAGE

Questions 144-146 refer to the following letter.

VL Architecture
101 Heralds Road,
Trenford Business Park, CA 90222

April 10

To whom it may concern:

I am writing to ------- VL Architecture's bid for the landscaping work at the

144. (A) request
(B) offer
(C) inquire
(D) accept

grounds of our new Calpine Valley office complex. We are particularly interested in your plans to include several water features, as well as the wide variety of shrubs and flowers you intend to use.

Would it be possible to provide us with your ------- by May 1? We have a

145. (A) quote
(B) model
(C) schedule
(D) directions

company-wide meeting on that day to discuss our relocation plans. I would like employees to be able to see for themselves how the gardens will look once the work has been completed. Please call me at your earliest convenience so that we can arrange a time to discuss ------- we should proceed with this project.

146. (A) whatever
(B) before
(C) further
(D) how

Best regards,
John Doubleton
John Doubleton

Questions 147-149 refer to the following advertisement.

Landing a job is not ------- as simple as responding to a job listing or submitting

> **147.** (A) almost
> (B) so
> (C) nearly
> (D) only

an application. You should be prepared to face harsh competition from other proficient candidates. *Career Advancement Basics*, the new educational software by Fluward Proware, will provide you with all the information you need to get an edge over others. In the program, you will learn how to determine what you want in a career and to focus your search ------- . You will get advice on creating

> **148.** (A) respectively
> (B) accordingly
> (C) consequently
> (D) prominently

winning résumés and cover letters, using the Internet, developing networks, and enhancing interview performance. ------- , *Career Advancement Basics* is the

> **149.** (A) In any case
> (B) Thereby
> (C) Provided that
> (D) In short

definitive guide to securing employment in the 21st century.

Purchase it for only $59.95!

GO ON TO THE NEXT PAGE

From: Skylark Tour <alicelee@skylarktour.com>
To: Milton Bernard <mbernard23@vmail.com>
Subject: Your vacation
Date: June 15

Dear Mr. Bernard,

Thank you for choosing Skylark Tour, and we hope your trip to the Emerald Resort in Cairns ------- up to your expectations. The Emerald Resort is a new addition

150. (A) lived
(B) will live
(C) lives
(D) is living

to our catalog. Therefore, we would be grateful for any comments that you may wish to offer regarding your trip. Specifically, we want to know whether anyone in particular provided superb service or if there was anything that you found ------- .

151. (A) disappointingly
(B) disappointed
(C) disappointment
(D) disappointing

As a token of our appreciation for the time you have taken to give us your comments, we will send you our complimentary travel atlas. We hope this -------

152. (A) option
(B) itinerary
(C) volume
(D) advice

will be of help to you in planning your next trip.

Thanks again for traveling with Skylark Tour.

Sincerely,
Alice Lee

Directions: In this part you will read a selection of texts, such as magazine and newspaper articles, letters, and advertisements. Each text is followed by several questions. Select the best answer for each question and mark the letter (A), (B), (C), or (D) on your answer sheet.

Questions 153-154 refer to the following notice.

Founded nearly ten years ago, Glasstar has quickly grown to be the premier purveyor of quality glass and crystal ornaments in the northeast of the country. We were recently described by industry journal *Giftware Today* as "the future of the industry," and last year won the prestigious Ornacom Golden Globe for an unprecedented fifth year. Starting later this year, we are expanding our operations across the country. We are therefore seeking a number of motivated, ambitious individuals to acquire franchises in our burgeoning business. Interested parties must have capital of €160,000 or more, and should contact Judi Alexandra at 759 0491 4413 for further details.

153. What is the purpose of the notice?

(A) To recruit workers for newly established locations

(B) To give an overview of an upcoming event

(C) To promote a retail space for potential shopkeepers

(D) To publicize an investment opportunity

154. What is indicated about Glasstar?

(A) It has been in business for a full decade.

(B) It is currently operating nationwide.

(C) It has received favorable reviews from a magazine.

(D) It provides product specifications over the telephone.

GO ON TO THE NEXT PAGE

Questions 155-156 refer to the following e-mail.

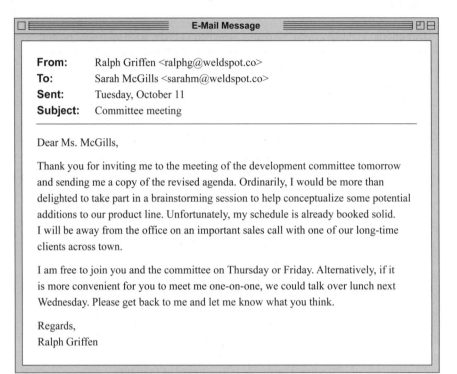

E-Mail Message

From: Ralph Griffen <ralphg@weldspot.co>
To: Sarah McGills <sarahm@weldspot.co>
Sent: Tuesday, October 11
Subject: Committee meeting

Dear Ms. McGills,

Thank you for inviting me to the meeting of the development committee tomorrow and sending me a copy of the revised agenda. Ordinarily, I would be more than delighted to take part in a brainstorming session to help conceptualize some potential additions to our product line. Unfortunately, my schedule is already booked solid. I will be away from the office on an important sales call with one of our long-time clients across town.

I am free to join you and the committee on Thursday or Friday. Alternatively, if it is more convenient for you to meet me one-on-one, we could talk over lunch next Wednesday. Please get back to me and let me know what you think.

Regards,
Ralph Griffen

155. What has Mr. Griffen been asked to do?

(A) Proofread an agenda for a future meeting
(B) Provide input for developing new products
(C) Inform committee members of a schedule change
(D) Join a discussion with production staff

156. What will Mr. Griffen most likely do on October 12?

(A) He will meet with Ms. McGills after lunch.
(B) He will consult with members of the committee.
(C) He will go out of town to speak with a corporate client.
(D) He will attempt to solicit business for the company.

BizPress New Release in April

Business and Pleasure in Europe, the new book to be published by us at BizPress, will be of interest to travel bookstore proprietors. Written by experienced travel writer Tim Foxheath, the book is the third in the best-selling series, which already has titles dealing with trips to North America and Asia. As always, there is an abundance of practical tips and fascinating pictures taken by the author himself. His anecdotes about sightseeing destinations close to the business centers of each location are noteworthy. Visit our Web site to view extracts from this new book, as well as to read professional reviews of Tim Foxheath's previously published work. *Business and Pleasure in Europe* would be an excellent addition to the shelves of your bookstore.

157. For whom is the information most likely intended?

(A) Publishing executives
(B) Foreign travelers
(C) Bookstore owners
(D) Travel writers

158. What is NOT indicated about *Business and Pleasure in Europe*?

(A) It contains the author's personal stories.
(B) It refers to current trends in the travel industry.
(C) Part of the book can be seen online.
(D) It includes photographs taken by Tim Foxheath.

GO ON TO THE NEXT PAGE

MEMORANDUM

From: Clarissa Hough, general manager
To: All employees
Date: November 6
Re: Survey

The date that WWD will launch its operations is only a few short weeks away. We have decided to conduct some research to gather detailed information about the listening preferences of the potential audience for the station. We have commissioned Bottomline, Inc., to produce a survey for us, in which we will ask local members of the public about their musical tastes and their radio listening habits in general.

Bottomline, Inc., will administer a written survey that will be sent directly to 3,000 households in the local area. However, as the response rate for direct-mail surveys is often quite low, we additionally plan to poll a smaller number of randomly chosen residents by telephone. These interviews will be based on the written questionnaire, but will have fewer questions and will last for no more than five minutes each. Bottomline, Inc., has said they could do the polling for us, but it will be more cost effective if we were to take care of it ourselves. Consequently, we need employees who are willing to assist us in this process on the weekend of December 10 and 11. Overtime payments will be made to those participating in this work.

If you are interested, please contact Stan Chadwick, the head of marketing, on extension 223 or at chadwick@wwd.co.wa.

159. Why was the memo most likely written?

(A) To enlist volunteers for a project
(B) To provide details about recent research
(C) To request feedback on a marketing plan
(D) To describe a customer satisfaction survey

160. What kind of company most likely is WWD?

(A) A music distribution firm
(B) An advertising agency
(C) A research firm
(D) A broadcasting company

161. What is suggested about the surveys?

(A) Both telephone and written surveys will be conducted by Bottomline, Inc.
(B) Telephone surveys will take place over two days.
(C) Written surveys will be more effective than telephone surveys.
(D) Telephone and written surveys will have exactly the same content.

GO ON TO THE NEXT PAGE

October 8

Dear Ms. Cartwright:

Your Publishers Direct Platinum membership is due to expire in the coming weeks. If you renew before your current membership runs out, you will be entitled to a reduction in the yearly Platinum member rate to only $60. Simply fill in and return the enclosed card by mail, or go to our Web site at www.publishersdirect.org to renew online.

We would also like to update you on our service. In light of rising ink and paper costs, we have decided to cease production of our printed catalog, and the last one will be published on November 1. Instead, we will expand our Web site. Not only will this streamline online ordering of paperback and hardcover books, but will give users access to an ever-widening variety of downloadable books, magazines and other content, including audio titles. This move will also enable us to continue offering our amazing everyday low prices.

Renew your membership before the November 30 and continue to take advantage of free expedited shipping, double loyalty points on all purchases, and the exclusive chance to buy books before they go on sale in other retail outlets. Also, make sure to visit our updated Web site after December 3 to check out our expanded selection. Please view exclusive special offers by logging on to the "Members Only" Web pages.

Yours sincerely,

Jim Sheffield

Jim Sheffield
Managing Director

162. What is one purpose of the letter?

(A) To inform a customer that their membership has been renewed

(B) To detail a change in company procedures

(C) To announce the upcoming expiration of a magazine subscription

(D) To explain which items have been discounted

163. What is mentioned about the printed catalog?

(A) It has become more expensive to create.

(B) Its circulation has increased.

(C) It can only be used until the end of October.

(D) It is not popular with Publishers Direct customers.

164. What is NOT indicated about the company's revised Web site?

(A) It will be accessible exclusively to Platinum members.

(B) It will be operational prior to the end of the year.

(C) It will make the ordering process simpler.

(D) It will feature audio versions of some books.

GO ON TO THE NEXT PAGE

Questions 165-167 refer to the following article.

Rapid economic development in India and other parts of Asia has led to a rise in competition among corporations for highly-skilled technical workers. This in turn is causing some companies to take more active measures in making themselves more appealing to prospective employees. Many companies are now offering schedule flexibility to let staff enjoy longer weekends without reducing their full-time work hours or increasing overall payroll expenses. One example, referred to as "summer hours," involves letting staff work an extra hour a day from Monday through Thursday. This means they can leave work at lunchtime on Fridays.

Businesses are also projecting a positive image to potential employees by demonstrating that they are interested in not only making a profit, but also in aiding the environment. Many of them cover part or all of employee public transportation costs or offer a gas subsidy for workers who car-pool from their homes. Companies are also creating workplaces that employees can be proud of by establishing office recycling programs, and cutting down on paper usage and electricity consumption.

254

165. What is the topic of the article?

(A) The impact of the growing economy in India on its surrounding countries

(B) Techniques for retaining highly-qualified workers

(C) Ways in which businesses are trying to gain an advantage in the labor market

(D) Methods for making full-time employees work more productively

166. According to the article, what has increased?

(A) The number of skilled workers who are applying for jobs

(B) The cost of the average worker's commute to the office

(C) The number of paid vacation days offered by employers

(D) The demand for employees with technical training

167. What is NOT mentioned as something companies are doing to help the environment?

(A) Consuming lower quantities of paper

(B) Making greater use of recycled materials in manufacturing

(C) Encouraging workers to use public transportation

(D) Reducing the amount of power used in the workplace

GO ON TO THE NEXT PAGE

The Halford Inn

Ranked by visitors as the second best hotel in the city of Kingsport and number one in the downtown area, the Halford Inn is perfect whether you are in town on business or pleasure. Although the hotel boasts ultra-modern decor, the building itself is a fine example of mid 19th-century architecture. Conveniently situated near the Kingsport Convention Center, it is also well connected to the public transportation system, with two train stations and numerous bus stops within walking distance.

Each room has wireless Internet access and a large flat screen television. All prices include continental breakfast in the dining room (breakfast in bed is available for a nominal fee), a free 24-hour shuttle bus to Somerton Airport, and use of the hotel's fitness center and pool. Given the expense of parking in the city center, the complimentary use of the garage is another huge plus.

There are two dining establishments on the premises. Chez Souris, owned by former professional musician Souris Lee, is a French restaurant serving classic cuisine in a congenial ambience. The newly remodeled Los Burrito is a Mexican restaurant that is more family oriented. They both have dishes and prices that are top of the line; however, there is a wealth of more affordable dining options in the center of the city.

Throughout the winter months patrons can take advantage of special rates. In addition, as the hotel is predominantly used by business travelers, reduced prices are often available on weekends.

168. What is included in the price of a stay at the Halford Inn?

(A) Breakfast delivery to each room
(B) A shuttle service to some airports
(C) Parking spaces for guests' vehicles
(D) A fitness consultation service

169. The word "boasts" in paragraph 1, line 4, is closest in meaning to

(A) contrasts
(B) incorporates
(C) acclaims
(D) exaggerates

170. What is NOT stated about the hotel?

(A) It is rated as the best hotel in downtown Kingsport.
(B) It is located next to the train station.
(C) It caters mainly to people traveling on business.
(D) It is in a historical building.

171. What is indicated about the hotel's restaurants?

(A) One of them occasionally features some live music.
(B) One of them has recently been constructed.
(C) They are more expensive than other local establishments.
(D) They serve the widest range of dishes in town.

GO ON TO THE NEXT PAGE

To: All Board Members

From: Tom Young, President

Date: February 15

Our offer for the vacant plot of land that runs adjacent to the south end of our processing facility in Glenbrook was accepted late last month. This, at long last, will allow us sufficient space to store chemical supplies on-site, rather than at the warehousing district in Kirkwood. Construction of the new storage unit has been slated to begin later this year. The blueprints for the building itself have already been drawn up and are available in the boardroom for you to look over. Ms. Cox of Dengle & Sprung, the person who created the designs for the building, will be attending a part of our next board meeting and will be able to address any concerns that you may have.

As this building will be used to house chemicals that pose a potential hazard to both local residents and area wildlife, we will need to secure approval from both the Health Department and the Department of the Environment before construction can commence. To do this we must submit an application form, along with a detailed analysis of the likely environmental impact of the project, to each of these government departments. Our legal department has been working on this paperwork, but I would now like to ask for your input. Please review the drafts of these documents that accompany this memo and focus on any issues which may require further attention or discussion. Be prepared to voice your thoughts when we gather next Wednesday.

The contents of the above are to remain strictly confidential and are not to be discussed outside of the boardroom. If you suspect that a member of your staff has seen any part of these documents, please notify me immediately.

Thank you for your cooperation on this matter.

172. What did the company do this year?

(A) Purchased some property
(B) Built a warehouse
(C) Leased a storage space
(D) Relocated some of its operations

173. What is most likely attached to the memo?

(A) An analysis of how the new policy will affect the working environment
(B) Architectural specifications for a construction project
(C) A report on how chemicals are stored
(D) A study of the potential effects of a new facility

174. According to the memo, why should someone contact Mr. Young?

(A) To inquire about a building's design
(B) To report unauthorized exposure of information
(C) To request a copy of the blueprints
(D) To give feedback on an application

175. What is NOT indicated about the proposed project?

(A) It will take place in Glenbrook.
(B) It must be approved by multiple government agencies.
(C) It is expected to begin by the end of the year.
(D) It is opposed by some local residents.

176. What will most likely happen next Wednesday?

(A) An application will be submitted.
(B) An architect will answer questions from board members.
(C) Work on a construction project will begin.
(D) The legal department will finalize work on required documents.

GO ON TO THE NEXT PAGE

Alpaca Plastics had only two employees when it was established, Andy Patel and Maurice Yates, the company's co-founders. Mr. Patel and Mr. Yates were roommates at Trapp University, where the former was enrolled in the plastics program and the latter was pursuing a degree in business management. Once Mr. Patel graduated, he took a job at Medford Molding, a small business in the plastic molding industry. He contacted Mr. Yates two years later with the idea of the two of them starting their own molding business. "I had only been out of college for a year at that time," says Mr. Yates, "and was working as a customer service representative for a communications firm."

This new company operated for nearly two years before the partners were able to hire their first additional employee, who was a supervisor at Medford Molding. For years the company struggled just to make ends meet and nearly had to shut down five years ago. "I concluded that the company would have to undergo radical restructuring if we were to keep on running the business," says Mr. Patel. They took out loans from banks, made substantial investments in technology, and broadened operations.

Since then, the company has purchased over $2 million worth of equipment and spent many thousands more on maintenance and product development. It has also paid a considerable amount to train its employees, some of whom are receiving company subsidies to pursue degree-level qualifications at local colleges. Alpaca now has 85 workers who are designing and molding plastic parts around the clock. The company's revenue has risen at the impressive rate of 55 percent annually for the past three years.

Both of the co-founders of the company will appear next week on a local television program *Business World Now* at 7 P.M. on December 1. It will feature an exclusive interview recorded in October.

177. What can be understood about Mr. Yates?

(A) He graduated from college later than his roommate.

(B) He acquired an academic background in plastics.

(C) He quit college before earning a degree.

(D) He held a management position before founding Alpaca Plastics.

178. What is mentioned about Mr. Patel?

(A) He was initially hesitant to partner with Mr. Yates.

(B) He currently owns most of Alpaca company shares.

(C) He recruited someone who worked for his previous employer.

(D) He has directly supervised Mr. Yates.

179. What has Alpaca Plastics done over the past five years?

(A) It has employed financial experts.

(B) It has helped employees participate in training outside the company.

(C) It has spent more money on advertising.

(D) It has increased its revenue by more than 50 percent every year.

180. What is NOT indicated about Alpaca Plastics?

(A) Its operations are conducted 24 hours a day.

(B) Its founders have been interviewed for a local television show.

(C) It operates several manufacturing facilities.

(D) It had financial problems for many years.

GO ON TO THE NEXT PAGE

	E-Mail Message	

From: ejackson@manderleyfest.com
To: hgallant@manderleyfest.com
Subject: Advance Ticket Sales

Dear Ms. Gallant,

Please find attached a copy of the latest ticket sales figures for the festival. These were updated this morning, based on the totals when the theater box offices closed yesterday.

By this time, we were aiming to have sold at least 70 percent of total seating capacity in Kelvin Theater and Cooper Theater, and 65 percent in Varley Hall. *Stormy Night* in particular has generated a lot of interest, most likely due to the popularity of the male lead. At the current rate that show should sell out, and the other on-target shows should be near capacity by the time the event starts.

During the time left before the start of the festival, I think you should focus our advertising on those shows that have not reached the sales target. I recommend that you pull the radio ads for *Stormy Night* and replace them with additional ads for the two below-target shows. If budget allows, you might also want to run extra ads in this weekend's newspapers.

Finally, I feel that we haven't done enough to advertise the street gala that concludes the event, which is scheduled for the day after the final performance at Kelvin Theater. My only suggestion here would be to hand out fliers to shoppers in the city center.

Thank you,

Edward Jackson
Managing Director

Manderley Drama Festival: Sales at end of day, October 27				
Venue	Show	Dates	Total seats	Percentage sold
Kelvin Theater	*Yesterday's News*	November 3-8	8,000	71%
	The Watchman	November 9-14	6,400	68%
Varley Hall	*Stormy Night*	November 1-6	4,000	73%
	The End of the Road	November 7-11	3,200	66%
Cooper Theater	*Behind the Mask*	November 4-8	4,050	58%
	The King's dream	November 9-13	3,500	75%

181. What most likely is Ms. Gallant's responsibility?

(A) Managing a theater's operations
(B) Directing a musical performance
(C) Increasing public awareness of the event
(D) Tracking ticket sales for the event

182. What does Mr. Jackson suggest doing?

(A) Purchasing additional print ads
(B) Focusing more attention on *Stormy Night*
(C) Modifying some of the sales targets
(D) Increasing the advertising budget

183. What is stated about the shows during the festival?

(A) Tickets to some shows are likely to sell out by the end of October.
(B) One of the shows features a well-known performer.
(C) Each show is performed at a different venue.
(D) The total number of seats for each show varies depending on the date.

184. Which show has yet to reach the sales target?

(A) *The End of the Road*
(B) *Stormy Night*
(C) *The Watchman*
(D) *Yesterday's News*

185. When does the festival most likely end?

(A) October 27
(B) November 3
(C) November 14
(D) November 15

GO ON TO THE NEXT PAGE

Sound Style, Inc.

About Us

Our founder and CEO, Laura Ann Casey, is an accomplished classical cellist. She was the chief administrator at the Institute of the Performing Arts in France, where she was instrumental in establishing the institution's highly renowned summer concert program for children. At Sound Style, Inc., we strive to continue this legacy of excellence by providing quality music education and recording services.

Our Courses

Private and group lessons include voice, piano, strings, percussion and wind instruments. From April 1, Sound Style is also pleased to announce the addition of jazz vocal lessons, taught by Wilbur Davis. Mr. Davis is best known for his work with The Pete Callaghan Experience, the group behind the award-winning soundtrack for the film *Misplaced*. We will also resume the popular intermediate cello class taught by our CEO from the same month.

Other Services

We offer state-of-the-art recording equipment for music and spoken-word projects. Studio A is a fully equipped digital studio and includes the largest recording room in the country. Studio B, which is currently being expanded to have all new equipment, will make an ideal setting for music and commercial recording when it reopens at the beginning of May this year. Studio C is the least spacious of our studios, but its unique acoustics produce exceptionally high quality sound. Patrons can also benefit from the considerable experience of our in-house sound engineer, Robert McGee. Never has recording in a professional studio space been so easy or affordable! To obtain more information about our services or for reservations, please contact us at reservation@soundstyle.com or 121, 4th Avenue, New York, NY 10562.

April 18
Mr. Kenneth Ellenbaum
247 East Mayweather Avenue
Lexington, NY 10472

Dear Mr. Ellenbaum:

Thank you for your application for renting studio space to create your album. Unfortunately, the studio you requested is not available until May 1. We do have a larger facility which is open on your specified dates of April 25 and 26. If you agree to book both days, we would be happy to rent the larger studio to you at no extra charge. Please let me know if this is acceptable to you.

In response to your request for support staff, we at Sound Style are able to provide you with the services of our professional sound engineer to assist you. I have sent you a document listing the approximate costs of the studio space, sound engineer and additional services you asked for. Also, please find a map giving directions to our studio printed on the reverse of this letter. Our opening hours and a full list of contact numbers are indicated below the map.

sincerely,

Sharon Li

Sharon Li
Customer Services
Sound Style Inc.

186. What is mentioned about Laura Ann Casey in the advertisement?

(A) She runs several educational institutions.

(B) She has a background in teaching.

(C) She established a business in France.

(D) She has received an award for her performances.

187. What is NOT indicated about Sound Style Inc.?

(A) It specializes in music education for children.

(B) It uses highly-advanced technology to provide its services.

(C) Its services are moderately priced.

(D) It plans to expand its range of courses.

188. What will Mr. Ellenbaum most likely do?

(A) Cancel a reservation for May

(B) Record a spoken-word project

(C) Work with Robert McGee

(D) Study sound engineering

189. Why is Mr. Ellenbaum unable to use the studio he requested?

(A) It lacks the necessary support staff.

(B) Its facilities are being upgraded.

(C) It is not large enough to accommodate his needs.

(D) It has already been reserved for his requested dates.

190. What information is indicated on the back of the letter?

(A) When the studio is open

(B) How much the project will cost

(C) Which services are currently available

(D) What time trains are run to the area

GO ON TO THE NEXT PAGE

March 20

Dear Mr. Michael Ayers:

Three years ago, the mayor of Lamford, Fred McCourt, first proposed the idea of building a 65-story tower in the city's Dockside district. At that time, his idea was heavily defeated in a public poll. He has worked hard to round up support from Dockside businesses as well as residents since then, and the proposal was finally passed last year. The Lamford Development Corporation was created to manage the project, and, after much discussion the final design was approved on March 4.

The basement mall will contain 108 individual shops, and once completed will be the largest shopping complex in the state. The offices on each of the first 62 floors will have stunning views not only of the city's rugged coastline, but also of the building's beautiful atrium. On top of these floors will be an aquarium housing a diverse collection of exotic marine life. Also there will be a lavishly decorated bar designed by Lamford-native interior designer Francesca Fortoni, and an observation deck with floor-to-ceiling windows. Overall, the project is expected to help revitalize the economy of the Dockside district, which has declined dramatically over the past twenty years.

The honor of your presence is requested at the Dockside Tower groundbreaking ceremony and reception we have organized for May 10. The ceremony is scheduled to start at 11 A.M., followed by a reception starting at 1 P.M. If you are able to attend, please contact us at the telephone number below by April 18.

Dockside Tower Groundbreaking Committee
The Lamford Development Corporation
555-8998

Landmark Event On Dockside

May 11—Work on Dockside Tower, Lamford's new development, got underway with a groundbreaking ceremony in front of over 400 guests. The ceremony was held on the grounds of Croston House, a historic building that will be integrated into the development. Mayor Fred McCourt broke the earth with a ceremonial spade. He then made a brief speech, thanking everyone for their assistance in making his ambition to build Dockside Tower a reality. Following the ceremony, the guests moved on to a reception at the Plaza Hotel, where Brian Russell, president of the Lamford Development Corporation, delivered an address outlining the development plan.

When finished, Dockside Tower will reach a height of 420 meters, making it the tallest structure in the city. The lower floors will house businesses, shops, restaurants and an entertainment complex, while the building's sole bar will take up the entire top story of the tower.

191. What is the purpose of the letter?

(A) To express gratitude to a local business owner

(B) To announce a winning bid for a construction project

(C) To extend an invitation to an official event

(D) To detail the history of the Dockside district

192. According to the letter, what has Fred McCourt already done?

(A) Proposed revisions to the design of a tower

(B) Approved new industry regulations

(C) Succeeded in changing public opinion on a project

(D) Implemented a new measure to improve the local economy

193. What is suggested about Croston House?

(A) It is situated close to the ocean.

(B) It has been used to teach history.

(C) It can accommodate over 400 people.

(D) It was recently demolished.

194. What happened on May 10?

(A) Local people gathered in front of a newly constructed building.

(B) Dockside residents were asked to make donations.

(C) A company president summarized a construction plan during the ceremony.

(D) A city representative marked the beginning of a construction project.

195. What can be understood about the 65th floor of the tower?

(A) It will house rare species of sea life.

(B) It will feature work by a local designer.

(C) It will be used as an observation deck.

(D) It will overlook the building's atrium.

GO ON TO THE NEXT PAGE

E-Mail Message

From: <travisc@powermail.com>
To: <c.richards@kentishsupplies.com>
Subject: Job vacancy

Dear Mr. Richards,

This e-mail is to express my interest in the vacancy for a marketing manager that you are currently advertising on your Web site. I believe that my employment history makes me an ideal candidate for this position.

I first realized that my future lay in marketing when I was a student. I took, and genuinely enjoyed, a summer job in the marketing department of one of your main competitors, AcePlate. Upon gaining my degree at Brimshire University, I took a job in the marketing department of FPL Enterprises. I played an integral role in creating their critically acclaimed "Appliances of Beauty" advertising campaign. After six years of service, I was offered the position of marketing manager. Although I only held this position for a year, company sales doubled during that period.

I left to take up a similar position with a newly founded company, Frompton Tech. I was hired to design its marketing strategy from the ground up, a task that I completed within the first year. As a result of my work, Frompton Tech was soon on a competitive footing with the more established companies in the industry.

My nine years of experience in the field, three of them in management, have furnished me with a thorough understanding of marketing practices, and I feel that I am perfectly qualified to help Kentish Supplies revitalize its marketing campaign.

Yours sincerely,
Conway Travis

From: <c.richards@kentishsupplies.com>
To: <m.singh@kentishsupplies.com>
Subject: Recruitment

Dear Ms. Singh,

I'm writing to update you on the progress that has been made in our search for a new marketing manager. My new assistant Ms. Schmidt has produced a list of the most suitable candidates that we have interviewed. Joanne Tempest is my preference for the position, as she performed exceptionally well in her interview and easily surpasses the minimum requirement of five years of marketing experience. She also has four years of managerial experience with AcePlate. Conversely, my assistant preferred Conway Travis, who was recommended by someone she knows. Mr. Travis displayed ingenious ideas along with a great deal of self-confidence. However, I'm unwilling to recommend him for the position as he is the only applicant who falls short of our minimum requirement for managerial experience. Therefore, I personally feel that he should be dropped from consideration.

I have sent the résumés of the remaining candidates together with this e-mail so that you can look them over. I would also like you to meet with the two other prospects, Gina Moon and Brian Scott. If you could let me know by the end of the day when you are available, I'll contact the candidates to arrange times for the second round of interviews.

Sincerely,
Charlie Richards

GO ON TO THE NEXT PAGE

196. What does Mr. Travis NOT mention in his e-mail?

(A) He has obtained a degree in marketing.

(B) He created a promotional campaign that received praise.

(C) He has marketing experience at three different companies.

(D) He was promoted by the company that first hired him after he graduated.

197. Who suggested Mr. Travis for the position?

(A) A professor of Brimshire University

(B) The president of Frompton Tech

(C) The hiring manager of FPL Enterprises

(D) An acquaintance of Ms. Schmidt

198. How much managerial experience is most likely required for the job opening?

(A) 3 years

(B) 4 years

(C) 5 years

(D) 9 years

199. In the second e-mail, the word "round" in paragraph 2, line 5, is closest in meaning to

(A) circle

(B) series

(C) visit

(D) chance

200. What can be understood about Joanna Tempest?

(A) She has met with Ms. Singh before.

(B) She displayed creative ideas throughout the interview.

(C) She has worked for a rival of Kentish Supplies.

(D) She did not make a good impression on Mr. Richards.

1

正解 ➤ (D)

(A) He's touching a keyboard.
(B) He's hanging up the telephone.
(C) He's glancing at a telephone directory.
(D) He has put on some footwear.

(A) 彼はキーボードに触れている。
(B) 彼は電話を切ろうとしている。
(C) 彼は電話帳をさっと読んでいる。
(D) 彼は靴を履いている。

正解 has put on という現在完了形で物をすでに身に着けている状態を表せるので，(D) が適切。He is putting some footwear.（靴を履いている最中だ）や，He has put some footwear on the table.（靴をテーブルに置いたままにしている）との違いに注意。**誤答** (C) は，directory を directly と聞き間違えないよう，文の最後まで集中力を維持しよう。

重要語句 □ hang up「電話を切る」 □ glance at ...「～をさっと見る，読む」 □ telephone directory「電話帳」

2

正解 ➤ (B)

(A) They're setting down some chairs.
(B) Their belongings are at their feet.
(C) They have their backs on the ground.
(D) They're seated opposite one another.

(A) 彼らはイスをいくつか下に置いているところだ。
(B) 彼らの持ち物は足元にある。
(C) 彼らは背中を地面につけている。
(D) 彼らは互いに向かい合って座っている。

正解 足元にモノが置いてあることから，(B) が正解だとわかる。**誤答** (A) の setting down は下にモノを置く最中であることを示す。(C) の backs [bǽks] を bags [bǽgz] と聞き間違えないように注意。(D) は，They're seated side by side. であれば正解となる。

重要語句 □ have one's back on ...「～に背をつけている」 ※have one's back to ...（～に背を向けている）も重要表現。 □ be seated「座っている」 □ opposite「～の反対側に，向こう側に」（= across from ...）

正解 ➤ (A)

(A) The man's performing repairs in a workshop.

(B) The man's adjusting a workbench.

(C) The man's rolling up his sleeves.

(D) The man's having a tool examined.

(A) 男性が作業場で修理をしている。

(B) 男性が作業台を調節している。

(C) 男性が袖をまくり上げているところだ。

(D) 男性が道具を点検してもらっている。

正解 男性が修理をしているのか確信が持てない場合は，他の選択肢が明らかに間違いであることを確認し，(A) を選ぼう。workshop は「研修会」のイメージが強いが，もとは「作業場」を意味する名詞であることも覚えておきたい。誤答 (C) は The man has his sleeves rolled up, (D) は The man's examining a tool. であればよい。

重要語句 □ perform「～を行う」(= carry out)　□ workbench「作業台」　□ have ... 過去分詞「…を～させる，してもらう」

 満点ポイント! 定番表現をおさえる

正解 ➤ (B)

(A) A server is taking a menu from a diner.

(B) A clerk is waiting on a customer.

(C) An employee is staffing a cashier booth.

(D) An attendant is serving refreshments.

(A) 給仕係が食事客からメニューを取り上げている。

(B) 店員が接客をしている。

(C) 従業員が料金ブースで働いている。

(D) 接客係が軽食を出している。

正解 飲食店の店員が接客をしている様子を言い表した (B) が正解。wait on *someone* は「人に接客をする」(= serve *someone*)の意味。誤答 (A) は taking an order であればよい。(C) の動詞 staff(～で働く)は重要語で，ここでは, An employee [A cashier] is staffing the counter. であれば正解。(D) は店員がこれから行うかもしれないが，Part 1 ではあくまで写真に写っている動作を選ぶ必要がある。

重要語句 □ server「給仕係」(= waiter/waitress)　□ booth「(小さく仕切られた) 小部屋，ブース」※「電話ボックス」は phone booth。　□ refreshments「軽食」

5 満点ポイント！ 現在進行形の受動態　　　　　　　　　　正解 ➤ (A)

(A) Garments are being stored on a rack.
(B) Coats are being hung on a hook.
(C) Boxes are being stacked on a cart.
(D) Some merchandise is being packaged.

(A) 衣服がコートかけに保管されている。
(B) コートがフックにかけられているところだ。
(C) 本がカートに積まれているところだ。
(D) 商品が梱包されているところだ。

正解 コートがかかった状態で保管されているので，この様子を言い表した (A) が正解。動詞 store は保管している「状態」を示せるので，is being stored が is stored と同じ意味を表すことになる。名詞 rack は，「商品棚」や「衣服かけ」など，物を入れたりかけたりする場所を幅広く指す重要語。誤答 (B) の動詞 hang は，... is hanging（〜がかかっている）という能動態も，... is [has been] hung（〜がかけられている）という受動態も同じ様子を表すことになるが，... is being hung とすると「今かけられている最中」を示すことに注意。

重要語句　□ garment「衣服」（= a piece of clothing）

6 満点ポイント！ 風景描写を極める　　　　　　　　　　　正解 ➤ (D)

(A) The beach is off-limits to the public.
(B) Some people are sitting on wooden crates.
(C) Some logs have been placed on end.
(D) A path runs alongside the beach.

(A) ビーチが立ち入り禁止になっている。
(B) 数人が木箱の上に座っている。
(C) 丸太が直立するように置かれている。
(D) 小道がビーチに沿って走っている。

正解 写真の手前に小道が写っていることを見逃さないようにし，(D) を選ぶ。誤答 (B) は，sitting on logs であれば正解。crate（箱）は Part 1 に頻出するので，必ず覚えておこう。

重要語句　□ off-limits to *someone*「人が立ち入り禁止の」（↔ open to *someone*）　□ crate「（運搬用の）箱」
　　　　　□ place [stand] ... on end「〜を直立させる」（= put ... in the upright position）

(A) The people have gathered to form a line.

(B) A trash bin is being set up on the runway.

(C) A vehicle is hovering near the front of the structure.

(D) A shelter has a slanted roof.

(A) 人々が集まって列をなしている。

(B) ゴミ箱が滑走路に設置されているところだ。

(C) 乗り物が建物の近くで空中にとどまっている。

(D) 小屋の屋根が傾斜している。

正解 写真手前の右側に屋根の傾斜した小屋状のものがあるので，(D) が適切。名詞 shelter は，天候などから人やモノを守る場所を指す語として Part 1 に登場する（バス停の雨よけスペースは bus shelter）。誤答 ちなみに，遠景の見える写真では，There is a mountain in the distance.（離れたところに山がある）のように，後方の目立たない景色を描写する文が正解になることもあるので注意。

重要語句 □ form a line「列になる」※form a circle「円になる」もおさえておこう。　□ trash bin「ゴミ箱」　□ runway「滑走路」　□ hover「空中にとどまる」　□ slanted「傾斜している」

(A) One of the women is reading to visitors.

(B) One of the men is folding some pamphlets.

(C) Some items have been laid out on display.

(D) Some men are stationed at a reception desk.

(A) 女性の一人が来場客に対して本を読み聞かせている。

(B) 男性の一人がパンフレットを折り畳んでいる。

(C) いくつかの物がテーブルの上に広げて展示されている。

(D) 男性の何人かが受付係をしている。

正解 テーブルの上にさまざまなモノが置かれている様子を表した (C) が正解。誤答 (B) は，folding「折りたたんでいる」を holding「手に持っている」と聞き間違えないように注意しよう。(D) の be stationed at ...（〜に配属されて働いている）は正解として登場することがある。

重要語句 □ read to *someone*「人に読み聞かせる」　□ lay out ...「〜を広げて置く」（= spread out ...）

(A) The pedestrians are looking over their shoulders.

(B) The walkway of the garden is bordered by the hedge.

(C) A trail is overgrown with plants.

(D) There are some trees between the passersby.

(A) 歩行者が後ろを振り返っている。
(B) 庭園の通路の境が生け垣で縁どられている。
(C) 道に植物が生い茂ったままになっている。
(D) 通行人の間に木が立っている。

正解▶ 庭を区切っている生け垣を hedge と言い，これが通路の両端にあることを描写した (B) を選ぶ難問。動詞 border（〜の境になる）も頻出語で，The hedge borders the walkway of the garden. という能動態で登場することもある。誤答▶ (C) の trail は山道など「踏みならされてできた道」を指す。(D) は，There are some passersby between the trees. であれば正解。

重要語句 □ pedestrian「（車に対して）歩行者」 □ look over *one's* shoulders「（肩ごしから）後ろを振り返る」 □ be bordered by ...「〜が境になっている」 □ overgrown with ...「〜が生い茂ったままの」 □ passerby「通行人」（複数形は passersby）

(A) Handrails are being installed in the stairwell.

(B) Shadows are being cast on a curb.

(C) A pillar stands on the landing of the steps.

(D) One of the doors is being opened.

(A) 手すりが吹き抜けの階段に設置されているところだ。
(B) 縁石に影がかかっている。
(C) 支柱が階段の踊り場に立っている。
(D) ドアのひとつが開けられているところだ。

正解▶ 踊り場の上に柱がある様子を示した (C) が正解となる難問。landing of the steps（階段の踊り場）は，flight of steps（一続きの階段）という表現とともに覚えておきたい。誤答▶ (A) と (D) は，is [are] being という現在進行形を絶対に聞き逃さないこと。(B) は，curb（縁石）を curve（曲線）と混同しないよう注意しよう。

重要語句 □ handrail「手すり」 □ stairwell「（建物内にある）階段の吹き抜けスペース」 □ pillar「（大きな）支柱，円柱」（= column）

11

正解 ➤ (C)

What was the weather like in Chicago?

(A) It depends on which airline I use.

(B) I'm not sure whether it did.

(C) It rained the entire time.

シカゴの天気はどうでしたか。

(A) どの航空会社を利用するかによります。

(B) そうしたのか定かではありません。

(C) ずっと雨が降っていました。

正解 What is ... like? は「〜はどのようなもの（人）ですか」と尋ねる表現で，天気について (C) が適切に答えている。**誤答** (A) は What's the airfare to Chicago? に対する応答。(B) は weather と whether（ともに [wéðər]）の音のひっかけをねらったもので，質問にまったく関連がない。実際の Part 2 は，誤答の選択肢にこうしたサウンドトリックを用いたものがかなり多くを占める。

重要語句 □ the entire time「ずっと」（= the whole time）

12

正解 ➤ (B)

Should I read this list of projects aloud?

(A) Yes, you're allowed to leave.

(B) No, we each have a copy.

(C) Sarah will make a great leader.

このプロジェクトのリストを声に出して読みましょうか。

(A) はい，退出して結構です。

(B) いいえ，みんな一部ずつ持っていますので。

(C) サラはすばらしいリーダーになりますね。

正解 Should I ...?（〜しましょうか）という申し出に対して，No と断り，「みんな一部持っている」とその理由を適切に伝えている (B) が正解。**誤答** (A) は aloud—allowed と read—leave，(C) は read—leader のサウンドトリック。こうした検討外れの応答を楽しみながら先に進もう。

重要語句 □ make ＋ポジティブな形容詞＋名詞「〜になる」

13

 場面を瞬時にイメージする

正解 ➤ (A)

Where did you learn bookkeeping?

(A) Actually, I taught myself.

(B) There were a few matters to attend to.

(C) About a year ago.

どこで簿記を習ったのですか。

(A) じつは独学なんです。

(B) 対処すべき問題がいくつかありました。

(C) 一年ほど前です。

正解 (A) の teach *oneself* は「独学で学ぶ」という意味なので，場所を答えていなくても応答が成り立っている。**誤答** (B) は attend（〜に出席する）と attend to（〜に対処する）の混同をねらったひっかけ。(C) は When に対する応答なので，絶対に冒頭の Where を聞き逃してはいけない。

重要語句 □ bookkeeping「簿記，経理」 □ attend to ...「〜に対処する」（= take care of ...）

14 満点ポイント！ 場面を瞬時にイメージする 正解 ➤ (C)

Who was at the banquet?

(A) More people were invited this year.

(B) We expected Garcia to come.

(C) Here's the list of attendees.

夕食会に誰がいましたか。

(A) 今年はさらに多くの人が招待されました。

(B) ガルシアが来ると思っていました。

(C) こちらが出席者リストです。

正解 出席者が誰だったかに対して，(C) はそのリストを見せているので，自然なやりとりになっている。**誤答** (A) は招待者数を答えているだけなので不適切。(B) にはガルシアという名前は出てくるが，「誰がいたか」の答えにはなっていない。

15 満点ポイント！ 場面を瞬時にイメージする 正解 ➤ (C)

He's the new head of finance, isn't he?

(A) He probably does.

(B) I interviewed for the position.

(C) You mean the man with a bow tie?

彼が新しい経理部長ですよね？

(A) おそらくそうすると思います。

(B) 私はその仕事の面接を受けました。

(C) 蝶ネクタイをしている男性のことですか。

正解 向こう側にいる男性を見て会話をしている場面。(C) がどの男性を指しているかを確認しており，応答が成立している。**誤答** (A) は He probably is. であればよいが，does を用いると He works in finance, doesn't he? などに対する応答になる。

重要語句 □ interview for ...「(仕事など)の面接を受ける」(= have an interview for ...) □ bow tie「蝶ネクタイ」

16 満点ポイント！ 発言を極める 正解 ➤ (A)

The delegates will be arriving any minute now.

(A) We'd better get ready to greet them.

(B) Sure, whenever they'd like.

(C) It's due at five this afternoon.

代表者たちが今すぐにでも到着します。

(A) 出迎える準備をしなくてはいけませんね。

(B) もちろん，希望する時でいつでもいいです。

(C) 今日の午後 5 時が期限です。

正解 今すぐ到着する代表者たちについて，(A) が「出迎える準備をすべきだ」と適切に答えている。**誤答** (B) は Is it all right if my staff visit your office?, (C) は，When should I send this report by? などに対する応答。

重要語句 □ delegate「(派遣されて来る) 代表者」※「代表団」は delegation（= group of delegates）と言う。
□ any minute now「今すぐにでも」

17 満点ポイント！ 場面を瞬時にイメージする 　　　　　正解 ➤ (B)

When did you buy that car?

(A) Not until later this week.

(B) It actually belongs to my company.

(C) At the dealership downtown.

あの車はいつ買ったのですか。

(A) 今週後半まではしません。

(B) じつはうちの会社のものなのです。

(C) ダウンタウンにある販売店でです。

正解 使用している車に関して、「会社のものだ」ということで、自分のものではないことを伝えている (B) が正解。When に対して「時」で答えない難問で、メッセージそのものをくみ取る力が求められる。**誤答** (A) の later this week は未来を示す表現なので、質問が When are you going to buy a car? であればよい。(C) は where に対する応答。

重要語句 □ dealership「特約販売店」(= dealer)

18 　　　　　正解 ➤ (A)

How much paper should I order?

(A) Three boxes should do.

(B) Fifty-nine dollars in total.

(C) Please check with me first.

用紙をどれくらい注文したらいいですか。

(A) 3 箱で足りるはずです。

(B) 合計で 59 ドルです。

(C) まず私に確認をとってください。

正解 注文すべき用紙の量について three boxes と答えている (A) が適切。この do は「事が足りる」(= be enough or suitable) という意味で、会話でよく用いられる。また、質問文と同じ語（ここでは should）が選択肢に含まれていても、必ずひっかけとは限らないので、あくまで自然な応答かをそのつど判断しよう。**誤答** (B) は How much is the paper? に対する応答。(C) は Please check with Mr. Kato first. であればよいが、ここではまさに相手に確認をとっているので不適切。

19 　　　　　正解 ➤ (A)

Did that package ever make it to the Paris branch?

(A) I was told they received it.

(B) Yes, they're all ready to be shipped.

(C) I wonder how much they weighed.

あの荷物はパリ支社にはたして着いたのでしょうか。

(A) 受け取ったとの報告を受けました。

(B) はい、すべて配送準備が整っています。

(C) どれくらいの重量だったのでしょう。

正解 make it to a place は「場所に（なんとか）着く」という意味。package が着いたかどうかについて、(A) は「受け取ったと報告を受けた」と答えている。they は people in the Paris branch を意味している。**誤答** (B) と (C) は they の指すべき「複数のモノ」が質問文になく、また質問に答えてもいない。

280

Disc 2 24 20

正解 ▶ (C)

Whose laptop is that on the table?

(A) Mr. Johnston's over there.

(B) Mostly for visitors to the store.

(C) The client must have left it by accident.

テーブルにあるのは誰のノートパソコンですか。

(A) ジョーンストンさんはあちら側にいます。

(B) 主に来店された方のためです。

(C) クライアントがうっかり置き忘れたのでしょう。

正解 laptop の持ち主について尋ねているのに対し，おそらくクライアントのものであることを伝えている (C) が適切。**誤答** (A) の Mr. Johnston's は Mr. Johnston is の省略形。これが It's Mr. Johnston's. であれば Mr. Johnston's laptop を指し，正解となる。(B) は用途を答えているので，What's that laptop on the table for? に対する応答。

重要語句 □ must have + 過去分詞「〜したに違いない」 □ by accident「うっかり，意図せずに」(= accidentally)

Disc 2 25 21

正解 ▶ (A)

Should we call it a day?

(A) I still have a thing or two to get done.

(B) He contacted us this morning.

(C) Well, it's Friday.

今日はここまでにしましょうか。

(A) まだひとつかふたつやるべき事が残っています。

(B) 彼は今朝連絡をしてきました。

(C) ええと，金曜日です。

正解 call it a day は「一日の仕事を切り上げる」という意味の慣用表現。まだ仕事が残っていることを伝えている (A) が応答として成り立つ。**誤答** (B) は Should we call the client today? に対する答えになる。(C) は a day—Friday のサウンドトリック。

重要語句 □ get ... done「〜を終わらせる」(= finish)

Disc 2 26 22 満点ポイント！ 発言を極める

正解 ▶ (B)

I'm having trouble with my car.

(A) That'd be a breakthrough.

(B) Why not take it to the shop?

(C) Do you know when it ended?

車の調子が悪いんです。

(A) それは大発見になりますね。

(B) 修理に出してはどうですか。

(C) いつ終わったかわかりますか。

正解 車の不具合について，(B) は修理に持っていくことを提案している。Why not ... は「〜したらどうか」(= Why don't you ...?)という提案表現。**誤答** (A) の breakthrough は「(研究などにおける)大発見，大躍進」の意味で，breakdown (故障)と混同しないように注意。(C) は，Do you know when it started? であれば，不具合がいつ起こり始めたかを尋ねる適切な応答になる。

重要語句 □ shop「修理工場 (= repair shop)」

23 満点ポイント! 場面を瞬時にイメージする
Disc 2 27

正解 ➤ (C)

Where do you want this stack of books?	この積み重なった本はどこに置けばいいですか。
(A) To a bookstore on the corner.	(A) 角の書店へです。
(B) Can you do it for me by Friday?	(B) 金曜日までにやってもらえますか。
(C) Let me make some room.	(C) 今スペースを確保します。

正解 質問文を聞いて，同僚が本の移動を手伝ってくれる場面が瞬時にイメージできただろうか。(C) は，本の置き場を確保すると伝えているので，これが正解と判断できる。誤答 (A) は方向を示す前置詞 to で始まっているので，Where do you want to take this stack of books? であればよい。(B) は when に対する応答。

重要語句 □ room「(不可算名詞で) スペース」(= space)

24
Disc 2 28

正解 ➤ (B)

How long have the technicians been working on the problem?	技術者たちはどれくらいの間この問題に取り組んでいますか。
(A) Just about a week ago.	(A) ちょうど1週間ほど前です。
(B) It hasn't been very long at all.	(B) ぜんぜん長くはありません。
(C) During the next three days.	(C) これから3日間のうちにです。

正解 how long で「継続の長さ」を尋ねているのに対し，(B) は問題に取り組み始めたばかりであることを示唆している。質問と選択肢の両方に long を登場させることで，逆に上級者を惑わせる問題になっている。誤答 (A) は When did the technicians start working on the problem?，(C) は When will the technicians work on the problem? に対する応答。

---

25 選択疑問文 満点ポイント! 場面をイメージする
Disc 2 29

正解 ➤ (B)

Could you spare some time to review the upcoming project now or would it be more convenient to do it later?	今度のプロジェクトについて確認する時間を今取れますか，それとも後のほうが都合がよいですか。
(A) I don't mind it, either.	(A) 私も気にしませんよ。
(B) Let me get something to eat first.	(B) まず何か食べる物を買いに行かせてください。
(C) It would be quite noisy in there.	(C) その中だと騒々しいですよ。

正解 プロジェクトの確認を今できるか後にするかを尋ねる選択疑問文。(B) は「まず食べ物を買いに行かせてほしい」と述べることで，その後でなら確認ができることを間接的に伝えている。誤答 (A) は，I don't mind either way.（どちらでも構いません）であれば正解になるので注意。(C) は Can we review the project in the break room? などに対する応答になる。

重要語句 □ spare time「時間を割く」

282

Disc 2 30 26 否定疑問文

Aren't you through with this computer?

(A) I'm nearly done with it.

(B) It should be the latest model.

(C) Let me show you how.

このパソコンを使い終わっていないのですか。

(A) もうすぐ終わります。

(B) 最新モデルのはずです。

(C) 方法を教えましょう。

正解 be through with ... は「〜をやり終える」(= be finished with ...; be done with ...) という意味。「(終わっていると思ったが)終わっていないのか」と驚きを示す相手に対して,(A) が「ほぼ終わっている」と適切に答えている。**誤答** (B) は computer と latest model という関連語を用いたひっかけの選択肢。(C) は Can you tell me how to use this computer? などに対する応答。

Disc 2 31 27

正解 ➤ (C)

Who told you to put a hold on the order of supplies?

(A) My secretary put them in order.

(B) I couldn't postpone it any longer.

(C) The manager said we had enough of everything.

誰が必要品の注文を保留にするよう指示したのですか。

(A) 私の秘書が順番どおりに揃えました。

(B) 私はこれ以上延期できませんでした。

(C) 部長がすべて十分あると言っていたのです。

正解 put a hold on ... は「〜を保留にする」(= suspend) の意味。(C) は「部長が必要品はすべてあると言っていた」と述べることで,注文の保留が部長の指示であることを伝えている。**誤答** (A) は put や order という同一語によるサウンドトリック。

重要語句 □ put ... in order「〜を順番どおりに揃える」

---

28 満点ポイント! 場面をイメージする

正解 ➤ (A)

 Disc 2 32 Why didn't you join us at the company picnic on Friday?

(A) A friend of mine dropped by unexpectedly.

(B) It was actually cancelled because of the rain.

(C) I must have forgotten to sign in.

なぜ金曜日の会社ピクニックに一緒に来なかったのですか。

(A) 友人が突然訪ねてきたのです。

(B) じつは雨で中止になったのです。

(C) ログインし忘れたに違いありません。

正解 ピクニックに来なかった同僚にその理由を尋ねており,(A) が適切に答えている。**誤答** (B) は質問文が Why didn't you go to the company picnic? であればよいが,ここでは join us という表現からイベントは実際に行われたとわかるので不適切。(C) は sign in の部分が質問に関連しない。

重要語句 □ drop by「立ち寄る」(= stop by) □ sign in「(ウェブサイトに) ログインする,(建物に) 署名して入る」

Disc 2
33

Ms. Huang will be back to work soon, won't she?

(A) For about a week or so.

(B) She said she'll get it back to us tomorrow.

(C) The date hasn't been decided yet.

ホアンさんはそろそろ職場に復帰しますよね？

(A) 1 週間かそこらです。

(B) 明日返してくれると言っていました。

(C) 日にちはまだ決まっていません。

正解▶ Ms. Huang の職場復帰の時期について，「復帰日が決まっていない」と答えている (C) が適切。
誤答▶ (A) は In about a week or so.（1 週間後かそこら）であればよいが，期間を答えているので会話が成立しない。(B) は get it back—get back の混同をねらったサウンドトリック。

重要語句 □ get A back to B「A を B の元に返す」

Disc 2
34

30 　　　　　　　　　　　　　　　　　　　　　　　正解 ▶ (B)

When is the award winner going to be announced?

(A) Since 5 o'clock.

(B) During the year-end reception.

(C) At the municipal auditorium.

受賞者はいつ発表される予定ですか。

(A) 5 時からずっと。

(B) 年末の祝賀会で。

(C) 市公会堂で。

正解▶ When で時を尋ねているのに対し，(B) は「発表される機会」を答えているので，会話が成立している。誤答▶ (A) の since は「過去のある時点から（今まで）」を意味するので，予定を尋ねる質問の答えとして不適切。(C) は Where に対する応答だが，Part 2 の後半で集中力を欠くあまり，冒頭を聞き落とすことが上級者でもあるので注意。

重要語句 □ municipal「市（営）の」 □ auditorium「講堂」

Disc 2
35

31 　　　　　　　　　　　　　　　　　　　　　　　正解 ▶ (B)

What if I want to end the lease agreement early?

(A) We'll end up rushing to finish on time.

(B) You may have to pay an extra fee.

(C) The first one leaves this morning.

リース契約を早く打ち切りたい場合どうなりますか。

(A) 期日に終わらすために急ぐことになるでしょう。

(B) 追加手数料を支払う必要があるかもしれません。

(C) 最初のは今朝出発します。

正解▶ What if ...? は「〜したらどうなるのか」と尋ねる慣用表現。契約を打ち切る場合について，手数料を支払う必要があると伝えている (B) が正解。誤答▶ (A) は，What if I move up the deadline?（期日を早めたらどうなるか）に対する応答。(C) は early と this morning という関連語はあるが，質問の内容にはまったく答えていない。

重要語句 □ end up doing「（結局）〜することになる」（= do ... eventually）

 **32** 満点ポイント！ 発言問題を極める　　　　　　　正解 ➤ (B)

I need a word with you about the Henderson contract.

(A) I've already signed for it.

(B) Is anything the matter with it?

(C) You can take it from my desk.

ヘンダーソン社との契約に関して話があります。

(A) すでに受領のサインをしました。

(B) 何か問題でもあるのですか。

(C) 私の机から取っていいですよ。

正解 need a word with *someone* は「〜と（折り入って）話がある」という意味。ここでは、「契約に関して話がある」と言われたのに対し、「問題があるのですか」と聞き返している (B) が自然な応答である。このように、「発言」→「質問」が答えになるパターンにぜひ慣れておきたい。誤答 (A) の sign for ... は「（配達物など）の受け取りのサインをする」という意味なので注意。(C) は I need a copy of the contract. に対する応答。

 33　　　　　　　　　　　　　　　　　　　　　　正解 ➤ (C)

Is there any way to have these charts ready for tomorrow's meeting?

(A) Why don't you ask Ms. Jones for some?

(B) He should be there by ten.

(C) I suppose so, if I work late.

これらの表を明日の会議までに仕上げる方法はありますか。

(A) ジョーンズさんに頼んでいくつかもらったらどうですか。

(B) 彼は 10 時までにはそこにいるはずです。

(C) 私が残業すればできると思います。

正解 charts を明日までに仕上げられるかについて、(C) は I suppose so.（そう思う）とまず肯定し、if I work late とその条件を述べているので、応答が成立している。誤答 (A) は Why don't you ask Ms. Jones for some help? であればよいが、ここでは some が some chart を指すので、作業中の charts を仕上げる答えになっていない。(B) は He の指す人物が質問文にない。

---

 34 付加疑問文 満点ポイント！ 一瞬たりとも聞き逃さない　　　正解 ➤ (B)

You haven't seen the updated list of suppliers, have you?

(A) I think I've seen him downstairs.

(B) It's still being compiled.

(C) I'll contact one of those companies.

販売業者を記載した最新のリストを見ていませんよね？

(A) 下の階で彼を見た気がします。

(B) まだ編集中です。

(C) それらの会社のひとつに連絡してみます。

正解 updated list を見ていないかを確認しているのに対し、(B) は「編集中だ」と答えることで list がまだできあがっていないことを伝えている。誤答 (A) は him ではなく it（= the list）であれば正解になるので、細部まで集中して聞こう。

重要語句 □ compile「〜をまとめる，編集する」（= put ... together）

285

35　満点ポイント！　一瞬たりとも聞き逃さない　　　　　正解 ▶ (A)

Why aren't more customers subscribing to our new online service?

(A) It seems that the menu is difficult to use.

(B) It's quite time-consuming for us.

(C) Because it's more efficient than our rival's.

なぜもっと多くの顧客が当社の新しいオンラインサービスに加入しないのでしょうか。

(A) メニュー画面が利用しづらいようです。

(B) かなり我々の時間がかかります。

(C) 競合他社のものよりも効率が良いからです。

正解 online service に顧客が加入しない理由について，menu の使いづらさを指摘している (A) が適切。誤答 (B) は It's quite time-consuming for them (= customers). であれば応答が成立する。(C) は aren't を are と聞き間違えると正解になってしまうので，すべて聞き逃さない集中力が必要。

重要語句　□ subscribe to ...「（サービス）に加入する」（= pay money regularly to receive a service）

36　選択疑問文　満点ポイント！　場面をイメージする　　　正解 ▶ (A)

Do you have everything you need or is there anything you want me to pick up from the store?

(A) I'm fine, thanks.

(B) I wish I had more time.

(C) Well, I didn't put in any order.

必要なものはすべてありますか，それともお店で何か買ってきてほしいですか。

(A) 結構ですよ，ありがとうございます。

(B) もっと時間があればいいのですが。

(C) ええと，私は何も注文していません。

正解 自分が買出しに出かけるときに尋ねる選択疑問文。(A) の I'm fine は I'm OK の意味で，特に必要がないことをお礼とともに伝えている。誤答 (B) は何をする時間が必要なのかが不明確。(C) は Are you expecting anything from the supplier? などに対する応答。

重要語句　□ pick ... up「（店で）〜を買う」（= buy）　□ put in an order「注文をする」（= place an order）

37　否定疑問文　　　　　　　　　　　　　　　　　　　　　正解 ▶ (C)

Won't there be a chance to give the visitors a tour of our production facility?

(A) Our plant was understaffed.

(B) Their flight has been delayed.

(C) As long as time permits.

来訪者に当社の生産施設を案内する機会はないのですか。

(A) 工場は人員不足でした。

(B) 彼らの便が遅れています。

(C) 時間が許す限りはあります。

正解 生産施設を visitors に案内する機会があるかどうかについて，(C) は「時間があれば（案内する機会がある）」と適切に答えている。as long as time permits は「時間が許せば，時間があれば」という重要表現。誤答 (A) は Why did we miss our production target?，(B) は Why are the visitors late for the tour? などに対する応答。

286

Disc 2 42 38 満点ポイント！ 場面をイメージする 正解 ➤ (B)

How do you account for the decline in attendance this year?

(A) I'm going to use the new software.

(B) The subject matter could have been more appealing.

(C) Almost 30 percent of the total figure.

今年の参加人数が減少した理由についてどう思いますか。

(A) 新しいソフトウェアを使う予定です。

(B) テーマをもっと興味深い内容にできたのかもしれません。

(C) 総数のほぼ 30 パーセントです。

正解 account for ... には「〜の理由を説明する」（＝ explain the reason of ...）の意味があり，How do you account for ...? で理由を尋ねる表現になる。ここでは参加者が減った理由について「テーマをもっと魅力的にできた」と答えている (B) が自然な応答。**誤答** account for ... には「割合を占める」という意味もあり，(C) は質問が What percentage of the attendees do men account for? であれば正解となる。

重要語句 □ could have been ...「〜になりえた」 □ appealing「魅力的な」（＝ attractive）

Disc 2 43 39 正解 ➤ (A)

Do you know whether the meeting has been rescheduled for Tuesday or Thursday?

(A) No, but I can find out.

(B) It depends on how many people attend.

(C) Could we do it both ways?

会議の変更日が火曜日になったか木曜日になったか知っていますか。

(A) いいえ，でも調べられますよ。

(B) どれくらいの人が出席するかによります。

(C) 両方のやり方でできませんか。

正解 会議の曜日について，No で「わからない」と答えながらも，I can find out（調べられます）と相手にオファーをしている (A) が適切。選択疑問文に Yes/No で答えることは原則できないが，ここでは Do you know ...? という Yes/No 疑問文が組み合わされていることに注意。**誤答** (B) の It depends on ...（〜次第だ）や (C) の both は選択疑問文に対する答えになることも多いが，ここでは応答が成立しない。

Disc 2 44 40 満点ポイント！ 発言問題を極める 正解 ➤ (C)

It'll be easier to understand if you put the figures beside each column.

(A) It's actually too heavy to move.

(B) I thought they were very understanding.

(C) I need more space on the page.

数値を各列の横に入れればもっとわかりやすくなりますよ。

(A) じつは重すぎて動かせないのです。

(B) とても理解のある人たちだと思いました。

(C) ページ上に余白がもっと必要なのです。

正解 「数値を横に入れればよい」という相手の提案に対して，(C) は「スペースがもっと必要だ」と提案に沿えない理由を適切に伝えている。**誤答** (A) は会話の「かみ合わなさ」を楽しもう。(B) は understand—understanding の混同をねらったひっかけで，understanding は「理解のある，同情心のある」（＝ sympathetic）という意味であることに注意。

重要語句 □ column「（縦の）欄，列」※column にはもともと「柱」の意味がある。

41-43

Questions 41 through 43 refer to the following conversation.

M: Hello, I recently moved here from overseas, and **Q41** I was wondering how I can get national health coverage.

W: **Q42** You need to be a resident for at least three months. After that, **Q43** you can send in an application by mail.

M: What kind of documentation do I need?

W: A copy of your passport and visa, as well as your banking details. Applications can be downloaded from our Web site. They usually take about two weeks to process. We'll notify you by mail when your health card is ready, and then you need to come and pick it up at our office.

重要語句 □ coverage「(保険による)補償」 □ send ... in「(提出書類など)を送る」

男性：こんにちは。海外から最近越してきたばかりなのですが、どうしたら国民健康保険に加入できるか知りたいんです。

女性：最低でも3か月間ここに住む必要があります。その後、郵送で申請書を送ってください。

男性：どのような書類が必要ですか。

女性：パスポートとビザのコピー、それと銀行の取引明細が必要です。申請書は私たちのウェブサイトからダウンロードできます。手続きには通常2週間ほどかかります。健康保険カードができ次第、郵送で通知します。その後で、カードを当事務所へ取りにきていただく必要があります。

41

正解 ➤ **(D)**

What does the man want to do?

(A) Receive a driver's license
(B) Apply for a resident visa
(C) Open a bank account
(D) Obtain health insurance

男性は何をしたいのですか。

(A) 免許証の取得
(B) 住居ビザの申請
(C) 銀行口座の開設
(D) 健康保険への加入

正解 男性の発言に注目。冒頭で I was wondering how I can get national health coverage. と述べていることから、(D) が正解だとわかる。後半で女性が「health card ができたら通知します」と話していることもヒント。

42 満点ポイント！ 「詳細問題」のヒントを聞き逃さない　　正解 ➤ (D)

How long must the man live in the country before applying? (A) Two weeks (B) Three weeks (C) Two months **(D) Three months**	申請する前に男性はこの国にどれだけ住んでいなければなりませんか。 (A) 2週間 (B) 3週間 (C) 2か月 (D) 3か月

正解 女性が You need to be a resident for at least three months. と期間を明確に述べているので，(D) を確実に選びたい。前の設問とヒントが連続するので，絶対に聞き逃さないようにしよう。
誤答 (A) は手続きの所要期間。

43 満点ポイント！ 「詳細問題」のヒントを聞き逃さない　　正解 ➤ (B)

How should the man submit his application? (A) Through a Web site **(B) By mail** (C) By fax (D) In person	男性は申請書をどのように提出しなければなりませんか。 (A) ウェブサイトを通して (B) 郵送で (C) ファクスで (D) 直接手渡しで

正解 提出方法について，女性が you can send in an application by mail と説明しているので，(B) が正解。誤答 (A) は申請書の入手方法，(D) は health card の受け取り方法。今回のように，前半の 2 ～ 3 文に 3 つの設問のヒントがすべて話されるパターンも実際の Part 3 に登場する。

44-46

Disc 2
48-49

Questions 44 through 46 refer to the following conversation.

M: Hello. I have a suit I'd like to have dry cleaned, but I'm checking out tomorrow morning. **Q44** Can your cleaning service take care of it that quickly?

W: It normally takes up to 48 hours for a suit, but we have **Q45** an in-house express service, which costs an extra five dollars. If we get the suit before noon, we can have it ready for you by 8:00 P.M.

M: I definitely need it for my meeting tomorrow, so I don't mind paying more.

W: **Q46** I'll send someone up to collect the suit now. May I have your room number?

重要語句 □ in-house「(他社に委託しているのではなく) 社内で行う」 ※on-site は「現地の，現場の」。

男性：こんにちは。クリーニングに出したいスーツがあるのですが，明朝にはチェックアウトする予定です。こちらのクリーニングはそのくらい早く仕上げることはできますか。

女性：通常であればスーツには最長 48 時間かかりますが，館内で行うお急ぎサービスがあり，5 ドルの追加料金でご利用いただけます。正午までにスーツをお預かりできれば，午後 8 時までにはお渡しできますよ。

男性：明日の会議に必ず必要なので，追加料金を払うのは構いません。

女性：では今お部屋までスーツを取りに行かせます。お部屋番号を教えていただけますか。

44

正解 ➤ **(B)**

Why is the man calling?

(A) To inquire about an express delivery

(B) To request a hotel service

(C) To reschedule an appointment

(D) To ask for a replacement part

男性が電話をしている理由は何ですか。

(A) 速達に関して問い合わせるため

(B) ホテルのサービスを依頼するため

(C) 予約の日程を変更するため

(D) 交換部品を取り寄せるため

正解 男性が冒頭で「スーツをクリーニングに出したいが明朝にはチェックアウトする」と状況を説明したうえで，Can your cleaning service take care of it that quickly? とサービスについて尋ねているので，(B) が正解。**誤答** (A) の express delivery と会話の中にある in-house express service を混同しないように注意。

290

What does the woman say about the express service?

(A) It is only available after 12 P.M.

(B) It is more expensive.

(C) It is not being offered today.

(D) It takes up to 48 hours.

お急ぎサービスについて女性は何と言っていますか。

(A) 午後 12 時以降のみ利用できる。

(B) 通常よりも高い。

(C) 今日は提供されていない。

(D) 最長で 48 時間かかる。

正解 an in-house express service について which costs an extra five dollars と説明を加えているので，(B) が適切。誤答 (A) は「正午までに出せば午後 8 時に仕上がる」とあるだけで，午後のみのサービスというわけではない。(D) は通常提供しているサービスのこと。

What does the woman offer to do?

(A) Send over a technician

(B) Transfer the man's call

(C) Change the man's room

(D) Have an item picked up

女性は何をすることを申し出ていますか。

(A) 技術者を送る

(B) 男性の電話を転送する

(C) 男性の部屋を代える

(D) 物を取りに行かせる

正解 女性のオファーの発言に注目。最後で I'll send someone up to collect the suit now. と申し出ているので，(D) がこれを適切に言い換えている。誤答 (A) は I'll send someone up to fix the air conditioner. などの文脈であれば正解になる。

Disc 2
50-51

47-49

Questions 47 through 49 refer to the following conversation.

W: Hello, **Q47** I'm wondering if anyone has turned in a pair of glasses. They were in a brown leather case. I thought I set them down around here while **Q48** I was looking for books.

M: I'm afraid no one has brought anything here to **Q48** the circulation desk. I'll call the security office and check with them. That's where lost items usually get taken.

W: Thanks. I'm heading up to **Q48** the periodicals room to look at some magazines. I'll stop by here again when I'm done.

M: Okay. **Q49** If anything turns up, you'll hear an announcement over the PA system.

重要語句 □ turn ... in「(紛失物)を届ける」 □ circulation desk「(図書館の)貸出返却デスク」 □ head up to ...「(上の階)に向かう」 □ periodical「定期刊行誌」(= magazine or newspaper) □ stop by「立ち寄る」 □ turn up「(偶然)起こる」(= happen) ※「(物が)見つかる」(= be found)という意味もある。 □ PA system (= public-address system)「場内放送」

女性：こんにちは。どなたかメガネを届けてきた方はいませんでしたか。茶色の皮のケースに入っています。本を探している間，この辺に置いたと思ったのですが。

男性：残念ながら，誰もここの貸出返却デスクに物品を持ってきた方はいません。警備室に電話をして調べてみます。紛失物はたいてい警備室に届けられますから。

女性：ありがとうございます。これから雑誌閲覧室へ雑誌を読みに行くので，終わったらまたここに寄ります。

男性：わかりました。何かあったら，館内放送でお伝えいたします。

---

47 満点 ポイント! 「詳細問題」のヒントを聞き逃さない　　　　正解 ➤ (D)

What is the woman looking for?

(A) Her briefcase

(B) Her gloves

(C) Her books

(D) Her eyeglasses

女性は何を探していますか。

(A) 自分の手提げかばん

(B) 自分の手袋

(C) 自分の本

(D) 自分のメガネ

正解 女性が冒頭で I'm wondering ... a pair of glasses と話しているのを絶対に聞き逃さないようにし，(D) を選ぶ。探し物を答える問題は 1 文目にヒントがあることが多いので，冒頭から集中力を高めておこう。**誤答** (C) は「本を探している間に glasses を置いた」と話しているだけで，自分の本を紛失したのではないことに注意。

292

48

正解 ➤ (C)

Where most likely are the speakers?	2人はおそらくどこにいると思われますか。
(A) At a bookstore	(A) 本屋
(B) At a hotel	(B) ホテル
(C) At a library	(C) 図書館
(D) At a doctor's office	(D) 診療所

正解 女性の I was looking for books という発言でまず (A) か (C) に絞れる。さらに，the circulation desk（貸出返却デスク）や the periodicals room（雑誌閲覧室）が図書館で用いる用語であることをおさえ，(C) を選択する。名詞 circulation は，他にも「発行部数」を意味する重要語。

49

満点ポイント！ 「詳細問題」のヒントを聞き逃さない 正解 ➤ (C)

According to the man, what should the woman do?	男性によると，女性は何をすべきですか。
(A) Go to the security office	(A) 警備室に行く
(B) Ask a clerk upstairs	(B) 上の階の係員に尋ねる
(C) Listen for an announcement	(C) 放送に耳を傾ける
(D) Wait in the lobby	(D) ロビーで待つ

正解 男性が最後に If anything turns up ... over the PA system.（何かあったら館内放送で伝える）と話しているので，女性がすべきことは (C) であると判断できる。listen for ... は「〜に気づくよう耳を傾ける，〜を聞き取る」という意味。誤答 (A) は，男性が I'll call the security office と述べているだけで，そこに行くことを指示してはいない。

Questions 50 through 52 refer to the following conversation.

W: Hi, Mr. Anderson, this is Kate Scholes at **Q50** Target Electronics. **Q50** I believe you worked with Mario Lobello on the sales campaign for our new line of computers last year.

M: That's right. It was a pleasure working with him. How is he doing these days?

W: Actually, **Q51** he's no longer with marketing and I've taken over his duties. **Q52** Jeff Barkley, the product manager for our computer products, spoke very highly of your work, so I'm calling to see if you would be available to work on our new mobile phone campaign.

重要語句 □ take over ...「~を引き継ぐ」(= take control of ...) □ speak highly of ...「~を称賛する」

女性：もしもし，アンダーソンさん。ターゲット・エレクトロニクス社のケイト・スコールズです。昨年，当社の新製品だったパソコンの販売キャンペーンでマリオ・ロベロと一緒にお仕事をなさったと思うのですが。

男性：ええ，彼とは楽しくお仕事をさせていただきました。彼は最近元気ですか。

女性：じつは彼はマーケティング部を離れ，私が彼の仕事を引き継いでいます。パソコン製品マネジャーのジェフ・バークリーがあなたの仕事ぶりを絶賛していましたので，当社の新しい携帯電話のキャンペーンをご担当いただけないかと思いお電話した次第です。

50

正解 ▶ (D)

According to the woman, what happened last year?	女性によれば，昨年何がありましたか。
(A) She participated in a sales campaign.	(A) 彼女が販売キャンペーンに参加した。
(B) Some merchandise was released overseas.	(B) 商品が海外で発売された。
(C) A campaign for new phones was started.	(C) 新しい電話のキャンペーンが開始された。
(D) The man worked with Target Electronics.	(D) 男性がターゲット・エレクトロニクス社と一緒に仕事をした。

正解 女性の last year に関する発言に注目。すると，まず自分の会社名を Target Electronics と述べ，さらに男性に関して「当社のキャンペーンで Mario Lobello と去年一緒に仕事をなさったと思います」と話していることから，(D) が正解。**誤答** (B) は，overseas に関する言及がない。(C) は，女性の最後の発言から，mobile phones のキャンペーンはこれから始まるものであるとわかる。

51·

In what department does the woman most likely work?	女性はおそらくどの部署で働いていますか。
(A) Production	(A) 製造部
(B) Sales	(B) 営業部
(C) Marketing	(C) マーケティング部
(D) Public Relations	(D) 広報部

正解 女性が Mario Lobello に関して he's no longer with marketing と説明した後，I've taken over his duties.（彼の仕事を引き継いだ）と話しているので，彼女が今 (C) のマーケティング部にいると判断できる。会話に登場する sales や production という語に惑わされないように注意。

52

What is mentioned about Jeff Barkley?	ジェフ・バークリーに関して何と述べられていますか。
(A) He designed a mobile phone.	(A) 携帯電話をデザインした。
(B) He is the woman's supervisor.	(B) 女性の上司である。
(C) He praised the man's work.	(C) 男性の仕事ぶりを絶賛した。
(D) He is coordinating an upcoming campaign.	(D) 今度のキャンペーンのコーディネートをしている。

正解 女性の Jeff Barkley ... spoke very highly of your work という発言を聞き逃さないようにし，spoke highly of ...（～を称賛した）を praised と言い換えている (C) を選ぶ。誤答 (D) は話し手の女性に関すること。

53-55

Questions 53 through 55 refer to the following conversation.

W: Jim, **Q53** I've heard that you're giving the opening speech at next month's conference. Are you looking forward to it?

M: I'm rather nervous. **Q53** I've never been very confident addressing a large audience, and I heard that they're expecting over 300 participants this year.

W: I used to feel the same way about speaking to large groups as well, **Q54** but I bought an excellent book on the subject by the actor David Reese. It really helped me a lot. **Q55** If you're working tomorrow, I can bring it in for you.

M: Actually, **Q55** I'll be out inspecting the plant all day. If you leave the book on my desk, I'll take a look at it when I'm back in the office on Thursday. Thanks—I need all the help I can get.

重要語句 □ address *someone*「～に向けてスピーチをする」（= speak to） □ subject「テーマ，主題」※ その前にある前置詞 on は「～に関して」（= about）というトピックを示す。

女性：ジム，来月の会議で開会のスピーチをすることになったと聞きました。楽しみですか。

男性：じつはかなり緊張しているのです。大人数の人たちに向けて話をするのに自信を持てたことがないですし。今年は 300 人を超える参加者がいると聞きました。

女性：私も大人数の前で話すことに対して同じように感じていましたが，それに関して俳優のデビッド・リースが書いた本を買って読んでみたら，すごく役に立ちました。もし明日出勤だったら，持ってきますよ。

男性：じつは明日は一日中工場の視察で外出する予定なんです。私のデスクに置いておいてもらえれば，木曜日にオフィスに戻ってきたときに見てみます。ありがとうございます。手に入るあらゆる助けが必要なので。

53

正解 ➤ **(C)**

What are the speakers discussing?

(A) Proposed topics for a conference

(B) The launch of a publication

(C) The man's public speaking skills

(D) Attendance at the recent event

2 人は何について話をしていますか。

(A) 会議のテーマ案

(B) 出版物の発売

(C) 男性の演説スキル

(D) 最近のイベントへの出席

正解 女性が「スピーチをすることになったと聞いた」と話しかけているのに対し，男性は「人前で話す自信がない」と不安を伝えている流れをつかみ，(C) を選ぶ。**誤答** (D) は Attendance at the upcoming event であれば正解。

54 満点ポイント！ 「詳細問題」のヒントを聞き逃さない　　　正解 ➤ (B)

Who most likely is David Reese?	デビッド・リースとはおそらく誰ですか。
(A) A conference attendee	(A) 会議の参加者
(B) An author	(B) 本の著者
(C) The speakers' colleague	(C) 話し手の同僚
(D) A film maker	(D) 映画監督

正解 女性が I bought an excellent book ... by the actor David Reese と話しているので，彼は actor であり，また (B) の author でもあることがわかる。actor は performer と言い換えられることもある。誤答 (D) の film maker は film director のこと。

55 満点ポイント！ 「詳細問題」のヒントを聞き逃さない　　　正解 ➤ (A)

What will the man do tomorrow?	男性は明日何をしますか。
(A) Visit a factory	(A) 工場を訪れる
(B) Give a speech	(B) スピーチをする
(C) Read a book	(C) 本を読む
(D) Work in his office	(D) オフィスで働く

正解 女性の「明日出勤するなら本を持ってくる」というオファーに対し，男性が I'll be out inspecting the plant all day と明日一日の予定を話していることから，plant を factory と言い換えている (A) が正解。正解のヒントが 2 文にまたがる難問パターンである。誤答 (B) は冒頭から next month のことだとわかる。(C) と (D) は Thursday に行われること。

56-58

Questions 56 through 58 refer to the following conversation.

W: Mr. Olson, **Q56** there's no Betafix cereal left. This is the second month in a row that we've run out before getting the next shipment.

M: It's certainly been selling very well since the manufacturer lowered its prices.

W: Customers have been asking for it. I told the cashiers to suggest other brands, but **Q57** maybe we should put in a bigger order next month.

M: That's a good idea. **Q58** I'd hate to lose business to other stores because of this. I'll tell the purchasing manager to order larger quantities of the cereal.

重要語句 □ run out (of ...)「(~が) 品切れになる, なくなる」 □ sell well「よく売れる」 □ put in an order「注文する」(= place an order)

女性：オルソンさん，ベータフィクスのシリアルの在庫がありません。次の入荷前に品切れになってしまうのはこれで 2 か月目です。

男性：メーカーが価格を下げてから飛ぶように売れていますね。

女性：お客さんから問い合わせがあるんです。レジ担当者には他のブランドを薦めるように言いましたが，来月は注文を増やしたほうがよさそうですね。

男性：それはいい考えですね。このために他の店に客を取られたくありませんから。購買部長にシリアルの注文を増やすように話しておきます。

56

正解 ➤ (A)

What problem is mentioned?

(A) A product is sold out.

(B) A delivery has been delayed.

(C) Sales have decreased.

(D) The merchandise is overpriced.

どのような問題が述べられていますか。

(A) 製品が売り切れている。

(B) 配送が遅れている。

(C) 売上が落ちている。

(D) 商品の値段が高すぎる。

正解 女性が冒頭で「cereal が残っていない」と話し，さらに This is the second month ... before getting the next shipment.（入荷前に品切れになるのは 2 か月目だ）と問題を伝えているので，(A) が正解。**誤答** (B) に関しては言及がなく，(C) と (D) は，男性の It's certainly been selling ... its prices.（メーカーが値下げしてから売上がよい）という発言内容に一致しない。

57 満点ポイント! 「詳細問題」のヒントを聞き逃さない　　正解 ➤ (B)

What does the woman recommend?

(A) Ordering a different brand

(B) Placing a larger order

(C) Offering a discount

(D) Rearranging the display

女性は何を勧めていますか。
(A) 他のメーカーの商品を注文する
(B) 注文を増やす
(C) 割引を提供する
(D) 陳列を組み直す

正解 女性の maybe we should put in a bigger order next month（注文を増やしたほうがよさそうだ）という提案表現に着目し，(B) を選ぶ。男性が最後に「部長に注文を増やすよう話しておく」と答えていることもヒントになる。**誤答** 女性は I told ... suggest other brands（レジ担当者に他のブランドを薦めるように言った）とも話しているが，女性が注文を提案しているわけではないので，(A) は不適切。

58 満点ポイント! 「詳細問題」のヒントを聞き逃さない　　正解 ➤ (B)

What is the man's concern?

(A) He received complaints from customers.

(B) Customers might go to competing stores.

(C) The purchasing manager is absent.

(D) Betafix is no longer being produced.

男性の心配事は何ですか。
(A) 彼は顧客から苦情を受けた。
(B) 顧客が他の競合店に足を運ぶかもしれない。
(C) 購買部長が休んでいる。
(D) ベータフィクスが製造中止になった。

正解 男性の I'd hate to lose business to other stores because of this. という発言から，客が他店に取られることを懸念していると考えられるので，(B) が適切。**誤答** 女性が Customers have been asking for it. と述べているが，男性が苦情を受けたわけではないので，(A) は選べない。

59-61

Disc 2
58-59

Questions 59 through 61 refer to the following conversation.

M: I heard that your department's bid for the Wapshot project was accepted. Well done.

W: Thanks. To be honest, though, **Q59** I'm a little concerned about our ability to finish the work on time. **Q60** Our department has secured a lot of new contracts lately, so everyone has a very hectic schedule, especially since Ron retired.

M: We're pretty busy in the accounting department these days as well. We're getting the annual expense report ready for the board meeting next week. But after that, **Q61** I could spare one or two staff members if you need help.

重要語句 □ bid「入札」(= offer to do work) □ secure「〜を確保・獲得する」(= obtain) □ hectic「多忙な，予定が詰まった」(= full of busy activity) □ spare「(時間・お金・人材など)を貸す，与える」(= give or lend)

男性：そちらの部署がワプショット・プロジェクトを落札したと聞きました。おめでとうございます。

女性：ありがとうございます。でも正直に言うと，期限内に仕事を終わらせられるか少し心配です。最近，うちの部署は新規契約をたくさんとったので，みんなとても多忙なスケジュールを抱えているんです。ロンが退職してからは特にね。

男性：うちの経理部も最近けっこう忙しいですよ。来週の役員会議に向けて年間経費報告をまとめているところなんです。それさえ終われば，人員が必要であれば一人か二人そちらに回せますよ。

59 満点ポイント! 「詳細問題」のヒントを聞き逃さない　　　正解 ➤ (D)

What is the woman worried about?

(A) Having a bid rejected
(B) Finishing tasks before the next meeting
(C) Approving a schedule change
(D) Meeting project requirements

女性は何を心配していますか。

(A) 入札を受け付けてもらえないこと
(B) 次の会議の前に任務を終わらせること
(C) スケジュール変更を承認すること
(D) プロジェクトの条件を満たすこと

正解 女性の懸念を示す発言に注目。すると，I'm a little concerned ... finish the work on time.（期限内に仕事を終わらせられるか心配だ）と話していることから，(D) が言い換えとして適切。**誤答** (B) は Finishing tasks まではよいが，会議があるのは男性のほうなので不適切。

300

60 満点ポイント! 「詳細問題」のヒントを聞き逃さない　　　　　　正解 ➤ (C)

What has the woman's department done recently?	女性の部署は最近何をしましたか。
(A) Hired more accountants	(A) 会計士を追加で雇った
(B) Completed a joint project	(B) 合同プロジェクトを完了した
(C) Received several new contracts	(C) 新規契約をいくつかとった
(D) Relocated to a new office	(D) 新しい事務所に移転した

正解 女性の発言の中で Our department has secured a lot of new contracts lately（新規の契約をたくさんとった）とあることから，secured を received と言い換えている (C) が正解。**誤答** (B) は，男性が冒頭で your department's bid ... was accepted と述べていることから，プロジェクトはこれから開始されることがわかる。

61 満点ポイント! 「詳細問題」のヒントを聞き逃さない　　　　　　正解 ➤ (C)

What does the man offer to do?	男性は何をすることを申し出ていますか。
(A) Train newly hired employees	(A) 新入社員の研修を行う
(B) Prepare documents for the board meeting	(B) 役員会議用の資料を準備する
(C) Assign people to work for the woman's department	(C) 女性の部署で働く人材を送る
(D) Organize a special event	(D) 特別なイベントを計画する

正解 男性の offer を示す表現に注意すると，多忙さを話す女性に対して I could spare one or two staff members（一人か二人そちらに回せる）と申し出ていることから，(C) が正解であると判断できる。**誤答** (B) は，男性の部署が現在取り組んでいること。

Questions 62 through 64 refer to the following conversation.

W: Q62 You certainly have impressive references and education, Mr. Garrett. My only concern is that Q63 you haven't worked in the airline industry before.

M: Well, that's true, but I do have experience as a store manager. The customer service skills I learned there would help me in dealing with the public as a member of Q62 your check-in staff.

W: Okay, And how do you feel about the location and hours? The schedule can be quite irregular, and Q64 you'll need your own car to get to the airport for early-morning shifts.

M: I don't mind the hours. And I don't have a car at the moment, but I would get one if I were offered the job.

重要語句 □ reference「推薦状（= a letter of reference），照会先」

女性：じつにすばらしい推薦状と学歴をお持ちですね，ガレットさん。ただ，航空業界での実務経験がないということだけが気になりますが。

男性：ええ，確かにそうですが，店長としての経験はあります。そこで学んだ顧客サービスのスキルは御社のチェックインカウンタースタッフのメンバーとして，お客様に対応する際にきっと役立ちます。

女性：わかりました。勤務地と勤務時間に関してはどう思いますか。勤務スケジュールはかなり不定期で，早朝シフトの際には空港まで自分の車での出勤となります。

男性：勤務時間は特に気になりません。今は車を持っていませんが，採用していただけたら購入します。

62
正解 ➤ **(C)**

Who most likely is the woman?

(A) A recruitment agency representative

(B) An airport security officer

(C) An employee of an airline

(D) An owner of a store

女性はおそらく誰ですか。

(A) 人材派遣会社の担当者

(B) 空港警備員

(C) 航空会社の従業員

(D) 店の経営者

正解 女性の最初の1～2文から，女性が男性に airline industry での採用面接をしているとわかる。さらに，男性の発言の中に your check-in staff とあることから，女性が航空会社の採用担当であると判断し，(C) を選ぶ。相手がその会社の採用担当者なのか派遣会社の担当者なのかを問う問題は過去にも登場したことがあるので，細かいヒントを聞き逃さないように注意。

63 満点ポイント! 「詳細問題」のヒントを聞き逃さない 　　　　正解 ➤ (D)

What does Mr. Garrett lack?	ガレット氏に欠けているものは何ですか。
(A) Customer service skills	(A) 顧客サービスのスキル
(B) Professional references	(B) 仕事の推薦状
(C) Education credentials	(C) 学歴
(D) Experience in the industry	(D) その業界での経験

正解 Mr. Garrett とは会話をしている男性のこと。女性が彼に対して you haven't worked in the airline industry before と懸念を伝えていることから，(D) が正解であるとわかる。誤答 (A) は，男性が「store manager の経験から身につけた」と述べている。(B) と (C) については，女性が始めに impressive と称賛している。

 64 満点ポイント! 「詳細問題」のヒントを聞き逃さない 　　　　正解 ➤ (B)

According to the woman, what is a requirement of the job?	女性によると，この職に必要な条件は何ですか。
(A) Frequent travel	(A) 頻繁に出張すること
(B) Owning a car	(B) 車を所有していること
(C) Regular overtime	(C) 通常の残業
(D) Managerial skills	(D) 経営管理能力

正解 女性が後半で you'll need your own car と述べているので，(B) が正解。誤答 (C) は，「スケジュールが irregular だ」とは話しているが，その後に early-morning shifts の話があることからも，残業が多いのではなく勤務シフトが不定期であることを意味しているとわかる。

Questions 65 through 67 refer to the following conversation.

W1: Q66 These floral arrangements aren't creating the right kind of visual impact. These tables are just too big by comparison. What should we do? We don't have much time Q65 before the reception starts.

W2: Q66 I was sure we'd ordered enough Q65 flowers, but you're right. We'll need some more to fill out the centerpieces. How are we doing on plates? We have enough Q65 place settings for all the attendees, don't we?

W1: Yes, we have ample dinnerware, but we could use a few extra Q65 chairs. Could you get about ten more in case any unexpected guests show up at the function?

W2: Sure. I'll go ask the staff if I can borrow a few from the hotel. In the meantime, Q67 Bob is headed to the restaurant to pick up the entrée right now. I'll give him a call and ask him to drop by the florist on his way back.

重要語句　□ floral arrangement「生け花，フラワーアレンジメント」　□ by comparison (with ...)「(〜と) 比較すると」　□ centerpiece「テーブル中央の装飾」　□ place setting「(一人分の) 食器一式」　□ ample「十二分の」(= more than enough; sufficient)　□ dinnerware「(ディナー用の) 食器類」　□ could use ...「〜があるとよい，〜があればありがたい」　□ function「式典」(= official event)　□ be headed to ...「〜に向かっている」(= be heading to ...)　□ entrée「主菜」(= main dish)

女性1：これらの生け花では適切な視覚効果が得られませんね。花に比べてテーブルが大きすぎるようです。どうしましょうか。パーティが始まるまであまり時間がありませんよ。

女性2：花は十分注文したと思っていたのですが，確かにそのとおりです。テーブル中央の装飾を埋めるのにもっと花が必要になりそうですね。お皿はどうですか。出席者全員分の食器は一式ありますよね？

女性1：食器類は十分すぎるほどあるのですが，イスがもう少し余分にあってもよいかもしれませんね。パーティに予定外のゲストが来たときに備えて，もう10個ほど取ってきてもらえますか。

女性2：もちろんです。ホテルからいくつか借りられないかスタッフに聞きに行ってきます。その間，ボブが今主菜を取りにレストランに向かっているところですので，彼に電話して，帰りに花屋に寄るようお願いしておきます。

65

正解 ➤ **(D)**

Who most likely are the speakers?

(A) Restaurant servers

(B) Store clerks

(C) Hotel receptionists

(D) Event coordinators

2人はおそらく誰ですか。

(A) レストランの給仕スタッフ

(B) 店の店員

(C) ホテルの受付係

(D) イベントコーディネーター

正解 会話全体から，reception の開始前に2人が flowers や place settings（食器一式），chairs

など会場全体のセッティングをしていることがわかるので，(D) がふさわしいと判断できる。話者が両方とも女性であることに惑わされず，場面展開をイメージしながらポイントを聞き取ろう。**誤答** (C) については，会場が hotel なのはわかるが，2 人がその receptionists（受付係）であるとは考えにくい。

66

What most likely is the problem?

(A) There are insufficient flowers.

(B) An order was not placed in time.

(C) The room is not large enough.

(D) Attendance is higher than expected.

何がおそらく問題となっていますか。

(A) 花が十分にない。

(B) 注文が時間内に行われなかった。

(C) 部屋の大きさが足りない。

(D) 出席者数が予測していたよりも多い。

正解 1 人目の女性が冒頭で floral arrangements について問題を指摘していること，また 2 人目の女性がそれに対し I was sure ... you're right.（十分花を注文したと思ったがそのとおりだ）や We'll need ... the centerpieces.（中央を埋めるのにもっと必要だ）と述べていることから，(A) が問題であるとわかる。**誤答** (D) は，in case any unexpected guests show up（予定外のゲストが来た場合に備えて）とあるだけで，実際の人数が予測より多いというわけではない。

67

満点 ポイント！ 「詳細問題」のヒントを聞き逃さない

What is Bob currently doing?

(A) Purchasing flowers

(B) Picking up some plates

(C) Borrowing a few chairs

(D) Collecting some food

ボブは今何をしていますか。

(A) 花を購入している

(B) お皿を取りに行っている

(C) イスをいくつか借りている

(D) 料理を取りに行っている

正解 2 人目の女性が Bob に関して Bob is headed to the restaurant to pick up the entrée（レストランに主菜を取りに向かっている）と述べているので，the entrée を some food と言い換えた (D) が正解。entrée [ɑ́:ntrei] という発音にも注意。**誤答** (A) は Bob にこれから依頼すること。(C) は 2 人目の女性がこれから行うこと。

68-70

Disc 2
64-65

Questions 68 through 70 refer to the following conversation.

M: I'm afraid that **Q68** our AccountTec software is already out-of-date.

W: Really? **Q68** We just launched the current edition a few months ago. What's the problem?

M: I just looked at Gigasoft's new EZBooks software, which was released last week. It's the same price as our AccountTec, but it has many more advanced features and is much more powerful. It looks like **Q69** it'll soon be outselling us in the market.

W: **Q68** Even if we start work on a new version immediately, it's going to take at least six months to develop. Well, **Q70** after I finish reviewing the sales data, I'll talk to the supervisor and ask what we can do about it.

重要語句 □ out-of-date「時代遅れの」 □ launch「〜を発売する」(= release) □ advanced「高性能の，進んだ」 □ feature「機能」 □ outsell「〜よりも多く売る，多く売れる」

男性：当社のアカウント・テクのソフトがもうすでに時代遅れになっているようです。

女性：本当ですか。最新バージョンを数か月前に発売したばかりですよ。何が問題なんですか。

男性：先週発売されたギガソフト社の新しい EZ ブックスというソフトを見てみたんです。金額は当社のアカウント・テクと同じですが，高度な機能をより多く備えてますし，高性能なのです。すぐにも当社の市場シェアを追い抜きそうな勢いですよ。

女性：今すぐに新しいバージョンに向けて始動したとしても，開発には少なくとも 6 か月かかります。販売データを確認したら，上司に話をして何ができるか相談してみることにします。

68

正解 ▶ (D)

What kind of company do the speakers work for?	2 人はどのような会社に勤めていますか。
(A) An accounting firm	(A) 会計事務所
(B) A computer manufacturer	(B) パソコンメーカー
(C) An electronics store	(C) 家電販売店
(D) A software developer	(D) ソフトウェア開発会社

正解 男性の our AccountTec software という発言，および女性の We just launched the current edition や Even if we start work ... to develop.（今すぐ新バージョンに向けて始動しても開発に 6 か月かかる）といった発言から，2 人は (D) の software developer に勤務していると判断できる。

69

What is suggested about EZBooks?

(A) It is currently less popular than AccountTec.

(B) Its price has recently been reduced.

(C) It runs faster than programs of rival companies.

(D) It is as powerful as AccountTec.

EZ ブックスに関して何が示唆されていますか。

(A) 今のところアカウント・テクよりも人気が低い。

(B) 最近価格が値下げになった。

(C) 競合他社のプログラムよりも動作が速い。

(D) アカウント・テクと同等の性能である。

正解 競合ソフトの EZBooks に関して，男性が it'll soon be outselling us in the market（すぐに当社の市場シェアを追い抜きそうだ）と話していることから，今の時点では AccountTec のほうが売れているとわかる。したがって，(A) が正解。誤答 (B) の価格については the same price as our AccountTec とあるのみ。(D) は，男性が much more powerful と述べている。

70

What will the woman do next?

(A) Start work on a new product

(B) Go over some figures

(C) Contact her supervisor

(D) Read reviews from customers

女性は次に何をしますか。

(A) 新製品の開発に着手する

(B) 数値を確認する

(C) 上司に連絡を取る

(D) 顧客の感想を読む

正解 次の行動は最後の発言にあることがほとんど。ここでは，女性が after I finish reviewing ... to the supervisor（データを確認してから上司に話をしてみる）と述べていることから，まず始めにするのは review the sales data であることをおさえ，これを言い換えた (B) を選ぶ。誤答 (C) は data を確認してから行うこと。

71-73

Questions 71 through 73 refer to the following telephone message.

Hello, Susan, this is Pete. **Q72** I'm hoping you could cover my **Q71** dinner shift next Friday. I'm off that weekend, so I was thinking if you could fill in for me, I'd be able to fly to Santa Cruz and go surfing for a few days. I'll be glad to return the favor next time you want to take time off. I'll be **Q71** waiting tables all day tomorrow if you want to call me on my mobile, and **Q73** we also have a shift together on Thursday, so we could discuss it then, if you like. Please let me know if you can help me out. Thanks, bye.

重要語句 □ cover「~を担う，扱う」(= deal with) □ fill in for *someone*「~の代理を務める」(= cover for *someone*; substitute for *someone*) □ wait tables「(レストランで) 給仕する」 □ call on *one's* mobile「~の携帯電話に連絡する」

71-73 の設問は次の電話メッセージに関するものです。

もしもし，スーザン。ピートです。来週金曜日のディナータイムの勤務を替わってもらえないかと思って電話しました。その週末は私が休みなので，もし替わってもらえれば飛行機でサンタ・クルーズへ行って数日間サーフィンに行けるのです。次にあなたが休みを取りたいときは，喜んでお返しをします。もし携帯電話に連絡をくれるなら明日は一日中レストランで給仕をしていますし，木曜日なら二人とも同じシフトなので，そのときに話し合っても結構です。替わってもらえるかどうか教えてください。ありがとうございます。それでは。

71

正解 ➤ (D)

Where does the speaker work?
(A) At a sports store
(B) At a travel agency
(C) At an airport
(D) At a restaurant

話し手はどこに勤めていますか。
(A) スポーツ用品店
(B) 旅行代理店
(C) 空港
(D) レストラン

正解 冒頭の dinner shift や，後半の waiting tables（給仕をしている）という表現から，(D) が正解であるとわかる。wait tables（給仕する）という表現は，waiter/waitress という名詞のイメージとともにおさえておこう。

満点 ポイント! 「詳細問題」のヒントを聞き逃さない　　　　正解 ➤ (C)

What does the speaker want Susan to do?	話し手はスーザンに何をして欲しいのですか。
(A) Take some time off work	(A) 仕事の休暇を取る
(B) Call back as soon as possible	(B) できるだけ早く折り返し電話をする
(C) Substitute for him	(C) 話し手の仕事を替わる
(D) Reserve a ticket by the end of the week	(D) 週末までにチケットを予約する

正解 冒頭にある I'm hoping you could ...（～してもらえないでしょうか）は丁寧な依頼表現。ここで cover my dinner shift と依頼しているので，これを substitute（代理を務める）で言い換えた (C) が適切。次の文にある fill in for も substitute for の言い換えとしてぜひ覚えておきたい。

誤答 (A) は話し手が行いたいこと。(B) は，「電話でも直接話し合ってもよい」と述べているので不適切。

満点 ポイント! 「詳細問題」のヒントを聞き逃さない　　　　正解 ➤ (C)

When will the speaker most likely meet Susan next?	話し手が次にスーザンに会うのはおそらくいつですか。
(A) Tomorrow	(A) 明日
(B) Tuesday	(B) 火曜日
(C) Thursday	(C) 木曜日
(D) Friday	(D) 金曜日

正解 後半で we also have a shift together on Thursday とあることから，次に会うのは (C) であると判断できる。誤答 (D) の Friday は勤務を替わってほしい曜日。ちなみに，next Friday と言う場合は通常 on Friday next week を指し，今週これからの金曜日は this (coming) Friday と言うことが多い。

74-76

Questions 74 through 76 refer to the following announcement.

Due to recent technical problems, **Q74** an inspection team will be here at the plant all morning tomorrow to look at the freight elevator. **Q75** The elevator will be out of service from 8 until at least 11. If repairs are needed, we may have to shut it down longer. While the team is working, we will be unable to move boxes from the second floor down to the loading deck on the first floor. During that time, **Q76** stack boxes against the wall to the left of the elevator. Once the elevator is working again, we will move the accumulated boxes down in batches.

重要語句 □ freight「積荷, 貨物」 □ loading deck「荷積み場」 □ accumulate「〜を積み上げる, 蓄積する」(= pile ... up; collect) □ in batches「数回に分けて」※batch は「(同時に処理する) 一回分, 一束分」の意味。

74-76 の設問は次のアナウンスに関するものです。

最近の技術的な問題により, 明日の午前中いっぱいは, 調査チームが荷物用エレベータの点検をしに工場に来る予定です。8 時から最短でも 11 時までは, エレベータは立ち入り禁止となります。もし修理が必要となれば, さらに長い時間, 使用停止にしなくてはなりません。調査チームが作業中, 2 階から 1 階の荷積み場まで箱を運ぶことができません。その間は, エレベータの左側の壁に箱を積み重ねるようにしてください。エレベータが再び稼動し始めましたらすぐに, 数回にわけて積まれている箱を下まで運びます。

74

正解 ➤ (A)

What will happen tomorrow?

(A) Some machinery will be inspected.

(B) Production will be suspended.

(C) New equipment will be installed.

(D) The employees will be evaluated.

明日何が起こりますか。

(A) 機械設備の点検がある。

(B) 製造が一時停止になる。

(C) 新しい機器が設置される。

(D) 従業員が評価される。

正解 明日の予定に関して, an inspection team ... to look at the freight elevator (調査チームがエレベータの点検をしに来る) と説明しているので, the freight elevator を some machinery と言い換えている (A) が正解。**誤答** elevator は停止になるが, 製造作業まで停止するとは述べていないので, (B) は不適切。

75 満点ポイント! 「詳細問題」のヒントを聞き逃さない   正解 ➤ (B)

When is the earliest time that the elevator will be accessible?

(A) At 8 A.M.

(B) At 11 A.M.

(C) At noon

(D) At 11 P.M.

エレベータの利用が可能になるのは一番早くていつですか。

(A) 午前 8 時

(B) 午前 11 時

(C) 正午

(D) 午後 11 時

正解 冒頭で「調査チームが all morning tomorrow に工場に来る」とあり，それを受けて The elevator will be out of service from 8 until at least 11. と述べていることから，午前 8 ～ 11 時が点検の予定時間帯であるとわかるので，(B) が正解。誤答 (A) は利用できなくなる予定時刻。

76 満点ポイント! 「詳細問題」のヒントを聞き逃さない   正解 ➤ (C)

What are listeners told to do with the boxes?

(A) Leave them in the elevator

(B) Carry them down the stairs

(C) Pile them next to the wall

(D) Show them to an inspector

聞き手は箱をどうするように指示されていますか。

(A) エレベータの中に置いておく

(B) 階段で下まで手で運ぶ

(C) 壁の横に積み上げておく

(D) 点検担当者に見せる

正解 箱について stack boxes against the wall（壁側に積み重ねるように）と指示しているので，stack を pile と言い換えている (C) が適切。誤答 (B) の carry は，人を主語に置くと「手で運ぶ」を意味する。エレベータ稼働後の話として move the ... boxes down（箱を下まで運ぶ）とあるので，ここではエレベータで降ろすことがわかる。

Questions 77 through 79 refer to the following announcement.

It is my pleasure to welcome you to this tour. I'll be your personal guide throughout the next hour. The building on the left is where Robson College was established in the early 19th century. The college became one of the most respected in the region, partly due to the innovative teaching techniques developed by the founder Joseph Chou, and partly due to a series of **Q77** famous alumni including Benn Monroe. With the expansion of public transport, however, students moved elsewhere, and it gradually lost its importance as an educational center. **Q78** The school itself has been relocated to a residential area on the outskirts of the city, but **Q79** the old school building is now the city's main tourist attraction and functions as a museum of local history. Now let's look around this building.

重要語句 □ innovative「斬新な」(= new and creative) □ partly due to ...「～がひとつの理由で」 □ alumni 「同窓生, 卒業生」※ 単数形は alumnus。 □ the outskirts of ...「(町)の外れ, 郊外」 □ function as ...「～として機能する」(= act as ...; serve as ...)

77-79 の設問は次のアナウンスに関するものです。

本ツアーにご参加いただきありがとうございます。これから1時間, 私が個人ガイドをさせていただきます。左側に見えます建物は, ロブソン・カレッジが19世紀初期に設立された場所です。この大学は, 創設者ジョセフ・チョウが斬新な教授方法を開発し, またベン・モンローを含む著名な卒業生を数々生み出したこともあり, 地域でもっとも権威のある大学のひとつに数えられました。しかしながら, 交通機関の拡大につれ, 学生は他の地域に移るようになり, 大学は徐々に教育中枢機関としての重要性を失いました。学校そのものは市の郊外の住宅地に移設されましたが, 学校の古い建物は現在, 市の主要な観光名所となっており, 地域の歴史を伝える博物館になっています。それでは, これから建物の中を見て回りましょう。

77 満点ポイント! 「詳細問題」のヒントを聞き逃さない　　　　正解 ➤ (B)

Who most likely is Benn Monroe?

(A) A founder of a school

(B) A graduate of a local college

(C) A renowned architect

(D) A curriculum developer

ベン・モンローとはおそらく誰ですか。

(A) 学校の創設者

(B) 地元大学の卒業生

(C) 著名な建築家

(D) カリキュラム開発者

正解 まず, ロブソン・カレッジに関して「地域でもっとも権威のある大学のひとつになった」と説明があり, その理由のひとつとして famous alumni including Benn Monroe を挙げていることから, 彼がこの大学に在籍していた人物だとわかるので, (B) が正解。名詞 alumni は the former students の意味。**誤答** (A) は Joseph Chou のこと。

What is mentioned about the college?	この大学に関して何が述べられていますか。
(A) It is situated in a coastal town.	(A) 海沿いの町にある。
(B) It has closed down completely.	(B) 完全に閉鎖されている。
(C) It is currently located in the suburbs.	(C) 現在は郊外にある。
(D) It is the most important college in the area.	(D) 地域でもっとも重要視されている大学である。

正解 ロブソン・カレッジに関する説明の中で The school itself ... on the outskirts of the city（学校は市の郊外に移設された）とあるので，on the outskirts（町の外れ）を in the suburbs（都心から離れた郊外）と言い換えた (C) を選ぶ。誤答 (D) は過去のことで，その後 it gradually lost ... an educational center（徐々に教育中枢機関としての重要性を失った）とある。

What will listeners most likely do next?	聞き手はおそらく次に何をしますか。
(A) Tour an educational center	(A) 教育センターを見学する
(B) Explore the city in groups	(B) グループになって町を散策する
(C) Visit a popular art gallery	(C) 人気のある画廊を訪れる
(D) View exhibits of historical importance	(D) 歴史的意義をもつ展示物を見る

正解 トークの最後で，現存の建物に関して「a museum of local history（地域の歴史を伝える博物館）になっている」と説明したうえで，Now let's look around this building. と話していることから，(D) が適切であると判断できる。誤答 学校自体は移転しているので，(A) は不適切。また，ここでの museum は「歴史博物館」なので，(C) の art gallery と混同しないように注意。

Questions 80 through 82 refer to the following telephone message.

Hi Josh, this is Valerie. I'm calling about the brochure that you asked me to send to the printers. I've been looking it over, and there seem to be several errors. First, the brochure lists the price of our J-50 portable heater as 78 dollars, but the company Web site has it listed as 68 dollars. Also, I believe **Q80** the picture above the HS-35 ceiling fan listing is actually a photo of the HS-40. Finally, the brochure has a listing for the A-70 air conditioner, but **Q81** that model was discontinued last year. Obviously, **Q82** I will hold off on sending in the brochure until I hear back from you, so please call me as soon as you get this.

重要語句 □ printer「印刷会社」(= printing company) □ look ... over「～に目を通す」(= examine)
□ hold off (on) *doing* ...「～するのを遅らせる，保留する」(= delay *doing* ...; put off *doing* ...)

80-82 の設問は，次の電話メッセージに関するものです。

もしもしジョシュ，バレリーです。印刷所にまわすよう頼まれたパンフレットについてお電話しています。ひととおり目を通したんですが，いくつか間違いがあるようです。まず，J50 携帯ヒーターの価格が 78 ドルとパンフレットには記載されていますが，会社のウェブサイトでは 68 ドルとなっています。また，HS-35 天井ファンの上に掲載されている写真は実際は HS-40 の写真です。最後に，パンフレットには A-70 エアコンが掲載されていますが，このモデルは去年販売中止になっています。もちろん，あなたから連絡があるまでパンフレットを送らずにいますので，これを聞いたらすぐに電話してください。

80 満点ポイント! 「詳細問題」のヒントを聞き逃さない 正解 ▶ (C)

What item's listing has an incorrect photograph?

(A) The printer
(B) The air conditioner
(C) The ceiling fan
(D) The portable heater

どの掲載商品の写真が間違っていますか。

(A) プリンター
(B) エアコン
(C) 天井ファン
(D) 携帯ヒーター

正解 掲載写真に関して，the picture ... a photo of the HS-40（ceiling fan の上にある写真は HS-40 の写真だ）と間違いを指摘していることから，(C) が正解とわかる。名詞 printer には「プリンター」と「印刷会社」の 2 つの意味があり，ここでは後者の意味で用いていることにも注意。

81

What does the speaker say about the A-70 model?	話し手は A-70 モデルに関して何と述べていますか。
(A) It was launched a year ago.	(A) 一年前に発売された。
(B) It has been discounted.	(B) 割引されている。
(C) It appears on a Web site.	(C) 会社のウェブサイトに掲載されている。
(D) It is no longer being sold.	(D) もう販売されていない。

正解 A-70 に関して that model was discontinued last year と説明している。discontinue は stop offering を意味するので，ここでは no longer being sold と言い換えた (D) が適切。誤答 (B) の discounted は discontinued と見間違えやすいので気をつけよう。

82

According to the message, what is the speaker going to do now?	メッセージによると，話し手は今から何をする予定ですか。
(A) Send out the brochures	(A) パンフレットを配る
(B) Contact a printing company	(B) 印刷会社に連絡を取る
(C) Wait for Josh to return a call	(C) ジョシュからの電話を待つ
(D) Update the company Web site	(D) 会社のウェブサイトを更新する

正解 これからの行動として，最後で I will hold off ... as soon as you get this.（パンフレットを送らずにいるからすぐに電話がほしい）と伝えている。電話の相手は Josh であることが冒頭部分でわかるので，(C) が正解。誤答 (A) の send out は distribute と同じで「多数の人の手に渡るよう配る」ことを意味する。

83-85

Questions 83 through 85 refer to the following talk.

Q83 I've completed my review of Spander Corporation's operations, and I'd like to start off by going over the main points. Overall, your company is run in an efficient manner that allows staff to use their skills and encourages new ideas and innovation. The work environment and employee compensation are better than average. **Q84** The main problem I observed was with the sharing of information. A lot of time is spent reading irrelevant e-mails or taking part in overly long meetings, and **Q84** there is also important information which is not shared with everyone. Accordingly, I have two key recommendations. First, I suggest appointing an employee to work as an inter-departmental liaison. Second, **Q85** I recommend implementing some guidelines regarding internal e-mails and meetings that will increase efficiency.

重要語句 □ innovation「斬新な考え，方法」 □ irrelevant「関連のない，不適切な」 □ overly「過度に」（= too） □ appoint *someone* to *do* ...「人を〜する仕事に任命する，選ぶ」（= choose *someone* to *do* ...） □ liaison「連絡役，橋渡し役」 □ implement「（新しいモノ）を導入する，実行に移す」（= put ... into effect）

83-85 の設問は次のトークに関するものです。

スパンダー・コーポレーションの業務調査が終わりましたので，まずは主要な点をみていきましょう。全体的に，貴社は従業員のスキルを十分に発揮させ，新しいアイデアや手法を奨励し，効率的に業務を遂行していると言えます。職場環境と従業員への給与は平均以上です。ただ，調査して一番の問題だったのは，情報の共有に関してです。業務とは関係のないメールを読んだり，必要以上に長い会議に参加したりするのに多くの時間が費やされ，重要な情報が全従業員に伝わっていないということもあります。従いまして，私からは重要な提言を 2 ついたします。まず 1 つは，部署間の連絡役になる従業員を選出することです。次に，社内メールと会議に関するガイドラインを新しく設け，効率を上げることです。

83

正解 ➤ (A)

What is the purpose of the talk?

(A) To present an analysis

(B) To train staff members

(C) To promote a company

(D) To announce a new schedule

このトークの目的は何ですか。

(A) 分析結果を発表すること

(B) スタッフに研修を行うこと

(C) 会社を宣伝すること

(D) 新スケジュールを発表すること

正解 冒頭部分で「会社の業務調査が終わった」と述べ，さらに社内の優れている点や改善点を説明しているので，(A) が目的としてふさわしい。**誤答** Spander Corportation という会社名を your company と言い換えていることや，後半で改善方法を提示していることからも，(C) が目的ではないことがわかる。

According to the speaker, what needs to be improved?

(A) Office communications

(B) Staff compensation

(C) Work environment

(D) Data confidentiality

話し手によれば，改善が必要なのは何ですか。

(A) 社内のコミュニケーション

(B) 従業員の給与

(C) 職場環境

(D) データの機密性

正解 改善点に関して The main problem ... the sharing of information.（主な問題は情報の共有に関してだ）と話し，さらに「重要な情報が全員に伝わっていない」と指摘しているので，(A) が問題点であるとわかる。誤答 (B) や (C) については better than average と述べられており，(D) は言及されていないので，確実に正解したい。

What does the speaker suggest?

(A) Installing a new computer system

(B) Hiring additional employees

(C) Holding meetings more often

(D) Instituting a new policy

話し手は何を勧めていますか。

(A) 新しいコンピュータシステムを導入すること

(B) 従業員を追加で雇うこと

(C) 会議をより頻繁に開くこと

(D) 新しい規則を設けること

正解 話し手は最後に「inter-departmental liaison（部署間の連絡役）となる人を選ぶこと」と「社内メールや会議に関する guidelines を設けること」という 2 つを提案しており，後者の提案が (D) と一致する。動詞 institute は「（制度やシステム）を設ける，実施する」（= establish; implement）の意味があることを覚えておこう。誤答 liaison となる人物を新たに雇うべきだとは述べていないので，(B) は不適切。

Questions 86 through 88 refer to the following excerpt from a news report.

According to the two-month survey that concluded in April, local residents are expected to spend a record amount on home-improvement projects this summer. The survey, **Q86** carried out by a local marketing firm, also found that people are becoming more careful about planning the budget to get that work done. **Q88** Home-improvement budgets are expected to rise to nearly 4,000 dollars later this year, up almost 60 percent from 10 years ago. People are choosing to spend less on vacation travel, dining out, and entertainment, although **Q87** travel still accounts for the largest portion of household expenses. At the same time, **Q88** homeowners are increasingly shopping in warehouse-style tool and supply stores which offer convenience as well as low prices.

重要語句 □conclude「終了する」(= end) □home improvement「家の修繕，日曜大工」 □carry out ...「～を行う」(= conduct; perform) □account for ...「(割合)を占める」 □A as well as B「A も B も」(= A and B)

86-88 の設問は次のニュース報道の一部に関するものです。

4月に終了した2か月の調査によれば，地域住民の日曜大工にかける金額は，この夏過去最高の数字になる見込みです。この調査は地域のマーケティング会社によって行われたもので，消費者はそのために予算をより慎重に検討するようになっているようです。日曜大工の予算は今年4000ドル近くまで上がると予想されており，これは10年前と比べて60%近い増加になります。消費者は，旅行，外食，娯楽については出費を抑える傾向にありますが，それでも旅行は家計出費の中でもっとも大きな割合を占めています。それと同時に，家を持つ人たちは，工具用品を扱う便利で安価な倉庫型店舗で買い物をする方が増えています。

86 満点ポイント! ▲「詳細問題」のヒントを聞き逃さない   正解 ▶ (D)

What does the speaker say about the survey?	調査に関して何が述べられていますか。
(A) It was started in April.	(A) 4月に開始された。
(B) It cost more than expected.	(B) 予測よりも費用がかかった。
(C) It targeted people nationwide.	(C) 全国の人々を対象とした。
(D) It was conducted by a local company.	(D) 地元企業によって行われた。

正解 調査に関して carried out by a local marketing firm と述べているので，これを言い換えた (D) が正解。**誤答** 冒頭から，(A) は April に終了したこと，(C) については local residents を対象にしたものであることがわかる。

満点 ポイント！ 「詳細問題」のヒントを聞き逃さない　　　　　　正解 ➤ (B)

According to the report, what do people spend the most money on? (A) Home improvements **(B) Vacation Travel** (C) Dining out (D) Entertainment	報道によると，人々が一番お金を費やしているのは何ですか。 (A) 日曜大工 (B) 旅行 (C) 外食 (D) 娯楽

正解 消費の割合について travel still accounts for the largest portion of household expenses とあるのを聞き逃さないようにし，(B) を選ぶ。誤答 (A) は，「過去最高の支出額になる」と述べているだけなので注意。

満点 ポイント！ 「詳細問題」のヒントを聞き逃さない　　　　　　正解 ➤ (B)

According to the report, what kind of business is becoming more popular? (A) Family restaurants **(B) Hardware stores** (C) Holiday resorts (D) Shopping malls	報道によると，どのようなビジネスが人気になってきていますか。 (A) ファミリー・レストラン (B) ホームセンター (C) リゾート施設 (D) ショッピングモール

正解 report の半ばで home-improvement budgets が増加していることや，最後で「工具用品を扱う倉庫型店舗で買い物をする人が増えている」と述べていることから，tool and supply（工具用品）を hardware（金物・工具）と言い換えている (B) が正解。ホームセンターはほかに，home-improvement stores や DIY（do-it-yourself）stores とも呼ばれる。

Questions 89 through 91 refer to the following excerpt from a talk.

With computer technology advancing at an incredible pace, **Q89** many people working freelance believe they need to purchase new equipment constantly to remain competitive. This can be a needless expense, as **Q90** many of them aren't using their existing computers and networks as efficiently as they could be. Before spending a fortune on new systems, it's worth looking at what you have now. **Q91** Internal memory can be upgraded at a fraction of the cost of a new computer, and regularly checking developers' Web sites for software updates can ensure that you always have the most recent version of your essential office software running.

重要語句 □ with *A doing*「Aが〜していて」 □ freelance「(特定の会社に所属せず) 自由契約で」 □ fortune「大金」(= a very large amount of money) □ a fraction of ...「ごくわずかな〜」(= only a small amount of ...)

89-91 の設問は次のトークの一部に関するものです。

コンピュータ技術が信じられない早さで進歩しているため，競争に勝ち残って行くためには常に新しい機器を購入しなくてはいけないとフリーランスで働く多くの人たちが考えています。彼らの多くは既存のコンピュータやネットワークをできる限りまで有効利用していないため，この費用は不要な経費であることがあります。新しいシステムに多額の資金を投入する前に，今あるものを確認してみる価値はあります。内部メモリのアップグレードは新しいパソコンを購入する価格のほんの一部の金額で行えますし，定期的に開発会社のウェブサイトをチェックしアップデートソフトを入手すれば，常にあなたのオフィスに必要なソフトを最新のものにしておくことができます。

89

正解 ➤ (D)

Who is the intended audience for the talk?	このトークは誰に向けられているものですか。
(A) Technical consultants	(A) 技術担当コンサルタント
(B) Business executives	(B) 会社の重役
(C) Software developers	(C) ソフトウェア開発者
(D) Self-employed workers	(D) 自営業者

正解 冒頭で「フリーランスで働く人たちは常に新しい機器を購入しなくてはいけないと考えている」とあり，そのうえで「不要な経費になりえる」「今あるものを確認してみる価値はある」とアドバイスをしているので，working freelance を self-employed と言い換えた (D) が対象者であると判断できる。

90

According to the speaker, what are many people doing?	話し手によると，多くの人が行っていることは何ですか。
(A) Launching new Web sites	(A) 新しいウェブサイトを開設している
(B) Creating their own software applications	(B) 独自のソフトを開発している
(C) Operating office equipment inefficiently	(C) オフィス機器を非効率的に使用している
(D) Applying for technology-related jobs	(D) 技術関係の職に応募している

正解 フリーランスで働く人たちに関して，many of them aren't using ... as efficiently as they could be（彼らの多くはコンピュータやネットワークを有効利用していない）と述べているので，(C) が正解。誤答 (B) は最終文の regularly checking developers' Web sites for software updates に関連してはいるが，多くの人が行っていることとして述べているわけではない。

91

What does the speaker say is available at a reasonable price?	話し手は何が手頃な価格で入手できると述べていますか。
(A) Memory upgrades	(A) メモリのアップグレード
(B) Regular maintenance work	(B) 定期メンテナンス
(C) New office software	(C) 新しいオフィス用ソフト
(D) Private consultation	(D) 個別相談

正解 Internal memory can be upgraded ... a new computer（内部メモリのアップグレードはごくわずかな金額で行える）の部分を聞き逃さないようにし，(A) を選ぶ。at a fraction of ...（ごくわずかな〜で）は重要表現。誤答 (C) は，「software updates（アップデートソフト）を開発会社のサイトでチェックする」とあるだけで，価格についての言及はない。

Questions 92 through 94 refer to the following radio broadcast.

Welcome to *Entertainment Talk*. Tonight we'll be speaking to members of the famous Attam Family. The Attam Family has performed at the Mackenzie Auditorium every summer, but this year **Q92** the concert will not feature the voice of Batima Attam. It'll instead be a guitar recital by her brothers. The music is taken from their upcoming album *Dance Without Words*. The brothers will speak on tonight's show about this album, and about guitarists that have inspired them. Later they will answer your questions and **Q93** play three of the tunes from the new album right here in the studio, **Q94** but first, we'll talk to actor-turned director Molly Hanson about her recent work.

重要語句 □ tune「曲」（= a piece of music）□ actor-turned「俳優から転身した」

92-94 の設問は次のラジオ放送に関するものです。
エンターテイメント・トークにようこそ。今夜は，有名なアッタム・ファミリーのメンバーにお話を伺います。アッタム・ファミリーは毎年夏にマッケンジー会館でコンサートを行ってきましたが，今年のコンサートにはボーカルのバティマ・アッタムは出演いたしません。そのかわり，兄弟によるギター・リサイタルとなります。彼らが演奏するのは近々発売される『ダンス・ウィザウト・ワーズ』の収録曲です。今夜の番組で，このアルバムや彼らが刺激を受けたギタリストについてお話しいただきます。後ほど皆さんからの質問にお答えし，まさにこのスタジオで新しいアルバムの収録曲を3曲演奏してくれることになっていますが，まずは，俳優出身の映画監督モリー・ハンソンさんから彼女の最近の作品についてお話を伺います。

92 満点ポイント！「詳細問題」のヒントを聞き逃さない　　　　正解 ➤ (A)

Who most likely is Batima Attam?

(A) A singer

(B) A concert promoter

(C) A dancer

(D) A guitar player

バティマ・アッタムはおそらく誰ですか。

(A) 歌手

(B) コンサート主催者

(C) ダンサー

(D) ギター奏者

正解 コンサートに関して，「今回は Batima Attam の声を含まない」と述べ，さらに「兄弟による guitar recital となる」と紹介されているので，彼女自身は (A) の singer であることがうかがえる。ラジオ番組は Part 4 にたびたび登場するので，日頃から聞き慣れておきたい。

93 満点ポイント! 「詳細問題」のヒントを聞き逃さない　　正解 ➤ (C)

What does the speaker say about the brothers?

(A) They started to play last year.

(B) They will not appear at the concert.

(C) They will perform live on the radio show.

(D) They released an album this year.

話し手は兄弟について何と言っていますか。

(A) 去年演奏を始めた。

(B) コンサートに出演しない。

(C) ラジオ番組で生演奏をする。

(D) 今年アルバムを発売した。

正解 brothers に関して後半で play three of the turns ... in the studio（スタジオで 3 曲演奏してくれる）と述べていることから，(C) が正解。この live は「（放送や演奏が）生で」という意味の副詞。**誤答** (D) については their upcoming album とあるので，これから発売されるものであるとわかる。

94 満点ポイント! 「詳細問題」のヒントを聞き逃さない　　正解 ➤ (C)

What will listeners most likely do next?

(A) Hear a radio advertisement

(B) Ask questions to special guests

(C) Learn more about a director

(D) Listen to some music

リスナーはおそらく次に何をしますか。

(A) ラジオ広告を聞く

(B) 特別ゲストに質問をする

(C) 監督に関する情報を得る

(D) 音楽を聞く

正解 Attam brothers の話の後に but first, we'll talk to actor-turned director Molly Hanson と述べているので，まずは director とのインタビューが行われると判断し，(C) を選ぶ。**誤答** (B) と (D) はその後に行われるもの。前の設問とヒントが連続しているので，絶対に聞き逃さないように注意しよう。

Questions 95 through 97 refer to the following introduction.

It is my pleasure to introduce to you Q95 the world-renowned author, Monica Kawamura. Ms. Kawamura is a graduate of our very own Dupont University. Interestingly enough, Ms. Kawamura's major was originally biology, and her plans were to become a researcher. However, while reading the works of novelist Shelly Austin, she became interested in creative writing. She Q96 switched departments and eight years ago graduated with a master's degree in English. Q95 Her first series of poems was published in *New York Today* five years ago, and Q97 last year her latest work *Waiting for Now* won the prestigious Paulter Prize. Now, please give her a warm welcome.

重要語句 □ major「(大学の) 専攻」※major in ... (〜を専攻する) という動詞の用法もおさえておこう。□ creative writing「文芸・小説や詩などの執筆」 □ department「(大学の) 学部」 □ master's degree「修士号」 □ poem「詩」 □ prestigious「名誉ある」(= admired and respected)

95-97 の設問は次の紹介に関するものです。

世界的に有名な作家モニカ・カワムラさんをご紹介できることを光栄に思います。カワムラさんは当デュポン大学の卒業生でもあります。興味深いことに，カワムラさんはもともと生物学を専攻しており，研究者になることを目指していました。しかしながら，小説家シェリー・オースティンの作品を読んでいるうちに，彼女は文芸の世界に興味を持ち始めたのでした。彼女は学部を変更し，8 年前に英文学の修士号を取得し当大学を卒業しました。5 年前には『ニューヨーク・トゥデイ』誌に詩集シリーズの第一弾が発表され，去年には最新作『ウェイティング・フォ・ナウ』で名誉あるポールター賞を受賞しました。それでは，どうぞ暖かい拍手で彼女をお迎え下さい。

95 満点ポイント！ 「詳細問題」のヒントを聞き逃さない　　　　正解 ➤ (B)

Who is the speaker introducing?

(A) A novelist

(B) A poet

(C) A researcher

(D) A journalist

話し手は誰を紹介していますか。

(A) 小説家

(B) 詩人

(C) 研究者

(D) ジャーナリスト

正解 まず冒頭で the world-renowned author と紹介されており，後半で Her first series of poems（初の詩集）について言及していることから，(B) が正解。**誤答** (A) は「Shelly Austin の小説を読んで文芸に興味を持った」とあるので，後半の poems を聞き逃すと選んでしまう難問である。

What did Ms. Kawamura do while attending university?

(A) She published a book.

(B) She changed her major.

(C) She met a famous author.

(D) She received a degree in biology.

カワムラさんは大学在学中に何をしましたか。

(A) 本を出版した。

(B) 専攻を変更した。

(C) 有名な作家と出会った。

(D) 生物学の学位を取得した。

正解 creative writing に興味を持ち始めた後，She switched departments（専攻を変えた）と述べているので，これを changed her major と言い換えた (B) が正解。誤答 (D) の biology はもともと専攻していた学科で，実際に取得したのは a master's degree in English と述べている。

When did Ms. Kawamura receive an award?

(A) Earlier this year

(B) One year ago

(C) Five years ago

(D) Eight years ago

カワムラさんが賞を受賞したのはいつですか。

(A) 今年

(B) 1 年前

(C) 5 年前

(D) 8 年前

正解 賞の名前が登場するのは Paulter Prize のみ。その一文で「last year に受賞した」と述べていることから，(B) を確実に正解したい。誤答 (C) は Her first series of poems が発表された年，(D) は大学卒業の年。

Questions 98 through 100 refer to the following talk.

I appreciate everyone finding the time to participate in this computer training workshop. **Q98** Before we adjourn, please take a few moments to complete the workshop assessment forms included inside your package of course materials. **Q98** Your input will be very beneficial in helping us refine our teaching techniques for the course. I'd also like to inform you of a seminar that will be introduced this fall: a full-day seminar entitled "Advanced Corporate Strategies". **Q99** It covers all the practical tips needed to accomplish your business objectives. It's certain to be a popular course, so be sure to register early if you're interested. **Q100** You can read about all the other workshops and training seminars available to **Q98** company staff in the document I'm passing out now.

重要語句 □ adjourn「(会議などを一時的に) 終了する，休止する」(= stop) □ assessment「評価，査定」(= evaluation; judgment) □ input「意見，感想」(= feedback; opinions) □ refine「～の精度を高める，洗練する」(= enhance) □ entitled「～と題された」 □ cover「～を扱う」(= include; deal with ...) □ objective「目標」(= goal)

98-100 の設問は次のトークに関するものです。

このパソコン研修ワークショップに参加するお時間をとっていただきありがとうございます。終了前に，資料一式の中にあるワークショップ評価用紙にご記入いただく時間をとっていただければ幸いです。みなさんのご意見は私たちが教授法を改善していくうえで大いに役立ちます。また今年の秋に行われる講座についてもお知らせしたいと思います。それは，「上級企業戦略」という終日セミナーです。このセミナーでは，ビジネス上の目標を達成するのに必要なあらゆる実践的アドバイスを伝授いたします。必ず人気のコースになると思いますので，ご興味がおありでしたら早めに申し込みをしてください。会社のスタッフが参加できるその他すべてのワークショップや研修会につきましては，今お配りしている書類でお読みいただけます。

98

正解 ➤ (C)

What is one purpose of the talk?

(A) To start a training workshop

(B) To recognize everyone's accomplishments

(C) To ask employees for feedback

(D) To outline a schedule of events

トークの目的のひとつは何ですか。

(A) 研修会を開始すること

(B) 全員の業績を認めること

(C) 会社の従業員に感想を求めること

(D) イベント日程の概要を説明すること

正解 前半で please take a few moments ... assessment forms（評価用紙にご記入ください）と促し，Your input will be very beneficial と述べていることがヒント。さらに，後半で company staff について言及があることから，聞き手が会社の従業員であることをおさえ，(C) を選ぶ。

誤答 冒頭の一文だけを聞くと (A) が正解に見えるが，次の文の adjourn は stop の意味であることに注意。(D) は，秋の終日セミナーの説明があるだけで，具体的な日程については何も示されていない。

99　満点ポイント!　「詳細問題」のヒントを聞き逃さない　　正解 ➤ (A)

What will be covered in the new program?	新しいプログラムでは何が教えられますか。
(A) Business planning	(A) ビジネス上の計画
(B) Training techniques	(B) 研修技術
(C) Sales strategies	(C) 販売戦略
(D) Project development	(D) プロジェクト開発

正解 新たに開始される Advanced Corporate Strategies というワークショップに関して，It covers all the practical tips ... business objectives.（ビジネス上の目標達成に必要なアドバイスをする）と説明しているので，(A) がこの内容に合致する。

100　満点ポイント!　「詳細問題」のヒントを聞き逃さない　　正解 ➤ (D)

What is being given to listeners by the speaker?	聞き手には何が与えられているところですか。
(A) Performance evaluation sheets	(A) 勤務評価シート
(B) Course material packages	(B) コース資料一式
(C) Workshop registration forms	(C) ワークショップ登録用紙
(D) Details about the upcoming events	(D) 将来のイベントに関する情報

正解 トークの最後の一文から，今配っているのは workshops and training seminars available to company staff（会社スタッフが参加できる研修会）の情報が入った書類だとわかるので, (D) が正解。
誤答 (B) は前半の inside your package of course materials の部分から，すでに参加者に配られているものであるとわかる。

101

⏱10秒　代名詞の格　　　　　　　　　　　　　　　　　正解 ➤ (D)

Fields of Clover, Gilda Vern's second
　　　　　　　 S
novel, helped <u>distinguish</u> ------- as one of
　　　　　　　　 V
the country's brightest new authors.

(A) hers

(B) she

(C) herself

(D) her

『フィールズ・オブ・クローバー』は，ギルダ・ベルンの 2 作目の小説であり，その作品によって彼女は国でもっとも有望な新人作家の一人として認知されることとなった。

(A) 所有代名詞

(B) 主格

(C) 再帰代名詞

(D) 所有格・目的格

正解 文の主語が *Fields of Clover*（= novel）で，空所が動詞 distinguish の目的語になっていることをおさえ，目的格の (D) her を入れる。《distinguish *A* as *B*》で「A を B として際立たせる，有名にする」という意味。

誤答 再帰代名詞の (C) herself は，Gilda Vern distinguished herself as ... のように動作主（主語）と目的語が同一のものを指す場合に用いられることに注意。

重要語句 □ bright「将来の明るい，有望な」（= promising）

102

⏱15秒　**満点** ポイント!　品詞　　　　　　　　　　　正解 ➤ (C)

Diamaz Jewelry offers free engraving
services for customers who want to have
their <u>purchases</u> ------- with their initials.
　　　　　　 O

(A) personally

(B) personal

(C) personalized

(D) to personalize

ダイアマズ宝石店は，購入した宝石に自分のイニシャルを入れたいと考える顧客のために，無料で彫刻サービスを提供している。

(A)「個人的に，みずから」

(B)「個人の」

(C)「個人仕様の」

(D)「個人仕様にするために」

正解 動詞 have には，《have ＋ O ＋過去分詞》で「O を（他人に）～させる」という使役動詞の語法があるので，過去分詞の (C) personalized を入れ，have purchases personalized（購入品を個人仕様にしてもらう）という構文を完成させる。

誤答 (A) は副詞で，「（仕事上ではなく）個人的に」（I know him personally.）や「みずから，直接」（He answered me personally.）という意味で用いる。また have は，《have ＋ O ＋形容詞》の形で「O を～の状態にする」という意味を表す（Please have your document ready.）が，(B) personal では意味を成さない。

重要語句 □ engraving「（文字などの）彫刻」　□ purchase「購入品，買い物」（この意味では可算名詞）

103 ⏱10秒 修飾 正解 ➤ (A)

The keynote speech at the international trade conference lasted ------- over two hours.

(A) well
(B) more
(C) all
(D) ever

国際貿易会議の基調講演は，2時間をはるかに超える長さだった。

(A)「はるかに，十分に」
(B)「より多く」
(C)「すべての」
(D)「今まで」

正解 空所がなくても文が完成するので，直後にある前置詞 over を修飾する機能をもつ副詞の (A) well（十分に）を選ぶ。well の修飾パターンとしてほかにも，well worth ...（〜の価値が十分ある）や well before [after] ...（〜よりはるか前に／〜をかなり過ぎて）をおさえておこう。また，last や wait の後ろでは，last (for) two hours のように期間を示す for がよく省略されることにも注意。

誤答 (B) more は，... lasted more than two hours. であれば OK。(C) all を入れた all over ... は「〜のいたるところに」という意味。(D) ever は，比較表現を除き，肯定文では通例用いられない。

重要語句 □ keynote speech「基調演説」（会議のテーマを提示する講演）

---

104 ⏱15秒 満点ポイント! 語法 正解 ➤ (A)

If the suggested policy change -------- with the supervisor's approval, it will be adopted as the new standard.

(A) meets
(B) complies
(C) satisfies
(D) consents

上司の承認を得られれば，規定変更の提案は新しい基準として採用されるだろう。

(A)「得る」
(B)「従う」
(C)「満たす」
(D)「合意する」

正解 空所直後の with とつながり，文意の通る動詞を選ぶ。(A) は，meet with approval [support/success] などの形で「(反応や結果) を得る」(= get or experience) という意味を表すことができるので，これが正解。

誤答 (B) は，comply with ... の形で「〜(規則など) に従う」(= obey; adhere to) の意味を表すが，ここでは文意に合わない。(C) satisfies (〜を満たす) は他動詞で，The policy change satisfies everyone's needs. のように用いて meet や fulfill の意味を表す。(D) consents は，The supervisor consented to the policy change. のように consent to ... の形で「〜に合意する」(= agree to ...) という意味になる。

重要語句 □ adopt「〜を採用する」(= accept formally)

105 ⏱ 15秒 満点ポイント！ 語彙　　　　正解 ➤ (C)

Although the new software seems exceptionally technical and complex, the fully illustrated user manual will give customers <u>peace of</u> -------.

(A) advice

(B) rationale

(C) mind

(D) reliability

その新しいソフトウェアは極めて専門的で複雑そうだが，詳細な図解入りの取扱説明書があるので，顧客は安心して利用できるだろう。

(A)「アドバイス」

(B)「（背後にある）理由，論理」

(C)「心」

(D)「信頼性」

正解 空所の前にある名詞 peace は，(C) mind を入れた peace of mind の形で「（心の平和＝）平穏，安心」という意味を表せるので，一文の文脈に合う。

誤答 (A) advice は，名詞 <u>piece</u> を用いて give customers a piece of advice とは言えるので，ふたつの名詞を混同しないように注意。(B) rationale（= reasons）は，the rationale for [behind] the new system（新システムを導入する理由）のように用いられる。

---

106 ⏱ 10秒 語法／慣用表現　　　　正解 ➤ (D)

While attending the convention in Lisbon, Mr. Burka will try to <u>remain</u> ------- <u>with</u> headquarters via e-mail.

(A) contacts

(B) to contact

(C) contacting

(D) in contact

リスボンで開かれる会議に参加している間，ブルカさんは本社とメールで連絡を保てるようにするつもりだ。

(A) 名詞・動詞

(B) 不定詞

(C) 動名詞・現在分詞

(D)「連絡をとって」

正解 空所直前にある remain（～のままでいる＝ keep; stay）は be 動詞と同じ働きをし，後ろに補語をとる。選択肢のうち，(D) は be in contact with ... の形で「～と連絡を取っている」（= be in touch with ...）という状態を表せるので，これが補語として適切。

誤答 動詞 contact は他動詞なので，直後に目的語が必要という観点から (B) と (C) はすぐに消去したい選択肢。

重要語句 □ while *doing*「～している間」

107

正解 ▶ (C)

As Manaluga Airways offers <u>two dining options</u> for its in-flight meal, passengers may choose ------- <u>a chicken dish</u> and <u>a vegetarian entrée</u>.

(A) both

(B) either

(C) between

(D) rather

マナルガ航空は機内食として2種類の料理を提供しており，乗客は鶏肉料理かベジタリアン料理かを選べる。

(A)「両方とも」

(B)「どちらか」

(C)「〜の間」

(D)「むしろ」

正解 (C) between を入れれば，choose between *A* and *B*（*A*と*B*から選ぶ）という形が完成し，文意も通ることがわかる。

誤答 空所直後に and があるので，(A) を反射的に入れて both *A* and *B*（*A*と*B*の両方とも）としたくなるが，文の前半に two dining options（選べる2つの料理）とあることから，both では文意が成立しないことに注意。(B) either は，choose either a chicken dish <u>or</u> a vegetarian entrée であればよい。(D) rather は *A* rather than *B*（= *A* instead of *B*）の形で用い，「*B* ではなくて *A*」という意味を表す。both や either を用いたひっかけは Part 5 にまれに登場するので，あくまで構文・文脈ともに成り立つものを選ぼう。

重要語句 □ entrée「メイン料理」（= main dish）

108

正解 ▶ (C)

------- to park in the employee garage, <u>S</u> which is on the basement level, <u>are</u> <u>V</u> obtainable from Ms. Lee in reception.

(A) Permission

(B) Permitted

(C) Permits

(D) Permitting

地下にある従業員駐車場の駐車許可証は，受付のリーさんから取得できます。

(A) 名詞

(B) 過去形・過去分詞

(C) 名詞・動詞

(D) 動名詞・現在分詞

正解 空所部分が主語で，are が述語動詞である構造をとらえる。1語で主語の位置に置ける名詞である (A) Permission と (C) Permits のうち，are に対応する複数名詞 (C) が正解。Permission（許可）が不可算名詞なのに対し，Permit（許可証）は可算名詞であることもおさえておこう。また，主語と述語の形を一致させる「主述の一致」は，上級者でも見落しがちになるので注意。

109

⏱ 15秒　満点ポイント!　語法　　　　　　　　　　　正解 ➤ (A)

While Banner Bridge is under repair, city officials plan to ------- traffic to the Sanger Tunnel.

(A) divert

(B) replace

(C) alternate

(D) facilitate

バナー・ブリッジの改修工事が行われている間, 市は交通をサンガー・トンネルに迂回させる予定である。

(A)「~をそらす」

(B)「~をとり替える」

(C)「~を交互に行う」

(D)「~を円滑にする」

正解 動詞の目的語として traffic があり, 後ろに to the Sanger Tunnel という〈方向〉が示されていることから,《divert A to B》(A を B〔違う方向〕に向ける)の形で用いられる (A) divert がふさわしいと判断する。

誤答 (B) replace は《replace A with B》で「A(古いもの)を B(新しいもの)に取り替える」, (C) alternate は《alternate A and B》で「A と B を交互に行う」, (D) facilitate は「(プロセス)を円滑に進める」という意味。ちなみに, make [take] a detour (迂回する)という表現もぜひ覚えておきたい。

重要語句 □ under repair「修理中の, 改修工事中の」

110

⏱ 30秒　前置詞　　　　　　　　　　　　　　　　　正解 ➤ (D)

The magazine decided to expand next year's summertime price promotion so that new subscribers would also be entitled to discounts ------- spring.

(A) within

(B) every

(C) since

(D) during

その雑誌社は, 新規の購読契約者が春の間も割引を受けられるようにするため, 来年の夏の割引期間を拡大することに決めた。

(A)「~以内に」

(B)「毎~」

(C)「~以来」

(D)「~の間」

正解 文の前半に「来年の夏の割引期間を延ばすことにした」とあり, その目的として so that ... entitled to discounts(新規契約者が割引を受けられるように)と述べているので, 割引期間を示す前置詞の (D) を入れ, during spring(春の間)とすれば文意が通る。

誤答 (A) within は, within a month(1か月以内に)など主に「時の長さ」を表す語をつなぐ。(B) every は文法的に入るが, ここでは next year の話をしているので文意が通らない。(C) since は過去の開始点を表す語をつなぐので, やはり一文の文意に合わない。

重要語句 □ be entitled to ...「~を得る権利がある」(= have the right to receive)

332

There is pressure on authors of fiction to <u>publish</u> ------- to ensure that they keep a large readership.

(A) regular

(B) regulation

(C) regulates

(D) regularly

フィクション作家には，多くの読者を確実に保つため，作品を定期的に発表しなければならないプレッシャーがある。

(A)「定期的な」形容詞

(B)「規定」名詞

(C)「規制する」動詞の現在形

(D)「定期的に」副詞

正解 動詞 publish は「作品を発表する」という意味で自動詞として用いることができるので，これを修飾する副詞の (D) regularly（定期的に）が入る。

誤答 publish は他動詞として目的語もとれるが，(B) regulation（規定＝ rule）では文意を成さない。また，通例 regulations という複数形で用いられることもおさえておこう。

重要語句 □ readership「読者（層）」（＝ readers）

<u>Artisan traditions</u> that date back hundreds
<small>S</small>
of years <u>have been</u> ------- to make each
<small>V</small>
replica of ancient handicraft displayed in the gallery as authentic as possible.

(A) delegated

(B) employed

(C) conformed

(D) emerged

ギャラリーに展示されている古代工芸品のレプリカをひとつひとつできるだけ本物に見せるため，何百年も遡る職人の伝統技術が用いられた。

(A)「任された」

(B)「用いられた」

(C)「従った」

(D)「現れた」

正解 文の主語が Artisan traditions（職人の伝統技術）で，空所には受動態を形成する過去分詞が必要。動詞 employ には「（方法・技術など）を用いる」（＝ use）という意味があるので，これの過去分詞である (B) employed を入れれば文意の通る受動態が完成する。

誤答 (A) は，《delegate ... to *someone*》の形で「（仕事）を人（部下など）に任せる」という意味になる他動詞で，ここでは文意を成さない。(C) は conform to ...（〜に従う，一致する）の形で用いる自動詞。(D) の emerge（現れる＝ appear; come out）も自動詞で，受動態では用いない。

重要語句 □ artisan「職人」（＝ craftsperson）　□ handicraft「手工芸品」（＝ artifact）　□ authentic「本物の，本場の」

113

Ms. Mapston is ideally suited for the management opening, in ------- she has <u>extensive</u> experience as a production supervisor.

（下線部: she has の下に s v の記号）

(A) that

(B) which

(C) itself

(D) as much

マップストンさんは，製造責任者として幅広い経験を有しているという点で，空いている管理職のポストに適任であると言える。

(A)「〜という点で」

(B) 関係代名詞

(C)「それ自体で」

(D)「同量だけ」

正解 前半で「Ms. Mapston は管理職に適任だ」と述べ，後半で「幅広い経験がある」とその根拠を示していることから，空所直前の in とともに《in that SV ...》（〜という点で）という接続詞表現を完成させる (A) that を入れる。

誤答 関係代名詞の (B) which を入れると，直前の名詞句 the management opening を先行詞にとることになり，文意を成さない。(C) を入れた in itself は副詞表現で，前後の節をつなぐ働きをもたない。

114

Appearing as a guest instructor, local entrepreneur Alfred Peterson told workshop attendees very ------- <u>stories</u> about business management.

(A) advance

(B) gainful

(C) engaging

(D) resourceful

ゲスト講師として登場した地元の起業家であるアルフレッド・ピーターソンは，経営管理に関してワークショップ参加者の心をつかむ非常に興味深い話をした。

(A)「事前の」

(B)「（仕事が）有益の，有給の」

(C)「人を引きつける，魅力的な」

(D)「機知に富む」

正解 空所直後にある名詞 stories を修飾するのに文脈上適切な形容詞は，(C) の engaging（= interesting and pleasant; attractive）。動詞 engage も，engage *one's* attention [interest] の形で「〜の注目・関心を引き付ける」という意味を表せる。

誤答 (A) advance は advance notice（事前の通知）といったフレーズで用いられる形容詞で，「高度な，上級の」という意味の advanced と混同しないよう注意。(D) resourceful（= skilled at solving problems）は人に関して用いられる。

重要語句　□ entrepreneur「起業家」

The board is planning to hold a special event as a ------- to the outgoing director after his thirty-year career at the firm.

(A) tribute
(B) respect
(C) celebration
(D) caliber

取締役会は，会社に 30 年勤め退職することになる重役に敬意を表して，特別なイベントを開催する予定だ。

(A)「敬意」
(B)「尊敬」
(C)「祝い」
(D)「能力，器量」

正解 as a ------- to ... という空所前後の形に合い，かつ一文の文意を成す名詞として，「敬意をささげる言葉・行為」を意味する (A) tribute が入る。as a tribute to ... （〜に敬意を表して＝ in honor of ...）のほか，pay tribute to ... （〜を称賛する＝ praise ... publicly）の形もおさえておこう。
誤答「尊敬の気持ち」を意味する (B) respect は不可算名詞で，to show respect for ... （〜に敬意を示すため）の形で用いることはできる。(C) は in celebration of ... で「（出来事）を祝って」という意味。(D) caliber は We need someone of his caliber. （彼ほどの実力のある人材が必要だ）のように用いられる。

重要語句 □ outgoing「辞職する」（= retiring）

Careful strategic planning prior to the relocation will ensure as ------ a transition as possible.

(A) easy
(B) easing
(C) ease
(D) easily

移転の前に慎重かつ戦略的な計画があれば，移行作業をできるだけスムーズに進められるだろう。

(A)「容易な」形容詞
(B) ease の動名詞・現在分詞
(C)「〜を容易にする，楽」動詞・名詞
(D)「容易に」副詞

正解 as ... as 構文の中では形容詞か副詞の原級を用いること，また空所の直後に a transition という名詞句があることから，名詞を修飾する形容詞の (A) easy を選ぶ。名詞句を伴う場合，《as ＋形容詞＋ (a/an) ＋名詞＋ as ...》の語順になることに注意しよう。
誤答 (C) ease は，Careful planning will ease the transition. のように動詞として「〜を容易にする」（= facilitate）という意味を表すほか，名詞として with ease （楽に＝ easily）や feel at ease （落ち着く＝ feel relaxed）などの形で用いられる。

117
⏱ 15秒 ┃満点ポイント!┃ 前置詞 vs. 接続詞 　　　　　　　　正解 ➤ (C)

Mr. Banks argued that the firm would be better off enlarging its existing production facilities, ------- constructing any new factories.

(A) in contrast

(B) other than

(C) as opposed to

(D) whereas

バンクスさんは，新工場を建設するのではなく現行の生産施設を拡張したほうが，会社にとってよいと主張した。

(A)「対照的に」

(B)「〜のほかには，〜を除いて」

(C)「〜と対照的に，〜ではなくて」

(D)「〜の一方で」

正解 前半に enlarging its existing production facilities（現行の生産施設を拡張する）とあるのに対し，カンマ以降では constructing any new factories（新工場を建設する）という対照的な考えを述べていることから, (C) の as opposed to（= instead of; rather than）が文脈に合うと判断する。

誤答 (A) は in contrast to ...（〜と対照的に）の形であればよい。(B) other than は「〜のほかには」（= apart from ...; except for ...）という意味なので，rather than ...（〜よりむしろ）と混同しないように注意。(D) whereas は接続詞で，後ろには節（SV）が必要。

重要語句 □ well off「うまくいく，困らない」（= in a good situation）

118
⏱ 15秒 ┃満点ポイント!┃ 品詞 　　　　　　　　　　　　　　　正解 ➤ (B)

Having surpassed his sales targets by a wide margin, Mr. En expects that his achievements will have a positive impact on his performance ------- this year.

(A) appraising

(B) appraisal

(C) appraisingly

(D) to appraise

エンさんは販売目標をかなり上回ったので，自分の業績が今年の業務評価に良い影響を与えるだろうと期待している。

(A)「見定めるような」

(B)「評価」

(C)「見定めるように」

(D)「評価するために」

正解 have a positive impact on ...（〜に良い影響を与える）の後ろに続く名詞句として，performance とともに複合名詞を形成する名詞の (B) appraisal（= evaluation; review; assessment）を入れれば performance appraisal（勤務評価）となり文意が通る。

誤答 (A) appraising は He gave an appraising look. のように形容詞的に用いられる。副詞の (C) appraisingly は文法的に空所の位置に入るが，文意が成立しない。(D) to appraise は不定詞。

重要語句 □ surpass「〜を上回る」（= exceed） □ by a wide margin「かなりの差で」※ 反対は by a narrow margin（わずかな差で）。

119 ⏱10秒　動詞形　　　　　　　　　　　　　　正解 ➤ (D)

After ------- to manager three years ago, Mr. Rodriguez went on to become the head of the eastern sales division of Maxiwell Corporation.

(A) promoting

(B) having promoted

(C) promoted

(D) being promoted

ロドリゲスさんは，3年前に部長職に昇進した後，マキシウェル・コーポレーションの東部営業部門の統括部長になった。

(A) 動名詞（能動態）

(B) 完了動名詞（能動態）

(C) 過去分詞（受動態）

(D) 動名詞（受動態）

正解 前置詞 After の後ろに置くのにふさわしい動詞の形は動名詞（-ing 形）であること，また「昇進する」の意味では be promoted という受動態で用いられることから，(D) being promoted が適切な形であると判断する。

誤答 (A) promoting と (B) having promoted は能動態の形なので，動詞 promote の目的語が直後に必要になる。過去分詞の (C) promoted は，after を接続詞として用いて After he was promoted to manager とすることはできるが，when/while などの接続詞とは違い，後ろの he was を省略することはできない。

重要語句 □ go on to *do*「さらに進んで〜する」（= proceed to *do*）

120 ⏱20秒　満点ポイント！　語彙　　　　　　　　　　正解 ➤ (B)

In his popular television program, renowned chef Justin Duval draws ------- 15 years of culinary experience to show viewers how to prepare gourmet food at home.

(A) back

(B) upon

(C) over

(D) aside

著名シェフのジャスティン・デュバルは，出演している人気のテレビ番組で，15年の料理経験を生かし，自宅でもできる高級料理の調理法を視聴者に披露している。

(A)「後ろに」

(B)「〜の上に」

(C)「〜以上」

(D)「かたわらに」

正解 空所直前に動詞 draws があり，後ろに 15 years of culinary experience という「経験」が来ていることから，(B) upon を入れて draw on [upon] ...（〔経験や資源など〕を生かす＝ make use of ...）という句動詞を完成させる。

誤答 (A) を入れた draw back は「引き下がる」（= move away）という意味。(C) は，over 15 years（15年以上）の形ができあがるが，ここでは動詞 draw とつながらない。(D) aside は set aside（〜を確保する）が TOEIC に出題される。

重要語句 □ culinary「料理に関する」（= cooking）

121 ⏱20秒 満点ポイント! 語彙 　　　　正解 ➤ (A)

George Ortega has served the citizens of Brownsville for twenty years in his ------- as the leader of the town council.

(A) capacity
(B) integrity
(C) authenticity
(D) majority

ジョージ・オルテガは，町議会会長として20年間ブラウンズビル町民のために働いてきた。

(A)「(仕事上の) 立場，職」
(B)「(信念に対する) 実直さ，誠実さ」
(C)「本物であること，信憑性」
(D)「大多数」

正解 空所の前までで「George Ortega が働いてきた」と述べ，直後に as the leader (of the town council) という立場が来ていることから，「(仕事上の) 立場」(= role; function) を意味する (A) capacity が適切。in one's capacity as ... (～としての立場で) の形のままおさえておこう。

誤答 (B) integrity は，He has a reputation for his professional integrity. (彼の仕事に対する実直さには定評がある) のように用いる。(C) authenticity は，形容詞 authentic (本物の) とともにおさえておきたい語。(D) majority は，a majority of ... (大多数の～) の形をおさえておこう。

122 ⏱10秒 修飾 　　　　正解 ➤ (A)

Recent declines in sales revenue and corresponding budget reductions make it likely that the company's expansion plans will have to wait for ------- another year.

(A) yet
(B) one
(C) again
(D) until

最近販売収益が落ち，それに伴って予算も削減されたため，会社の事業拡大計画はさらにもう一年持ち越しにせざるを得なくなるだろう。

(A)「さらに」
(B)「ひとつの」
(C)「再び」
(D)「～までずっと」

正解 空所がなくても for another year という表現が完成するので，直後の another を修飾する機能をもつ (A) yet を入れる。yet another ... で「さらにまた～」という意味。yet にはほかにも，「これまでで (もっとも)」(This is the best camera yet manufactured.) や「それでも，だが= but」(a cheap yet stylish jacket) などさまざまな用法がある。

誤答 (B) one を入れると one another (お互い= each other) という代名詞の表現ができあがるが，直後の名詞を修飾できない。(C) again は，for another year again のように通例語尾に置かれる。前置詞の (D) until は，for の代わりに用いて wait until next year とすればよい。

重要語句 □ corresponding「それに伴った」 □ wait「(物事が) 後回しになる」

338

123 ⏱10秒 　満点ポイント!　品詞　　　　　　　　　正解 ➤ (D)

Only the applicants showing the most ---
<u>V-ing</u>　　　　<u>O</u>
---- will be called back for the second
screening process held at the firm's head
office.

(A) promising
(B) promises
(C) promisingly
(D) promise

有望さをもっとも発揮した応募者のみが，本社で行われる二次審査に呼ばれることになる。

(A)「有望な」形容詞
(B)「約束」名詞
(C)「有望な様子で」副詞
(D)「有望さ」名詞

正解 空所の前にある showing の目的語として名詞が必要であることをおさえる。名詞 promise は不加算名詞として用いると「有望さ，見込み」(= potential) を意味することから，単数形の (D) promise を入れて show(ing) the most promise（もっとも有望さを発揮する）とするのが適切であると判断する。

誤答 複数形の (B) promises では「約束」の意味になり，また「約束する」という場合は <u>make</u> promises となることもおさえたい。最近の Part 5 ではこのように，加算・不加算の「感覚」を問う上級者向けの品詞問題がたびたび登場する。

重要語句 □ call *someone* back「［人］を呼び戻す」(= ask *someone* back)　□ screening「審査」(= check)

124 ⏱10秒 代名詞の格　　　　　　　　　　　　　　正解 ➤ (A)

Mr. Navari won ------- support by
　　　　　<u>won</u>　<u>O₁</u>　　<u>support</u>
　　　　　　　　　　O₂
presenting a very persuasive case for his
proposal to company directors.

(A) himself
(B) them
(C) its
(D) theirs

ナバリさんは，提案に対するじつに説得力のある主張を会社役員に展開し，支持を得ることができた。

(A) 再帰代名詞
(B) 目的格
(C) 所有格
(D) 所有代名詞

正解 空所直前にある won に着目。動詞 win には《win O₁ O₂》で「O₁ に O₂ を勝ち取らせる」という意味を表す語法があるので，主語 Mr. Navari を再び目的語 O₁ の位置で受けるのにふさわしい再帰代名詞の (A) himself を入れる。win *oneself* ... で「～をみずから勝ち取る」という意味。

誤答 名詞 support の前に所有格がくる場合は，the directors' [their] support のように「support する人」を置く必要があるので，(C) its は不適切。実際の Part 5 では，名詞の前は，所有格がほぼ正解になるが，今回のように所有格以外が正解になるパターンも過去に数回出題されたことがある。

重要語句 □ persuasive「説得力のある」(= convincing)　□ case「(議論の) 主張，根拠」(= argument)

125

⏱15秒　時制　　　　　　　　　　　　　　　　正解 ➤ (B)

Economic indicators suggest that
worldwide demand for consumer
　　　　　S
electronics ------- exponentially in the year
ahead.　　　　　V

(A) increase

(B) will be increasing

(C) has been increased

(D) to increase

経済指標は，家電製品に対する需要が来年世界
的に急激に高まることを示している。

(A) 原形・現在形

(B) 未来進行形

(C) 現在完了形

(D) 不定詞

正解 一文の構造上，that 節内の主語 worldwide demand に対応する述語動詞が求められている
ことをおさえ，空所の後ろにある in the year ahead という未来を示す語句に合う未来進行形の (B)
will be increasing を選ぶ。ここでの動詞 suggest は「〜を示す」(= indicate) の意味。

誤答 suggest が「提案する」を意味する場合は，The manager suggests that we increase the
price next year. のように that 節内で原形動詞を用いることに注意（仮定法現在）。

重要語句 □ indicator「指標」(= sign)　□ exponentially「急激に，指数関数的に」　□ ahead「(時間が) 先に」

126

⏱15秒　満点ポイント！ 語彙　　　　　　　　　　　　正解 ➤ (B)

Traffic congestion was expected on Fifth
Avenue from 3 P.M. to 5 P.M. on Wednesday,
but Ms. Petrelli had to use that road -------.

(A) otherwise

(B) nevertheless

(C) likewise

(D) meanwhile

水曜日の午後 3 時から 5 時の間，5 番街が渋滞
する予測が出されていたが，それでもペトレリ
さんはその道を使わざるをえなかった。

(A)「さもないと」

(B)「それでもやはり」

(C)「同様に」

(D)「その間」

正解 Traffic congestion was expected（渋滞が予測されていた）という事実に対し，カンマの
後ろで but Ms. Petrelli ... that road（その道路を使わざるをえなかった）という対照的な結果が
述べられていることから，対照を強調する副詞の (B) nevertheless (= anyway) が入る。副詞
nevertheless は however の意味で文頭に置くことも多いが，but ... nevertheless の形で文尾にも
置けることは多くの上級者が見落としがちな点。

誤答 (A) otherwise (= if not) と (C) likewise (= in the similar way) は文意に合わない。(D)
meanwhile は通例，文頭に置かれる。

127 ⏱10秒 満点ポイント! 品詞 正解 ▶ (C)

While many felt that the suggestion was a reasonably ------- solution to the problem, the president opposed it vigorously.

(A) soundly

(B) sounded

(C) sound

(D) sounding

その提案が問題を解決するのに十分妥当な策だと多くの人が感じたが，社長は強く反対した。

(A)「十分に」副詞

(B)「鳴らされる，発音される」過去分詞

(C)「適切な，妥当な」形容詞

(D)「聞こえる」現在分詞

正解 空所の前にある副詞 reasonably が修飾でき，かつ直後の名詞 solution を修飾する形容詞の (C) sound（妥当な）を選択する。この reasonably は fairly や quite の意味。

誤答 (A) soundly は sleep soundly（熟睡する＝ have a sound sleep）のように用いられる。過去分詞の (B) sounded が名詞を修飾する場合は「(音が) 鳴らされる，発音される」という意味になり，文意を成さない。(D) sounding は，《形容詞＋ -sounding》の形で「〜に聞こえる，〜のような」という意味を表す。

重要語句 □ oppose「〜に反対する」 □ vigorously「激しく，力強く」（＝ strongly; energetically）

---

128 ⏱30秒 満点ポイント! 前置詞 vs. 接続詞 正解 ▶ (A)

------- the ten sales representatives
<u>名詞句</u>
(enrolled in the company's online negotiating techniques workshop), Mr. Durand was the only one who completed the course within the specified period.

(A) Out of

(B) Notwithstanding

(C) As soon as

(D) Altogether

会社のオンライン交渉技術研修に登録していた10人の営業担当者のうち，期日どおりにコースを修了したのはデュランドさんだけだった。

(A)「〜のうちで」

(B)「〜に関わらず」

(C)「〜するとすぐに」

(D)「合わせて」

正解 空所の後ろにある enrolled が，representatives (which were) enrolled のように過去分詞として用いられていることを見極め，名詞句をつなぐ前置詞の (A) Out of ...（〜のうちで）を入れる。enroll in は「登録する」(=register for) という意味を表すほか，be enrolled という受け身の形で「登録されている状態」を表せることをおさえよう。

誤答 enrolled を過去形と考えると，the ... representatives (S') enrolled (V') という節ができあがるが，接続詞の (C) As soon as では文脈がつながらない。(B) Notwithstanding は in spite of と同じ意味のフォーマルな前置詞で，過去に一度正解になったことがある。

129

Decisions regarding promotions within the department are left to the ------ of the supervisor.

(A) discretion
(B) perspective
(C) liability
(D) insistence

部門内部での昇進に関する決定は，部門責任者の判断にゆだねられる。

(A)「判断力」
(B)「（独自の）見方，観点」
(C)「（法的な）責任」
(D)「主張，強い勧め」

正解 主語 Decisions に関して，are left to the ...（〜にゆだねられる）と続いていることから，「（どうするかを決める）判断力」を意味する (A) discretion が適切。leave ... to one's discretion（〜を〔人〕の判断にゆだねる）の形でよく用いられる。

誤答 (B) は perspective on ...（〜に対する見方・観点）の形で TOEIC に頻出する。(D) は at one's insistence（〔人〕の強い勧めで）の形をおさえておこう。

130

Despite being created by the same architect, there are some ------- differences in the design of the two buildings.

(A) oblivious
(B) enduring
(C) attentive
(D) marked

同じ建築家によって設計されたものだが，その2つの建物のデザインには顕著な違いが見られる。

(A)「無関心の」
(B)「持続的な」
(C)「注意を払っている」
(D)「顕著な」

正解 直後の名詞 difference と結びつき，かつ一文の文意に合う形容詞は，「顕著な，際立った」という意味の (D) marked（= striking）である。

誤答 (A) oblivious（無関心の）は obvious（明確な）と混同しないよう注意。(B) enduring（持続的な）は enduring effect（持続効果）の形をおさえておこう。(C) attentive は「注意を払っている，気配りのある」の意味。

重要語句 □ architect「建築家」

Owing to his hard work in the past year, Mr. Bernard ------ a prominent role on the design team.

(A) assigned
(B) was assigned
(C) has been assigning
(D) assigning

バーナードさんは，過去 1 年の努力が実り，デザインチームでの重要な役割を任された。

(A) 能動態
(B) 受動態
(C) 能動態
(D) 現在分詞

正解 冒頭の Owing to ... in the past year（過去 1 年の努力により）という文脈から，主語の Mr. Bernard は a prominent role を assign される側であることを見極め，受動態の (B) was assigned を選択する。動詞 assign には《assign O₁ O₂》（O₁ に O₂ を任せる）という語法があり，受動態にした場合も O₁ be assigned O₂ のように目的語がひとつ残る。態の問題は，目的語があれば能動態となるパターンがほとんどだが，満点を目指すのであれば目的語が残る受動態もマスターしたい。

誤答 (A) assigned と (C) has been assigning は能動態で，ここでは文意が通らない。

重要語句 □ owing to ...「〜が原因で」（= because of ...; due to ...; on account of ...）　□ prominent「重要な」（= important），「目立つ」（= noticeable）

A variety of artists performed commendably at the annual concert this past weekend, the last of ------- was by far the most well-known in the country.

(A) which
(B) whose
(C) all
(D) whom

さまざまなアーティストが先週末，毎年恒例のコンサートですばらしい演奏をしたが，最後の出演者が国内でずば抜けて有名なアーティストだった。

(A) 関係代名詞［モノ・主格；目的格］
(B) 関係代名詞［所有格］
(C) 代名詞
(D) 関係代名詞［人・目的格］

正解 カンマの前までで文が完成しているので，カンマ以下の節をつなぐために関係詞が必要。前置詞 of の目的語が空所になっていることから，目的格の (A) which と (D) whom が候補に残るが，空所に入れて文意が通るのは主語の (a variety of) artists なので，人を受ける (D) を選ぶ。先行詞が直前にない関係詞の難問。

誤答 the annual concert を (A) which で受けることもできるが，文意が通らない。所有格の (B) whose は，《whose ＋名詞》の形をとる。(C) all は代名詞なので，カンマ前後の節をつなぐことができない。

重要語句 □ commendably「立派に，すばらしく」　□ this past weekend「（過ぎたばかりの）先週末」 ※ これから来る週末は this coming weekend。　□ by far ＋最上級「はるかに，ずば抜けて」《最上級の強調》

133

⏱ 10秒 　満点ポイント! 　語彙（句動詞） 　　　　　　　　　正解 ➤ (D)

Several of the items reported missing from the warehouse have yet to be -------.

(A) shown up

(B) looked into

(C) turned out

(D) accounted for

倉庫からなくなっていると届出のあった品物のうち，数点の所在がまだわかっていない。

(A) 「現れる」（= appear）

(B) 「（問題など）を探る」（= investigate）

(C) 「［他］〜を生産する，［自］（イベントに）現れる，集まる」

(D) 「（紛失物）の所在がわかる」

正解 選択肢に並ぶ句動詞のうち，「（紛失物）の所在がわかる」という意味のある (D) が文脈に合う。account for はほかに，「〜の割合を占める」（= form a particular amount）や「〜の説明になる」（= explain the reason of ...）などさまざまな意味を持つ重要表現。

誤答 (A) は自動詞的な表現で，受動態で用いない。(B) は The problem has yet to be looked into. とは言える。(C) は，他動詞として「〜を生産する」（= produce），自動詞として「イベントに現れる，集まる」（= appear）という意味があり，ここから派生した名詞 turnout（出席者= attendance）も重要。

重要語句 □ have yet to *do*「まだ〜していない」（= have not yet *done*）

134

⏱ 15秒 　満点ポイント! 　品詞 　　　　　　　　　　　　　　正解 ➤ (B)

The proposal for expansion of the entire ground floor of the building has been rejected, as such an undertaking would have ------- high costs.

(A) prohibited

(B) prohibitively

(C) prohibiting

(D) prohibitive

一階全体を拡張する提案は却下されたが，それはそれほどの規模の工事を行うのに法外な費用がかかるからだ。

(A) 過去形・過去分詞

(B) 「法外に」副詞

(C) 現在分詞・動名詞

(D) 「（金額が）法外に高い」形容詞

正解 空所を取っても文が成り立つので，直後の形容詞 high を修飾するのにふさわしい副詞の (B) prohibitively が入る。prohibitively high [expensive]（〔金額が〕法外に高い）の形のままおさえておきたい。

誤答 形容詞の (D) prohibitive は prohibitive costs とは言えるが，ここでは同じ意味を表す high がすでにあるため不適切。動詞 prohibit（〜を禁止する）の過去分詞である (A) prohibited を入れると would have prohibited で「（もし〜だったら）禁止しただろう）」という仮定法過去完了になり，文意が通らない。

重要語句 □ undertaking「大変な仕事，事業」（= important or difficult task）

135 ⏱15秒 満点ポイント! 語法 　　　　　　　　　　　　正解 ➤ (A)

The executive committee ------- the success (of the promotional campaign) to the hard work (of the marketing staff).

(A) credited

(B) appreciated

(C) rewarded

(D) acknowledged

取締役会は，販促キャンペーンの成功がマーケティングスタッフの努力のおかげであると称えた。

(A) 「(功績) を認めた」
(B) 「〜に感謝した」
(C) 「〜に報酬を与えた」
(D) 「〜を (正式に) 認めた」

正解 動詞が 4 つ並んでいるので語法に着目。空所の後ろに the success ... to the hard work と *A to B* の形が続くことから，credit *A* to *B* で「A (功績) が B のおかげだと認める」(= attribute *A* to *B*) という語法をもつ (A) credited を選択する。

誤答 他の選択肢は語法上，いずれも to 以下とつながらない。(C) は reward *someone* for ... で「人に〜に対する報酬を与える」，reward *someone* with ... で「人に報酬として〜を与える」のように人を目的語にとることが多く，ここでは The committee rewarded the staff for their hard work. とは言える。

---

136 ⏱15秒 満点ポイント! 語彙 　　　　　　　　　　　　正解 ➤ (B)

Due to predicted inclement weather, there is a ------- possibility that the organizers will have to move tomorrow's event to an indoor venue.

(A) decisive

(B) distinct

(C) profuse

(D) dependent

悪天候が予測されているので，主催者が明日のイベントを屋内の会場に移す可能性が非常に高い。

(A) 「決定づける」
(B) 「確実な」
(C) 「大量にあふれる」
(D) 「依存している」

正解 空所直後の名詞 possibility を修飾するのにふさわしい形容詞は，「はっきりした，確実な」(= definite) という意味のある (B) distinct。反対の意味を表す remote possibility (わずかな可能性) とセットでおさえておこう。distinct はほかにも，distinct voice で「明瞭な」(= clear)，The two cities are distinct from each other. のように用いて「はっきり異なる」(= clearly different) という意味になる。

誤答 (A) decisive は decisive role (決定的役割) や decisive factor (決定要因) のように用いる。(C) profuse は He made profuse apologies. (平謝りした) の形でよく用いる。(D) dependent は dependable (頼れる) との混同をねらった不正解の選択肢としてよく登場する。

重要語句 □ inclement weather「悪天候」

345

137

MGO Travel promises to deliver vacations that are both reasonably priced and -------.

（s' / v'）

(A) memories

(B) memorized

(C) memorable

(D) memorably

	MGO トラベル社は，手頃な価格でかつ思い出に残る休暇プランを提供することを約束している。

(A) 「記憶，思い出」名詞

(B) 「暗記される」過去分詞

(C) 「記憶に残る」形容詞

(D) 「印象的に」副詞

正解 空所の前には vacations を先行詞にとる関係代名詞 that があり，さらに are が続いている。そこで，vacations とイコールの関係になる補語が必要と判断し，形容詞の (C) memorable（記憶に残る）を入れる。

誤答 過去分詞の (B) memorized も文法的に入るが，文意が通らない。直前の priced に惑わされて，同じ形を反射的に選ばないようにしよう。

重要語句 □ promise to *do* ...「～すると約束する」 □ reasonably priced「手頃な価格」

138

Duplication or redistribution of this film or any of its content without the written consent of Globoflix Entertainment, Inc., is ------- forbidden.

(A) expressly

(B) vastly

(C) adamantly

(D) exclusively

本映画やその内容の複製および再配給は，グロボフリックス・エンターテイメント社の書面による承諾のない限り，固く禁じられております。

(A) 「明確に，絶対に」（= clearly; definitely）

(B) 「大いに」（= very much）

(C) 「頑固に」

(D) 「それだけに限定して」（= only）

正解 空所直後の過去分詞 forbidden を適切に修飾できる副詞は，「明確に，絶対に」という意味の (A) expressly。expressly forbidden（固く禁じられる）の形でよく用いられる。

誤答 (B) vastly（非常に= very much）は vastly improved（大いに改善した）や vastly different（非常に異なった）など，「違いの大きさ」を強調する。(C) adamantly（頑固に）は上級者を惑わすためのハイレベル単語。(D) exclusively（= only）は The content can be accessed exclusively by members. のように用いられる。

重要語句 □ consent「同意，承諾」（= approval; permission; authorization）

139 ⏱ 15秒　語法 正解 ➤ (D)

Although numerous proposals have been submitted from the research and development staff, ------- have been discussed at recent committee meetings.

(A) little

(B) much

(C) neither

(D) none

研究開発スタッフから数多くの提案が出されたが，どれも最近の委員会で議論されていない。

(A) 「わずか」

(B) 「多く」

(C) 「(ふたつの) どちらも～ない」

(D) 「何も～でない」

正解 空所直後に have があるので，複数扱いをする代名詞が必要。(D) の none（＝ not any）は，指している名詞が加算か不加算かにより扱いが変わり，ここでは none of the proposals を指すことから，proposals に合わせて複数扱いになる。

誤答 (A) little，(B) much，(C) neither は，いずれも主語として用いられるが，必ず単数扱いになることに注意。一方，必ず複数扱いをする代名詞として，few と several をおさえておこう。

重要語句 □ numerous「数多くの」（＝ very many; countless）

---

140 ⏱ 15秒　満点ポイント!　語彙 正解 ➤ (C)

When Mr. Phelps summarized the research findings, he inadvertently left out some ------- details.

(A) apparent

(B) contingent

(C) pertinent

(D) subsequent

フェルプスさんが調査結果を要約した際，関連情報の一部を誤って抜かしてしまった。

(A) 「おそらくの，見かけ上の」

(B) 「将来起こる，～次第の」（＝ dependent）

(C) 「関連する，状況に合った」（＝ relevant）

(D) 「次に来る」（＝ next; following）

正解 空所直後にある名詞 details を修飾するのに適切な形容詞は，(C) の pertinent（関連する）である。動詞形の pertain to ...（～に関連する＝ relate to ...）と合わせておさえておこう。

誤答 (A) apparent は，「おそらくの，見かけ上の」という意味を表すほか，it is apparent that SV の形で「(事実) が明白な」（＝ obvious）という意味になる。(B) の contingent はハイレベルな語で，不正解の選択肢に登場する。(D) subsequent は the subsequent business day（翌営業日）のように用いる TOEIC 頻出の重要語。

重要語句 □ inadvertently「不注意にも，誤って」（＝ accidentally; mistakenly）　□ leave out ...「～を省く」（＝ omit）

Questions 141-143 refer to the following article.

The Canberra Museum of Natural History will soon begin extensive renovations in order to create a brighter, more spacious environment. The curator of the museum announced yesterday that the initial phase of the project, ------- to continue

141. (A) expecting

(B) which expected

(C) having been expected

(D) expected

for the next three months, will entail an overhaul of the Goldberg Wing of the museum. All exhibits of the wing will be ------- while the work is in progress.

142. (A) displayed

(B) replaced

(C) inspected

(D) stored

Following the renovations, the Goldberg Wing will offer a much-improved experience to museum visitors. All artwork will be reclaimed from the warehouse facility and reinstalled in a way that takes full advantage of the renovated area. ------- the inconvenience to patrons, during the renovation period the regular

143. (A) So as to

(B) As part of

(C) In accordance with

(D) In light of

admission price of $5 will be waived.

重要語句 □ curator「(図書館や博物館の) 館長」 □ phase「段階」(= stage) □ entail「~を伴う」(= involve; require) □ in progress「進行中の」(= underway) □ reclaim「~を取り戻す」(= take ... back) □ waive「(料金など) を免除する」

141-143 の設問は次の記事に関するものです。
キャンベラ自然博物館は、より明るく広々とした空間を作り出す目的で、まもなく大規模な改修工事に取り掛かる。同博物館館長が昨日発表したところによると、今後3か月続くと見込まれる工事の第1段階において、ゴールドバーグ棟の総改修を行うとのことだ。同棟の展示品は、工事期間中すべて倉庫に保管されることになる。
工事の終了後、来館者はゴールドバーグ棟においてより一層すばらしい体験ができるようになる。展示品はすべて倉庫から再び取り出され、新しい空間を十分活用した展示がなされる予定だ。来館者にかかる不便を考慮し、改修期間中は通常の入場料5ドルが無料となる。

141 ⏱30秒 構文（一文完結型） 正解 ➤ (D)

The curator of the museum announced yesterday that the initial phase of the project, **expected** to continue for the next three months, will entail an overhaul of the Goldberg Wing of the museum.

正解 空所前にある the initial phase (of the project) は「expect される」ものなので,過去分詞の (D) expected を入れれば,「〜すると予期されて」と受身の意味を補足する分詞構文ができあがる。この形は, the initial phase, (which is) expected ... の which is が省略された形と見ることもできる。
誤答 現在分詞の (A) expecting は「予期して」という能動の意味を表すため,態（する・させる）が合わない。(B) which expected の expected は過去形なので,やはり能動の意味になり不適切。(C) having been expected のような完了分詞構文《having ＋過去分詞》は, The project, having been overseen by Mr. Kato, ended successfully.（カトウ氏の監督下で行われたので〜）のように,明確な因果関係がある場合に用いられる。

142 ⏱40秒 語彙 満点ポイント! 全文読む・文脈依存型 正解 ➤ (D)

All exhibits of the wing will be **stored** while the work is in progress.

正解 空所の一文までに,exhibits に関する言及がないので,次の段落も読んでいく。すると, All artwork will ... the warehouse facility（展示品が倉庫から再び取り出される）の部分から,工事中は倉庫に収められるのだと判断し,(D) stored（保管される）を選ぶ。
誤答 空所の前の文にある名詞 overhaul は「(総点検による) 修理」のことで,ここでは「Goldberg Wing の改修工事」を意味するので,(C) inspected（検査される）を入れることはできない。また,exhibits とともによく用いられる (A) displayed（展示される）や (B) replaced（取り替えられる）も文脈に合わない。

143 ⏱15秒 慣用表現（一文完結型） 正解 ➤ (D)

In light of the inconvenience to patrons, during the renovation period the regular admission price of $5 will be waived.

正解 空所の後ろに続く名詞句 the inconvenience to patrons をつなぎ,かつともに用いて一文の文意を成すのは,「〜を考慮して」という意味を表す (D) の In light of（= in consideration of; because of）である。
誤答 (A) So as to は,《so as to ＋原形動詞》の形で「〜するために」（= in order to）の意味を表す。(B) As part of（〜の一環として）は, as part of the project [plan/initiative]（プロジェクト［計画／策略］の一環として）という組み合わせでよく用いる。(C) In accordance with（〜に従って＝ in compliance with）は,規則や条件を示す語を後ろにとる。

144-146

Questions 144-146 refer to the following letter.

VL Architecture
101 Heralds Road,
Trenford Business Park, CA 90222

April 10

To whom it may concern:

I am writing to ------- VL Architecture's bid for the landscaping work at the grounds of our new

144. (A) request
(B) offer
(C) inquire
(D) accept

Calpine Valley office complex. We are particularly interested in your plans to include several water features, as well as the wide variety of shrubs and flowers you intend to use.

Would it be possible to provide us with your ------- by May 1? We have a company-wide

145. (A) quote
(B) model
(C) schedule
(D) directions

meeting on that day to discuss our relocation plans. I would like employees to be able to see for themselves how the gardens will look once the work has been completed. Please call me at your earliest convenience so that we can arrange a time to discuss ------- we should proceed with this project.

146. (A) whatever
(B) before
(C) further
(D) how

Best regards,
John Doubleton
John Doubleton

重要語句 □ landscaping work「造園工事」 □ water feature「水をあしらったもの(噴水など)」 □ shrub「低木」 (= bush) □ see ... for *oneself*「~を直接見て確かめる」 □ once the work has been completed 「工事が完了したら」(= once the work is completed) ※once や when など時を示す接続詞の中では, 未来に関しても現在形や現在完了形が用いられる。 □ at *one's* earliest convenience「できるだけ早 急に」(as soon as possible の丁寧表現) □ proceed with ...「~を進める, 続ける」(= continue)

144-146 の設問は次の手紙に関するものです。

VL アーキテクチャー社

ヘラルズロード 101

トレンフォード・ビジネス・パーク　カリフォルニア州 90222

4 月 10 日

ご担当者様

このたび, 弊社が新たに移転を予定しておりますカルパイン・バレーのオフィスビル敷地内における造園工事に 関しまして, 貴社 VL アーキテクチャーからの入札をお受けすることにいたしました。中でも, 水をモチーフに したものや, 多種多様な低木や花を取り入れるという貴社のご提案に特に興味があります。

つきましては, 模型を 5 月 1 日までにご用意いただくことは可能でしょうか。その日に弊社で全社会議があり, 移転計画について話し合う予定になっております。そこで, 工事の終了後に庭園がどのような外観になるかを従

業員に直接目で見て確認してほしいと考えています。本工事の今後の進め方について話し合う機会を設定したいと思いますので，ご都合がつき次第お電話いただければと存じます。

敬具

ジョン・ダブルトン

144　⏱30秒　語彙　満点ポイント！　文脈依存型　正解 ➤ (D)

I am writing to **accept** VL Architecture's bid for the landscaping work at the grounds of our new Calpine Valley office complex.

正解 空所の後ろにある VL Architecture は，手紙の左上にある宛先から相手の会社であるとわかる。さらに，次の文からこの会社が具体的な plans をすでに提示していることをおさえ，(D) accept（～を受諾する）を入れて文脈を完成させる。bid は「入札」（= offer to do work）を意味し，TOEIC に頻出。

誤答 (A) request（～を依頼する）を入れると bid がまだ提示されていないことになり，文脈に合わない。(B) offer（～を差し出す）は請負会社である VL Architecture がすでに行ったこと。(C) inquire は通例 inquire about ...（～について問い合わせる）の形で用いられる。

145　⏱40秒　語彙　満点ポイント！　全文読む・文脈依存型　正解 ➤ (B)

Would it be possible to provide us with your **model** by May 1?

正解 May 1 までに何が必要になるかを考えながら文章を読み進める。すると，次の文に「その日に会議がある」とあり，さらに次の文で I would like ... the gardens will look（庭がどのような外観になるか直接従業員に見てもらいたい）と述べていることから，概観を目で確かめられるものとして (B) model（見本，模型）がふさわしいと判断する。

誤答 (A) quote（見積もり），(C) schedule（予定），(D) directions（指示，道順）は，いずれも空所の一文だけでは正解に見えるので，必ず全文を読もう。

146　⏱15秒　構文（一文完結型）　正解 ➤ (D)

Please call me at your earliest convenience so that we can arrange a time to discuss **how** we should proceed with this project.

正解 空所の後ろには，他動詞 discuss（～を話し合う）の目的語が必要。ここでは，後ろに we (S') should proceed (V') という文の要素が揃った節が続いているので，この節全体を動詞 discuss の目的語（名詞節）にする働きのある疑問副詞の (D) how（どのように～か）を入れる。proceed が自動詞であることも重要。

誤答 複合関係代名詞の (A) whatever（～は何でも）を用いる場合，discuss whatever we should do (with this project) のように，後ろの節に主語や目的語が欠けることになる。(B) before（～の前に）は副詞節を導く接続詞。(C) further（さらに）は副詞なので，節をつなぐ機能をもたない。

Questions 147-149 refer to the following advertisement.

Landing a job is not ------- as simple as responding to a job listing or submitting

147. (A) almost
(B) so
(C) nearly
(D) only

an application. You should be prepared to face harsh competition from other proficient candidates. *Career Advancement Basics*, the new educational software by Fluward Proware, will provide you with all the information you need to get an edge over others. In the program, you will learn how to determine what you want in a career and to focus your search ------- . You will get advice on creating

148. (A) respectively
(B) accordingly
(C) consequently
(D) prominently

winning résumés and cover letters, using the Internet, developing networks, and enhancing interview performance. ------- , *Career Advancement Basics* is the

149. (A) In any case
(B) Thereby
(C) Provided that
(D) In short

definitive guide to securing employment in the 21st century.

Purchase it for only $59.95!

重要語句 □ land a job「仕事を得る」(= get a job)　□ proficient「熟練の」(= skillful)　□ get an edge over ...「〜より優位に立つ」(= get an advantage over ...)　□ determine「〜を見極める, 判断する」(= judge; find out)　□ definitive「(本などが) 決定版の」(= considered to be the best of its kind)　□ secure「〜を獲得する, 確保する」(= get)

147-149 の設問は次の広告に関するものです。
職を得るということは, ただ求人広告を見て連絡を取ったり応募用紙を提出したりすることほど単純では決してありません。他の有能な候補者たちと厳しい競争に立ち向かう準備ができていなければならないのです。フルワード・プロウェア社から新発売の教育ソフト『キャリアアップの基本』は, 他の候補者より優位に立つために必要な情報をすべて提供します。このソフトのプログラムの中で, 自分のキャリアに求めるものをどのように見極め, またそれにしたがってどのように就職活動の的を絞ればいいかを学びます。採用される履歴書やカバーレターの書き方, インターネットの活用法, 人脈

の広げ方，そして面接での受け答えを向上させるためのアドバイスも満載です。『キャリアアップの基本』はすなわち，21 世紀における就職ガイドの決定版と言えます。販売価格はたった 59.95 ドルですので，今すぐお買い求めください！

147 ⏱ 20 秒　修飾　満点ポイント！　文脈依存型　　　　　　　正解 ➤ (C)

Landing a job is not **nearly** as simple as responding to a job listing or submitting an application.

正解▶ 次の文で You should be prepared ... proficient candidates.（他者との競争に立ち向かう準備が必要だ）と職を得る大変さを述べているので，(C) nearly を入れて not nearly（決して〜でない = not at all）とすれば，「決して simple なことではない」となり前後の文脈が通る。not nearly はこのように，as ... as 構文の否定形を強調する際に用いられる。

誤答▶ (A) almost は「ほぼ，あと少しで」の意味では nearly と言い換えられる。(B) so は，not so simple as ... とは言える。not を見ると (D) only を入れて not only ...（〜であるだけではない）としたくなるが，ここでは次の文と意味がつながらないことに注意。

148 ⏱ 40 秒　語彙（一文完結型）　　　　　　　　　　　　正解 ➤ (B)

In the program, you will learn how to determine what you want in a career and to focus your search **accordingly**.

正解▶ 空所の前にある to determine what you want in a career（キャリアに求めることを見極める）と to focus your search（求職活動の的を絞る）というふたつの事柄を文脈上つなぐのは，(B) の accordingly（それに従って）である。

誤答▶ (A) respectively（〔述べられた順に〕それぞれ）は，Paul and Brad are British and American, respectively. のように用いる。(C) の consequently（その結果，従って= as a result）は，文修飾をする副詞なので，文尾には置けない。(D) の prominently（目立つように，際立って）は，prominently displayed（目立つように置かれている）という形でよく用いられる。

149 ⏱ 30 秒　接続副詞　満点ポイント！　文脈依存型　　　　正解 ➤ (D)

In short, *Career Advancement Basics* is the definitive guide to securing employment in the 21st century.

正解▶ それまでの文章全体でソフトの内容を説明しているのに対し，空所の文で *Career Advancement Basics* is ... in the 21st century（21 世紀における就職ガイドの決定版だ）と一言で要約されていることから，(D) In short（手短に言うと，すなわち= In summary）が適切。

誤答▶ (A) In any case（〔何があっても〕とにかく）は whatever happens の意味で，In any case, you should buy this software. のように用いる。(B) Thereby（それによって）は，主に thereby doing ... の形で用いられる副詞。(C) Provided that（〜であれば，〜を条件として）は if と同様の意味を表す接続詞。

150-152

Questions 150-152 refer to the following e-mail.

From: Skylark Tour <alicelee@skylarktour.com>
To: Milton Bernard <mbernard23@vmail.com>
Subject: Your vacation
Date: June 15

Dear Mr. Bernard,

Thank you for choosing Skylark Tour, and we hope your trip to the Emerald Resort in Cairns -------

150. (A) lived
(B) will live
(C) lives
(D) is living

up to your expectations. The Emerald Resort is a new addition to our catalog. Therefore, we would be grateful for any comments that you may wish to offer regarding your trip. Specifically, we want to know whether anyone in particular provided superb service or if there was anything that you found ------- .

151. (A) disappointingly
(B) disappointed
(C) disappointment
(D) disappointing

As a token of our appreciation for the time you have taken to give us your comments, we will send you our complimentary travel atlas. We hope this ------- will be of help to you in planning your next trip.

152. (A) option
(B) itinerary
(C) volume
(D) advice

Thanks again for traveling with Skylark Tour.

Sincerely,
Alice Lee

重要語句 □ superb「すばらしい」(= excellent) □ as a token of ...「~のしるしとして」 □ complimentary 「無料の」(= free) □ atlas「地図帳」(= map book)

150-152 の設問は次のメールに関するものです。
送信者：スカイラーク・ツアー <alicelee@sylarktour.com>
宛先：ミルトン・バーナード <mbernard23@vmail.com>
件名：お客様のご旅行
日付：6月15日

バーナード様

このたびはスカイラーク・ツアーをお選びいただきありがとうございました。ケアンズのエメラルド・リゾートへの旅がお客様のご期待に沿うものであったことを願っております。エメラルド・リゾートは弊社カタログに新しく加わったものですので、ご旅行に関してどんなことでもご意見をいただければ幸いです。例えば、特にすばらしいサービスを提供した者や、何かご期待に添えなかった点などがあればお伝えいただければと存じます。

ご感想をいただいたお客様には，お時間を割いていただいたことへの感謝といたしまして，弊社の観光地図帳を無料で差し上げております。バーナード様が次回旅行の計画を立てる際に，この冊子がお役に立てば幸いです。スカイラーク・ツアーをご利用いただきましたことに重ねてお礼申し上げます。

敬具
アリス・リー

150 ⏱ 40秒 時制 満点ポイント！ 全文読む・文脈依存型 正解 ➤ (A)

Thank you for choosing Skylark Tour, and we hope your trip to the Emerald Resort in Cairns **lived** up to your expectations.

正解 動詞 hope の後ろが常に未来とは限らないことに注意。そのまま読み進めると，Specifically, we want to know ... の一文で過去形を用いていること，またメールの最終文で Thanks again for traveling と感謝していることから，旅行後のメールであると判断し，過去形の (A) lived を選ぶ。live up to one's expectations は「〔人〕の期待に沿う」（＝ meet one's expectations）という意味。
誤答 (B) will live は未来形，(C) lives は現在形。動詞 hope の後ろでは，近い未来に関して We hope your trip lives [will live] up to your expectations. のようにどちらの形も用いることをおさえておきたい。(D) is living は現在進行形。

151 ⏱ 20秒 品詞・構文（一文完結型） 正解 ➤ (D)

Specifically, we want to know whether anyone in particular provided superb service or if there was anything that you found **disappointing**.

正解 空所前の関係代名詞 that は anything を受けているので，you found anything ------- という形に置き換えて考えるとよい。find には find O C（O が C だと思う）という語法があるので，目的語 anything を説明する補語として適切な形容詞の (D) disappointing（がっかりさせる，期待はずれの）が入る。
誤答 (B) の disappointed（残念に思う）は人の気持ちを表す形容詞なので，anything という物事に対して用いない。(A) の disappointingly（がっかりさせるように）は副詞，(C) の disappointment（失望）は名詞。

152 ⏱ 30秒 語彙 満点ポイント！ 文脈依存型 正解 ➤ (C)

We hope this **volume** will be of help to you in planning your next trip.

正解 空所の直前にある指示代名詞 this に着目し，これが何を指しているかを前の文から見極める。すると，「travel atlas（旅行地図帳）を送る」とあるので，これを一語で言い換えた (C) volume（本，巻＝ book）がふさわしい。
誤答 (A) option（選択肢），(B) itinerary（旅程表＝ travel schedule），(D) advice（アドバイス）は，いずれも travel atlas の言い換えとして不適切。

Questions 153-154 refer to the following notice. （語数：105 語）

Founded nearly ten years ago, Glasstar has quickly grown to be the premier purveyor of quality glass and crystal ornaments in the northeast of the country. We were recently described by industry journal *Giftware Today* as "the future of the industry," and last year won the prestigious Ornacom Golden Globe for an unprecedented fifth year. Starting later this year, we are expanding our operations across the country. We are therefore seeking a number of motivated, ambitious individuals to acquire franchises in our burgeoning business. Interested parties must have capital of €160,000 or more, and should contact Judi Alexandra at 759 0491 4413 for further details.

---

153. What is the purpose of the notice?

(A) To recruit workers for newly established locations

(B) To give an overview of an upcoming event

(C) To promote a retail space for potential shopkeepers

(D) To publicize an investment opportunity

154. What is indicated about Glasstar?

(A) It has been in business for a full decade.

(B) It is currently operating nationwide.

(C) It has received favorable reviews from a magazine.

(D) It provides product specifications over the telephone.

重要語句 □premier「主要な，大手の」（= main; leading; prominent） □purveyor「販売会社」（= supplier; retailer） □ornament「装飾品」 □prestigious「名誉ある」（= important and respected） □unprecedented「先例のない」 □franchise「フランチャイズ権」（会社の一店舗として商品を販売する権利） □burgeoning「急成長している」（= rapidly growing） □shopkeeper「店の経営者」（= shop owner）

153-154 の設問は次の通知に関するものです。

グラスター社はほぼ 10 年前に設立され，国の北東部髄一の高品質なガラスやクリスタルの装飾品販売会社へと急成長しました。当社は最近，業界誌『ギフトウェア・トゥデイ』で「この産業の未来」と評され，昨年は名誉あるオーナコム・ゴールデン・グローブ賞を先例のない 5 年連続で受賞しました。今年の後半には，全国展開を始める予定です。したがって，急成長している当社事業のフランチャイズ権を取得する意欲と野心のある人材を多数募集しています。応募希望の方は，16 万ユーロ以上の資本金が必要です。詳細については，ジュディ・アレクサンドラ，759 0491 4413 までお電話ください。

153 ⏱ 15 秒　　　　　　　　　　　　　　　　　　　正解 ➤ (D)

この通知の目的は何ですか。
(A) 新たに設立された店舗で働く人材を募集すること
(B) これから行われるイベントの概要を伝えること
(C) 店の経営を考えている人に店舗スペースを宣伝すること
(D) 出資の機会を宣伝すること

正解 Glasstar 社に関して，4 文目で We are therefore seeking ... to acquire franchises（フランチャイズ権を取得する人材を募集中）とあり，さらに次の文で Interested parties ... €160,000 or more（16 万ユーロ以上の資本金が必要）と具体的な金額が提示されていることから，これを investment opportunity と言い表した (D) が正解。副詞 therefore は，文書の結論や目的を示すキーワードになる。
誤答 (A) は，通知の中で「今年これから全国展開していく」とあるので，newly established locations ではないことに注意。(C) は，通知が potential shopkeepers 向けのものと考えることはできるが，retail space に関しては何も伝えていない。

154 ⏱ 10 秒　　　　　　　　　　　　　　　　　　　正解 ➤ (C)

グラスター社に関して何が述べられていますか。
(A) 丸 10 年間ビジネスをしてきた。
(B) 現在全国展開している。
(C) 雑誌から肯定的な評価を受けた。
(D) 電話を通じて製品の詳細情報を提供している。

正解 第 2 文目の We were recently described ... "the future of the industry" から，*Giftware Today* という業界誌で高い評価を受けたことがわかるので，この内容と一致する (C) が適切。
誤答 (A) は，冒頭の Founded nearly ten years ago の部分から，10 年には満たないことがわかる。(B) は 3 文目に Starting later this year とあるので現在ではなくこれからのこと。(D) は，最終文に contact ... for further details とあるので，製品情報ではなくフランチャイズの出店に関する情報だとわかる。

Questions 155-156 refer to the following e-mail. （語数：117 語）

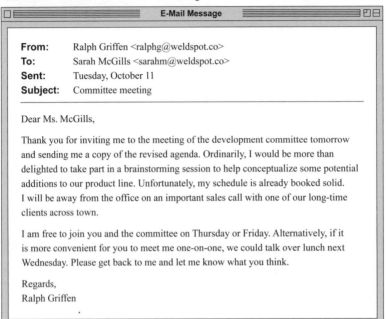

```
┌─┬─────────────────────────┬───────┐
│ □│▤▤▤▤▤▤▤▤   E-Mail Message  ▤▤▤▤▤▤▤ │▱▯▤│
```

From:	Ralph Griffen <ralphg@weldspot.co>
To:	Sarah McGills <sarahm@weldspot.co>
Sent:	Tuesday, October 11
Subject:	Committee meeting

Dear Ms. McGills,

Thank you for inviting me to the meeting of the development committee tomorrow and sending me a copy of the revised agenda. Ordinarily, I would be more than delighted to take part in a brainstorming session to help conceptualize some potential additions to our product line. Unfortunately, my schedule is already booked solid. I will be away from the office on an important sales call with one of our long-time clients across town.

I am free to join you and the committee on Thursday or Friday. Alternatively, if it is more convenient for you to meet me one-on-one, we could talk over lunch next Wednesday. Please get back to me and let me know what you think.

Regards,
Ralph Griffen

155. What has Mr. Griffen been asked to do?
(A) Proofread an agenda for a future meeting
(B) Provide input for developing new products
(C) Inform committee members of a schedule change
(D) Join a discussion with production staff

156. What will Mr. Griffen most likely do on October 12?
(A) He will meet with Ms. McGills after lunch.
(B) He will consult with members of the committee.
(C) He will go out of town to speak with a corporate client.
(D) He will attempt to solicit business for the company.

重要語句 □ conceptualize「～に関するアイデアを練る」(= form an idea of ...) □ booked solid「予定で埋まっている」(= fully booked) □ proofread「～を校正する」(= read and check for mistakes) □ solicit「～を求める，得ようとする」(= ask for ...; try to get) ※solicit business で「売り込みをする，営業する」という意味。

155-156 の設問は次のメールに関するものです。

差出人：ラルフ・グリフィン <ralphg@weldspot.co>

宛先：サラ・マクギルズ <sarahm@weldspot.co>

日付：10月11日，火曜日

件名：委員会会議について

マクギルズさん

明日行われる開発委員会の会議に呼んでいただき，また議題の修正版を送っていただき，ありがとうございました。本来ならば，新製品に加えうる製品についてのアイデアを練るため，ぜひともブレインストーミングに参加したいところですが，残念ながら明日はすでに予定が埋まっています。長年付き合いのある顧客を営業で訪問するため町の反対側に行く大事な予定があるので，オフィスにいません。

木曜日か金曜日なら，あなたと委員の皆さんの話し合いに参加することができます。あるいは，二人だけで会ったほうがよろしければ，来週の水曜日に昼食をご一緒するというのはいかがでしょうか。ご都合を知らせてください。

敬具
ラルフ・グリフィン

155 ⏱ 20秒   正解 ➤ (B)

グリフィンさんは何をするよう求められていますか。
(A) これから行われる会議の議題を校正する
(B) 新製品の開発に関してアイデアを出す
(C) 開発委員会のメンバーに予定の変更を知らせる
(D) 製造スタッフとの話し合いに参加する

正解 メールの冒頭部分から Mr. Griffen が会議に呼ばれていること，さらに次の Ordinarily, I would be ... to our product line. という一文から会議の目的が新製品のアイデアの構築であることをおさえ，(B) を選ぶ。
誤答 (A) は，proofread でなく read や review であれば正解。また，会議は development committee によるもので，(D) の production staff については言及されていない。

156 ⏱ 30秒   正解 ➤ (D)

グリフィンさんは 10 月 12 日におそらく何をしますか。
(A) 昼食の後にマクギルズさんと直接打ち合わせをする。
(B) 委員会のメンバーたちと話をする。
(C) 法人顧客と話をするため町を出る。
(D) 会社のために営業に出かける。

正解 October 12 はメールが送付された日の翌日なので，第 1 文目から会議に呼ばれている日であることをおさえる。さらに，第 1 段落後半で，その日の予定に関して I will be away from the office ... across town.（顧客を営業訪問する予定がありオフィスにいない）と説明していることから，(D) がこの内容に一致する。sales call に「営業訪問」（＝ sales visit）の意味があることをおさえておこう。
誤答 across town は on the other side of town という意味なので，(C) の out of town と一致しないことに注意。

Questions 157-158 refer to the following information. （語数：123語）

BizPress New Release in April

Business and Pleasure in Europe, the new book to be published by us at BizPress, will be of interest to travel bookstore proprietors. Written by experienced travel writer Tim Foxheath, the book is the third in the best-selling series, which already has titles dealing with trips to North America and Asia. As always, there is an abundance of practical tips and fascinating pictures taken by the author himself. His anecdotes about sightseeing destinations close to the business centers of each location are noteworthy. Visit our Web site to view extracts from this new book, as well as to read professional reviews of Tim Foxheath's previously published work. *Business and Pleasure in Europe* would be an excellent addition to the shelves of your bookstore.

---

157. For whom is the information most likely intended?

(A) Publishing executives
(B) Foreign travelers
(C) Bookstore owners
(D) Travel writers

158. What is NOT indicated about *Business and Pleasure in Europe*?

(A) It contains the author's personal stories.
(B) It refers to current trends in the travel industry.
(C) Part of the book can be seen online.
(D) It includes photographs taken by Tim Foxheath.

重要語句　□ of interest to *someone*「[人] にとって興味深い」(= interesting to *someone*) □ proprietor「(店の) 経営者，オーナー」(= business owner) □ an abundance of ...「豊富な量の〜」(= a large quantity of ...; plenty of ...) □ anecdote「逸話」(= real story) □ noteworthy「特筆すべき」□ extract「抜粋」(= excerpt)

157-158 の設問は次の情報に関するものです。

ビズ・プレスの 4 月新刊

弊社ビズ・プレスより出版予定の新刊『ヨーロッパでの仕事と楽しみ』は，旅行関連の書籍を扱う書店経営者の方にとって興味深いものです。本書は経験豊富な旅行記者のティム・フォクスヒース氏による著書で，すでに北アメリカとアジアの旅行を取り上げているベストセラーシリーズ第 3 作目です。前作同様，実践的なアドバイスや著者自身が撮影した美しい写真が満載です。各地のビジネス街周辺にある観光スポットの話は特筆すべきものです。弊社ウェブサイトにアクセスいただければ，この新刊の抜粋，およびティム・フォクスヒースの過去の著書に関する専門家のレビューもご覧いただけます。『ヨーロッパでの仕事と楽しみ』は，書店の本棚に加えるのに最適な本になることは間違いありません。

157 ⏱ 10 秒　満点ポイント!　文章をすべて先読みする　　正解 ▶ (C)

この情報はおそらく誰を対象としたものですか。

(A) 出版社の重役

(B) 海外旅行者

(C) 書店経営者

(D) 旅行記者

正解 読み手が誰かを示す語句に着目。冒頭文に to travel bookstore proprietors とあることや，最終文に to the shelves of your bookstore とあることから，proprietors を owners と言い換えた (C) の Bookstore owners が対象者であるとわかる。

誤答 本そのものは (B) に向けて書かれたものなので，必ず先に全文を読み，「書き手」「読み手」「文書の目的」をあらかじめ把握しておこう。

158 ⏱ 50 秒　　　　　　　　　　　　　　　　　　　　　正解 ▶ (B)

『ヨーロッパでの仕事と楽しみ』に関して述べられていないのは何ですか。

(A) 著者個人の話を含んでいる。

(B) 旅行業界における最近の動向を記している。

(C) 本の一部がオンラインで見られる。

(D) ティム・フォクスヒースの撮影した写真が掲載されている。

誤答 (A) は，4 文目の His (= author's) anecdotes，(C) は 5 文目の Visit our Web site to view extracts from this new book，(D) は 3 文目の fascinating pictures taken by the author (= Tim Foxheath) himself の部分とそれぞれ一致する。正解 旅行業界の動向に関する記述はないため，(B) が正解。各選択肢の該当箇所を正確に突き止めよう。

Questions 159-161 refer to the following memo. （語数：215 語）

MEMORANDUM

From: Clarissa Hough, general manager
To: All employees
Date: November 6
Re: Survey

The date that WWD will launch its operations is only a few short weeks away. We have decided to conduct some research to gather detailed information about the listening preferences of the potential audience for the station. We have commissioned Bottomline, Inc., to produce a survey for us, in which we will ask local members of the public about their musical tastes and their radio listening habits in general.

Bottomline, Inc., will administer a written survey that will be sent directly to 3,000 households in the local area. However, as the response rate for direct-mail surveys is often quite low, we additionally plan to poll a smaller number of randomly chosen residents by telephone. These interviews will be based on the written questionnaire, but will have fewer questions and will last for no more than five minutes each. Bottomline, Inc., has said they could do the polling for us, but it will be more cost effective if we were to take care of it ourselves. Consequently, we need employees who are willing to assist us in this process on the weekend of December 10 and 11. Overtime payments will be made to those participating in this work.

If you are interested, please contact Stan Chadwick, the head of marketing, on extension 223 or at chadwick@wwd.co.wa.

---

159. Why was the memo most likely written?

(A) To enlist volunteers for a project
(B) To provide details about recent research
(C) To request feedback on a marketing plan
(D) To describe a customer satisfaction survey

160. What kind of company most likely is WWD?

(A) A music distribution firm
(B) An advertising agency
(C) A research firm
(D) A broadcasting company

161. What is suggested about the surveys?

(A) Both telephone and written surveys will be conducted by Bottomline, Inc.
(B) Telephone surveys will take place over two days.
(C) Written surveys will be more effective than telephone surveys.
(D) Telephone and written surveys will have exactly the same content.

重要語句 □ commission ... to *do*「…に～する仕事を委託する」(= ask ... officially to do a task) □ administer「～を管理・実施する」(= manage; take care of ...) □ poll *someone*「人にアンケート調査を行う」(= survey *someone*) □ no more than ...「せいぜい，たったの」(= only; at most) □ enlist「～の協力を求める」

159-161 の設問は次の社内連絡に関するものです。

社内連絡

差出人：クラリッサ・ヒュー，総支配人

宛て先：全従業員

日付：11 月 6 日

件名：アンケート調査

WWD の営業開始までわずか数週間です。そこで，将来当局の視聴者となる可能性がある人達が何を聴きたいかに関して詳細な情報を集めるため，調査を行うことにしました。ボトムライン社にアンケートの作成を委託しましたが，アンケートでは，地元に住んでいる一般の人たちを対象に，音楽の好みとラジオを聴く習慣全般について調査する予定です。

ボトムライン社は，地元の 3000 世帯に直接郵送する書面のアンケートを実施することになります。しかし，ダイレクトメールによるアンケートの回答率はかなり低いことも多いので，さらにより少数の住民を無作為に抽出して，電話によるアンケートを実施する予定です。この聞き取り調査は，書面によるアンケートの内容に沿ったものですが，質問数は少なく，所要時間はわずか 5 分です。ボトムライン社から電話アンケートも実施できる旨の申し出がありましたが，当社で実施するほうが経済的だと考えています。したがいまして，12 月 10 日と 11 日の週末にこの調査を実施するにあたり進んで協力してくれる従業員の方が必要になります。この仕事に参加していただける方には，残業代が支払われます。

興味のある方は，当社マーケティング部長スタン・チャドウィック（内線 223 または chadwick@wwd.co.wa）にご連絡ください。

159 ⏱ 15 秒　満点ポイント!　文章をすべて先読みする　　　正解 ▶ (A)

この社内連絡の書かれた理由はおそらく何ですか。

(A) プロジェクトに進んで協力してくれる人を求めるため

(B) 最近行われた調査に関する情報を伝えるため

(C) マーケティング計画に関して意見を求めるため

(D) 顧客満足度調査について説明するため

正解 第 2 段落最後から 2 文目で Consequently, we need employees ... in this process（調査の実施に進んで協力してくれる従業員が必要だ）と助けを求めていることから，(A) が目的としてふさわしい。名詞 volunteer は「（無給の）ボランティア」だけでなく，このように「（同じチームや団体の中で）進んで協力してくれる人」を意味することもある。

誤答 調査はこれから行われるので，(B) は upcoming research であれば正解。第 1 段落で「音楽の好みや習慣を尋ねる」とあるので，(D) の customer satisfaction survey ではない。

160 ⏱ 20秒　　　　　　　　　　　　　　　　　　　　　　正解 ➤ (D)

WWD はどんな会社だと思われますか。

(A) 音楽配給会社

(B) 広告代理店

(C) 調査会社

(D) 放送会社

正解 第1段落でまず，WWD の営業開始にあたって We have decided ... for the station.（視聴者になる可能性のある人が何を聞きたいか調査を行うことにした）と述べている。さらに，調査内容として radio listening habits（ラジオを聴く習慣）が挙げられていることから，WWD がラジオ放送会社であると判断できるので，(D) が正解。誤答 (C) は，調査の委託先である Bottomline, Inc のこと。

161 ⏱ 50秒　　　　　　　　　　　　　　　　　　　　　　正解 ➤ (B)

調査について何が示唆されていますか。

(A) 電話調査と書面調査の両方ともボトムライン社によって実施される。

(B) 電話調査は2日にわたって行われる。

(C) 書面調査は電話調査よりも効果的である。

(D) 電話調査と書面調査の内容はまったく同じである。

正解 第2段落4文目で it will be more cost-effective ... take care of it ourselves（電話調査は当社で実施したほうが経済的だ）と述べ，それにあたり the weekend of December 10 and 11 に助けが必要だとあるので，(B) が適切。ここでの over は「～にわたって」という意味で期間を表す。誤答 電話調査は社内で行うため (A) は不適切。また，書面の調査に関して2文目に the response rate ... is often quite low（アンケートの回答率は低い）とあるので (C) も一致しない。(D) は，電話調査に関して These interviews will be based ... fewer questions（書面調査をもとにしているが質問数は少ない）と説明されていることから，まったく同じではないことがわかる。

Questions 162-164 refer to the following letter.　（語数：219 語）

October 8

Dear Ms. Cartwright:

Your Publishers Direct Platinum membership is due to expire in the coming weeks. If you renew before your current membership runs out, you will be entitled to a reduction in the yearly Platinum member rate to only $60. Simply fill in and return the enclosed card by mail, or go to our Web site at www.publishersdirect.org to renew online.

We would also like to update you on our service. In light of rising ink and paper costs, we have decided to cease production of our printed catalog, and the last one will be published on November 1. Instead, we will expand our Web site. Not only will this streamline online ordering of paperback and hardcover books, but will give users access to an ever-widening variety of downloadable books, magazines and other content, including audio titles. This move will also enable us to continue offering our amazing everyday low prices.

Renew your membership before the November 30 and continue to take advantage of free expedited shipping, double loyalty points on all purchases, and the exclusive chance to buy books before they go on sale in other retail outlets. Also, make sure to visit our updated Web site after December 3 to check out our expanded selection. Please view exclusive special offers by logging on to the "Members Only" Web pages.

Yours sincerely,

Jim Sheffield

Jim Sheffield
Managing Director

162. What is one purpose of the letter?
(A) To inform a customer that their membership has been renewed
(B) To detail a change in company procedures
(C) To announce the upcoming expiration of a magazine subscription
(D) To explain which items have been discounted

163. What is mentioned about the printed catalog?
(A) It has become more expensive to create.
(B) Its circulation has increased.
(C) It can only be used until the end of October.
(D) It is not popular with Publishers Direct customers.

164. What is NOT indicated about the company's revised Web site?
(A) It will be accessible exclusively to Platinum members.
(B) It will be operational prior to the end of the year.
(C) It will make the ordering process simpler.
(D) It will feature audio versions of some books.

重要語句 □ due to *do*「〜することになる」（= expected to *do*）　□ run out「期限が切れる」（= expire）
□ in light of ...「〜を踏まえて」（= after considering）　□ cease「〜をやめる」（= stop）
□ streamline「〜を合理化する，シンプルにする」（= simplify）　□ ever-「常に〜する」※
ever-widening で「常に広がっていく」という意味。　□ title「出版物」（= book; publication）
□ expedite「〜を速める，促進する」（= speed up）　□ loyalty point「会員ポイント」　□ retail
outlet「販売店，小売店」（= retail store）　□ circulation「発行部数」

162-164 の設問は次の手紙に関するものです。

10 月 8 日

カートライト様

お客様のパブリシャーズ・ダイレクト社のプラチナ会員権の期限が切れる時期が近づいて参りました。現在の会員権の期限が切れる前に更新いただきますと，年間プラチナ会員の会費がわずか 60 ドルと割引になります。同封の葉書に必要事項をご記入のうえご返送いただくか，弊社ウェブサイト www. publishersdirect.org でインターネットによる更新を行ってください。

また，弊社のサービスに関して重要なお知らせがございます。インクや紙にかかる費用が増加しているため，印刷カタログの作成を取り止めることにいたしました。最後のカタログの発行日は 11 月 1 日になります。その代わりに，弊社のウェブサイトをより充実させます。これによりペーパーバックやハードカバーの本のインターネットによるご注文が簡単になるだけでなく，種類が日に日に増えていくダウンロード可能な書籍や雑誌，オーディオブックを含むその他のコンテンツをユーザーの方にご利用いただけます。また，この変更により，弊社は常時驚くべき低価格で商品をご提供し続けることができます。

11 月 30 日までに更新いただければ，引き続き商品が無料で迅速に発送されるだけでなく，すべてのお買い物につき 2 倍のポイントが付き，他の販売店で発売されるより前に本を購入できる会員様限定のサービスをご利用いただけます。また，12 月 3 日にアップデートされる弊社ウェブサイトにぜひアクセスし，さらに豊富になった品揃えをご覧ください。その際には，「会員限定」のウェブページにログインいただき，会員限定特典を忘れずにご確認ください。

敬具
ジム・シェフィールド
常務取締役

162 ⏱ 20 秒　満点ポイント！　▲文章をすべて先読みする　　　　正解 ➤ (B)

この手紙の目的の一つは何ですか。
(A) 会員資格が更新されたことを顧客に知らせること
(B) 会社の従来のやり方の変更に関して詳しく説明すること
(C) 雑誌の定期購読契約の期限がまもなく切れることを知らせること
(D) 割引価格で購入できる商品について説明すること

正解 第 1 段落には membership の期限が切れることについて，第 2 段落には printed catalog の中止と Web site の充実について，第 3 段落には契約更新後のさまざまなサービスについて説明があ

る。この中で，(B) が第2段落のテーマに一致する。

誤答 (A) は，第1段落冒頭から更新がまだ済んでいないことをおさえよう。(C) は，定期購読の更新ではないことに注意。

163 ⏱ 20秒   正解 ➤ (A)

印刷カタログに関して何が述べられていますか。

(A) 作成するのにより多くの費用がかかるようになった。

(B) 発行部数が増えた。

(C) 10月末までしか使用できない。

(D) パブリッシャーズ・ダイレクトの利用客に人気がない。

正解 printed catalog に関する記述のある第2段落2文目で，In light of ... our printed catalog（インクや紙の費用が増加しているため，作成を取り止めることした）と明確に述べているので，(A) を即答したい。

誤答 (C) に関しては，the last one will be published on November 1（最後の発行日は11月1日になる）とあるだけなので，10月末までしかカタログを使用できないわけではない。(B) や (D) に関してはまったく述べられていない。

164 ⏱ 60秒   正解 ➤ (A)

会社の新しくなったウェブサイトに関して述べられていないことは何ですか。

(A) プラチナ会員のみアクセスできる。

(B) 年末までに利用できるようになる。

(C) 注文方法がよりシンプルになる。

(D) オーディオブックも取り扱う。

正解 (A) に関して，第3段落の最終文で "Members Only" Web pages を見るよう促しているが，サイトへのアクセス自体が Platinum 会員限定であるとは述べていないので，これが正解。

誤答 (B) は，第3段落2文目の visit our updated Web site after December 3 と，(C) は第2段落4文目の Not only will this streamline online ordering と，それぞれ内容が一致する。(D) も，同じ文で「audio titles（= audio books）を含むコンテンツを利用できる」とある。NOT 問題では，正解となる選択肢が判断しづらい場合もあるので，本文に述べられている3つの選択肢を確実に消去するようにしよう。

Questions 165-167 refer to the following article.　（語数：174 語）

Rapid economic development in India and other parts of Asia has led to a rise in competition among corporations for highly-skilled technical workers. This in turn is causing some companies to take more active measures in making themselves more appealing to prospective employees. Many companies are now offering schedule flexibility to let staff enjoy longer weekends without reducing their full-time work hours or increasing overall payroll expenses. One example, referred to as "summer hours," involves letting staff work an extra hour a day from Monday through Thursday. This means they can leave work at lunchtime on Fridays.

Businesses are also projecting a positive image to potential employees by demonstrating that they are interested in not only making a profit, but also in aiding the environment. Many of them cover part or all of employee public transportation costs or offer a gas subsidy for workers who car-pool from their homes. Companies are also creating workplaces that employees can be proud of by establishing office recycling programs, and cutting down on paper usage and electricity consumption.

---

165. What is the topic of the article?

(A) The impact of the growing economy in India on its surrounding countries

(B) Techniques for retaining highly-qualified workers

(C) Ways in which businesses are trying to gain an advantage in the labor market

(D) Methods for making full-time employees work more productively

166. According to the article, what has increased?

(A) The number of skilled workers who are applying for jobs

(B) The cost of the average worker's commute to the office

(C) The number of paid vacation days offered by employers

(D) The demand for employees with technical training

167. What is NOT mentioned as something companies are doing to help the environment?

(A) Consuming lower quantities of paper

(B) Making greater use of recycled materials in manufacturing

(C) Encouraging workers to use public transportation

(D) Reducing the amount of power used in the workplace

重要語句 □ in turn「それにより，その結果」（= as a result）　□ referred to as ...「～と呼ばれている」（= called）　□ subsidy「補助金」（= financial support）　□ car-pool「車を相乗りする」　□ cut down on ...「～を減らす」（= reduce）

165-167 の設問は次の記事に関するものです。

インドや他のアジアの地域における急速な経済発展によって，高度な技術力を持つ従業員を獲得しようと企業間の競争が高まっている。そのため，将来の従業員にとって自社をより魅力的なものにするための措置を積極的に講じている企業もある。現在多くの企業は，融通のきく勤務スケジュールを採用しており，常勤従業員の労働時間を減らしたり，給与支払総額を増やすことなく，従業員が週末の休みをより長く取れるようにしている。その一例として「summer hours」と呼ばれているものがあるが，この制度では，従業員は月曜日から木曜日まで一日 1 時間長く働くことができる。そうすれば，金曜日には昼食時に退社できるというわけだ。

また，企業は利益を上げることだけでなく環境保護にも関心を持っていることを示すことによって，将来の従業員に好印象を与えようとしている。多くの企業は，従業員の公共交通機関の運賃の一部または全額を負担したり，自宅から相乗りして出勤する従業員に対してガソリン代を補助したりもしている。さらに，企業はオフィスのリサイクルプログラムを設けたり，紙の使用量や電気の消費量を減らすことによって，従業員が誇りを持てるような職場作りに励んでいる。

165　⏱ 30 秒　　　　　　　　　　　　　　　　　　　　　正解 ▶ (C)

この記事のテーマは何ですか。

(A) インドの経済発展が周辺諸国に与える影響

(B) 能力の高い従業員を引きとめる方策

(C) 企業が労働市場で優位に立つために講じている措置

(D) 正社員をより生産的に働かせるための方法

正解 第 1 段落 1 文目で「有能な従業員を獲得する競争の激化」について触れ，2 文目で「企業が自社をより魅力的に見せる措置を講じている」と述べているので，(C) が一致する。labor market とは，企業が労働力を求める場のこと。

誤答 (B) は，potential employees を引き付けることが記事のテーマなので，retaining（= keeping）ではなく obtaining であれば正解。(D) は，第 1 段落 3 文目に schedule flexibility に関する記述はあるが，生産性を高めるためではなく，企業を魅力的に見せる方法として触れられていることに注意。

166 ⏱ 45秒 　　　　　　　　　　　　　　　　　　正解 ➤ (D)

この記事によると，何が増加しましたか。

(A) 職を求める熟練労働者の数

(B) 従業員の通勤費用の平均

(C) 雇用主が与える有給休暇の日数

(D) 技術的な訓練を受けた人材の需要

正解 第1段落の冒頭文にある a rise in competition ... for highly-skilled technical workers（高度な技術をもつ従業員を獲得する競争の激化）を，(D) が適切に言い換えている。

誤答 企業間の競争が高まっているだけで，求職者数が増えているとは述べていないので (A) は不適切。(C) は，第1段落の schedule flexibility に関する説明の中で，without reducing their full-time work hours とあることから，休暇の日数は変わらないことがわかる。どの選択肢も記事の内容に関連しているので，他の選択肢が不正解である理由を文中から必ず突き止めよう。

---

167 ⏱ 50秒 　　　　　　　　　　　　　　　　　　正解 ➤ (B)

企業が環境保護のためにしていることとして述べられていないものは何ですか。

(A) 紙の消費量を減らすこと

(B) 製造過程でリサイクル素材をより多く使用すること

(C) 従業員に公共交通機関を利用するよう奨励すること

(D) 職場での電気消費量を減らすこと

誤答 environment に関して述べられている第2段落の内容と一致する選択肢を消去していく。(A) と (D) は，最終文の cutting down on paper usage and electricity consumption の内容と一致している。(C) も，環境保護策として2文目に cover part or all of employee public transportation costs とあるので，公共交通機関の利用を促していると考えられる。

正解 (B) は，最終文に establishing office recycling programs とあるので，manufacturing（製造）の部分が本文の内容に合致しないと判断し，これを正解として選ぶ。

Questions 168-171 refer to the following except from a brochure.　（語数：244 語）

The Halford Inn

Ranked by visitors as the second best hotel in the city of Kingsport and number one in the downtown area, the Halford Inn is perfect whether you are in town on business or pleasure. Although the hotel boasts ultra-modern decor, the building itself is a fine example of mid 19th-century architecture. Conveniently situated near the Kingsport Convention Center, it is also well connected to the public transportation system, with two train stations and numerous bus stops within walking distance.

Each room has wireless Internet access and a large flat screen television. All prices include continental breakfast in the dining room (breakfast in bed is available for a nominal fee), a free 24-hour shuttle bus to Somerton Airport, and use of the hotel's fitness center and pool. Given the expense of parking in the city center, the complimentary use of the garage is another huge plus.

There are two dining establishments on the premises. Chez Souris, owned by former professional musician Souris Lee, is a French restaurant serving classic cuisine in a congenial ambience. The newly remodeled Los Burrito is a Mexican restaurant that is more family oriented. They both have dishes and prices that are top of the line; however, there is a wealth of more affordable dining options in the center of the city.

Throughout the winter months patrons can take advantage of special rates. In addition, as the hotel is predominantly used by business travelers, reduced prices are often available on weekends.

---

168. What is included in the price of a stay at the Halford Inn?

(A) Breakfast delivery to each room

(B) A shuttle service to some airports

(C) Parking spaces for guests' vehicles

(D) A fitness consultation service

169. The word "boasts" in paragraph 1, line 4, is closest in meaning to

(A) contrasts

(B) incorporates

(C) acclaims

(D) exaggerates

170. What is NOT stated about the hotel?

(A) It is rated as the best hotel in downtown Kingsport.

(B) It is located next to the train station.

(C) It caters mainly to people traveling on business.

(D) It is in a historical building.

171. What is indicated about the hotel's restaurants?

(A) One of them occasionally features some live music.

(B) One of them has recently been constructed.

(C) They are more expensive than other local establishments.

(D) They serve the widest range of dishes in town.

重要語句 □ decor「（建物などの）内装」 □ fine example「好例」（= great example） □ continental breakfast「コンチネンタルブレックファスト（パンやコーヒーだけの簡単な朝食）」 □ nominal「小額の」（= small） □ given ...「～を考えると」（= considering） □ dining establishment「飲食施設、レストラン」 □ cuisine「料理」（= cooking） □ congenial「心地よい、気の合う」（= pleasant） □ ambience「雰囲気」（= atmosphere） □ top of the line「最高級の」（= best of its kind） □ a wealth of ...「豊富な～」（= an abundance of ...） □ predominantly「主に」（= mainly; mostly） □ cater to *someone*「人（の要望）に応える」

168-171 の設問は次のパンフレットの抜粋によるものです。

ハルフォード・イン

ハルフォード・インは、宿泊客によるランキングがキングスポート市内では 2 位、市の中心部では 1位のホテルであり、滞在目的が仕事でも娯楽でも、申し分のないホテルと言える。内装は時代の最先端をいくものだが、建物そのものは 19 世紀半ばの建築物の好例だ。キングスポート・コンベンション・センターに近いうえに、徒歩圏内に 2 つの駅と多くのバス停があるため、公共交通機関も利用しやすい。

各客室では無線インターネットが利用でき、大きな薄型テレビもある。料金には、食堂でのコンチネンタルブレックファスト（小額料金で朝食のルームサービスも可）、24 時間運行しているソマートン空港への無料シャトルバス、ホテルのフィットネスセンターおよびプールの利用料が含まれる。市の中心部の駐車料金を考えると、無料で駐車場を利用できることも大きな利点である。

ホテル内には 2 つのレストランがある。元プロ音楽家のソーリス・リーがオーナーを務めるチェス・ソーリスは、心地よい雰囲気で伝統的な料理を提供するフレンチレストランである。また、最近改装されたばかりのロス・ブリトは、家族向けのメキシカンレストランである。どちらのレストランも料理と料金は最高級だ。もっとも、市の中心部には料金がより手頃なレストランが数多くある。
冬期には特別料金で宿泊することができる。また、ホテルの主な利用客は出張客なので、週末には割引料金で利用できることも多い。

168 ⏱ 40 秒　　　　　　　　　　　　　　　　　　　　　　正解 ▶ (C)

ハルフォード・インの宿泊料金に含まれているのは何ですか。

(A) 各部屋に朝食を届けるサービス

(B) 複数の空港へのシャトルサービス

(C) 宿泊客の車を駐車する駐車場

(D) 健康相談サービス

正解 料金に関する記述のある第 2 段落の内容と各選択肢を照らし合わせる。すると、最終文に the complimentary use of the garage（無料で駐車場を利用できること）とあることから、(C) が正解。complimentary（= free）は Part 7 頻出のキーワード。

誤答 (A) は、breakfast in bed について 2 文目に for a nominal fee（= for a small fee）とあること、(B) はシャトルサービスについて Somerton Airport しか挙げられていないこと、(D) は use of the hotel's fitness center とあるだけで相談サービスが受けられるとは述べていないので、いずれも消去したい選択肢。

169 ⏱30秒 満点ポイント！ 同義語問題 正解 ➤ (B)

第1段落4行目にある "boasts" にもっとも意味の近い語は

(A) 〜を比較する

(B) 〜を組み込む

(C) 〜を称賛する

(D) 〜を誇張する

正解 動詞 boast(s) は，場所や組織を主語に置いて「〜を（誇りとして）持つ」（= have *something* impressive; feature）という意味を表すので，ここでは (B) の incorporate(s)（= include）がふさわしい。

誤答 He is boasting about his success. のように人を主語に置くと「自慢げに話す」（= speak with too much pride）という意味になり，(D) exaggerates とニュアンスが近くなる。

---

170 ⏱60秒 正解 ➤ (B)

ホテルに関して述べられていないことは何ですか。

(A) キングスポート市の中心部にあるホテルのランキングで1位である。

(B) 駅の隣にある。

(C) 主に出張客にサービスを提供している。

(D) ホテルの建物は歴史建造物である。

誤答 各選択肢の該当箇所を本文から慎重に探していく。(A) は，第1段落冒頭の Ranked by visitors ... number one in the downtown area の部分，(C) は最終段落の the hotel is predominantly used by business travelers の部分，(D) は第1段落2文目の the building itself is ... architecture の部分と，それぞれ内容が一致する。

正解 (B) は，第1段落後半に well connected to the public transportation system とはあるが，well connected（アクセスしやすい）は「隣にある」という意味ではないので，これが正解。

---

171 ⏱30秒 正解 ➤ (C)

ホテル内のレストランに関して何が述べられていますか。

(A) レストランのひとつは時々音楽の生演奏を行っている。

(B) レストランのひとつは最近建設されたものである。

(C) その地域にある他のレストランよりも料金が高い。

(D) 市内でもっとも豊富なメニューを取り揃えている。

正解 レストランに関する記述があるのは第3段落全体。ここに登場するふたつのレストランに関して，They both have ... top of the line（料理も価格も最高級だ）とあり，さらに there is ... in the center of the city（中心部にはより手頃なレストランが数多くある）と述べているので，(C) が正解。

誤答 (A) はオーナーが「元音楽家」とあるだけで，生演奏を行っていると判断するのは禁物。(B) は，newly constructed と文中の newly remodeled との混同をねらったひっかけ。

Questions 172-176 refer to the following memo. （語数：292語）

To: All Board Members
From: Tom Young, President
Date: February 15

Our offer for the vacant plot of land that runs adjacent to the south end of our processing facility in Glenbrook was accepted late last month. This, at long last, will allow us sufficient space to store chemical supplies on-site, rather than at the warehousing district in Kirkwood. Construction of the new storage unit has been slated to begin later this year. The blueprints for the building itself have already been drawn up and are available in the boardroom for you to look over. Ms. Cox of Dengle & Sprung, the person who created the designs for the building, will be attending a part of our next board meeting and will be able to address any concerns that you may have.

As this building will be used to house chemicals that pose a potential hazard to both local residents and area wildlife, we will need to secure approval from both the Health Department and the Department of the Environment before construction can commence. To do this we must submit an application form, along with a detailed analysis of the likely environmental impact of the project, to each of these government departments. Our legal department has been working on this paperwork, but I would now like to ask for your input. Please review the drafts of these documents that accompany this memo and focus on any issues which may require further attention or discussion. Be prepared to voice your thoughts when we gather next Wednesday.

The contents of the above are to remain strictly confidential and are not to be discussed outside of the boardroom. If you suspect that a member of your staff has seen any part of these documents, please notify me immediately.

Thank you for your cooperation on this matter.

---

172. What did the company do this year?
(A) Purchased some property
(B) Built a warehouse
(C) Leased a storage space
(D) Relocated some of its operations

173. What is most likely attached to the memo?
(A) An analysis of how the new policy will affect the working environment
(B) Architectural specifications for a construction project
(C) A report on how chemicals are stored
(D) A study of the potential effects of a new facility

174. According to the memo, why should someone contact Mr. Young?
(A) To inquire about a building's design
(B) To report unauthorized exposure of information
(C) To request a copy of the blueprints
(D) To give feedback on an application

175. What is NOT indicated about the proposed project?

(A) It will take place in Glenbrook.

(B) It must be approved by multiple government agencies.

(C) It is expected to begin by the end of the year.

(D) It is opposed by some local residents.

176. What will most likely happen next Wednesday?

(A) An application will be submitted.

(B) An architect will answer questions from board members.

(C) Work on a construction project will begin.

(D) The legal department will finalize work on required documents.

重要語句 □ plot「(土地の) 一画」(= small piece of land) □ adjacent to ...「〜に隣接する」(= next to ...) □ at long last「ついに」(= finally; at last) □ on-site「現地で」 □ slated to *do*「〜する予定の」(= planned to *do*) □ blueprint「設計図，青写真」 □ draw ... up「〜を (入念に) 作成する」(= write ... with careful planning) □ address「〜に応える，対処する」(= deal with ...; respond to ...) □ pose *A* to *B*「*A* (問題など) を *B* に引き起こす」(= cause; present) □ commence「開始する」(= begin) □ voice「〜を (言葉で) 伝える」(= express)

172-176 の設問は次の社内連絡に関するものです。

宛先：全取締役

差出人：トム・ヤング，社長

日付：2月15日

グレンブルックにある当社加工施設の南端に隣接している空き地の購入申し込みが，先月下旬に承諾されました。これによりやっと，カークウッドの保管施設区域を利用せずに，化学薬品を保管するのに十分なスペースを現地で確保できることになります。新しい保管施設の建設は，年内に開始される予定です。建物自体の青写真はすでにできあがっており，重役用会議室で閲覧することができます。建物の設計を手がけたデングル・アンド・スプラング社のコックスさんが次回の取締役会議に一部同席し，皆さんの懸念点に答えます。

この施設は，地域住民や周辺の野生生物に危険を及ぼしうる化学薬品を保管するために使用されるので，着工前に保健省と環境省から許可を得なくてはなりません。それにあたり，申請書と，このプロジェクトによって環境にどのような影響が及ぶ可能性があるかを詳しく分析した書類を両省に提出する必要があります。現在法務部が書類の作成に取り組んでいますが，皆さんにも意見を提供いただきたいと思います。書類の草稿を添付しておりますので，ご確認のうえ，配慮や議論がさらに必要な事項がないか注意を向けてください。次の水曜日に会議で集まる際に，意見を発表できるよう準備をしておいてください。

以上の内容は極秘であり，重役用会議室の外では話さないようお願いします。以上の書類が一部でも従業員の目に触れたことがわかった場合には，すぐに私に知らせてください。

この件に関しまして，ご協力のほどよろしくお願いします。

172 ⏱ 20秒　　　　　　　　　　　　正解 ➤ (A)

会社は今年何を行いましたか。

(A) 地所を購入した

(B) 倉庫を建設した

(C) 保管施設の賃貸借契約を結んだ

(D) 事業の一部を移転した

正解 冒頭にある Our offer for ... はここでは Our offer to buy ... のこと。この一文で「空き地購入の申込が先月下旬に受諾された」とあることから，(A) が正解。

誤答 (B)は，同段落3文目に Construction ... later this year. とあるので，これから行われるとわかる。

173 ⏱ 50秒　　　　　　　　　　　　正解 ➤ (D)

この社内連絡にはおそらく何が添付されていますか。

(A) 新規定が労働環境に与える影響に関する分析

(B) 建設工事の建築仕様書

(C) 化学薬品の保管方法に関する報告書

(D) 新しい施設が及ぼしうる影響に関する調査書

正解 第2段落4文目に Please review ... these documents that accompany this memo（memoに添付されている書類の草稿をご確認ください）とあるので，these documents が何を指すかをおさえる。すると，倉庫の建設に際して，同段落2文目で a detailed analysis of the likely environmental impact of the project（このプロジェクトが環境に及ぼしうる影響を詳しく分析した書類）の提出が必要だと述べていることから，この部分を言い換えた (D) が適切。

誤答 (B) は，第1段落4文目で The blueprints ... are available in the boardroom とあるので，添付書類ではない。「添付物」問題では通常，Please find attached ... や I've attached ... という慣用表現がキーになることが多いが，今回のように動詞 accompany も用いられることをおさえよう。

174 ⏱ 30秒　　　　　　　　　　　　正解 ➤ (B)

社内連絡によると，どのような場合にヤンさんに連絡すべきですか。

(A) 建物の設計に関して尋ねる場合

(B) 情報が権限のない人の目に触れたことを報告する場合

(C) 設計図のコピーを請求する場合

(D) 申請書に関する意見を伝える場合

正解 Mr. Young が memo の差出人であることに着目。第3段落で，If you suspect ... these documents, please notify me immediately.（一部でも従業員の目に触れた場合は私に知らせてください）と要請していることから，(B) が正解。exposure は，ここでは「（外にさらされること＝）人の目に触れること」という意味。

175 ⏱ 60秒 　　　　　　　　　　　　　　正解 ➤ (D)

予定されているプロジェクトに関して述べられていないことは何ですか。

(A) グレンブルックで行われる。

(B) 複数の政府機関の許可を得なければならない。

(C) 年末までに開始される予定である。

(D) 一部の地元住民が反対している。

誤答 ▶ the proposed project とは，倉庫の建設のこと。(A) は第1段落冒頭の adjacent to ... our processing facility in Glenbrook と，(C) は3文目の Construction ... begin later this year. とそれぞれ内容が一致する。(B) は，第2段落冒頭で we will need ... both the Health Department and the Department of the Environment と2つの機関について述べ，次の文で these government departments と言い換えていることから，正しい記述であるとわかる。

正解 ▶ (D) は，第2段落冒頭文で As this building ... local residents and area wildlife（施設が地域住民や野生生物に危険を及ぼしうる化学薬品を保管するために使用される）とあるだけで，実際に反対を受けているとの記述はないので，これが正解。

176 ⏱ 50秒 　　　　　　　　　　　　　　正解 ➤ (B)

来週の水曜日に何が起こると思われますか。

(A) 申請書が提出される。

(B) 建築家が取締役の質問に答える。

(C) 建設工事が始まる。

(D) 法務部が必要書類の作成を完了させる。

正解 ▶ Next Wednesday に関して，第2段落最終文で Be prepared to voice your thoughts when we gather next Wednesday. とあり，メモの宛先が All Board Members であることから，この集まりが第1段落最終文にある our next board meeting を指していると見極める。この文で，「設計を手がけた Ms. Cox が懸念点に答える」とあるので，「建物を設計した人」を architect（建築家）と言い表した (B) を選ぶ。

誤答 ▶ (D) の required documents に関しては第2段落で述べているが，この日に最終原稿が完成するかどうかは判断できない。

Questions 177-180 refer to the following article. （語数：309 語）

Alpaca Plastics had only two employees when it was established, Andy Patel and Maurice Yates, the company's co-founders. Mr. Patel and Mr. Yates were roommates at Trapp University, where the former was enrolled in the plastics program and the latter was pursuing a degree in business management. Once Mr. Patel graduated, he took a job at Medford Molding, a small business in the plastic molding industry. He contacted Mr. Yates two years later with the idea of the two of them starting their own molding business. "I had only been out of college for a year at that time," says Mr. Yates, "and was working as a customer service representative for a communications firm."

This new company operated for nearly two years before the partners were able to hire their first additional employee, who was a supervisor at Medford Molding. For years the company struggled just to make ends meet and nearly had to shut down five years ago. "I concluded that the company would have to undergo radical restructuring if we were to keep on running the business," says Mr. Patel. They took out loans from banks, made substantial investments in technology, and broadened operations.

Since then, the company has purchased over $2 million worth of equipment and spent many thousands more on maintenance and product development. It has also paid a considerable amount to train its employees, some of whom are receiving company subsidies to pursue degree-level qualifications at local colleges. Alpaca now has 85 workers who are designing and molding plastic parts around the clock. The company's revenue has risen at the impressive rate of 55 percent annually for the past three years.

Both of the co-founders of the company will appear next week on a local television program *Business World Now* at 7 P.M. on December 1. It will feature an exclusive interview recorded in October.

177. What can be understood about Mr. Yates?

(A) He graduated from college later than his roommate.

(B) He acquired an academic background in plastics.

(C) He quit college before earning a degree.

(D) He held a management position before founding Alpaca Plastics.

178. What is mentioned about Mr. Patel?

(A) He was initially hesitant to partner with Mr. Yates.

(B) He currently owns most of Alpaca company shares.

(C) He recruited someone who worked for his previous employer.

(D) He has directly supervised Mr. Yates.

179. What has Alpaca Plastics done over the past five years?

(A) It has employed financial experts.

(B) It has helped employees participate in training outside the company.

(C) It has spent more money on advertising.

(D) It has increased its revenue by more than 50 percent every year.

180. What is NOT indicated about Alpaca Plastics?

(A) Its operations are conducted 24 hours a day.

(B) Its founders have been interviewed for a local television show.

(C) It operates several manufacturing facilities.

(D) It had financial problems for many years.

重要語句 □ mold「(型を用いて) ～を形作る, 成形する」 □ make ends meet「収支を何とか合わせる」 □ radical「根本的な」(= very new and different) □ take out a loan「ローンを組む」 □ subsidy「補助金」 □ around the clock「昼夜問わず, 24 時間体制で」(= all day and all night)

177-180 の設問は次の記事に関するものです。

アルパカ・プラスチックス社は設立当時, 2 人の従業員しかいなかった。会社の共同創設者であるアンディ・パテルとモーリス・イエイツである。パテル氏とイエイツ氏はトラップ大学のルームメイトであり, パテル氏はプラスチック工学科に在籍し, イエイツ氏は企業経営学の学位取得を目指していた。パテル氏は卒業後すぐに, プラスチック成形業を営む小企業のメドフォード・モールディング社に就職した。その 2 年後, 彼はイエイツ氏に連絡をとり, 2 人で成形加工の会社を設立するアイデアを持ちかけた。「当時は大学を出てまだ 1 年しか経っていない頃で, 私は通信会社の顧客サービス担当として働いていました」とイエイツ氏は語る。

この新しい会社がほぼ 2 年間操業をした後, 共同経営者のふたりは初めて 3 人目の従業員として, メドフォード・モールディング社の管理職だった人を雇うことができた。会社はただ収支を合わせることに何年も苦労し, 5 年前には操業停止に追い込まれる寸前だった。「操業を続けるならば, 会社は根本的な改革が必要になるとの結論に至りました」とパテル氏は話す。ふたりは銀行から資金を調達し, 技術に多大な投資をして, 事業を拡大した。

会社はそれ以来, 200 万ドル以上に相当する機械類を購入し, さらに数万ドルもの資金を機械のメンテナンスと製品開発に費やしてきた。また, 従業員の研修にも多額の資金を充てており, 中には会社から補助金を受け, 地元の大学で学位レベルの資格の取得を目指している従業員もいる。アルパカ社は現在, 85 人の従業員を抱えるまでになり, 24 時間体制でプラスチック部品の設計と成形加工を行っている。会社の収益は, 過去 3 年間で毎年 55 パーセントという目覚ましい割合で伸びてきた。

この会社の共同創設者の 2 人は来週, 12 月 1 日午後 7 時から放送される地元のテレビ番組『ビジネス・ワールド・ナウ』に出演する。この番組では, 10 月に収録された独占インタビューを取り上げる。

177 ⏱ 55秒 正解 ➤ (A)

イエイツさんに関して何がわかりますか。

(A) ルームメイトよりも遅く大学を卒業した。
(B) プラスチック工学の分野で学歴を得た。
(C) 学位を取得する前に大学を中退した。
(D) アルパカ・プラスチックス社の設立前に管理職に就いていた。

正解 第1段落の2文目から Mr. Yates と Mr. Patel が roommates であったことをおさえる。さらに，Mr. Patel に関して4文目に He contacted Mr. Yates two years later（= two years after Mr. Patel graduated）とあるのに対し，Mr. Yates は I had only been out of college for a year at that time と話していることから，(A) が正しいことがわかる。

誤答 (B) は Mr. Patel に関する記述。(D) は，Mr. Yates が「a customer service representative として働いていた」と述べているので，management position（管理職）ではない。

178 ⏱ 40秒 正解 ➤ (C)

パテルさんに関して何が述べられていますか。
(A) イエイツさんと共同経営者となることに当初はためらいがあった。
(B) 現在アルパカ社株の過半数を保有している。
(C) 以前の会社に勤務していた人物を採用した。
(D) イエイツさんを直接指導してきた。

正解 第2段落の冒頭文でふたりが first additional employee を雇ったと述べられ，その人物の説明として who was a supervisor at Medford Molding とあることに着目。ここで，Medford Molding は Mr. Patel が卒業後に勤めていた会社であると第1段落でわかるので，(C) が適切。

179 ⏱ 45秒 正解 ➤ (B)

アルパカ・プラスチックス社は過去5年にわたり何を行ってきましたか。
(A) 財務の専門家を雇用してきた。
(B) 従業員が会社外部で研修を受ける手助けをしてきた。
(C) 広告に対してより多くのお金を費やしてきた。
(D) 毎年50パーセント以上収益を伸ばしてきた。

正解 第2段落2文目で nearly had to shut down five years ago とあることから，それ以降の出来事を探し出す。すると第3段落2文目の It has also paid ... at local colleges. という一文から，資格の取得を会社が支援しているとわかるので，(B) が正解。

誤答 (D) は，第3段落最終文に The company's revenue ... for the past three years. とあるので，過去5年間ではない。

180 ⏱ 80秒

正解 ➤ (C)

アルパカ・プラスチックス社に関して述べられていないのは何ですか。

(A) 操業は 24 時間体制で行われている。

(B) 創設者が地元のテレビ番組の取材を受けた。

(C) 複数の製造施設を操業している。

(D) 何年も財政困難を抱えた。

誤答▶ (A) は，第 3 段落 3 文目にある around the clock（昼夜問わず）が 24 hours a day と同じ意味であることをおさえる。(B) は，最終段落で「co-founders が番組に出演する」とあり，番組の内容に関して an exclusive interview recorded in October（10 月に収録された独占インタビュー）とあることから，すでに取材を受けているとわかる。(D) は，第 2 段落 2 文目の For years ... to make ends meet の部分と一致する。

正解▶ (C) の several（＝ more than a few）は，少なくても 3 つ以上のモノに用いる。第 2 段落最終文に broadened operations とはあるが，それだけでは manufacturing facilities の数を判断できないので，これが正解。

Questions 181-185 refer to the following e-mail and chart. （語数：213語＋64語）

From: ejackson@manderleyfest.com
To: hgallant@manderleyfest.com
Subject: Advance Ticket Sales

Dear Ms. Gallant,

Please find attached a copy of the latest ticket sales figures for the festival. These were updated this morning, based on the totals when the theater box offices closed yesterday.

By this time, we were aiming to have sold at least 70 percent of total seating capacity in Kelvin Theater and Cooper Theater, and 65 percent in Varley Hall. *Stormy Night* in particular has generated a lot of interest, most likely due to the popularity of the male lead. At the current rate that show should sell out, and the other on-target shows should be near capacity by the time the event starts.

During the time left before the start of the festival, I think you should focus our advertising on those shows that have not reached the sales target. I recommend that you pull the radio ads for *Stormy Night* and replace them with additional ads for the two below-target shows. If budget allows, you might also want to run extra ads in this weekend's newspapers.

Finally, I feel that we haven't done enough to advertise the street gala that concludes the event, which is scheduled for the day after the final performance at Kelvin Theater. My only suggestion here would be to hand out fliers to shoppers in the city center.

Thank you,

Edward Jackson
Managing Director

Manderley Drama Festival: Sales at end of day, October 27

Venue	Show	Dates	Total seats	Percentage sold
Kelvin Theater	*Yesterday's News*	November 3-8	8,000	71%
	The Watchman	November 9-14	6,400	68%
Varley Hall	*Stormy Night*	November 1-6	4,000	73%
	The End of the Road	November 7-11	3,200	66%
Cooper Theater	*Behind the Mask*	November 4-8	4,050	58%
	The King's dream	November 9-13	3,500	75%

181. What most likely is Ms. Gallant's responsibility?

(A) Managing a theater's operations
(B) Directing a musical performance
(C) Increasing public awareness of the event
(D) Tracking ticket sales for the event

182. What does Mr. Jackson suggest doing?

(A) Purchasing additional print ads
(B) Focusing more attention on *Stormy Night*
(C) Modifying some of the sales targets
(D) Increasing the advertising budget

183. What is stated about the shows during the festival?

(A) Tickets to some shows are likely to sell out by the end of October.

(B) One of the shows features a well-known performer.

(C) Each show is performed at a different venue.

(D) The total number of seats for each show varies depending on the date.

184. Which show has yet to reach the sales target?

(A) *The End of the Road*

(B) *Stormy Night*

(C) *The Watchman*

(D) *Yesterday's News*

185. When does the festival most likely end?

(A) October 27

(B) November 3

(C) November 14

(D) November 15

重要語句 □ lead「主役」(= main actor) □ near capacity「ほぼ定員の状態で」※「定員に達している」場合は filled to capacity。 □ pull「〜を取り除く, とりやめる」(= remove) □ if ... allows「〜が許せば」(= if ... permits) ※budget のほか, weather/time/space などにも用いる。 □ gala「(祝いの) 祭り」(= public celebration) □ flier「ビラ, チラシ」

181-185 の設問は次のメールと表に関するものです。

送信者：ejackson@manderleyfest.com
宛て先：hgallent@manderleyfest.com
件名：前売券の売上

ギャラントさん

フェスティバルのチケットの売上に関する最新の数字を添付しましたのでご確認ください。この数字は, 劇場チケット売場の昨日の営業終了時における合計枚数に基づいて, 今朝更新されたものです。

現時点までに, ケルビン・シアターとクーパー・シアターで定員数の最低 70 パーセント, バーリー・ホールで定員数の最低 65 パーセントのチケットの販売達成を目標としていました。主演男優の人気によるものと思われますが, 『嵐の夜』は特に高い関心を集めています。現在のペースでいけば, この演劇のチケットは完売するでしょう。また, チケットの販売が予定どおり進んでいる他の演劇も, イベント開始までにはほぼ満席の状態になると思われます。

フェスティバル開始までの残された時間で, まだ売上目標に達していない演劇を集中的に宣伝すべきだと思います。『嵐の夜』のラジオ広告を止め, その代わりに目標に達していない 2 つの演劇の広告を増やすことをお勧めします。予算に余裕があれば, 今週末の新聞にも追加の広告を掲載するとよいと思います。

最後に, イベントの締めくくりとしてストリートフェスティバルがケルビン・シアターでの最終上演の翌日に予定されていますが, これについては十分な宣伝が行われていないように思います。中心街の買い物客にビラ配りをするのがよいのではないでしょうか。

よろしくお願いします。

エドワード・ジャクソン
運営部長

上演会場	演目	上演日	全座席数	販売済みの割合
ケルビン・シアター	『昨日のニュース』	11月3日〜8日	8,000	71%
	『見張り人』	11月9日〜14日	6,400	68%
バーリー・ホール	『嵐の夜』	11月1日〜6日	4,000	73%
	『この道の果てに』	11月7日〜11日	3,200	66%
クーパー・シアター	『仮面の下』	11月4日〜8日	4,050	58%
	『王の夢』	11月9日〜13日	3,500	75%

マンダリー演劇フェスティバル：10月27日営業終了時における売上

181　⏱30秒　正解 ➤ (C)

ギャラントさんの仕事はおそらく何ですか。

(A) 劇場の業務運営
(B) ミュージカルの演出
(C) イベントに対する一般市民の関心を高めること
(D) イベントチケットの売上の記録

正解 Ms. Gallent はメールの受取人。送信者の Mr. Jackson が彼女に対し，第2段落で ticket sales の現状について説明をし，第3段落で advertising に関する提案をしていることから，Ms. Gallent が広告・宣伝の担当者であることをおさえ，(C) を選択する。increase awareness は「関心を高める」という意味の重要表現。

182　⏱40秒　正解 ➤ (A)

ジャクソンさんは何をすることを提案していますか。

(A) 追加で紙媒体の広告を出すこと
(B) 『嵐の夜』にもっと集中すること
(C) 売上目標を修正すること
(D) 広告予算を増やすこと

正解 提案をしている第3段落に着目。この最終文で you might also want to run extra ads in this weekend's newspapers と述べているので，(A) がこの内容に一致する。
誤答 (B) の Stormy Night に関しては，第2段落で完売が見込まれると説明し，第3段落2文目で you pull the radio ads for Stormy Night と広告の取りやめを提案していることに注意。(D) は，if budget allows（予算があれば）と前置きをしていることから，予算を増やす提案はしていないと判断できる。

183 ⏱ 40秒 正解 ➤ (B)

フェスティバルで上演される演劇について何が述べられていますか。

(A) いくつかの演劇のチケットが 10 月末までに完売する見込みである。

(B) 演劇のひとつは有名な俳優が主演する。

(C) 演劇ごとに上演会場が異なる。

(D) 演劇ごとの座席数は上演日によって異なる。

正解 (B) の well-known performer に関して，第 2 段落で「the popularity of the male lead（= main actor）のおかげで *Stormy Night* が関心を集めている」と述べているので，これが正解。

誤答 (A) は，次の文で *Stormy Night* のチケットが完売しそうであることはわかるが，他の on-target shows に関しては should be near capacity とあるだけなので不適切。(C) と (D) は，下の chart からどちらも一致しないことがわかる。

184 ⏱ 60秒 両文書参照型 正解 ➤ (C)

売上目標にまだ達していない演劇はどれですか。

(A)『この道の果てに』

(B)『嵐の夜』

(C)『見張り人』

(D)『昨日のニュース』

正解 sales target については，メールの第 2 段落冒頭に at least 70 percent ... Kelvin Theater and Cooper Theater, and 65 percent in Varley Hall と記述がある。この内容と下の chart を照らし合わせると，達していないのは Kelvin Theater 上演の *The Watchman*（68%）と Cooper Theater 上演の *Behind the Mask*（58%）であることがわかるので，選択肢にある (C) が適切。

185 ⏱ 40秒 両文書参照型 正解 ➤ (D)

演劇フェスティバルの最終日はおそらくいつですか。

(A) 10 月 27 日

(B) 11 月 3 日

(C) 11 月 14 日

(D) 11 月 15 日

正解 メールの最終段落で the street gala that concludes the event（イベントを締めくくるストリートフェスティバル）とあり，その開催日として scheduled for the day after the final performance at Kelvin Theater と述べていることに着目。下の chart を見ると，Kelvin Theater の最終上演は November 14 だとわかるので，その翌日である (D) が正解。

誤答 始めから chart の Dates だけを見てしまうと (C) が正解に見えるので，両文書参照型問題でミスを犯さないために，最低でも上の文章は先に全文読むようにしよう。

Questions 186-190 refer to the following advertisement and letter. (語数：259 語＋156 語)

Sound Style, Inc.

About Us
Our founder and CEO, Laura Ann Casey, is an accomplished classical cellist. She was the chief administrator at the Institute of the Performing Arts in France, where she was instrumental in establishing the institution's highly renowned summer concert program for children. At Sound Style, Inc., we strive to continue this legacy of excellence by providing quality music education and recording services.

Our Courses
Private and group lessons include voice, piano, strings, percussion and wind instruments. From April 1, Sound Style is also pleased to announce the addition of jazz vocal lessons, taught by Wilbur Davis. Mr. Davis is best known for his work with The Pete Callaghan Experience, the group behind the award-winning soundtrack for the film *Misplaced*. We will also resume the popular intermediate cello class taught by our CEO from the same month.

Other Services
We offer state-of-the-art recording equipment for music and spoken-word projects. Studio A is a fully equipped digital studio and includes the largest recording room in the country. Studio B, which is currently being expanded to have all new equipment, will make an ideal setting for music and commercial recording when it reopens at the beginning of May this year. Studio C is the least spacious of our studios, but its unique acoustics produce exceptionally high quality sound. Patrons can also benefit from the considerable experience of our in-house sound engineer, Robert McGee. Never has recording in a professional studio space been so easy or affordable! To obtain more information about our services or for reservations, please contact us at reservation@soundstyle.com or 121, 4th Avenue, New York, NY 10562.

April 18
Mr. Kenneth Ellenbaum
247 East Mayweather Avenue
Lexington, NY 10472

Dear Mr. Ellenbaum:

Thank you for your application for renting studio space to create your album. Unfortunately, the studio you requested is not available until May 1. We do have a larger facility which is open on your specified dates of April 25 and 26. If you agree to book both days, we would be happy to rent the larger studio to you at no extra charge. Please let me know if this is acceptable to you.

In response to your request for support staff, we at Sound Style are able to provide you with the services of our professional sound engineer to assist you. I have sent you a document listing the approximate costs of the studio space, sound engineer and additional services you asked for. Also, please find a map giving directions to our studio printed on the reverse of this letter. Our opening hours and a full list of contact numbers are indicated below the map.

sincerely,

Sharon Li

Sharon Li
Customer Services
Sound Style Inc.

186. What is mentioned about Laura Ann Casey in the advertisement?
(A) She runs several educational institutions.
(B) She has a background in teaching.
(C) She established a business in France.
(D) She has received an award for her performances.

187. What is NOT indicated about Sound Style Inc.?
(A) It specializes in music education for children.
(B) It uses highly-advanced technology to provide its services.
(C) Its services are moderately priced.
(D) It plans to expand its range of courses.

188. What will Mr. Ellenbaum most likely do?
(A) Cancel a reservation for May
(B) Record a spoken-word project
(C) Work with Robert McGee
(D) Study sound engineering

189. Why is Mr. Ellenbaum unable to use the studio he requested?
(A) It lacks the necessary support staff.
(B) Its facilities are being upgraded.
(C) It is not large enough to accommodate his needs.
(D) It has already been reserved for his requested dates.

190. What information is indicated on the back of the letter?
(A) When the studio is open
(B) How much the project will cost
(C) Which services are currently available
(D) What time trains are run to the area

重要語句 □ accomplished「熟練の，有能な」(= highly skilled) □ chief administrator「事務局長，運営責任者」 □ instrumental in ...「〜に欠かせない，役立つ」(= essential; helpful) □ legacy「受け継がれたもの，遺産」 □ state-of-the-art「最新鋭の」(= very modern or advanced) □ make an ideal setting「理想的な場所になる」※ この make は become と同じ意味。 □ Never has recording in a professional studio space been ... もともと Recording in a professional studio space has never been ... という文で，否定語 never が文頭に来たため倒置した形。 □ in response to ...「〜に答えて」 □ list「〜を記載する」

186-190 の設問は次の広告と手紙に関するものです。

サウンド・スタイル社
当社について
当社の創設者であり CEO でもあるローラ・アン・ケイシーは，熟練のクラシックチェリストです。彼女は，フランス舞台芸術学院の理事としての経験もあり，非常に有名な子ども向けサマーコンサートを開始するのに重要な役割を果たしました。弊社は，この受け継がれた卓越性を維持すべく，質の高い音楽教育と録音サービスの提供に尽力しております。

当校の講座

声楽・ピアノ・弦楽器・打楽器・管楽器などの個人レッスンやグループレッスンを行っております。また，4月1日からは，ウィルバー・デイビス氏によるジャズボーカルレッスンも加わります。彼は，受賞歴のある映画『ミスプレイスト』のサウンドトラックに携わったグループ，ザ・ピート・カラガン・エクスペリエンスを担当したことでもっとも知られています。また，同月には，CEO が講師を務める人気のチェロ中級レッスンも再開する予定です。

その他のサービス

当社は，音楽や朗読録音のための最先端の録音設備を提供しております。スタジオ A は，設備が完備したデジタルスタジオで，全国最大のレコーディングルームもあります。スタジオ B は現在拡張工事中で，全機材を新しく入れ替えています。今年の5月初頭に再オープンする時には，音楽や商業用レコーディングを行うのに理想的な設備をご提供できます。スタジオ C は，当社スタジオの中では最小規模になりますが，独特の音響環境により極めて高い音質を生み出します。さらには，経験豊富な音響技師ロバート・マクギーがお客様のお手伝いをいたします。専門的なスタジオでのレコーディングがこれほど容易に手頃な価格でできたことはかつてありません！　サービスの詳細やご予約をご希望の方は，reservation@soundstyle.com，または 121，4 番通り，ニューヨーク，NY 10562 までご連絡ください。

4 月 18 日
ケネス・エレンバウム様
イースト・メイウェザー通り 247 番地
レキシントン　ニューヨーク 10472

エレンバウム様

アルバム製作のために弊社レコーディングスタジオのレンタルのお申し込みをいただき，ありがとうございました。残念ながら，ご希望のスタジオは5月1日までご利用いただけません。もっとも，ご指定いただいた4月25日と26日にご利用いただけるさらに広いスタジオはございます。両日共にご予約される場合は，追加料金なしでこの広いほうのスタジオを提供させていただきます。以上の条件でよろしいかどうかについてご連絡いただければと思います。

サポートスタッフのご要望につきましては，弊社にはレコーディングをお手伝いするプロの音響技師によるサービスがございます。スタジオや音響技師，希望される追加サービスに要する費用の概算をお送りいたしましたのでご確認ください。また，本状の裏側には弊社スタジオへの道順を記した地図が印刷されておりますので，合わせてご確認ください。弊社の営業時間と連絡先につきましては，地図の下部に記載されております。

敬具
シャロン・リ
カスタマー・サービス部
サウンド・スタイル社

186 ⏱ 35秒 　　　　　　　　　　　　　正解 ➤ (B)

広告の中でローラ・アン・ケイシーに関して何が述べられていますか。

(A) いくつかの教育施設を運営している。

(B) 教えた経験がある。

(C) フランスで会社を設立した。

(D) 演奏に関して受賞歴がある。

正解 Laura Ann Casey について，第1段落冒頭で founder and CEO とあり，第2段落最終文の We will also resume the ... class taught by our CEO の部分から以前クラスを教えていたことがわかるので，これら2か所の情報を組み合わせて (B) が正解であると判断する。

誤答 (C) に関しては，第1段落で「the chief administrator を務めていた」とはあるが，設立したとは述べていない。また，冒頭文で an accomplished classical cellist とあるが，accomplished（= highly skilled）という記述だけでは受賞歴があるかどうかを判断できないため (D) も不適切。

---

187 ⏱ 50秒 　　　　　　　　　　　　　正解 ➤ (A)

サウンド・スタイル社に関して述べられていないのは何ですか。

(A) 子どもの音楽教育を専門に扱っている。

(B) サービスを提供するのに最新鋭の技術を駆使している。

(C) 手頃な価格でサービスを提供している。

(D) コース内容を拡大する計画がある。

誤答 (B) は第3段落冒頭の We offer state-of-the-art recording equipment と，(C) は同段落後半の Never has recording ... so easy or affordable と，(D) は第2段落2文目の From April 1, ... the addition of jazz vocal lessons と，それぞれ内容が一致する。

正解 (A) の children は，第1段落で CEO が summer concert program for children に携わったとあるだけなので，Sound Style 社が子ども向けのサービスを専門にしていることの根拠にはならず，これが正解としてふさわしい。

---

188 ⏱ 60秒 両文書参照型 　　　　　　　　正解 ➤ (C)

エレンバウムさんはおそらく何をしますか。

(A) 5月の予約をキャンセルする

(B) 朗読の録音を行う

(C) ロバート・マクギーさんと作業をする

(D) 音響技術を学ぶ

正解 Mr. Ellenbaum は手紙の宛て先。手紙の第2段落冒頭で In response to your request ... our professional sound engineer to assist you. とあることから，彼が sound engineer によるサポートを望んでいるとわかる。ここで，広告の第3段落5文目に our in-house sound engineer, Robert McGee と名前が紹介されているので，(C) が正解であると判断する。

誤答 (A) は，手紙の第1段落に your specified dates of April 25 and 26 とあるので，5月には予約していない。

189

エレンバウムさんが希望したスタジオを利用できないのはなぜですか。

(A) 必要なサポートスタッフがいない。

(B) 設備の改良工事が行われている最中である。

(C) 彼の要望に応えられるほどスタジオが広くない。

(D) 彼が希望した日にちにすでに予約が入っている。

正解 手紙の冒頭で「スタジオが May 1 まで利用できない」とあり，さらに広告の第 3 段落において Studio B の再オープンが the beginning of May とあることをおさえる。この一文に currently being expanded to have all new equipment（現在機材を新しくする工事が行われている）と説明があるので，スタジオを利用できない理由が (B) であることを見極める。

誤答 手紙にある a larger facility だけを見ると (C) が正解に見えるので，他の選択肢がいずれも本文の内容に一致しないことを常に確認できるようにしたい。

190

どのような情報が手紙の裏側に印刷されていますか。

(A) スタジオの営業時間

(B) プロジェクトにかかる費用

(C) 現在利用可能なサービス

(D) 現地に行く電車の運行時間

正解 on the back of the letter の情報を探すと，手紙の第 2 段落 3 文目に a map ... printed on the reverse（＝ back）of this letter とあり，さらに次の文で Our opening hours ... are indicated below the map（営業時間が map の下部に記載されている）と述べていることから，(A) が正解であると判断できる。

誤答 第 2 段落 2 文目に I have sent you a document listing the approximate costs とあるので，(B) は手紙に同封されているものである。

Questions 191-195 refer to the following letter and article.　（語数：246 語＋ 148 語）

March 20

Dear Mr. Michael Ayers:

Three years ago, the mayor of Lamford, Fred McCourt, first proposed the idea of building a 65-story tower in the city's Dockside district. At that time, his idea was heavily defeated in a public poll. He has worked hard to round up support from Dockside businesses as well as residents since then, and the proposal was finally passed last year. The Lamford Development Corporation was created to manage the project, and, after much discussion the final design was approved on March 4.

The basement mall will contain 108 individual shops, and once completed will be the largest shopping complex in the state. The offices on each of the first 62 floors will have stunning views not only of the city's rugged coastline, but also of the building's beautiful atrium. On top of these floors will be an aquarium housing a diverse collection of exotic marine life. Also there will be a lavishly decorated bar designed by Lamford-native interior designer Francesca Fortoni, and an observation deck with floor-to-ceiling windows. Overall, the project is expected to help revitalize the economy of the Dockside district, which has declined dramatically over the past twenty years.

The honor of your presence is requested at the Dockside Tower groundbreaking ceremony and reception we have organized for May 10. The ceremony is scheduled to start at 11 A.M., followed by a reception starting at 1 P.M. If you are able to attend, please contact us at the telephone number below by April 18.

Dockside Tower Groundbreaking Committee
The Lamford Development Corporation
555-8998

Landmark Event On Dockside

May 11—Work on Dockside Tower, Lamford's new development, got underway with a groundbreaking ceremony in front of over 400 guests. The ceremony was held on the grounds of Croston House, a historic building that will be integrated into the development. Mayor Fred McCourt broke the earth with a ceremonial spade. He then made a brief speech, thanking everyone for their assistance in making his ambition to build Dockside Tower a reality. Following the ceremony, the guests moved on to a reception at the Plaza Hotel, where Brian Russell, president of the Lamford Development Corporation, delivered an address outlining the development plan.

When finished, Dockside Tower will reach a height of 420 meters, making it the tallest structure in the city. The lower floors will house businesses, shops, restaurants and an entertainment complex, while the building's sole bar will take up the entire top story of the tower.

191. What is the purpose of the letter?

(A) To express gratitude to a local business owner

(B) To announce a winning bid for a construction project

(C) To extend an invitation to an official event

(D) To detail the history of the Dockside district

192. According to the letter, what has Fred McCourt already done?

(A) Proposed revisions to the design of a tower

(B) Approved new industry regulations

(C) Succeeded in changing public opinion on a project

(D) Implemented a new measure to improve the local economy

193. What is suggested about Croston House?

(A) It is situated close to the ocean.

(B) It has been used to teach history.

(C) It can accommodate over 400 people.

(D) It was recently demolished.

194. What happened on May 10?

(A) Local people gathered in front of a newly constructed building.

(B) Dockside residents were asked to make donations.

(C) A company president summarized a construction plan during the ceremony.

(D) A city representative marked the beginning of a construction project.

195. What can be understood about the 65th floor of the tower?

(A) It will house rare species of sea life.

(B) It will feature work by a local designer.

(C) It will be used as an observation deck.

(D) It will overlook the building's atrium.

重要語句 □ story「(建物の)階」(= floor) □ defeat「〜を敗北させる，挫かせる」(= make ... fail) □ public poll「世論調査」 □ round ... up「〜をかき集める」(= collect) □ stunning「見事な」(= very impressive) □ rugged「起伏に富んだ，ゴツゴツした」(= rough and uneven) □ atrium「(ビルの中央に設けられた) 吹き抜けの広場，アトリウム」 □ lavishly「ふんだんに，豪華に」(= expensively or generously) □ The honor of your presence is requested.「ご出席いただきますようお願いいたします」(招待の丁寧な表現) □ groundbreaking ceremony「着工式」 □ get underway「開始になる」(= start) □ integrate A into B「A を B に組み込む」(= incorporate) □ spade「(穴掘り用の) 鋤 (すき)」 □ deliver an address「スピーチをする」(= make an address [speech]) □ sole「唯一の」(= only) □ take ... up「(時間や空間など)を取る」(= use; occupy) □ demolish「〜を取り壊す」(= destroy; pull down) □ mark「〜を記念する，祝う」(= celebrate)

191-195 の設問は次の手紙と記事に関するものです。

3月20日

マイケル・エイヤーズ様

ラムフォード市長であるフレッド・マコート氏は3年前，市のドックサイド地区に65階のタワーを建設する計画を最初に提案いたしました。当時，市長の考えは世論調査で圧倒的な反対を受けていました。それ以来市長は，ドックサイド市内の企業や市民から支持を得るため懸命な努力を続け，去年ついに案が可決されました。このプロジェクトを管理するためにラムフォード開発社が設立され，多くの議論を経て，最終的な設計案が3月4日に承認されました。

地下のモールには108店舗を含む予定で，建設が完了すれば州で最大のショッピング施設となります。1階から62階までの各階にあるオフィスからは，市の起伏に富む海岸線を見事に一望できるだけでなく，タワー内の美しい吹き抜け広場も見ることができます。さらに上の階には，多種多様な珍しい海洋生物を収容する水族館もできる予定です。また，特筆すべき点として，ラムフォード出身のインテリアデザイナーであるフランチェスカ・フォルトニの手掛けた豪華な装飾を施したバーや，床から天井まで窓で覆われた展望台フロアもあります。総合的に見て，このプロジェクトが過去20年間著しく低迷しているドックサイド地区の経済活性化に役立つと期待されています。

5月10日に開催されるドックサイド・タワー着工式と祝賀会にぜひお越しいただきたく存じます。式は午前11時に開始される予定で，その後，午後1時が祝賀会の開始予定となっております。ご出席いただける場合は，4月18日までに下記の電話番号にご連絡ください。

ドックサイド・タワー起工式委員会
ラムフォード地域開発会社
555-8998

ドックサイドの画期的なイベント

5月11日 — 400人を超える招待客が見守る中行われた着工式でラムフォード市に新しく開発されるドックサイド・タワーの工事が始まった。式はクロストン・ハウスの敷地で行われたが，この建物は，開発タワーの一部に組み込まれる予定の歴史的建築物である。フレッド・マコート市長は着工式用の鋤（すき）で地面を掘った。その後彼は短いスピーチを行い，彼の夢であるドックサイド・タワー建設の実現を支持してくれたことに対して，すべての人々に感謝した。着工式の後，招待客はプラザ・ホテルでの祝賀会へと移動し，そこでラムフォード開発社の社長であるブライアン・ラッセル氏が開発計画の概要を説明するスピーチを行った。

ドックサイド・タワーが完成すれば，高さは420メートルに達し，市内でもっとも高い建造物となる。ドックサイド・タワーの低層階には，企業，店舗，レストラン，娯楽施設が入り，一方最上階は建物唯一のバーが全体を占めることになる。

191

手紙が書かれた目的は何ですか。

(A) 地元の経営者に感謝の意を伝えること

(B) 建設プロジェクトを勝ち取った入札を発表すること

(C) 公式のイベントに招待すること

(D) ドックサイド地区の歴史を詳しく説明すること

正解 letter の第2段落まででタワー建設の説明をした後，最終段落冒頭の The honor of your presence ... for May 10. で着工式や祝賀会への参加を招待している流れをつかみ，(C) を選択する。手紙の目的は第1段落冒頭で書かれることが多いが，今回のように背景的な出来事をまず述べてから，最後に主旨を伝えることもある。

192

手紙によると，フレッド・マコート氏がすでに行ったことは何ですか。

(A) タワーの設計の修正を提案した

(B) 新しい産業規定を承認した

(C) プロジェクトに関する一般市民の意見を変えることに成功した

(D) 地域経済の改善策を新たに実施した

正解 Fred McCourt に関して，第1段落2文目でまず his idea was heavily defeated in a public poll とあり，その後で He has worked hard to round up support ... finally passed last year.（企業や市民から支持を得る努力を続け，去年ついに案が可決された）と説明しているので，(C) が適切。

誤答 (A) は，第1段落冒頭に「建設の案を出した」とはあるが，設計の修正を提案したわけではない。

193

クロストン・ハウスについて何が示唆されていますか。

(A) 海の近くに位置している。

(B) 歴史教育のために使用されてきたものである。

(C) 400人以上を収容できる。

(D) 最近取り壊されたものである。

正解 Croston House に関して，記事の第1段落2文目で，a historic building that will be integrated into the development（タワーの一部に組み込まれる予定の歴史建築物）とあることから，建設地に所在するものであるとわかる。ここで，手紙の第2段落2文目において，タワーの62階までのオフィスについて「the city's rugged coastline が一望できる」と説明していることから，海に近い場所にあることを見極め，(A) を選ぶ。

誤答 (C) は記事の冒頭で出席者が over 400 guests とあるが，Croston House の建物内で式が行われたとは書かれていない。

194 ⏱60秒 両文書参照型 正解 ➤ (D)

5月10日に何が起こりましたか。
(A) 地域住民が新しく建設されたビルの前に集まった。
(B) ドックサイド地区の住民が寄付を要請された。
(C) 会社の社長が式の中で建設計画の概要を説明した。
(D) 市の代表者が建設工事の開始を祝った。

正解 まず，手紙の第3段落冒頭から，May 10 が groundbreaking ceremony and reception の開催日であることをおさえる。ここで，記事の第1段落3文目に Mayor Fred McCourt ... a ceremonial spade.（市長が着工式用のすきで地面を掘った）や He then made a brief speech とあることから，mayor を city representative と言い換えた (D) が正解。

誤答 (A) は，建設予定地に集まったことに注意。(C) は during the ceremony ではなく during the reception であれば，記事の第1段落最終文の Brian Russell ... outlining the development plan と一致する。

195 ⏱70秒 両文書参照型 正解 ➤ (B)

タワーの65階について何がわかりますか。
(A) 珍しい海洋生物を収容する場所になる。
(B) 地元のデザイナーが手がけることになる。
(C) 展望台として利用される。
(D) 建物の大広場が見下ろせる。

正解 手紙の冒頭に 65-story tower とあるので，65階は最上階である。ここで，記事の最終文で the building's sole bar will take up the entire top story（= floor）of the tower と述べていることから，bar に関する記述を選べばよいとわかる。すると，手紙の第2段落4文目で Also, there will be ... bar designed by Lamford-native interior designer とあるので，(B) が正解であるとわかる。

誤答 (A) や (C) に関しては，on top of these（= the first 62）floors とあることから，63階と最上階の間にできるものと考えられる。(D) は the offices on each of the first 62 floors に関する記述。

Questions 196-200 refer to the following two e-mails. （語数：228 語＋ 203 語）

From: <travisc@powermail.com>
To: <c.richards@kentishsupplies.com>
Subject: Job vacancy

Dear Mr. Richards,

This e-mail is to express my interest in the vacancy for a marketing manager that you are currently advertising on your Web site. I believe that my employment history makes me an ideal candidate for this position.

I first realized that my future lay in marketing when I was a student. I took, and genuinely enjoyed, a summer job in the marketing department of one of your main competitors, AcePlate. Upon gaining my degree at Brimshire University, I took a job in the marketing department of FPL Enterprises. I played an integral role in creating their critically acclaimed "Appliances of Beauty" advertising campaign. After six years of service, I was offered the position of marketing manager. Although I only held this position for a year, company sales doubled during that period.

I left to take up a similar position with a newly founded company, Frompton Tech. I was hired to design its marketing strategy from the ground up, a task that I completed within the first year. As a result of my work, Frompton Tech was soon on a competitive footing with the more established companies in the industry.

My nine years of experience in the field, three of them in management, have furnished me with a thorough understanding of marketing practices, and I feel that I am perfectly qualified to help Kentish Supplies revitalize its marketing campaign.

Yours sincerely,
Conway Travis

From: <c.richards@kentishsupplies.com>
To: <m.singh@kentishsupplies.com>
Subject: Recruitment

Dear Ms. Singh,

I'm writing to update you on the progress that has been made in our search for a new marketing manager. My new assistant Ms. Schmidt has produced a list of the most suitable candidates that we have interviewed. Joanne Tempest is my preference for the position, as she performed exceptionally well in her interview and easily surpasses the minimum requirement of five years of marketing experience. She also has four years of managerial experience with AcePlate. Conversely, my assistant preferred Conway Travis, who was recommended by someone she knows. Mr. Travis displayed ingenious ideas along with a great deal of self-confidence. However, I'm unwilling to recommend him for the position as he is the only applicant who falls short of our minimum requirement for managerial experience. Therefore, I personally feel that he should be dropped from consideration.

I have sent the résumés of the remaining candidates together with this e-mail so that you can look them over. I would also like you to meet with the two other prospects, Gina Moon and Brian Scott. If you could let me know by the end of the day when you are available, I'll contact the candidates to arrange times for the second round of interviews.

Sincerely,
Charlie Richards

196. What does Mr. Travis NOT mention in his e-mail?
(A) He has obtained a degree in marketing.
(B) He created a promotional campaign that received praise.
(C) He has marketing experience at three different companies.
(D) He was promoted by the company that first hired him after he graduated.

197. Who suggested Mr. Travis for the position?
(A) A professor of Brimshire University
(B) The president of Frompton Tech
(C) The hiring manager of FPL Enterprises
(D) An acquaintance of Ms. Schmidt

198. How much managerial experience is most likely required for the job opening?
(A) 3 years
(B) 4 years
(C) 5 years
(D) 9 years

199. In the second e-mail, the word "round" in paragraph 2, line 5, is closest in meaning to
(A) circle
(B) series
(C) visit
(D) chance

200. What can be understood about Joanna Tempest?
(A) She has met with Ms. Singh before.
(B) She displayed creative ideas throughout the interview.
(C) She has worked for a rival of Kentish Supplies.
(D) She did not make a good impression on Mr. Richards.

(重要語句) □ vacancy「(仕事の) 空き」(= opening)　□ genuinely「実に, 本当に」(= truly)　□ upon *doing*「〜した直後に」　□ integral「不可欠な」(= essential)　□ take up ...「〜を始める, (仕事) に就く」(= start)　□ from the ground up「基盤からすべて」　□ on a competitive footing with ...「〜と競争的な立場になる, 肩を並べる」 ※ この footing は position の意味。　□ established「確立した, 認められた」　□ furnish *someone* with ...「人に (必要なもの) を与える」(= provide; supply)　□ practice「慣習, やり方」　□ surpass「〜を上回る」(= exceed)　□ conversely「逆に」(= on the other hand)　□ ingenious「独創的な」(= innovative; inventive; creative)　□ fall short of ...「〜に達しない」　□ prospect「見込みのある候補者」

397

196-200 の設問は次の２つのメールに関するものです。

送信者： 〈travisc@powermail.com〉
宛て先： 〈c.richards@kentishsupplies.com〉
件名： 求人

リチャーズ様

貴社のウェブサイトで現在募集しているマーケティング部長職について興味がありご連絡申し上げました。自分の職歴から，私はこの職にふさわしいと考えております。

自分の将来の方向性がマーケティングにあると初めて実感したのは，学生の時でした。当時私は，貴社の競合企業のひとつであるエイスプレイト社のマーケティング部門で夏の間アルバイトをし，心から楽しみを覚えました。ブリムシア大学で学位を取得した後，私は FPL エンタープライジズ社のマーケティング部門に就職しました。そこで，専門家から好評を得た「美しい電化製品」という名の広告キャンペーンを手掛けるのに不可欠な役割を果たしました。６年間勤務した後，マーケティング部長職のオファーを受けました。この役職に就いたのは一年間のみでしたが，会社の売上はその期間２倍に伸びました。

それから私は同社を辞職し，設立間もないフロンプトン・テク社にて同種の職に就きました。会社のマーケティング戦略を基盤から作り上げるために採用されましたが，勤務最初の一年でこれを成し遂げました。私の業績により，フロンプトン・テク社はその後すぐ，業界の他のより確立された企業と競争的な関係を築くに至りました。

３年間の管理職の経験を含む当該分野での９年間の経験により，私はマーケティング業務を深く理解することができましたので，ケンティッシュ・サプライズ社の広告キャンペーンをさらに良いものにしていく仕事に適任であると考えます。

敬具
コンウェイ・トラビス

送信者： 〈c.richards@kentishsupplies.com〉
宛て先： 〈m.singh@kentishsupplies.com〉
件名： 採用活動

シンさん

新しいマーケティング部長の求人に関する進捗状況の報告です。私の新しいアシスタントであるシュミットが，これまで面接をした中でもっともこの職に適していると思われる候補者のリストを作成しました。私はジョアン・テンペストが良いと考えていますが，それは彼女が面接で非常に優れた受け答えをし，またマーケティング経験５年という最低条件をはるかに上回っているからです。さらには，エイスプレイト社で４年にわたる管理職の経験もあります。一方，私のアシスタントは，知人に推薦された人物であるコンウェイ・トラビスが良いと思ったようです。彼は独創的なアイデアを発揮し，自信も大いに見せていました。ただ，管理職経験の最低条件を満たしていない唯一の候補者でもあり，私は彼を勧めることができません。したがって，個人的には彼を検討の対象から外すべきではないかと考えています。

残りの候補者の履歴書をメールに添付しておりますので，ご確認ください。他の２人の有望な候補者であるギナ・ムーンとブライアン・スコットとの面接にも立ち会っていただければと思っています。ご都合を今日中にお知らせいただければ，候補者に連絡をとり，第二次面接の時間を設定したいと思います。

敬具
チャーリー・リチャーズ

196 ⏱ 60秒 正解 ➤ (A)

トラビスさんがメールの中で述べていないことは何ですか。

(A) マーケティングの学位を取得している。
(B) 称賛された宣伝キャンペーンを手掛けた。
(C) 異なる3社でマーケティングの経験がある。
(D) 卒業後に初めて雇われた会社で昇進した。

誤答▶ (B) は，第2段落4文目の I played an integral role ... advertising campaign.（専門家から好評を得た広告キャンペーンを手掛けた）とあるので，内容が一致する。(C) も，第1段落から Aceplate 社と FPL Enterprises 社で，第3段落から Frompton Tech 社で，それぞれマーケティング部門における経験があることがわかる。(D) は，第1段落で「学位取得後すぐに FPL Enterprises 社に就職した」とあり，さらに同じ会社で after six years of service, I was offered the position of marketing manager と述べているので，これも内容が一致している。

正解 (A) は，第2段落3文目に my degree at Brimshire University とあるが，学位名が具体的に記されていないので，これが正解。

197 ⏱ 30秒 正解 ➤ (D)

トラビスさんを推薦したのは誰ですか。
(A) ブリムシア大学の教授
(B) フロンプトン・テク社の社長
(C) FPL エンタープライジズ社の採用担当部長
(D) シュミットさんの知人

正解 下のメールの第1段落5文目で，my assistant preferred Conway Travis, who was recommended by someone she（= my assistant）knows とあることに着目。第2文目から my assistant = Ms. Schmidt であるとわかるので，(D) を選ぶ。設問だけでは上下どちらのメールに情報があるか判断しづらいが，最初に全文を読んでいれば該当箇所をすぐに特定できるはず。

198 ⏱ 70秒 両文書参照型 正解 ➤ (B)

どれくらいの管理職の経験がおそらく求人職に求められていますか。
(A) 3年 　　(C) 5年
(B) 4年 　(D) 9年

正解 下のメールの第1段落4文目で，Joanne Tempest に four years of managerial experience があること，また8文目の he is the only applicant ... for managerial experience で，Conway Travis が管理職の条件を満たしていないことをおさえる。ここで，上のメールの第4段落冒頭文で，Mr. Travis が My nine years of experience in the field, three of them（= those nine years）in management（3年の管理職の経験を含む9年間の経験）と述べていることから，求められる最低年数が (B) であることを見極める。

199 ⏱20秒 満点ポイント! 同義語問題 正解 ▶ (B)

2つ目のメールの第2段落5行目にある "round" にもっとも意味の近い語は

(A) 周期 　　　(C) 訪問

(B) 一巡 　　　(D) 機会

正解 the second round of interviews は「二次面接」のこと。この round は「（連続して行われる出来事の）一巡，一回」を意味するので，(B) series が適切。

誤答 The doctor is on his daily rounds. のように用いた場合は round が「巡回」を意味し，(C) visit と言い換えられる。(D) chance は「（偶然得られる）チャンス，機会」という意味で，round の言い換えにはならないので注意。

---

200 ⏱70秒 両文書参照型 正解 ▶ (C)

ジョアン・テンペストに関して何がわかりますか。

(A) シンさんに以前会ったことがある。

(B) 面接の間創造的な考えを発揮した。

(C) ケンティッシュ・サプライズ社の競合企業における勤務経験がある。

(D) リチャーズさんにあまり良い印象を与えなかった。

正解 下のメールの第1段落4文目で，Joanne Tempest に関して She also has ... experience with AcePlate. と述べている。ここで，上のメールの第2段落で AcePlate 社について one of your (= Kentish Supplies) main competitors とあることから，(C) が正解とわかる。

誤答 (A) の Ms. Singh は下のメールの宛て先。冒頭の一文で Mr. Richards が「求人に関する進捗状況の報告をするために連絡している」と伝えていることから，今までの面接には携わっていないことがうかがえる。(B) や (D) は，どちらも Conway Travis に関する記述。

おわりに

　満点トレーニング，いかがだったでしょうか。最後に皆さんに思い出していただきたいのは，TOEIC の問題の大半は英語の「基礎力」を試すものだということです。そうした基本問題をいかにすばやく解けるかが，何よりも大切です。本書で究極レベルの力をつけた後は，公式問題集や『TOEIC® テスト究極の模試600問』（ヒロ前田著／アルク）など，本番と同レベルの問題に感覚を慣らしておくことをオススメします。

　それでは，本書を閉じる前に，990 点をすでに達成した自分をイメージしてみてください。どのパートもペースを乱されることなく，自信をもって全問解き終わる自分です。そして，一か月後の結果を見たとき，990 の数字が目に飛び込んでくる瞬間を思い浮かべてください。そのときに沸き起こる胸の高鳴りを，今感じてみましょう。この「高揚感」が，夢を目標に，目標を現実に呼び寄せる力になってくれます。皆さんが目標を達成し，そこから新たに広がる世界で一層ご活躍されることを，心より応援しています。

ANSWER SHEET

LISTENING SECTION

Part 1

NO.	ANSWER A B C D
1	Ⓐ Ⓑ Ⓒ Ⓓ
2	Ⓐ Ⓑ Ⓒ Ⓓ
3	Ⓐ Ⓑ Ⓒ Ⓓ
4	Ⓐ Ⓑ Ⓒ Ⓓ
5	Ⓐ Ⓑ Ⓒ Ⓓ
6	Ⓐ Ⓑ Ⓒ Ⓓ
7	Ⓐ Ⓑ Ⓒ Ⓓ
8	Ⓐ Ⓑ Ⓒ Ⓓ
9	Ⓐ Ⓑ Ⓒ Ⓓ
10	Ⓐ Ⓑ Ⓒ Ⓓ

Part 2

NO.	ANSWER A B C
11	Ⓐ Ⓑ Ⓒ
12	Ⓐ Ⓑ Ⓒ
13	Ⓐ Ⓑ Ⓒ
14	Ⓐ Ⓑ Ⓒ
15	Ⓐ Ⓑ Ⓒ
16	Ⓐ Ⓑ Ⓒ
17	Ⓐ Ⓑ Ⓒ
18	Ⓐ Ⓑ Ⓒ
19	Ⓐ Ⓑ Ⓒ
20	Ⓐ Ⓑ Ⓒ

NO.	ANSWER A B C
21	Ⓐ Ⓑ Ⓒ
22	Ⓐ Ⓑ Ⓒ
23	Ⓐ Ⓑ Ⓒ
24	Ⓐ Ⓑ Ⓒ
25	Ⓐ Ⓑ Ⓒ
26	Ⓐ Ⓑ Ⓒ
27	Ⓐ Ⓑ Ⓒ
28	Ⓐ Ⓑ Ⓒ
29	Ⓐ Ⓑ Ⓒ
30	Ⓐ Ⓑ Ⓒ

NO.	ANSWER A B C
31	Ⓐ Ⓑ Ⓒ
32	Ⓐ Ⓑ Ⓒ
33	Ⓐ Ⓑ Ⓒ
34	Ⓐ Ⓑ Ⓒ
35	Ⓐ Ⓑ Ⓒ
36	Ⓐ Ⓑ Ⓒ
37	Ⓐ Ⓑ Ⓒ
38	Ⓐ Ⓑ Ⓒ
39	Ⓐ Ⓑ Ⓒ
40	Ⓐ Ⓑ Ⓒ

Part 3

NO.	ANSWER A B C D
41	Ⓐ Ⓑ Ⓒ Ⓓ
42	Ⓐ Ⓑ Ⓒ Ⓓ
43	Ⓐ Ⓑ Ⓒ Ⓓ
44	Ⓐ Ⓑ Ⓒ Ⓓ
45	Ⓐ Ⓑ Ⓒ Ⓓ
46	Ⓐ Ⓑ Ⓒ Ⓓ
47	Ⓐ Ⓑ Ⓒ Ⓓ
48	Ⓐ Ⓑ Ⓒ Ⓓ
49	Ⓐ Ⓑ Ⓒ Ⓓ
50	Ⓐ Ⓑ Ⓒ Ⓓ

NO.	ANSWER A B C D
51	Ⓐ Ⓑ Ⓒ Ⓓ
52	Ⓐ Ⓑ Ⓒ Ⓓ
53	Ⓐ Ⓑ Ⓒ Ⓓ
54	Ⓐ Ⓑ Ⓒ Ⓓ
55	Ⓐ Ⓑ Ⓒ Ⓓ
56	Ⓐ Ⓑ Ⓒ Ⓓ
57	Ⓐ Ⓑ Ⓒ Ⓓ
58	Ⓐ Ⓑ Ⓒ Ⓓ
59	Ⓐ Ⓑ Ⓒ Ⓓ
60	Ⓐ Ⓑ Ⓒ Ⓓ

NO.	ANSWER A B C D
61	Ⓐ Ⓑ Ⓒ Ⓓ
62	Ⓐ Ⓑ Ⓒ Ⓓ
63	Ⓐ Ⓑ Ⓒ Ⓓ
64	Ⓐ Ⓑ Ⓒ Ⓓ
65	Ⓐ Ⓑ Ⓒ Ⓓ
66	Ⓐ Ⓑ Ⓒ Ⓓ
67	Ⓐ Ⓑ Ⓒ Ⓓ
68	Ⓐ Ⓑ Ⓒ Ⓓ
69	Ⓐ Ⓑ Ⓒ Ⓓ
70	Ⓐ Ⓑ Ⓒ Ⓓ

Part 4

NO.	ANSWER A B C D
71	Ⓐ Ⓑ Ⓒ Ⓓ
72	Ⓐ Ⓑ Ⓒ Ⓓ
73	Ⓐ Ⓑ Ⓒ Ⓓ
74	Ⓐ Ⓑ Ⓒ Ⓓ
75	Ⓐ Ⓑ Ⓒ Ⓓ
76	Ⓐ Ⓑ Ⓒ Ⓓ
77	Ⓐ Ⓑ Ⓒ Ⓓ
78	Ⓐ Ⓑ Ⓒ Ⓓ
79	Ⓐ Ⓑ Ⓒ Ⓓ
80	Ⓐ Ⓑ Ⓒ Ⓓ

NO.	ANSWER A B C D
81	Ⓐ Ⓑ Ⓒ Ⓓ
82	Ⓐ Ⓑ Ⓒ Ⓓ
83	Ⓐ Ⓑ Ⓒ Ⓓ
84	Ⓐ Ⓑ Ⓒ Ⓓ
85	Ⓐ Ⓑ Ⓒ Ⓓ
86	Ⓐ Ⓑ Ⓒ Ⓓ
87	Ⓐ Ⓑ Ⓒ Ⓓ
88	Ⓐ Ⓑ Ⓒ Ⓓ
89	Ⓐ Ⓑ Ⓒ Ⓓ
90	Ⓐ Ⓑ Ⓒ Ⓓ

NO.	ANSWER A B C D
91	Ⓐ Ⓑ Ⓒ Ⓓ
92	Ⓐ Ⓑ Ⓒ Ⓓ
93	Ⓐ Ⓑ Ⓒ Ⓓ
94	Ⓐ Ⓑ Ⓒ Ⓓ
95	Ⓐ Ⓑ Ⓒ Ⓓ
96	Ⓐ Ⓑ Ⓒ Ⓓ
97	Ⓐ Ⓑ Ⓒ Ⓓ
98	Ⓐ Ⓑ Ⓒ Ⓓ
99	Ⓐ Ⓑ Ⓒ Ⓓ
100	Ⓐ Ⓑ Ⓒ Ⓓ

READING SECTION

Part 5

NO.	ANSWER A B C D
101	Ⓐ Ⓑ Ⓒ Ⓓ
102	Ⓐ Ⓑ Ⓒ Ⓓ
103	Ⓐ Ⓑ Ⓒ Ⓓ
104	Ⓐ Ⓑ Ⓒ Ⓓ
105	Ⓐ Ⓑ Ⓒ Ⓓ
106	Ⓐ Ⓑ Ⓒ Ⓓ
107	Ⓐ Ⓑ Ⓒ Ⓓ
108	Ⓐ Ⓑ Ⓒ Ⓓ
109	Ⓐ Ⓑ Ⓒ Ⓓ
110	Ⓐ Ⓑ Ⓒ Ⓓ

NO.	ANSWER A B C D
111	Ⓐ Ⓑ Ⓒ Ⓓ
112	Ⓐ Ⓑ Ⓒ Ⓓ
113	Ⓐ Ⓑ Ⓒ Ⓓ
114	Ⓐ Ⓑ Ⓒ Ⓓ
115	Ⓐ Ⓑ Ⓒ Ⓓ
116	Ⓐ Ⓑ Ⓒ Ⓓ
117	Ⓐ Ⓑ Ⓒ Ⓓ
118	Ⓐ Ⓑ Ⓒ Ⓓ
119	Ⓐ Ⓑ Ⓒ Ⓓ
120	Ⓐ Ⓑ Ⓒ Ⓓ

NO.	ANSWER A B C D
121	Ⓐ Ⓑ Ⓒ Ⓓ
122	Ⓐ Ⓑ Ⓒ Ⓓ
123	Ⓐ Ⓑ Ⓒ Ⓓ
124	Ⓐ Ⓑ Ⓒ Ⓓ
125	Ⓐ Ⓑ Ⓒ Ⓓ
126	Ⓐ Ⓑ Ⓒ Ⓓ
127	Ⓐ Ⓑ Ⓒ Ⓓ
128	Ⓐ Ⓑ Ⓒ Ⓓ
129	Ⓐ Ⓑ Ⓒ Ⓓ
130	Ⓐ Ⓑ Ⓒ Ⓓ

NO.	ANSWER A B C D
131	Ⓐ Ⓑ Ⓒ Ⓓ
132	Ⓐ Ⓑ Ⓒ Ⓓ
133	Ⓐ Ⓑ Ⓒ Ⓓ
134	Ⓐ Ⓑ Ⓒ Ⓓ
135	Ⓐ Ⓑ Ⓒ Ⓓ
136	Ⓐ Ⓑ Ⓒ Ⓓ
137	Ⓐ Ⓑ Ⓒ Ⓓ
138	Ⓐ Ⓑ Ⓒ Ⓓ
139	Ⓐ Ⓑ Ⓒ Ⓓ
140	Ⓐ Ⓑ Ⓒ Ⓓ

Part 6

NO.	ANSWER A B C D
141	Ⓐ Ⓑ Ⓒ Ⓓ
142	Ⓐ Ⓑ Ⓒ Ⓓ
143	Ⓐ Ⓑ Ⓒ Ⓓ
144	Ⓐ Ⓑ Ⓒ Ⓓ
145	Ⓐ Ⓑ Ⓒ Ⓓ
146	Ⓐ Ⓑ Ⓒ Ⓓ
147	Ⓐ Ⓑ Ⓒ Ⓓ
148	Ⓐ Ⓑ Ⓒ Ⓓ
149	Ⓐ Ⓑ Ⓒ Ⓓ
150	Ⓐ Ⓑ Ⓒ Ⓓ

NO.	ANSWER A B C D
151	Ⓐ Ⓑ Ⓒ Ⓓ
152	Ⓐ Ⓑ Ⓒ Ⓓ
153	Ⓐ Ⓑ Ⓒ Ⓓ
154	Ⓐ Ⓑ Ⓒ Ⓓ
155	Ⓐ Ⓑ Ⓒ Ⓓ
156	Ⓐ Ⓑ Ⓒ Ⓓ
157	Ⓐ Ⓑ Ⓒ Ⓓ
158	Ⓐ Ⓑ Ⓒ Ⓓ
159	Ⓐ Ⓑ Ⓒ Ⓓ
160	Ⓐ Ⓑ Ⓒ Ⓓ

Part 7

NO.	ANSWER A B C D
161	Ⓐ Ⓑ Ⓒ Ⓓ
162	Ⓐ Ⓑ Ⓒ Ⓓ
163	Ⓐ Ⓑ Ⓒ Ⓓ
164	Ⓐ Ⓑ Ⓒ Ⓓ
165	Ⓐ Ⓑ Ⓒ Ⓓ
166	Ⓐ Ⓑ Ⓒ Ⓓ
167	Ⓐ Ⓑ Ⓒ Ⓓ
168	Ⓐ Ⓑ Ⓒ Ⓓ
169	Ⓐ Ⓑ Ⓒ Ⓓ
170	Ⓐ Ⓑ Ⓒ Ⓓ

NO.	ANSWER A B C D
171	Ⓐ Ⓑ Ⓒ Ⓓ
172	Ⓐ Ⓑ Ⓒ Ⓓ
173	Ⓐ Ⓑ Ⓒ Ⓓ
174	Ⓐ Ⓑ Ⓒ Ⓓ
175	Ⓐ Ⓑ Ⓒ Ⓓ
176	Ⓐ Ⓑ Ⓒ Ⓓ
177	Ⓐ Ⓑ Ⓒ Ⓓ
178	Ⓐ Ⓑ Ⓒ Ⓓ
179	Ⓐ Ⓑ Ⓒ Ⓓ
180	Ⓐ Ⓑ Ⓒ Ⓓ

NO.	ANSWER A B C D
181	Ⓐ Ⓑ Ⓒ Ⓓ
182	Ⓐ Ⓑ Ⓒ Ⓓ
183	Ⓐ Ⓑ Ⓒ Ⓓ
184	Ⓐ Ⓑ Ⓒ Ⓓ
185	Ⓐ Ⓑ Ⓒ Ⓓ
186	Ⓐ Ⓑ Ⓒ Ⓓ
187	Ⓐ Ⓑ Ⓒ Ⓓ
188	Ⓐ Ⓑ Ⓒ Ⓓ
189	Ⓐ Ⓑ Ⓒ Ⓓ
190	Ⓐ Ⓑ Ⓒ Ⓓ

NO.	ANSWER A B C D
191	Ⓐ Ⓑ Ⓒ Ⓓ
192	Ⓐ Ⓑ Ⓒ Ⓓ
193	Ⓐ Ⓑ Ⓒ Ⓓ
194	Ⓐ Ⓑ Ⓒ Ⓓ
195	Ⓐ Ⓑ Ⓒ Ⓓ
196	Ⓐ Ⓑ Ⓒ Ⓓ
197	Ⓐ Ⓑ Ⓒ Ⓓ
198	Ⓐ Ⓑ Ⓒ Ⓓ
199	Ⓐ Ⓑ Ⓒ Ⓓ
200	Ⓐ Ⓑ Ⓒ Ⓓ

ANSWER SHEET

READING SECTION

Part 5

NO.	ANSWER A B C D	NO.	ANSWER A B C D	NO.	ANSWER A B C D	NO.	ANSWER A B C D
101	A B C D	111	A B C D	121	A B C D	131	A B C D
102	A B C D	112	A B C D	122	A B C D	132	A B C D
103	A B C D	113	A B C D	123	A B C D	133	A B C D
104	A B C D	114	A B C D	124	A B C D	134	A B C D
105	A B C D	115	A B C D	125	A B C D	135	A B C D
106	A B C D	116	A B C D	126	A B C D	136	A B C D
107	A B C D	117	A B C D	127	A B C D	137	A B C D
108	A B C D	118	A B C D	128	A B C D	138	A B C D
109	A B C D	119	A B C D	129	A B C D	139	A B C D
110	A B C D	120	A B C D	130	A B C D	140	A B C D

Part 6

NO.	ANSWER A B C D	NO.	ANSWER A B C D
141	A B C D	151	A B C D
142	A B C D	152	A B C D
143	A B C D	153	A B C D
144	A B C D	154	A B C D
145	A B C D	155	A B C D
146	A B C D	156	A B C D
147	A B C D	157	A B C D
148	A B C D	158	A B C D
149	A B C D	159	A B C D
150	A B C D	160	A B C D

Part 7

NO.	ANSWER A B C D	NO.	ANSWER A B C D	NO.	ANSWER A B C D	NO.	ANSWER A B C D
161	A B C D	171	A B C D	181	A B C D	191	A B C D
162	A B C D	172	A B C D	182	A B C D	192	A B C D
163	A B C D	173	A B C D	183	A B C D	193	A B C D
164	A B C D	174	A B C D	184	A B C D	194	A B C D
165	A B C D	175	A B C D	185	A B C D	195	A B C D
166	A B C D	176	A B C D	186	A B C D	196	A B C D
167	A B C D	177	A B C D	187	A B C D	197	A B C D
168	A B C D	178	A B C D	188	A B C D	198	A B C D
169	A B C D	179	A B C D	189	A B C D	199	A B C D
170	A B C D	180	A B C D	190	A B C D	200	A B C D

LISTENING SECTION

Part 1

NO.	ANSWER A B C D
1	A B C D
2	A B C D
3	A B C D
4	A B C D
5	A B C D
6	A B C D
7	A B C D
8	A B C D
9	A B C D
10	A B C D

Part 2

NO.	ANSWER A B C
11	A B C
12	A B C
13	A B C
14	A B C
15	A B C
16	A B C
17	A B C
18	A B C
19	A B C
20	A B C

NO.	ANSWER A B C
21	A B C
22	A B C
23	A B C
24	A B C
25	A B C
26	A B C
27	A B C
28	A B C
29	A B C
30	A B C

NO.	ANSWER A B C
31	A B C
32	A B C
33	A B C
34	A B C
35	A B C
36	A B C
37	A B C
38	A B C
39	A B C
40	A B C

Part 3

NO.	ANSWER A B C D	NO.	ANSWER A B C D	NO.	ANSWER A B C D
41	A B C D	51	A B C D	61	A B C D
42	A B C D	52	A B C D	62	A B C D
43	A B C D	53	A B C D	63	A B C D
44	A B C D	54	A B C D	64	A B C D
45	A B C D	55	A B C D	65	A B C D
46	A B C D	56	A B C D	66	A B C D
47	A B C D	57	A B C D	67	A B C D
48	A B C D	58	A B C D	68	A B C D
49	A B C D	59	A B C D	69	A B C D
50	A B C D	60	A B C D	70	A B C D

Part 4

NO.	ANSWER A B C D	NO.	ANSWER A B C D	NO.	ANSWER A B C D
71	A B C D	81	A B C D	91	A B C D
72	A B C D	82	A B C D	92	A B C D
73	A B C D	83	A B C D	93	A B C D
74	A B C D	84	A B C D	94	A B C D
75	A B C D	85	A B C D	95	A B C D
76	A B C D	86	A B C D	96	A B C D
77	A B C D	87	A B C D	97	A B C D
78	A B C D	88	A B C D	98	A B C D
79	A B C D	89	A B C D	99	A B C D
80	A B C D	90	A B C D	100	A B C D

加藤 優（かとう　まさし）

青山学院大学英米文学科卒業。
バンクーバー・コミュニティ・
カレッジで国際TESOL（英語教
授法）ディプロマを取得。大手
英会話スクールでの講師を経て
現在，エッセンス イングリッシュ スクール主任講師。
TOEIC990点。TOEICを毎回受験して積み重ねてき
た研究と分析をもとに，つねに最新の傾向を反映した
授業を行っている。わかりやすい解説と独自のティー
チングスタイルで多くの生徒から支持を得ている。著
書に『新TOEIC® TEST990点特急パート5&6』（朝
日新聞出版）がある。週刊ST（ジャパンタイムズ）
ではTOEICコーナーのPart 6の執筆を担当。ユーキャ
ンの『はじめて受けるTOEIC®講座』では主任担当
講師として参加している。

[英文校正協力]
Paul McConnell
Bradley Towle

© Masashi Kato, 2012, Printed in Japan

**全問正解する
新 TOEIC® TEST 990 点対策**

2012 年 8 月 1 日　初版第 1 刷発行

著　者　加藤　優
制　作　ツディブックス株式会社
発行者　田中　稔
発行所　株式会社 語研
　　　　〒101－0064
　　　　東京都千代田区猿楽町 2－7－17
　　　　電　話 03－3291－3986
　　　　ファクス 03－3291－6749
　　　　振替口座 00140－9－66728
組　版　ツディブックス株式会社
印刷・製本　日経印刷株式会社

ISBN978-4-87615-257-5 C0082
書名　ゼンモンセイカイスル　シントーイックテスト
　　　キュウヒャクキュウジュッテンタイサク
著者　カトウ　マサシ
著作者および発行者の許可なく転載・複製することを禁じます。

定価はカバーに表示してあります。
乱丁本，落丁本はお取り替えいたします。

株式会社語研
語研ホームページ http://www.goken-net.co.jp/

[付属 CD について]
2 枚の CD は同じ袋の中に
入っています。

CD 収録時間：
　　66 分 12 秒（Disc 1）
　　48 分 34 秒（Disc 2）

学習レベル
初級~中級

新TOEIC®TEST
文法・語彙問題
秒速解答法

中村 紳一郎＋Susan Anderton＋森田 鉄也 [著]
定価1,680円(税込) A5判 384頁
ISBN978-4-87615-199-8

　パート5・6に出題される52問を26分以内(=1問30秒以内)に解くための【秒速解答法】を習得できます。TOEIC®受験指導の「全国優秀校」エッセンス イングリッシュ スクールが授業で行っている図解解説を紙面に再現。解答力を鍛える練習問題(260問)についても全問図解で解説しています。

初級~中級

1問30秒で解くための解答力を鍛える

新TOEIC®TEST
文法・語彙問題
完全攻略580問

白野 伊津夫 [監]
定価1,890円(税込) A5判 464頁
ISBN978-4-87615-208-7

初級~中級

フレーズ形式で必須語彙をマスター

目標スコア600-900
TOEIC®TEST
完全攻略3000語

Susan Anderton＋
中村 紳一郎 [著]
定価2,940円(税込) 四六判 640頁
ISBN978-4-87615-053-3 CD2枚付き

初級~中級

正攻法で攻略する頻出出題パターン24

新TOEIC®TEST
リスニング
完全攻略

宮野 智靖＋妻鳥 千鶴子＋
Miguel E. Corti [著]
定価2,310円(税込) A5判 352頁
ISBN978-4-87615-221-6 CD2枚付き

初級~中級

秒速で解き進む頻出出題パターン21

新TOEIC®TEST
リーディング
完全攻略

宮野 智靖＋Miguel E. Corti＋
松井 こずえ＋三宅 淳子 [著]
定価2,100円(税込) A5判 472頁
ISBN978-4-87615-222-3

お買い求めは全国の書店またはオンライン書店で。オンライン書店でのご購入にはISBNコード検索が便利です。定価は本書奥付に記載した最新刷発行日時点の消費税率を用いて算出しております。

語研 GOKEN
TEL:03-3291-3986
FAX:03-3291-6749
〒101-0064 東京都千代田区猿楽町2-7-17
http://www.goken-net.co.jp/